D1525393

Educational
Performance of the Poor

A World Bank Book

Educational
Performance of the Poor

Lessons from Rural Northeast Brazil

Ralph W. Harbison
Eric A. Hanushek

Published for the World Bank
Oxford University Press

Oxford University Press

OXFORD NEW YORK TORONTO DELHI
BOMBAY CALCUTTA MADRAS KARACHI
PETALING JAYA SINGAPORE HONG KONG
TOKYO NAIROBI DAR ES SALAAM
CAPE TOWN MELBOURNE AUCKLAND
and associated companies in
BERLIN IBADAN

Manufactured in the United States of America
First printing March 1992

Library of Congress Cataloging-in-Publication Data

Harbison, Ralph W.
    Educational performance of the poor : lessons from rural northeast
Brazil / Ralph W. Harbison, Eric A. Hanushek.
        p.   cm.
    Based on research by the World Bank.
    Includes bibliographical references (p.   ) and index.
    ISBN 0-19-520878-1
    1. Programa de Expansão e Melhoracão da Educacão no Meio Rural do
Nordeste (Brazil) 2. School improvement programs—Brazil—Statistics.
3. Education, Primary—Economic aspects—Brazil—Statistics. 4. Poor
children—Education (Primary—Brazil—Statistics). 5. Education,
Rural—Brazil—Statistics. 6. Academic achievement—Brazil—Statistics.
7. Educational surveys—Brazil.   I. Hanushek, Eric Alan, 1943–
II. World Bank.   III. Title.
LB2822.84.B6H37   1992
370.19'346'0981—dc20   91-47492
                                                          CIP

Contents

TABLES AND FIGURES

Tables

Figures

Cover photograph by Stephen P. Heyneman

Acknowledgments

THIS BOOK BUILDS UPON the painstaking work of many people. They include colleagues too numerous to be listed as authors but too important to the intellectual content and to the conduct of the research to be mentioned only in the customary long list of pro forma acknowledgments.

The entire research project followed largely uncharted paths. The goal was deceptively simple: Find out whether a new educational development project jointly sponsored by the Brazilian government and the World Bank worked. To address this question, however, a research team, whose composition changed over time, had to design and implement a multiyear project of unprecedented scope. The entire enterprise involved the combined efforts of a Brazilian group and a World Bank group. Only Ralph W. Harbison, who designed the study in 1980 and directed the work throughout, managed to stay with the project at every stage, and even he was pulled during much of the late period by changed responsibilities at the World Bank.

The task began with the always challenging chore of primary data collection. In this instance, the data development effort involved testing academic achievement in a large sample of young children and gathering extensive complementary information directly from the students, their teachers, and their parents. All of this was done in the extremely deprived and isolated rural areas of northeast Brazil. Extensive data of remarkable quality were collected over a six-year period in four massive sample surveys. Underlying this effort were the difficult requirements of instrument construction and pretesting, sample selection, interviewer training, quality control, and the logistics of survey administration. None of this would have been possible without the efforts, the unflagging interest, and the continual encouragement of the Brazilian members of the team.

The research itself spanned the entire decade of the 1980s and involved a wide variety of analytical forays. This book reports on one set of investigations but by no means the only one. More important, the analysis here has been heavily influenced by the other pieces of research and by extensive discussions with the other participants about the operation of the sampled schools, about the interpretation of our results, and about the overall schooling context.

The Brazilian research team was headed by Raimundo Helio Leite who was then, and for most of the period of field research in Brazil, professor of education at the Federal University of Ceará (UFC) and executive director of UFC's research foundation, Fundação Cearense de Pesquisas e Cultura (FCPC). He recently completed a four-year term as president of UFC. At one time or another, the team comprised dozens of people. They came from the UFC Department of Education and the Department of Statistics and Applied Mathematics, from the Fundação Carlos Chagas in São Paulo and from the secretariats of education in the Brazilian states of Piaui, Ceará, and Pernambuco (the states where the data were collected). The professionalism and dedication of the leading figures in this Brazilian team are reflected in the bibliography, which lists a portion of their written contributions.

Three specific individuals made indispensable contributions to this research, first as integral members of the field team in Brazil, later as major actors in the early rounds of data analysis and writing in Fortaleza and at the World Bank in Washington.

João Batista Ferreira Gomes-Neto, professor and, in 1981–85, chairman of the Statistics and Applied Mathematics department at UFC, was responsible for the design and management of the huge data bases that resulted from the surveys. He was also key to the data analysis conducted both on the UFC mainframe computer and later at the World Bank, where he spent two years in residence. In Washington, Gomes-Neto wisely and quickly weaned us from the Bank's costly mainframes and indoctrinated us all in the glories of desktop data analysis of large empirical data sets. He was the manager of the 1987 Ceará fieldwork and undertook the early analytical work and writing on the relationship between health status and achievement. Finally he led us rigorously through the mathematical relations underlying the calculations of partial benefit cost ratios and was a constant source of wisdom in our struggle to invest cold analytical findings with Brazilian reality.

Donald Holsinger provided senior scientific and technical advice and on-the-scene professional colleagueship to the Brazilian team. Until 1986 he was a professor of sociology of education at the State University of New York at Albany; now he is a member of the staff of the World Bank's Education and Employment Division. He made his contribution on repeated short trips and summer-long stays in Fortaleza and by hosting a stream of short visits by Brazilian team members to Albany for intensive stretches of work. In addition, Holsinger did the original technical writing on variable specifications and measurement, on the sample design and characteristics, and on the contextual background of the study. Both in

Albany and at the World Bank, his deep knowledge of education and other sociopolitical institutions in the Brazilian northeast and his disciplinary background in sociology rather than economics have been an absolutely essential counterpoint to our biases as economists.

Jane Armitage spent twenty-two months in Fortaleza working daily with the Brazilian team on the 1983 and 1985 field surveys, on organization of the massive empirical data bases, and on the manifold analytical tasks conducted in Fortaleza. She was solely responsible for gathering the data on the costs of educational inputs and for the initial cost-effectiveness analyses, as well as for our early forays into value-added specifications of achievement models. Her vision of how all the pieces would fit together and her perseverance in the day-to-day struggles to move the work forward were an inspiration to her colleagues in Brazil and Washington. She is currently a member of the staff of the World Bank Country Operations Division for Southern Africa.

Together, Armitage, Gomes-Neto, Harbison, Holsinger, and Leite produced the project's first major working paper in English in 1984, updated it in 1986, and presented its findings on several occasions in the United States and Brazil. Discussions at those times revealed how imperfect was the analysis to date, and stimulated the extension and expansion of the research presented in this volume.

The substantial costs of the project were covered from two sources. Data collection and analysis in Brazil, including all the psychometric work by researchers at the Fundação Carlos Chagas, were paid by the Federal Government of Brazil from proceeds of Loan 1867-BR in support of the Northeast Rural Primary Project (EDURURAL). Funding approved by the Research Committee of the World Bank from the Bank's administrative budget provided consultant inputs to the study and made possible the more sophisticated multivariate exploitation of the data.

Many others have been subjected to reading and discussing draft material in various states of completion, and they have made substantial contributions to the analytical approaches and the clarity of the arguments. With some fear of slighting other individuals who have devoted energy to this, we wish to acknowledge the particularly helpful comments of Bruce Fuller, Dean Jamison, Marlaine Lockheed, Richard Murnane, and Richard Sabot, and the research assistance of Richard Pace and Dan Williams. The materials also received the constructive scrutiny of seminars at the World Bank, University of Rochester, Texas A&M University, and Yale University. The suggestions in five anonymous reviews arranged by the World Bank's Editorial Committee were also insightful and are gratefully acknowledged. Robert Faherty edited the entire manuscript. Stephanie Soutouras, perhaps the person outside our families who was most interested in seeing the project completed, was our production manager. She organized the many different versions of the tables, typed each of the several drafts, produced the myriad analytical tables, and generally undertook to impose order on the flow of written materials over a three-year period. But, much as we owe to others, we alone are responsible for remaining deficiencies.

Finally, Irene Harbison and Nancy Hanushek contributed immensely to this project by their gentle forbearance as we followed the trail of educational research in rural northeast Brazil. Thanks.

PART I

Background

1

Introduction and Overview

HUMAN RESOURCES ARE just as much the basis of the wealth of poor nations as of rich. Recognizing this, developing countries spend heavily on education, which is typically the second largest claimant on public budgets after the military. But recognizing the importance of education is not the same as knowing how to get the most out of expenditure on it.

Strategies to expand the coverage and improve the quality of schooling typically emphasize, in developing countries no less than elsewhere, the provision of school inputs. The strategies concentrate on school buildings, furniture and equipment, teachers and their training, new curricula and syllabi, textbooks and other instructional materials that assist in delivering the curriculum, and administrative services at all levels. The presumption is that increased abundance and quality of such things improve educational performance as measured by how many children enter school, how long they stay there, how fast they move through the grades, what they actually learn, and the social and private utility of what they learn. This book investigates that presumption.

The Policy Process

Designing and implementing strategies to improve education in developing countries is not easy. The preponderance of evidence on effectiveness—that is, on what level and quality and mix of inputs best serve performance objectives—refers to environments that are profoundly different from those in developing countries. Furthermore, the reliability of that evidence is questionable. Conclusions from different studies are sometimes ambiguous, often inconsistent, and nearly always subject to methodological challenge. More important, evidence on the efficiency of alternative development strategies—that is, on effectiveness of input mixes relative to their costs—is even scarcer and less reliable. Thus, the basic information on which to build educational policies is lacking.

3

Yet policy decisions must be made, and the only alternative in such circumstances is to plow ahead. The best that appears generally possible is to apply liberal doses of common sense, professional judgment, and knowledge of the local scene to whatever lessons can be distilled from documented experience and conventional wisdom elsewhere. Education planners and managers in developing countries and their supporters in international development assistance agencies regularly operate on just such a "best guess, make do" basis. It should come as little surprise then that the results often fall short of expectations and desires.

The pressures of the day and the difficulty of making truly informed decisions need not, however, be a perpetual and inescapable reality, as many would imply. The policy process is played out over and over again. Decisionmakers should be able to learn from experience and thereby to refine and improve those best guesses. To improve on policies and the policy process, we must build up knowledge of what works and what does not, trace the effects of differing environments and costs, and, along the way, perfect analytical tools for accumulating such knowledge.

This book reports on one sizable effort to develop the essential in-gredients for informed educational policy. It presents results from an eight-year investigation into the relationship between inputs to primary schools and educational performance in one of the world's poorest re-gions, the rural areas of the northeastern states of Brazil. The study was motivated by a specific educational improvement project undertaken in Brazil with assistance from the World Bank, but its scope goes far beyond that.

The large-scale empirical effort that is the analytical core of the book tests a set of fundamental propositions about how to improve educational performance in developing countries. The findings are potentially im-portant and interesting for three reasons. First, they pertain to environ-ments of extreme rural poverty in which little is known about improving educational performance. Second, they were generated by research de-signed explicitly to test the validity and reliability of previous empirical inquiry into educational performance. Third, and most important, these research results provide clear guidance for a number of policies that could have revolutionary effects on education in developing countries.

The Scope of the Work

This research comprises two distinct, but interrelated inquiries. The more straightforward can be viewed as a pure evaluation effort. Did a specific educational intervention project—the Northeast Rural Primary Project (EDURURAL)—accomplish its goals? The second inquiry, however, is both more important and more central to the work here. This involves a detailed effort to expand our knowledge of what works in education and what educational policies flow from this. The second inquiry is not fundamentally tied to the assumptions behind the EDURURAL program. It aims explicitly to develop information about how other programs might be designed. We begin with an overview of the issues considered in this policy research effort and then consider the evaluation component.

The Central Issues of Policy Research

This work focuses on a subset of the essential educational policy concerns. We adopt the simple perspective that the most important objective is to have policies that will lead to maximum performance within the available budget. In other words, our concern is efficiency. For the most part, we ignore the larger issues of how much should be spent on education and how educational resources should be distributed.[1]

Educational policy operates at two fundamental levels. First, an institutional structure is established for the conduct of schooling. In most of the world, the central element of this structure is the establishment of a series of publicly financed and publicly operated schools. But the institutional structure goes much deeper to set the goals of the schooling system, the rules of student attendance and promotion, the operating procedures for the schools, the curriculum, and so forth. Second, within this institutional structure, policies are developed for financing the system, hiring teachers and other personnel, making expenditures on other educational resources from buildings to paper and pencils, and attending to the details that define more precisely just what the schooling system looks like. These two levels obviously interact and at times are difficult to distinguish from each other. We distinguish between them, however, because they point to specific aspects of the analysis that are important for generalizing the results to other settings.

Our research has most to say about detailed policies applied within a specific institutional structure. The reason for this is simple: We do not observe schools within other kinds of institutional structures, so any conclusions about policies outside the current structure are based more on extrapolation and speculation than on evidence. While we do conclude that certain aspects of the overall schooling system in the northeast of Brazil appear inefficient and even counterproductive, we must necessarily be cautious in applying these results. As we discuss later, the degree to which institutional structures resemble each other in Brazil and in developing countries in general is important to the consideration of how well our results generalize.

Beneath the superficial listing of features of the system just given lies the message that school decisions are so complicated that setting policy requires an enormous amount of information if it is to be done correctly. The other side of the coin, the starting point for this book, is that we currently lack much of the information that is key to optimal decision-making.

Certain data are required to assess efficiency. The first requirement is information on the relationship between school inputs and student performance. For example, how do different inputs that policymakers can manipulate affect educational performance? If we improve schools by providing a given resource—say, a teacher with complete secondary schooling as opposed to only primary schooling—by how much will student performance increase? Second, we need information about the costs of altering these different inputs. How much, for example, would it cost to attract teachers with secondary schooling? With information on these two factors, effectiveness and cost, policies can be designed for the efficient use of resources in the schools.

A primary purpose of the research reported here is to supply the data needed to address such efficiency questions. For this, we do not restrict ourselves to the particular educational intervention of the EDURURAL project. We use the data generated by a sample of students in schools inside and outside the project to estimate the relationships between educational resources and student performance. Although data generated by the evaluation component of the EDURURAL project are superior to any previously available to investigate performance of schools in developing countries, the specifics of the intervention are not central to this superiority.

Policy considerations depend critically on how school performance is gauged. Our primary measure is student performance on basic tests of literacy and numeracy. The overall evaluation design for the EDURURAL project led to development of new criterion-referenced tests of performance in Portuguese and mathematics. The new tests were designed to measure student progress on state curricular objectives and were therefore appropriate for primary school students in the impoverished northeast states of Brazil. As indicators of educational performance, such measures of cognitive achievement clearly surpass simple quantitative, or pupil count-based, measures such as years of school completed or rate of progression by students through different grade levels. The common shorthand descriptions of these different outcome measures are simply "quality" and "quantity." This terminology is potentially confusing. Analyses of quality differences—such as the achievement tests employed here—rely on quantitative, statistical analysis. Moreover, student time in school, which is what years of schooling measures, is best thought of as an input into the educational process—not an output. Nevertheless, because of its common usage, we will at times describe the different approaches simply as quality and quantity analyses.

Achievement measures are, however, not very commonly used, and there is independent interest in understanding the quantitative dimensions of primary schools. Therefore, we also investigate promotion and dropout behavior in the sampled schools.[2]

The inquiry into student flows is important for two reasons. First, from a policy perspective, it provides direct information about one of the most commonly discussed issues of school policy in developing countries: how to approach the presumptive tradeoff between quantity (the numbers of children who can attend schools) and quality (assumed for the moment to be reflected in how many resources are devoted to each child)? Second, from a research perspective, the analysis of quality differences must take into account the fact that students who are still in higher levels of schooling are often very special compared with those who entered school with them. In particular, those who remain in school are almost certainly systematically different—in motivation, ability, or what-have-you—from those dropping out. In order to generalize from these selected samples about the influences of resources on student performance, it is essential to understand what determines who remains in school—that is, what behavior influences the observed student flows.

This analysis is predicated on the institutional structure that exists in rural northeast Brazil. Though we make some efforts to investigate how certain institutions affect the observed operations of schools, for the most part we simply take the prevailing structure as given. Thus, for example, we can analyze how the current institutions determine the salaries paid to teachers with varying characteristics to obtain insights into the efficiency of teacher personnel practices. We cannot, however, say much about what would happen if an entirely different wage structure were employed. We also delve into how the current support for schools affects the dynamics of their survival and, implicitly, access of individual students to primary schools. But we must again stop short of considering how different programs of support for local schools might lead to different patterns of access.

Combining information about the effects of resources and organization on performance and about the costs of the alternatives allows us to formulate a set of policies that would dramatically improve the efficiency of resource use. In this strictest sense, these conclusions relate only to a restricted sample of primary school students in the rural northeast of Brazil. We will argue, however, that many of the results can be generalized to other settings—other rural regions, the remainder of Brazil, and even other developing countries.

Evaluation of the EDURURAL Program

This research was an immediate outgrowth of the EDURURAL project, an effort of the Brazilian government that received support from the World Bank. The data were collected to provide a means of assessing the assumptions and implementation of that program. The second major facet of this work is then the evaluation of that specific project. Such evaluations are, however, fiendishly difficult to do correctly. We argue in the end that major interventions like the one in rural Brazil cannot be evaluated without more fundamental research such as that reported in this book.

The program for educational improvement in Brazil's northeast depended for its success on two plausible but unproven assumptions: that the designated resources would be delivered to dispersed and often remote project schools; and that those resources would improve learning achievement and reduce educational wastage (repetition and dropout) within the schools. Testing these assumptions is the heart of the evaluation effort.

The fundamental difficulty in doing such evaluation is knowing what would happen if the project did not exist. To deal with this, we employed a common quasi-experimental design. In that approach, a set of control schools is selected to indicate the counterfactual situation that would have occurred. But the use of such natural experiments vastly complicates the analysis. The selection of schools is seldom truly random. And the treatment of these schools after selection is typically not the same as it would have been if there had been no intervention. The control schools are in effect contaminated by the program, either through actual changes in resource flows or through information and organizational changes.

As a result, answering the question "did it work?" seldom amounts to the simple comparison of mean performance called for under a pure experimental design. Instead, differences in resources and performance over time must be compared in the project and nonproject schools, and doing this requires the prior estimation of the determinants of scholastic performance.

The evaluation effort thus has two components. The first is development of methodology for the evaluation of complicated natural experiments that continue over several years. The second is actually answering the question of whether or not the specific intervention appeared to work.

Alternative Paths through the Book

This book combines extensive new empirical evidence on schooling with a discussion of specific policy recommendations. Some readers may be less interested in the details of the evidence and the statistical analyses than in the overall conclusions. Hence, the book is written in self-contained sections to allow readers to take alternative paths based on their interests or technical expertise. It is important to note that the background materials in

Part I and the discussion of policy implications in Part III *do not* presume
technical knowledge of the analytical procedures. Readers interested only
in the educational and policy context and in the conclusions can safely skip
Part II, the detailed presentation of the evidence.

The remainder of Part I sets the stage for our story. Chapter 2 summarizes what is generally known about the determinants of educational
achievement (or "education production") and about student flows. Chapter 3 describes EDURURAL, the particular education improvement project
that was the focus of our work, presents the overall research design from
which our findings emerge, and provides a sketch of the desperately poor
environment of northeast Brazil in which EDURURAL and other education
improvement projects operated.

Part II summarizes the research and program evaluation findings on
educational performance in the Brazilian northeast. Chapter 4 focuses
on how much schooling children receive, examining determinants of
access to schools and promotion within them. This chapter provides
unique insights into the relationship between student achievement and
student progress in schools. Chapter 5 concentrates on school quality,
exploring the relationship between inputs to schooling and learning
achievement. By taking advantage of the special aspects of the research
design employed for this work, chapter 5 extends and enriches the standard production function approach to analysis of learning determinants.
The results of this statistical inquiry provide the material for much more
precise policy guidance than previously possible.

Chapter 6 introduces costs into the discussion, shifting the focus from
the comparative effectiveness of different inputs to schooling to their
relative efficiency. In so doing it provides a novel analysis of the potential
interaction between quantity and quality of schooling, through empirical
estimates of the relationship between educational wastage and achievement increases induced by more informed resource allocations to
schools.

Chapter 7 assesses whether EDURURAL as an educational improvement
program had a discernable effect. This chapter describes a methodological approach to evaluation of quasi-experiments (such as the EDURURAL
research) in which the evidence on induced input differences is summarized according to the previously estimated statistical models.

Chapters 4 to 7, the analytical heart of the book, are inevitably technical
and are not meant for every reader. These chapters provide a discussion
of methodology and detailed statistical findings. They are meant to document the evidence and to explain the analytical approach. Readers interested just in the conclusions and policy implications can skip directly
to Part III.

Part III contains lessons for educational policy. Chapter 8 consolidates
the evidence on major factors affecting educational performance (quan-

tity and quality of schooling) in a manner comprehensible to the lay reader. The discussion of policy implications highlights findings that can be generalized to educational improvement programs in other poor countries. It concludes with additional findings about how evaluation and research can be incorporated in ongoing educational programs in order to expand our knowledge about appropriate educational policies. Throughout chapter 8, page references are provided to the supporting evidence in the previous chapters. Overall, the research provides a number of findings about what does and does not affect educational performance. These findings, which contribute directly to current policy debates worldwide, are developed throughout the book.

A Fundamental Policy Insight

To orient the reader we highlight below the most fundamental finding. This conclusion could only have been derived from an integrated analysis of academic achievement, student progression, and resource costs such as we develop here.

Some inputs actually induce resource savings substantially larger than their original investment cost.

The implications of this finding cannot be overstated. It suggests the possibility of a kind of "free lunch" embedded in the current inefficiencies of the most needy school systems. Investment in quality schooling is typically described as being profitable because of the increased future earnings to skilled individuals. Now, however, we suggest that savings in school operating costs *alone* could justify investments in quality enhancements for schools. Far from being constrained by a tradeoff between quantity and quality, decisionmakers in impoverished areas of the world may take advantage of a mutually reinforcing positive interaction.

If this conclusion is taken seriously, policymakers should begin moving rapidly away from the subminimal schools currently operated in many developing countries. Here is a clear strategy of educational improvement—both for fundamental development reasons and as a device for improving the overall efficiency of the educational system. Such a movement would, in turn, free resources to expand schools to populations currently underserved.

We delineate this startling result now, in part because it highlights the fact that the primary objective of this research is to find ways of altering policies in order to improve educational performance. An underlying, albeit implicit, theme of this book is that systematic analysis, built on sound scientific principles, provides one of the most likely paths to improved policy and practice. The analytical sections are indeed long, perhaps even tedious in places. But arrival at such a fundamental—and unexpected—policy finding requires the integrated approach followed here. The conclusion described above relies on the following: identifying the increased achievement that comes from providing specific added resources (chapter 5); analyzing the effect of the resultant increased achievement on promotion rates (chapter 4); and comparing the costs of the added resources to the savings that accrue from less grade repetition (chapter 6). The background, the evidence, the qualifications, the uncertainties are identified and developed in the ensuing chapters.

2

Education Production: What We Know

EDUCATIONAL POLICY IS forever hampered by fundamental gaps in our knowledge about the educational process. Improving educational performance through governmental policy interventions requires a basic understanding of the underlying behavioral and technical relationships that govern student performance. What kind of teacher will best tap the potential of the poor rural student? How should materials be designed for students who get no reinforcement of language skills at home? How can schools best be organized to provide proper incentives to teachers? The list of questions that the policymaker might like to ask goes on and on. Unfortunately, the available answers are few and frequently uncertain.

In this chapter, we review the current state of knowledge about the educational process with special reference to resources and other attributes that policymakers can readily manipulate. The ultimate concerns are the quantity of schooling obtained and the quality of that schooling. If we understand the determinants of these, we can design policies with efficiency and equity objectives, and can take into account any possible tradeoffs between them, on a rational basis. The information on determinants is drawn from a variety of circumstances, many of which bear little resemblance to the situation of profound rural poverty in northeast Brazil, the laboratory for our work. Nevertheless, given the overall paucity of information, we have searched broadly for clues about the educational process.

Research into education has been most extensive in developed countries and specifically in the United States. While the typical American school looks very different from the rural school in northeast Brazil, lessons about the educational process drawn from American experience may at least suggest hypotheses worthy of exploration in other settings.

Before going into the specifics of studies, however, a somewhat larger perspective is needed. The studies we review here, and the work reported in this book, ask how characteristics of schools and teachers affect academic achievement of students measured during schooling. But the real concern is not performance on some standardized test of language or mathematics achievement. Rather it is how students perform in the labor market and in society after leaving school. The reason for concentrating on achievement in school is, however, straightforward. The policy question centers on how different teachers and school resources affect student performance. It would be generally impractical to have to wait a decade or two after observing educational inputs to measure the outcomes that will be related to those inputs.

In our study and most others, data and analytical necessities dictate concentration on immediate measures of student performance such as test scores. Other research, however, indicates that these measures are related to subsequent performance in the labor market and that they are thus reasonable proxies of economically pertinent skills. One rather commonly held presumption is that the better individuals are educated, the better able they are to perform more complicated tasks or to adapt to changing conditions and tasks (see Welch 1970; Nelson and Phelps 1966).[3] The testing of this has followed two general approaches. First, test measures have been included in standard models that explain earnings differences in the population. Studies of adult earnings in developed countries typically show significant, but quantitatively limited, direct effects of achievement. These come, however, in statistical models that also include years of schooling, and test achievement is an important determinant of continuation in schooling, implying an important additional indirect effect.[4] The evidence on returns to different measured skills has tended to be stronger in developing countries.[5] Second, studies have found direct links with productivity, particularly in agriculture.[6] In short, there is reasonably broad support for the notion that school quality as measured during schooling is directly related to productivity and earnings when students enter the labor force.

Thus, although our attention is focused on the ability of schools to raise students' academic performance, there is reason to interpret this in the broader context of increasing economic performance of the students and of the overall economies.

Schooling in the United States

The pertinent research on primary schooling in developed countries deals with qualitative differences, or differences in the performance of students, not questions of continuation in school (repetition and dropouts).[7] In developed countries essentially 100 percent of the eligible population completes at least primary school. The evidence on promotion and retention in these countries, such as it is, pertains mostly to upper secondary and higher education and is of limited relevance for the primary education issues to be considered here.[8]

Although research into the determinants of students' achievement takes various approaches, one of the most appealing and useful is what economists call the *production function* approach, or in other disciplines the *input-output* or *cost-quality* approach. In this, attention is focused primarily on the relationship between school outcomes and measurable inputs into the educational process.[9] If the production function for schools were known, it would then be possible to predict what would happen if resources were added or subtracted and to analyze what actions should be taken if the prices of various inputs were to change. The problem, of course, is that the production function for education is not known and must be inferred from data on students and their schools.

The origin of estimating input-output relations in schools is usually traced to the monumental U.S. study, *Equality of Educational Opportunity*, or, more commonly, the Coleman Report (Coleman and others 1966). Designed explicitly to study equity, this report was the U.S. Office of Education's response to a requirement of the Civil Rights Act of 1964 to investigate the extent of inequality (by race, religion, or national origin) in the nation's schools. The study's fundamental contribution was to direct attention to the distribution of student performance—the outputs with which we are concerned. Instead of addressing questions of inequality simply by producing an inventory of differences among schools and teachers by race and region of the country, the Coleman Report sought to explain those differences; it delved into the relationship between inputs and outputs of schools. Even though it was not the first such effort, the Coleman Report was much larger and more influential than any previous (or subsequent) input-output study. The study surveyed and tested 600,000 students in some 3,000 schools across the United States.

The report captured attention not, however, because of this innovative perspective or because of its unparalleled description of schools and students. Instead, it was much discussed because of its major conclusion. The Coleman Report was widely interpreted as finding that schools are not very important in determining student achievement. Families and, to a lesser extent, peers were seen to be the primary determinants of variations in performance. The findings were clearly controversial and immediately led to a large (but diffuse) research effort to compile additional evidence about the relationship between school resources and school performance.[10]

The underlying model guiding the Coleman Report and most subsequent studies is very straightforward. It postulates that the output of the educational process—that is, the achievement of individual students— is related directly to a series of inputs. Policymakers directly control some of these inputs—for instance, the characteristics of schools, teachers, and curricula. Others, those of families and friends plus the innate endowments or learning capacities of the students, generally cannot be affected by public policy. Further, although achievement is usually measured at discrete points in time, the educational process is cumulative; past inputs affect students' current levels of achievement.

Starting with this model, statistical techniques, typically some form of regression analysis,[11] are employed to identify the specific determinants of achievement and to make inferences about the relative importance of the various inputs into student performance. The accuracy of the analysis and the confidence the answers warrant depend crucially on a variety of issues regarding measurement and technical estimation. This summary sets aside these issues.[12] Instead it highlights the overall findings and major unanswered questions from this research.

Most studies of educational production relationships measure output by students' scores on standardized achievement tests, although significant numbers have used other quantitative measures, such as student attitudes, school attendance rates, and college continuation or dropout rates. The general interpretation is that they are all plausible indicators of future success in the labor market.

Empirical specifications have varied widely in details, but they have also had much in common. Family inputs tend to be measured by sociodemographic characteristics of the families such as parental education, income, and family size. Peer inputs, when included, are typically aggregate summaries of the sociodemographic characteristics of other students in the school. School inputs include measures of the teachers' characteristics (education level, experience, sex, race, and so forth), of the schools' organization (class sizes, facilities, administrative expenditures, and so forth), and of district or community factors (for example, average expenditure levels). Except for the original Coleman Report, most empirical work has relied on data, such as the normal administrative records of schools, that were compiled for other purposes.

Schools, Expenditures, and Achievement in the United States

The production function approach has been employed broadly to investigate the effect on school performance of the core factors that determine expenditure on education. Instructional expenditures make up about two-thirds of total school expenditures. Instructional expenditures are, in turn, determined mostly by teacher salaries and class sizes. Finally, in most U.S. school districts, teacher salaries are directly related to the years of teaching experience and the educational level of the teacher. Thus, the basic determinants of instructional expenditures in a district are teacher experience, teacher education, and class size. Most studies, regardless of what other school characteristics might be included, analyze the effect of these factors on outcomes. (These are also the factors most likely to be found in any given data set, especially if the data come from standard administrative records.)

Because the analyses have such common specifications, the effects of the expenditure parameters can easily be tabulated. A reasonably exhaustive search uncovered 187 separate qualified studies found in thirty-eight separate published articles or books. (Qualified studies satisfy certain minimal quality standards and provide direct information about the effects of school resources on student performance.)[13] These studies, while restricted to public schools, cover all regions of the United States, different grade levels, different measures of performance, and different analytical and statistical approaches. About one-third draw their data from a single school district, while the remaining two-thirds compare school performance across multiple districts. A majority of the studies (104) use individual students as the unit of analysis; the remainder rely upon aggregate school, district, or state level data. The studies are split about evenly between primary schooling (grades 1–6) and secondary schooling (grades 7–12). Over 70 percent of the studies measure school performance by some kind of standardized test. However, those that use nontest measures (such as dropout rates, college continuation, attitudes, or performance after school) are for obvious reasons concentrated in studies of secondary schooling. There is no indication that differences in sample and study design lead to differences in conclusions.[14]

Table 2-1 summarizes the expenditure components of the 187 studies. Since not all studies include each of the expenditure parameters, the first column in the table presents the total number of studies for which an input can be tabulated. For example, 152 studies provide information about the relationship between the teacher-pupil ratio and student performance. The available studies all provide regression estimates of the partial effect of given inputs, holding constant family background and other inputs. These estimated coefficients have been tabulated according to two pieces of information: the sign and the statistical significance (5 percent level) of the estimated relationship. Statistical significance is included to indicate confidence that any estimated relationship is real and not just an artifact of the sample of data employed.[15, 16]

According both to conventional wisdom and to generally observed school policies, each tabulated factor should have a positive effect on student achievement. More education and more experience on the part of the teacher cost more and are presumed to improve individual student learning. Smaller classes (more teachers per student) are also expected to be beneficial.[17] More spending in general, higher teacher salaries, better facilities and better administration should also lead to better stu-

Table 2-1. Summary of Estimated Expenditure Parameter Coefficients from 187 Studies of Educational Production Functions: United States

Input	Number of studies	Statistically significant			Statistically insignificant			
		Total	+	−	Total	+	−	Unknown sign
Teacher/pupil ratio	152	27	14	13	125	34	46	45
Teacher education	113	13	8	5	100	31	32	37
Teacher experience	140	50	40	10	90	44	31	15
Teacher salary	69	15	11	4	54	16	14	24
Expenditure per pupil	65	16	13	3	49	25	13	11
Administration	61	8	7	1	53	14	15	24
Facilities	74	12	7	5	62	17	14	31

Source: Armor and others 1976; Beiker and Anschel 1973; Behrendt, Eisenach, and Johnson 1986; Boardman, Davis, and Sanday 1977; Bowles 1970; Brown and Saks 1975; Burkhead 1967; Cohn 1968; Cohn and Millman 1975; Dolan and Schmidt 1987; Dynarsky 1987; Eberts and Stone 1984; Hanushek 1971, 1972; Heim and Perl 1974; Henderson, Mieszkowski, and Sauvageau 1976; Jencks and Brown 1975; Katzman 1971; Keisling 1967; Kenny 1982; Levin 1970, 1976; Link and Mulligan 1986; Link and Ratledge 1979; Maynard and Crawford 1976; Michelson 1970, 1972; Murnane 1975; Murnane and Phillips 1981; Perl 1973; Raymond 1968; Ribich and Murphy 1975; Sebold and Dato 1981; Smith 1972; Strauss and Sawyer 1986; Summers and Wolfe 1977; Tuckman 1971; Winkler 1975.

dent performance. The quantitative magnitudes of estimated relationships are ignored here; only the direction of any effect is analyzed.[18]

Having a positive sign in a production function is clearly a minimal requirement for justifying a given input or expenditure. Policy conclusions should also incorporate information on the quantitative magnitude of effects and the costs of inputs. However, as we shall soon see, the results on effects do not justify pursuing detailed cost effectiveness calculations.

Of the 152 estimates of the effects of class size, only 27 are statistically significant. Of these, only 14 show a statistically significant positive relationship, whereas 13 display a negative relationship.[19] An additional 125 estimates show that class size is not significant at the 5 percent level. Nor does ignoring statistical significance help to confirm the benefits of small classes. By a 46 to 34 margin the insignificant coefficients are negative, the wrong sign according to conventional wisdom.[20]

The entries for teacher education tell a similar story. The statistically significant results are split between positive and negative relationships, and in a vast majority of cases (100 out of 113) the estimated coefficients are statistically insignificant. Forgetting about statistical significance and looking just at estimated signs again does not make a case for the importance of added schooling for teachers.[21]

Teacher experience is possibly different. A clear majority of estimated coefficients point in the expected direction, and about 29 percent of the estimated coefficients are both statistically significant and of the conventionally expected sign. But these results are hardly overwhelming; they only appear strong relative to the other school inputs. Moreover, they are subject to interpretive questions. Specifically, these positive correlations may result from senior teachers having the ability to locate themselves in schools and classrooms with good students (Greenberg and McCall 1974). In other words, causation may run from achievement to experience and not the other way around.[22]

Overall, the results are startlingly consistent. No compelling evidence emerges that teacher-pupil ratios, teacher education, or teacher experience have the expected positive effects on student achievement. We cannot be confident that hiring teachers with more education or having smaller classes will improve student performance. Teacher experience appears only marginally stronger in its relationship.

The remaining rows of table 2-1 summarize information on other expenditure components, including administration, facilities, teacher salaries, and total expenditure per student.[23] The quality of administration is measured in a wide variety of ways, ranging from characteristics of the principal to expenditure per pupil on noninstructional items. Similarly, the quality of facilities is identified through both spending and many specific physical characteristics. The absence of a strong relationship between these two components and performance may result in part from variations in how these factors are measured. If only because of the preponderance of positive signs among the significant coefficients, administration appears marginally stronger in its relationship than facilities. Nevertheless, the available evidence on both again fails to support convincingly the conventional wisdom.

Finally, and not surprisingly, explicit measures of teacher salaries and expenditure per student do not suggest that they have a currently important role in determining achievement.[24] After all, the underlying components of this expenditure were themselves unrelated to achievement.[25]

Without systematic tabulation of the results of the various studies, it would be easy to conclude that the findings are inconsistent. But there is a consistency, though not with the conventional wisdom.

The research reveals no strong or systematic relationship between school expenditures and student performance.

This is the case both when expenditure is decomposed into underlying determinants and when it is considered in the aggregate.

There are several obvious reasons for caution in interpreting this evidence. For any individual study, incomplete information, poor quality data, or faulty research could distort the statistical results. Even without such problems, the actions of school administrators could mask any relationship. For example, if the most difficult students to teach were consistently put in smaller classes, any independent effect of class size could be difficult to disentangle from mismeasurement of the characteristics of the students. Finally, the statistical insignificance of estimates can reflect no relationship, but it also can reflect a variety of data problems, including high correlations among the different measured inputs. In other words, as in most research, virtually any of the studies is open to some sort of challenge.

Just such uncertainties about individual results motivated this tabulation of estimates. If the studies' common parameters were in fact central to variations in student achievement, the tabulations would almost certainly show more of a pattern in the expected direction. The reasons for caution are clearly more important in some circumstances than others. But the consistency across these very different studies is still striking. Furthermore, given the general biases toward publication of statistically significant estimates, the paucity of such results is notable. Although individual studies may be affected by specific analytical problems, the aggregate data provided by the 187 separate estimates lead relentlessly to the conclusion that, after family backgrounds and other educational inputs are considered, differences in educational expenditures are not systematically related to student performance.

Other Inputs into Education

Since the publication of the Coleman Report, intense debate has surrounded the fundamental question of whether schools and teachers are important to the educational performance of students. That report has been commonly interpreted as finding that variations in school resources explain only a negligible portion of the variation in students' achievement. If true, it would not matter which particular teacher a student had or which school a student attended—a conclusion most people would have difficulty accepting.

A number of studies provide direct analyses of this overall question of differential effectiveness of teachers and schools. They do this by estimating differences in the average performance of each teacher's (or school's) students after allowing for differences in family backgrounds and initial achievement scores.[26] The findings are unequivocal: teachers and schools differ dramatically in their effectiveness. The formal statistical tests employed in these studies confirm that there are striking differences in average gain in student achievement across teachers.

The faulty impressions left by the Coleman Report and by a number of subsequent studies about the importance of teachers have resulted primarily from a confusion between the measures of effectiveness and true effectiveness itself. In other words, existing measures of characteristics of teachers and schools are seriously flawed and thus are poor indicators of their true effects; when these measurement errors are avoided, schools are seen to have important effects on student performance. While a number of implications and refinements of that work still need to be explored,[27] this conclusion that schools and teachers are important is very firm.[28]

These production function analyses have also investigated a wide variety of other school and nonschool factors. Although it is difficult to be specific in any summary of other factors because the specifications are quite idiosyncratic, three generalizations are possible.

First, family background is clearly very important in explaining differences in achievement. Virtually regardless of how measured, more educated and more wealthy parents have children who perform better on average, even after taking into account the effect of other factors. The studies, however, have seldom gone into any detail about the mechanisms by which families influence education. Generally they have stopped with the introduction of proxies for family differences in education.[29] From a policy perspective, it is essential to understand whether or not a change in identifiable and manipulable inputs will engender improved performance, in either the short run or the long run. This requires understanding the underlying causal structure.[30]

Second, considerable attention has been given to the characteristics of peers or other students within schools. This line of inquiry was pressed in the Coleman Report and pursued in a number of subsequent studies.[31] The question is especially important in considering school desegregation where the racial composition of schools is at issue. The educational effect of differing student bodies has also been important in the debate about public versus private schooling. Nevertheless, the findings are ambiguous, in large part because of data and measurement questions.[32] For example, one important critique of the estimated importance of private schools asserts that the effect of private schools is inflated because of mismeasurement of student body characteristics.[33]

Finally, studies have examined many additional measures of the effects of schools, teachers, curricula, and especially instructional methods on achievement. Various studies have included indicators of schools' organizational aspects, including specific curricula or educational process choices, and of time spent by students working at different subject matter. Others have compiled detailed information on teachers' cognitive abilities, their family backgrounds, and such educational factors as where they went to school, what their majors were, what their attitudes are about education of different kinds of students, and so forth. Similarly detailed information has been gathered about school facilities, school administrators, and other personnel. Although table 2-1 presents some evidence on facilities and administrators, disparities in the measurement of all of these factors certainly add to difficulties in uncovering any consistent relationships.

Perhaps the closest thing to a consistent conclusion across the studies is that "smarter" teachers, ones who perform well on verbal ability tests, do better in the classroom. Even there, however, the evidence is not overly strong.[34]

While not systematically addressed by existing research, one plausible interpretation of the combined results of these studies is that an important element of skill is involved in being a successful teacher.[35] Skill refers simply to the ability of some teachers to promote higher achievement of students. The evidence previously presented then indicates that it is currently impossible to identify, much less to measure, specific components of this skill with any precision. Moreover, the direct evidence also casts doubt on whether any form of teacher training could be organized to foster high skill levels in teachers. These interpretations of the data involve, however, speculation that extends beyond currently available evidence.

Schooling in Developing Countries

Past research on school achievement in developing countries is less extensive, less rigorous, and more difficult to interpret than that for the United States. Nevertheless, we can develop some information about school operations in developing countries from such research.

Dissimilar findings about the determinants of school performance in developing countries, as contrasted to developed countries, might indeed be expected. The dramatic differences in the level of educational support provided by families and schools imply that the educational production process could be very different in developed and developing countries. In particular, while the effect of marginal resources on achievement may be hard to discern when average school expenditure is $5,000 per year, it might be much larger and more noticeable when expenditure is one-tenth or one-hundredth that level.[36] The following section investigates whether or not such alternative conclusions can be found in existing work.

Schools, Expenditures, and Achievement in Developing Countries

Input-output studies in developing countries allow insights into aspects of the educational process that are difficult to observe in the United States. The restricted range of inputs and school organization found in the United States and other developed countries inhibits estimating the importance of many factors. For example, virtually all United States teachers have a baccalaureate degree, and variations in their education relate essentially to differences in the amount of graduate school instruction individual teachers have. Similarly, textbooks and a wealth of supplementary instructional materials are universally available in developed country classrooms, but not in developing countries. Finally, the near universal use of standard classroom instruction does not permit analysis of how radio instruction or other means of distance education affect student performance. In developing countries, where natural variations in schooling inputs are much larger, estimating the effects of such factors is feasible and more likely to yield reliable results.[37]

At the same time, the standards of data collection and analysis are so variable that the results from this work tend to be quite uncertain. Much of the analysis of input-output relationships for developing countries is not published in standard academic journals, and thus it does not have that basic level of quality control. Even more important, the data for many of these studies do not come from regular collection schemes, are difficult to check for quality, and miss key elements of the educational process. Therefore, even if the analytical approaches were state-of-the-art, many questions would remain.

Different researchers have attempted to summarize key aspects of these studies, frequently providing qualitative discussions of the analyses, their results, and their interpretation.[38] Here, however, we present an overall quantitative summary of the available analyses, which parallels that for the U.S. studies. Our starting point is the comprehensive review of studies by Bruce Fuller (1985). This is supplemented by additional studies appearing since that review or omitted from it. There are limitations, however. Because this discussion and analysis relies chiefly on secondary materials, we cannot alter the reporting of results. Consequently, the results cannot be presented in the same depth as those for the United States. Additionally, there is virtually no control over the selection of papers (that is, according to explicit minimal quality standards), over the interpretation of the statistical results, and the like.

A total of ninety-six underlying studies form the basis for the analysis (about half the number utilized in the U.S. analysis). Table 2-2 divides the available studies into statistically significant (by sign) and statistically insignificant. (The insignificant findings, unfortunately, cannot be divided by direction of effect.) The table is laid out similarly to that for the U.S. studies. It begins with the characteristics directly related to instructional expenditure per student and then goes to other attributes of schools.[39]

These studies differ from the U.S. studies in terms of the overall significance of the estimated school effects. Simply put, compared with the results presented in table 2-1, a higher proportion of the tabulated coefficients for the ninety-six studies in developing countries is statistically significant. (It must be emphasized, however, that the proportion of re-

Table 2-2. Summary of Estimated Expenditure Parameter
Coefficients from Ninety-six Studies of Educational Production
Functions: Developing Countries

Input	Number of studies	Statistically significant		Statistically insignificant
		+	−	
Teacher/pupil ratio	30	8	8	14
Teacher education	63	35	2	26
Teacher experience	46	16	2	28
Teacher salary	13	4	2	7
Expenditure per pupil	12	6	0	6
Facilities	34	22	3	9

Source: Avalos and Haddad 1979; Birdsall 1985; Carnoy 1971; Fuller 1985; Jimenez and Lockheed 1989; Jimenez, Lockheed, and Wattanawaha 1987; Lee and Lockheed 1990; Lockheed 1987; Lockheed and Komenan 1987; Ngay 1984; Schiefelbein and Farrell 1982.

sults that are "correct"—statistically significant by conventional standards and in the right direction—never reaches two-thirds; and, the general conclusion of no strong evidence of a systematic relationship between these factors and performance will not change.) The relative robustness in statistical findings could reflect analysis of settings where there is either greater variation in the tabulated educational inputs or greater sensitivity to these inputs by students. Alternatively, the differences could reflect attributes and, specifically, biases of the analyses themselves.[40] While it would be useful to distinguish among these possible reasons for differences, we are unable to do so at this point.

The evidence in table 2-2 from developing countries provides no support for policies of reducing class sizes. Of the thirty studies investigating teacher-pupil ratios, only eight find statistically significant results supporting smaller classes; an equal number are significant but have the opposite sign; and almost half are statistically insignificant.[41] These findings are particularly interesting because class sizes in the developing country studies are considerably more varied than those in the U.S. studies and thus pertain to a wider set of environments.[42]

The analysis of the effect of teacher experience yields results that are roughly similar to those in the U.S. studies. Although 35 percent of the studies display significant positive benefits from more teaching experience (the analogous figure for U.S. studies is 29 percent), the majority of the estimated coefficients still are statistically insignificant. The primary difference between the two sets of tabulations arises from the relative support implied for the different school inputs. The U.S. studies are the most supportive of the conventional wisdom regarding the effects of teacher experience on performance. In developing country studies, teachers' experience is not such a significant factor.

The results for teacher education, on the other hand, diverge in relative terms from those seen for the United States. A majority of the studies (thirty-five out of sixty-three) support the conventional notion that providing more education for teachers is valuable. In the U.S. studies, teacher education provided the least support of all the inputs for the conventional wisdom. Although still surrounded by considerable uncertainty (since twenty-six estimates are insignificant and two display significantly negative effects), these noticeably stronger results in developing countries clearly suggest a possible differentiation by stage of development and general level of resources available.

The teacher salary findings in developing countries contain no compelling support for the notion that better teachers are systematically paid more. Since they aggregate studies across very different countries, school organizations, and labor markets, however, it is difficult to take these results too far. For policy purposes, one would generally want information on what happens if the entire salary schedule is altered (as opposed to simply moving along a given schedule denominated, say, in experience, education, or other attributes of teachers). It is not possible to distinguish, however, between studies reflecting differences in schedules and those reflecting movements along a schedule.

Data for total expenditure per pupil are rarely available in analyses of developing countries. The twelve studies for which estimates can be found are evenly split between statistically significant and statistically insignificant. Given questions about the quality of the underlying data, not too much should be inferred from the findings for direct expenditure measures.

One of the clearest divergencies between the two sets of findings is for facilities, again suggesting that differences in school environments are of some importance. The measures of facilities in developing countries (which incorporate a wide range of actual variables in specific studies) indicate more likely effects on student performance than found in U.S. studies. Some twenty-two of the thirty-four investigations demonstrate support for the provision of quality buildings and libraries.

In summary, the results of studies in developing countries do not make a compelling case for specific input policies. They do, however, indicate that direct school resources might be important in developing countries. Nevertheless, as in the U.S. research, the estimated models of educational performance undoubtedly fail to capture many of the truly important inputs to the educational process.

Other Factors

As with the U.S. studies, a variety of other factors has been investigated in the course of the developing country analyses, including an assortment of curriculum issues, instructional methods, and teacher training programs. Many of these are difficult to assess (at least in a quantitative, comparative way) given the multicountry evidence and the probable importance of local institutions.

One intervention that has widespread endorsement, although as much for conceptual reasons as for solid empirical ones, is the provision of textbooks. The relationship of textbooks and writing materials to student performance is found with reasonable consistency to be important in developing countries, but there are relatively few studies of this.[43]

Investigations of technological or organizational differences have led to mixed results. Because of scattered settlement in many rural areas, several approaches to *distance education* have been investigated. In three extensive investigations (Nicaragua, Kenya, and Thailand), the use of interactive radio has proved effective.[44] However, this conclusion should not be generalized to all possible uses of new technology. In particular, there is little evidence at this time that the widespread introduction of computers is sensible (Lockheed and Verspoor 1991).

Student Flows and School Quality

The central focus of many education policy debates in developing countries is the quantity of schooling received by students, rather than its quality (learning achievement). The substantive reasons behind such a concentration are clear. In the poorest countries, high proportions of students drop out not only of secondary schools but also of primary schools; and many existing schools are filled with grade repeaters. This emphasis on quantitative aspects of schools is also natural from an analytical viewpoint, because quantity—which is based on simple counts of students—is easily observed and measured. Standard governmental statistics invariably record the years of school received by the population. These statistics combined with aggregate cost information provide a tempting opportunity for some sort of efficiency analysis. We argue, however, that the policy debate on quantitative issues has not been informed very much by relevant evidence.

The standard efficiency discussion concentrates on wastage—that is, the number of students who repeat grades or drop out of school. Data on wastage can then be translated into *flow efficiency* or the number of student years required to produce a graduate relative to the number of years that would be required with regular annual promotion and no dropouts.[45] In a simple cost framework, increased wastage (decreased flow efficiency) clearly translates into increased costs of obtaining any target number of graduates. Indeed, a common way to phrase the issue is to note that each extra year a student spends in school denies some other child access to the school. If wastage could be reduced, the argument goes, the schools would become more efficient, and the savings could be used to expand access to schools.

Despite the importance of flow efficiency to policy discussions, remarkably little relevant research is available. Policy discussions typically begin with data about the magnitude of the wastage problem and immediately turn to conceptual issues about the importance of efficiency improvements and then to proposed policies. But the central problem in making policy decisions has been a lack of understanding of the underlying determinants of wastage. Without such information policy prescriptions are likely to be quite misguided.

The existing policy debates in fact highlight a series of fundamental measurement problems, problems so severe that some researchers and policymakers eschew altogether the use of quantity measures of school output. Without an understanding of the underlying determinants of wastage, the most direct policy interventions are restricted to such actions as imposing mandatory attendance laws or regulations dictating automatic grade promotion. But if wastage is highly related to student performance, such regulatory changes are likely simply to change de facto the definition of grade completion without improving true flow efficiency. In other words, there is no clear definition of a "year of schooling," and what is implied could differ across schools and over time.

The dominant questions that must be addressed in considering alternative policies revolve around the relationship between student performance on the one hand and promotion, repetition, and dropout behavior on the other. Providing such information requires measurement of student performance and the development of longitudinal data for individual students. Such data have been extremely rare, particularly in developing countries. As a result, the far-ranging review of wastage by Haddad (1979) cites very little direct evidence on the key questions, and much of that evidence actually relates to developed countries.[46]

One of the few direct investigations of the linkage between promotion and student achievement is found in the analyses of radio-based instruction in mathematics (Jamison 1978, 1980). In those analyses, Jamison demonstrates that academic achievement, as measured by standardized mathematics test scores, is a powerful predictor of student promotion. Although the data were collected as part of a special project in mathematics instruction, the basic findings about promotion patterns can likely be generalized to other settings.

Implications for Policy and Research

Somewhat surprisingly, perhaps, the available research from both developed and developing countries leads to many of the same conclusions. These provide a backdrop for our investigations of education in rural northeast Brazil and the benchmarks for our conclusions.

Two potential policy conclusions spring immediately from the overall results. First, since within the current institutional structure expenditures are not systematically related to performance, policies should not be dictated simply on the basis of expenditure. Second, since common surrogates for teacher and school quality—class size, teachers' education, and teachers' experience among the most important—are not systematically related to performance, policies should not be dictated simply on the basis of such surrogates.

Before leaving this interpretation of the results, however, it is important to refer again to the overall caveat that applies. All of these results reflect generalizations based upon the structure and operating procedures of schools observed in different settings. A different organizational structure with different incentives could produce very different results. For example, almost every economist would support the position that increasing teacher salaries would expand and improve the pool of potential teachers. However, whether this improves the quality of teaching depends on whether or not schools can systematically choose and retain the best teachers from the pool. The results on salary variations presented previously might be very different if schools faced a greater incentive to produce student achievement and if mechanisms for teacher selection were altered. In other words, there seems little question that money *could* count. It just does not systematically do so in the current organization of schools.

Moreover, the consistency criterion used to judge the results and the potential for policy improvements does not suggest that money never counts. The results are entirely compatible with some schools using funds effectively and others not.

Research on developing countries diverges most from that for developed countries in the consideration of specific resource inputs. Past results suggest that the quality of facilities and the availability of textbooks and other software inputs may be quite important in more deprived settings.[47] This set of findings implies that research in developing country settings must be more sensitive to the measurement of such factors.

3

The EDURURAL Project
and Evaluation Design

BEGINNING IN THE EARLY 1980s, the federal government of Brazil and the nine state governments in the country's northeast region increased their investment in the area's schooling.[48] This increased investment reflected a growing realization of education's importance for development and of how far welfare in this region lagged behind the rest of the country.[49]

We begin with a discussion of the socioeconomic context of education in the northeast of Brazil. We then turn to the EDURURAL program (the specific investment program that occasioned this research), the organization and design of the research, and the characteristics of the data base for our study.

The Socioeconomic Context

The significance of research findings reported later cannot be grasped without an appreciation of the unusual context from which they are derived, a picture sketched in the next section. Later sections then turn to the extent to which the areas where we sampled rural schools faithfully reflect educational reality in Brazil, in its northeast, and in the rural areas of the northeast. Underscored are several important ways in which the sampled schools represent extreme characteristics.

Brazil's Northeast

Brazil is big by any standard. With a land area of 8.5 million square kilometers, slightly larger than Western Europe, and population by the mid-1980s of about 135 million, Brazil is the world's tenth largest economy, second only to China among developing countries.

Brazil is also a country of sharp socioeconomic contrasts. High tech-

29

nology industrial, agricultural, and service sectors have produced living standards in the south close to European levels. By contrast, the northeast has fallen far behind the rest of Brazil. Epitomizing the boom and bust character of Brazil's economic history, the northeast enjoyed a heyday derived from short-lived but bounteous sugarcane harvests during the colonial period. Indeed, through the middle of the nineteenth century, the northeast was the wealthiest part of Brazil. But even before the abolition of slavery in 1888, the wealth of the nation began to drift south. The growing importance there of coffee production fueled by migrant labor from Central Europe accelerated the shift in the years before World War I. The drive for industrialization after that war further increased the economic disparities. The northeast found itself ever more at the margin of the Brazilian economy and grew increasingly dependent upon the south.[50]

The nine states of the northeast are today among the poorest regions in the world. Estimates for 1985 suggest that the bottom 50 percent of the population of the northeast had per capita annual incomes of less than US$300, which is roughly equivalent to West Africa, China, or South Asia.[51] This is the largest concentration of poor in Latin America.

The disparities within the country as a whole are immense. The northeast had about 29 percent of Brazil's population in 1980 (35 million inhabitants) but generated only 13 percent of the national product. Some 64 percent of northeastern households had earnings lower than the rough poverty level of US$320 in 1979,[52] whereas only 29 percent of families elsewhere in Brazil were as poor. Just under half the population of the northeast live in rural areas, whereas only 21 percent of the population in the rest of Brazil does. According to the 1980 census, mean earnings in the northeast were 58 percent of the national average. Estimates for 1985 suggest only slight changes. Income per capita in the northeast was US$992, or 61 percent of the national average of US$1,635 and less than half that in the south.

Although generally poor, the northeast is not a homogeneous region. The disparities among states in the northeast, as well as between urban and rural areas generally, are substantial. Table 3-1 contains data for the three states from which our samples are drawn (Ceará, Pernambuco, and Piauí), as well as for the region and for Brazil as a whole. Estimated per capita gross domestic product (GDP) in Piauí for 1985 is less than half that for Pernambuco, with Ceará about midway between the two. Disparities in basic living conditions are obvious: over 70 percent of families in Piauí lack electricity or sanitary facilities, again much worse than the situation in Pernambuco. Even Pernambuco, however, is noticeably below the national average in income and housing conditions.

Table 3-1. Basic Economic Indicators for the Three EDURURAL Research States, the Northeast Region, and Brazil, Selected Years

Indicator	Piaui	Ceará	Pernambuco	Northeast region	Brazil
Population in 1985 (thousands)	2,425	5,868	6,755	39,005	135,539
Percentage rural in 1980	58	47	38	49	31
Population growth rate, 1970–85 (percent)	2.48	2.00	1.80	2.21	2.43
Estimated per capita GDP in 1985 (U.S. dollars)	578	843	1,182	992	1,635
Percentage of households in 1980 without:					
Electric light	71	56	43	56	33
Sanitary facilities of any kind	72	56	33	52	23
Any source of clean water	55	44	35	42	16

Note: Data for 1988 are from 3 percent public use sample of the 1980 census.
Source: IBGE 1980.

Education in Rural Northeast Brazil

Basic education in Brazil is divided officially into two cycles: lower primary, which includes grades one to four (nominally for students seven to ten years old) and upper primary, which includes grades five to eight (for students eleven to fourteen years old). There are also kindergartens, which have as their objective educational readiness. In the rural northeast, however, rather than going to formal kindergarten, children often attend the local primary school for a period of literacy training (*ano de alfabetização*) before being counted as enrolled in first grade.[53]

The minimal educational objectives of the lower primary cycle are functional literacy and numeracy. The objective of upper primary schooling is adequate academic preparation for secondary education. The Education Reform Law of 1971 mandated free and compulsory education for all children between the ages of seven and fourteen—a goal still far from realized.

Data from Brazilian household surveys and censuses provide eloquent evidence that northeast Brazil is educationally disadvantaged compared with the rest of the nation, and that the rural areas are more deprived than urban areas. The comparative educational indicators for 1982 presented in table 3-2 locate rural northeast Brazil at the same place as the income comparisons did—firmly among the most disadvantaged worldwide. Throughout the table, the disparities within the country are also dramatic. Two-thirds of the rural northeast population is illiterate, and almost as many have less than one year of schooling. Outside the northeast, by contrast, only one-fifth of the population is illiterate. The situation

Table 3-2. Comparative Educational Indicators, 1982
(percentage)

Indicator	Rural northeast	Total northeast	Rest of Brazil
Illiteracy rate (population over five years)	65.5	50.2	21.6
Less than one year of education (population over ten years)	58.9	41.7	16.5
More than eight years of education (population over ten years)	1.1	7.9	15.0
Enrollment rate in grades 1–8 (population seven to fourteen years)	74.2	92.8	100.9
Enrollment rate in grades 1–4 (population seven to fourteen years)	67.6	72.2	67.0
Primary enrollment in			
Grades 1–2	71.1	55.3	39.9
Grades 1–4	91.1	77.9	66.5
Grades 5–8	8.9	22.1	33.5
Primary school teachers with incomplete primary education	59.8	25.3	5.9
Enrollment rate in grades 9–12 (population fifteen to nineteen years)	3.3	15.2	23.9

Source: IBGE, various years.

is actually much bleaker than implied by these literacy differentials alone, because the enrollment rates suggest that the problem will persist well into the future. Only 74 percent of rural northeastern children who by law should be attending school were actually attending in 1982. Moreover, 71 percent of all enrollment is stuck in the first two grades.

An additional source of the persistence of these unsatisfactory conditions is the evidently poor quality of schools in the northeast. Only 40 percent of the primary school teachers in rural northeast Brazil in 1982 had themselves completed primary school.

Tables 3-3 and 3-4, constructed from the 3 percent public use sample of the 1980 Brazilian census, refer exclusively to primary school age children—those seven to fourteen years old—who should be in school.[54] Table 3-3 shows that a striking 65 percent of rural northeast school age children had never attended school. Only 31 percent of school age children in the rural northeast actually attended school in the twelve months preceding the 1980 census and only 28 percent can read and write. The corresponding figures for attendance and reading in Brazil as a whole are more than double, at 69 percent. The clear implication of these numbers is that the educational disadvantage of youth in Brazil will continue to be concentrated to a very large extent in the northeast, especially in its rural areas, unless large changes are introduced.

*Table 3-3. Education Indicators for Children Aged
Seven to Fourteen, 1980*
(percentage)

Indicator	Brazil	Total northeast	Rural northeast
Attended school in last 12 months	69.2	52.4	30.7
Knows how to read and write	69.3	44.9	28.4
Never attended school	22.8	43.8	64.9
Mean years of schooling (years)	2.4	1.5	0.8

Source: Psacharopoulos and Arriagada 1989. Data source IBGE 1980.

As shown in table 3-4, when the raw data on attendance are adjusted for differences in a variety of intervening characteristics of households, parents, and children, the relative deprivation of the rural northeast, especially compared with the urban northeast, is even more stark. The probability of a rural-northeast school age child having attended school in the previous twelve months is less than half, and his grade attainment only one-quarter, that of his urban-northeast counterpart. His probability of having dropped out of school is three times greater, and of having to work four times greater, than his urban counterpart.

Children in the rural northeast are also very different from their peers elsewhere in Brazil in their rate of progression up through the grades once enrolled in school. As shown in table 3-5, promotion rates in the rural northeast are about half, and repetition rates at least double, those prevailing outside the northeast.[55] In the rural northeast, it takes between eighteen and twenty-three student-years of schooling services to ensure the entry of one student to fourth grade; the analogous figure for the

*Table 3-4. Adjusted Education Indicators for Children Aged
Seven to Fourteen, 1980*
(percentage)

Indicator	Brazil	Urban northeast	Rural northeast
Predicted percentage having attended school in last twelve months	69.2	74.0	30.7
Predicted mean grade attainment (years)	2.4	2.4	0.6
Predicted percentage having dropped out of school	10.2	4.3	13.3
Predicted percentage working	7.3	3.0	13.2

Note: Figures are partial coefficients from separate regressions of various characteristics of households, parental education, and parental occupations, on children's attendance, attainment, dropout, and employment, with all other variables set at mean values. Those stated as percents are properly interpreted as conditional probabilities.
Source: Psacharopoulos and Arriagada (1989). Data source IBGE 1980.

*Table 3-5. Flow Efficiency Indicators for Brazilian
Primary Schools, 1982*

Indicators	Northeast	Rural northeast	Low-income rural northeast	Rest of Brazil
Promotion rates				
Grade 2	0.486	0.368	0.339	0.690
Grade 3	0.542	0.364	0.318	0.725
Grade 4	0.521	0.275	0.209	0.650
Repetition rates				
Grade 2	0.449	0.514	0.524	0.277
Grade 3	0.366	0.477	0.504	0.212
Grade 4	0.315	0.437	0.486	0.158
Overall efficiency[a]				
Grade 2	3.2	4.5	5.0	1.9
Grade 4	9.2	18.0	22.6	5.1
Average years between grades 2 and 4[b]	4.3	6.6	7.8	3.0

a. Number of student-years of schooling services required to produce an entrant to the grade indicated.
b. Average time in grades 2 and 3 for an entrant to grade 4.
Source: Appendix tables C3-3 and C3-4.

rest of Brazil is five years. A perfectly efficient system would require three years. To move a student through second and third to fourth grade, which ought to require two student-years of schooling, requires about seven in the rural northeast, and three outside the northeast.

The EDURURAL Project

An important component of intensified Brazilian educational efforts in the 1980s was the Northeast Basic Education Project (EDURURAL), an integrated educational program instituted in 18 percent of the counties (*municipios*) in the northeast region. Planned in 1978—79 and launched in 1980, EDURURAL involved total incremental investment costs of US $92 million, of which US $32 million was financed with a loan from the World Bank. EDURURAL was designed to expand children's access to primary schooling, to reduce wastage of educational resources inherent in grade repetition and dropout as children progress through the system, and to increase achievement by improving the quality of instruction. Further, a hierarchical relationship was assumed among these three objectives. Improving learning achievement would reduce repetition and dropouts, which in turn would make it possible to enroll additional students in existing schools.[56]

There were 218 rural counties in the EDURURAL program. They were selected because they were thought to be the least developed areas (especially in educational terms) in their respective states, and because they were not receiving special educational attention through other programs. The underlying principle was to concentrate sufficient resources in the most disadvantaged areas to make a real difference. In these counties, only schools outside the county seat—often itself only a small town— received the full range of EDURURAL inputs. Those incremental investments in instructional quality included the following: construction and refurbishment of schools, provision of furniture, training of teachers, development of curricula especially adapted to the poor rural environment, provision of textbooks and other student learning materials, and the strengthening of the county school administrative apparatus through a new institutional structure, the *orgão municipal de educação*, or OME.[57]

During the period (1981–87) when the EDURURAL project was implemented in the 218 counties, a range of other educational improvement programs with similar objectives were under way elsewhere in the rural northeast. These other efforts typically sought at least one of the same three objectives and involved some, and occasionally all, of the same general kinds of inputs. But they differed among themselves and from EDURURAL in potentially important ways. The precise nature and mix of inputs varied from one project to another in different areas. One school might benefit from participating in the school lunch program. The teacher(s) in another might receive a salary supplement designed to reward their qualifications or simply to enhance their dedication to their jobs. Or teacher(s) might receive either general training in the form of academic upgrading and pedagogical techniques, or specific training on a newly developed curriculum. Still other schools might receive textbooks, or other instructional material, or furniture, or rehabilitation of the physical plant.

EDURURAL sought within given counties in each state to provide to the selected schools a reasonably integrated and concentrated package of all essential inputs in a planned and rational manner. To meet the enormous managerial challenge of doing so, EDURURAL supported strengthening the agencies involved in delivering public education at federal, state, and county levels. Where appropriate institutions did not exist, EDURURAL encouraged their establishment. In contrast, for example, to the primary schooling components of integrated rural development projects executed in several areas (frequently with separate World Bank support), EDURURAL was characterized by a certain focus and coherence as a single-purpose educational program. This, and the substantial participation of the World Bank, ensured that EDURURAL enjoyed a relative abundance of financial resources and other forms of special attention. Once EDURURAL was launched, counties not included because they were participating in some other program eagerly sought to be incorporated into EDURURAL.[58] In short, EDURURAL was the premier program among several education development programs for the lower grades being implemented simultaneously in the region. Together these programs offered an unusually attractive natural laboratory for learning how to improve educational performance among the rural poor.

The Research Project and Data Base

Given the program's size and importance, EDURURAL's sponsors—the federal Ministry of Education and Culture in Brasilia, the secretariats of education in the nine northeastern states, and the World Bank—agreed upon an unusually comprehensive program of data collection and analysis to assess whether EDURURAL was meeting its objectives.[59]

Two evaluation questions were paramount. The first concerned implementation: did the planned inputs actually get produced and delivered in the targeted schools? The second concerned effects: did those improved learning resources result in higher academic achievement of pupils, in less educational wastage, and in expanded access to schooling? A rigorous approach to this second question also promised substantial rewards in terms of more general understanding of the determinants of educational performance in very poor environments.

Key Design Characteristics

The EDURURAL evaluation research project established a plan for data collection that represented a compromise between what would be desirable for assessment purposes and what was reasonably obtainable given constraints of human and financial resources. This plan, as originally conceived in 1980–81, had seven important characteristics.

First, the data used for monitoring implementation and assessing effects would be collected over a substantial period in order to capture the full extent of project outcomes. The research design called for data collection in 1981 before the effective start of EDURURAL, in 1983 and 1985 as EDURURAL inputs were being diffused within designated project areas, and in 1987 when EDURURAL would have reached full implementation. (Yearly collection would have been superior, but was impractical for financial and administrative reasons.) In each case, data were to be collected in October-November, toward the end of the academic year.

Second, the grade-sampling scheme would be linked to the biennial data collection. Taking advantage of the decision to conduct a survey every other year, the evaluation research design called for data collection on each occasion from second and fourth graders in the *same* schools, originally selected randomly within counties in 1981.[60] As described below, this design made possible the observation of the same student in multiple years; that is, it generated panel data on individual students.

Third, data collection and evaluation would also involve a set of control schools, setting up a quasi-experimental design. In the absence of the project, no school system would be expected to stand still economically or educationally. In order to develop a comparison group—to provide information on what might have happened to EDURURAL schools had the program not been instituted—the evaluation research design called for data collection in a control group from OTHER counties not included in EDURURAL.[61] Counties in both categories were selected in 1981, using cluster sampling techniques.

Fourth, evaluation resources—again, for financial reasons—would be concentrated in a sample of participating states. Thus, the evaluation research design called for data collection in three of the nine EDURURAL states. Pernambuco, Ceará, and Piaui were selected purposely to represent, respectively, the most economically developed, the average, and the least developed areas of the northeast region (see table 3-1, above).

Fifth, the project evaluation would be based on the multitude of factors affecting the individual student's educational performance. The evaluation research design called for the meticulous measurement of the school and teacher resources provided to the child, and of his academic achievement. It also required data collection of a comprehensive set of variables designed to capture key characteristics of the child, his family, and his community. Further, the survey procedures would have to ensure that information about a child's community, family, school, and teacher could be associated easily with data on the child himself.

Sixth, student achievement would be measured by specially designed achievement tests that related to the school curriculum. The criterion referenced tests in Portuguese and mathematics, described in chapter 5 and appendix A, were intended to identify qualitative differences in student learning.

Seventh, information would be collected, separately from the field surveys, on the disaggregated costs of school inputs. The objective was to do so in sufficient detail to permit the statistically derived effects on achievement of packages of inputs to be linked directly to the costs of those packages. This would lead to an analysis of the cost-effectiveness of differing packages of inputs.

Sampling Outcomes and the Resulting Data Base

The data actually collected, representing the most comprehensive field survey of rural education ever attempted in a developing country, provide high quality information on large samples, as summarized in table 3-6.[62] In each year, data were available for analysis from between 585 and 670 schools and between 5,500 and 6,400 students.

Table 3-6. *Size of Samples, 1981, 1983, 1985, and 1987*

Sample	1981		1983		1985		1987 [Ceará only]	
	EDURURAL	OTHER	EDURURAL	OTHER	EDURURAL	OTHER	EDURURAL	OTHER
Counties	30	30	30	30	30	30	6	5
Schools	397	189	404	195	447	195	48	32
Teachers	463	231	499	278	606	291	n.a.	n.a.
Students								
Second grade	3,037	1,681	2,619	1,350	2,950	1,418	25	7
Third grade	n.a.	n.a.	n.a.	n.a.	n.a.	n.a.	68	44
Fourth grade	1,075	639	997	580	1,273	631	103	107
Dropouts	n.a.	n.a.	n.a.	n.a.	n.a.	n.a.	22	4

n.a. = Not applicable.
Note: These numbers refer to the schools, teachers, and students for which reasonably complete and reliable information was obtained in our surveys. Because some data are missing on individuals, the samples on which the various analyses are based are typically a little smaller than the numbers reported here.
Source: EDURURAL research sample.

Some of the outcomes of the sampling and data collection efforts did not, however, match original expectations. Each divergence has an effect on the analysis and on the reliability of any policy conclusions. In order to set the stage for the subsequent analysis, we identify several key differences here.

Schools disappeared over time. Between 1982 and 1984, the notoriously precarious circumstances of schools in the rural northeast were aggravated by two events unforeseen when EDURURAL was launched. The worst drought in the region's history reached its peak in 1983. Large numbers of families were forced off the land. Also in 1983, as the first step in a process of redemocratization in Brazil, elections for county executive (*prefeito*) were held. The staffing of rural primary schools is the exclusive prerogative of the county executive and the major form of patronage at the county level. So, after each change of county executive, not only are many teachers and administrative staff released but often entire schools are closed—especially those situated in the homes of teachers who have fallen out of favor.[63]

The confluence of these two events resulted in the disappearance by October-November 1983 of one-third of the schools originally sampled in 1981 (see table 3-7). Neither drought nor elections intervened between 1983 and 1985. Still, 17 percent of the schools sampled in 1983 could not be found in 1985. (Note that in an attempt to maintain similar sample sizes over time, schools that could not be found from one data round to the next were replaced in the sample by nearby schools in the same county.)

Further, we learned that even when a school survived the two years from one data round to the next, there was no guarantee that a surviving school would actually offer fourth-grade instruction.[64] If no students were available for fourth grade, the school did not offer fourth grade. And in schools with graded classrooms, if only one or two students were fit for the fourth grade, it is possible that the teacher simply refused to cater to the demand of such a small number. (Such a complication apparently is not a problem with multigraded classrooms.) Thus, over 100 surviving schools in 1983 and in 1985 failed to have a fourth grade, making it impossible to observe any students in those schools who progressed from the second to the fourth grade.

One striking aspect of these data is that both school survival and existence of fourth grades is dramatically lower in Ceará than in either Piauí or Pernambuco. This holds between 1981 and 1983—years affected by elections and drought—and between 1983 and 1985—years unaffected by these factors. Of the sampled schools in Ceará in 1983, only two-thirds survived until 1985 and less than 40 percent offered fourth-grade instruction in 1985. In contrast, over 80 percent of the 1983 sample

Table 3-7. School Survival by State and Program Status, 1981 and 1983

Schools	Piauí		Ceará		Pernambuco		Total		
	EDURURAL	OTHER	EDURURAL	OTHER	EDURURAL	OTHER	EDURURAL	OTHER	Total
1981									
Number in base year	124	47	164	77	109	65	397	189	586
Still operating two years later	82	37	92	60	76	45	250	142	392
Still operating two years later and had 4th grade	78	35	32	37	63	40	173	112	285
1983									
Number in base year	129	48	164	80	111	67	404	195	599
Still operating two years later	124	47	94	70	100	62	318	179	497
Still operating two years later and had 4th grade	106	44	48	47	88	55	242	146	388

Source: EDURURAL research sample.

schools in Piaui and Pernambuco provided fourth-grade instruction in 1985. Further, across all states and both time periods, schools surviving and offering a fourth grade are less likely to be found in EDURURAL counties than in the comparison (OTHER) counties.

Fewer students than anticipated were matched in adjoining survey cross sections. The original design called, insofar as possible, for sampling the same schools in each data round. No specific attempt was planned to follow individual students. However, the initial expectation was that many of the same individuals would appear at more than one phase of the data collection as they proceeded naturally from second to fourth grade over the two-year interval between data collections.

The survival record of schools obviously imposed limits on what could be expected in terms of students appearing in more than one survey. Repetition and dropout within schools that did survive from one survey to the next further reduced the numbers of students who could turn up in two successive surveys.

Table 3-8 reveals that hopes for large numbers were indeed unrealized between 1981 and 1983. Only 258 of the sampled fourth graders in 1983 (of the overall total of 1,557 fourth graders tested that year) had been in the 1981 sample of 4,677 second graders; in addition 39 fourth-grade students in 1983 had also been in the fourth-grade sample two years earlier. Despite intensified efforts to maximize the number of matches, the outcome for the matches between 1983 and 1985 was not much

Table 3-8. Distribution of Initial-Year Second-Grade Students by Follow-Up Year Status, 1981–83 and 1983–85

	Initial year	
Student distribution	*1981*	*1983*
Total second graders in initial year[a]	4,677	3,918
School missing in follow-up year	1,936	1,141
School present in follow-up year	2,741	2,777
Initial/follow-up total matched		
Second grade–second grade match	n.a.	126
Second grade–fourth grade match	258	379
Fourth grade–fourth grade match	39	41

a. Of those students tested in second grade (as in table 3-6), a few in each year were in schools whose status—continued existence or demise—at the succeeding testing round could not be verified from long distance several years after the fact, when the attempt was made. They are not included in these numbers, which thus differ slightly from those in table 3-6. However, student counts in this table do include some cases for which crucial analytical data are missing. Therefore, the numbers here also differ from those in figures 4-2 and 4-3.

Source: EDURURAL research sample.

better. Only 379 of the sampled fourth graders in 1985 (of an overall total of 1,904 fourth graders tested that year) had appeared in the 1983 sample of 3,918 second graders. In addition, the 1985 survey identified 126 students from the 1983 second graders who were still in second grade in 1985, and 41 students who were in fourth grade in both 1985 and 1983.[65]

The 1987 survey had to be altered substantially from the prior surveys. The 1987 survey retreated from the comprehensive cross sections of 1981, 1983, and 1985 to a more focused special purpose effort. The data collection was limited to a reduced sample of EDURURAL and OTHER counties in a single state (Ceará). Furthermore, the 1987 fieldwork did not involve, as had been the case on the three earlier occasions, collection of contemporaneous information on the full range of family, school, and other background variables. Unanticipated constraints after 1985 on research leadership, staff availability, and finances, in Brazil and in Washington, forced these limitations.

The 1987 data, however, are unique in three ways. First, the 1987 data collection was designed to reveal more clearly and precisely the patterns of retention and dropout. This change resulted in part from the discouraging outcomes on the matches in 1983 and 1985 that reinforced the concern with retention in the schools of Brazil's rural northeast. Second, they include anthropometric information on all sampled children, facilitating an analysis of the relationship between nutritional and health status and achievement. Finally, earlier years had employed separate achievement tests for second and fourth graders. In 1987, however, exactly the same achievement tests that had been administered to second graders in 1985 were given to all the children in the 1987 sample irrespective of their 1987 grade level. This produces true longitudinal gain scores for children who appear in both the 1985 and 1987 samples. In prior years, achievement measurements on matched children in fourth grade refer to the fourth grade tests administered in those years instead of to the second grade tests they had taken two years earlier.

Some important characteristics were unexpectedly difficult to measure accurately. The most serious deficiency was the incompleteness and crudeness of information on actual school attendance, expected to be an important determinant of achievement and retention. Difficulties in measuring attendance bedeviled the research from the start. The Brazilian research team insisted that attendance records are not typically kept in the rural schools of the northeast. The survey instruments as originally constructed and used in 1981 asked the teacher to recall whether the child had been absent less than half or more than half the school days in the two months preceding testing. The analytical results from 1981 suggested that even this crude measurement of attendance was significant. But the Brazilian survey team had very low confidence in its reliability and excluded it from the instruments in the 1983 and 1985 surveys. The information gathered in those years on the reasons for student absences was interesting but unfortunately no substitute for a quantitative measure of actual attendance.[66]

A second measurement shortfall concerned the costing of individual inputs to schooling. Primary attention in the EDURURAL evaluation was focused on measuring real inputs to the educational process. Even though resource costs are an important ingredient in educational policy, developing appropriate cost data on their real inputs is itself a major research challenge. Constraints of time and money permitted collecting data of the required detail and reliability in only one state in one period—Ceará in late 1984 and 1985. The data obtained were then used to proxy the situation in all states and years.[67] To the extent relative costs of inputs vary significantly by state or year, the reliability of the estimates of cost effectiveness is reduced.

Third, the indicators of socioeconomic conditions in the county do not come from our surveys, but from cross-sectional data obtained from the Brazilian Institute for Geography and Statistics (IBGE) for various years around 1980. Thus, although these indicators may be reasonable proxies for relative conditions in the early 1980s, they cannot capture any changes in those conditions over the decade. Although it is likely that conditions did change appreciably, there is no compelling reason to assume that changes affected EDURURAL and OTHER counties differently within each state.

Finally, experience gained in the 1981 and 1983 field surveys suggested that measurement of some variables could be improved by reformulating the questions or modifying the precoded categories of the responses. Several of the school quality variables (and a few others as well) are thus not perfectly comparable over time. Reliance upon normalized indices in the analysis ameliorates this complication but makes direct interpretation of some factors difficult.

While the sampling outcomes were less than perfect, the analytical samples remain adequate. The initial sampling and the replenishing of nonsurviving schools led to some oversampling and undersampling of schools and students in different subsamples. The study design called for random selection of schools with fourth grades in 1981, followed by visits to exactly the same schools in subsequent years. Disappearing schools were replaced by the nearest one in the county with a fourth grade. For each school visited, the field teams were trained to select randomly for interview ten students each from both the second and the fourth grades. If fewer than ten pupils were available in any grade—a frequent occurrence in small rural schools—all present were to be interviewed.

Table 3-9. Sample Proportions Actually Obtained for Schools and Pupils, by Year, State, and Program Status, 1981, 1983, and 1985 (as percentage of total number of schools and of total pupils enrolled in grades 1 to 4 in the sixty research counties)

Year	Piauí EDURURAL	Piauí OTHER	Ceará EDURURAL	Ceará OTHER	Pernambuco EDURURAL	Pernambuco OTHER	Total EDURURAL	Total OTHER
1981								
Schools	11.5	8.3	8.5	13.9	20.7	8.9	11.2	10.2
Pupils	2.9	2.3	1.9	2.7	7.1	3.3	3.3	2.8
1983								
Schools	12.1	7.3	9.9	15.4	20.8	8.2	12.4	9.8
Pupils	3.1	2.1	1.9	3.0	3.9	1.8	2.8	2.2
1985								
Schools	14.4	7.0	11.7	17.6	25.3	8.9	14.8	10.3
Pupils	3.4	2.1	2.3	3.7	4.9	1.9	3.2	2.4

Source: Calculated from tables 3-13 and 3-14, and from appendix table C3-1.

Table 3-9 shows that roughly 10 percent of schools and 3 percent of all students in the sixty-county research area were in fact surveyed. By comparison to the other two states, the fieldwork team in Pernambuco appears to have somewhat oversampled schools in EDURURAL counties at the expense of the OTHER counties, especially in 1981. Differences in sampling outcomes over time are minor and reflect the changing numbers of schools and students.

Table 3-10 shows that, within schools included in the samples, 40 to 60 percent of the students reported by the teacher as attending the school typically were surveyed. The anomalous situation in Pernambuco in 1981 is again evident. Surprisingly, the second-grade proportions are almost always higher than those for fourth grade, even though we expected the total number of students in the fourth grade to be systematically lower. Given the special nature of our schools—all had fourth grade when originally included in the sample—it is likely that this is a reflection both of relatively even enrollment across grades (after first grade) and of a higher propensity of fourth-grade students to be absent at the time of the school visit. Finally, it is worth noting that about one-fifth of the students in all the rural schools of the sixty counties actually attends schools from which we sampled second and fourth graders.

It would be useful for some analytical purposes to have had perfectly equal effective sampling proportions across states, years, and program status, but the variations on the whole are not large. The samples are broadly representative of the universe of second- and fourth-grade students in complete lower primary schools outside county seats in rural northeast Brazil.

Education in the EDURURAL Sample Counties

This section contains a snapshot of the economic and educational poverty of the actual research area, which comprised sixty rural counties in three states. There are two purposes for presenting these data. First, they provide additional insights into the economic and educational deficits of the area. Second, by facilitating comparison of census with sample data, they allow the implications of the data collection scheme to be better understood.

The sixty counties participating in the EDURURAL evaluation research appear from table 3-11 to be only slightly more disadvantaged educationally than the northeast in general. The differences are not large enough to conclude that the counties used in our study reflect only the most extreme circumstances in the northeast. The sample may be broadly representative of the region as a whole. The aggregate county-level indicators presented in table 3-12 further confirm both the socioeconomic heterogeneity of the region and the fact that the sixty counties

Table 3-10. Sample Proportions Actually Obtained for Second- and Fourth-Grade Students within Sampled Schools, by Year, State, and Program Status, 1981, 1983, and 1985 (as percentage of students in sampled schools in each grade)

Year	Piaui		Ceará		Pernambuco		Total	
	EDURURAL	*OTHER*	*EDURURAL*	*OTHER*	*EDURURAL*	*OTHER*	*EDURURAL*	*OTHER*
1981								
Second grade	41.9	50.3	66.0	55.6	75.9	89.9	58.2	66.0
Fourth grade	36.1	42.1	46.3	35.7	73.5	85.1	50.1	55.1
1983								
Second grade	38.4	45.6	62.5	51.3	55.5	43.4	48.7	46.8
Fourth grade	38.8	37.8	45.3	31.0	47.3	39.0	42.4	36.0
1985								
Second grade	34.8	46.3	55.9	49.9	46.6	44.8	43.3	47.1
Fourth grade	35.2	41.3	42.5	57.4	42.6	39.7	39.4	37.4
Memo item:								
Enrollment in sampled schools as percent of total enrollment in rural schools in sixty counties								
1981	21.9	24.0	11.7	18.6	22.1	11.2	17.6	17.1
1983	25.2	16.3	15.3	21.8	22.9	10.8	20.7	15.2
1985	26.7	15.1	18.6	28.5	29.0	12.0	23.6	17.0

Source: Calculated from tables 3-13 and 3-14, and from appendix table C3-1.

*Table 3-11. Selected Characteristics of Counties Participating
in the* EDURURAL *Evaluation Research and the Northeast in General*

Characteristic	60 EDURURAL evaluation study counties	Northeast in general
Percent of population in rural areas (1982)	100.0	47.0
Enrollment in grades 1–4 (percent of those 7–14 years 1982)	63.6[a]	72.2
Economically active literate population (percent with 1–3 years education 1981)	25.5	22.7
Teachers with incomplete primary education (percent of all teachers 1983)[b]	38.3	25.3
School operated by county (percent of total)	84.0	83.0
Female enrollment (percent enrollment in grades 1–4)	62.8	50.5
Overage in grade (percent in first grade over age 10)	35.8	32.6

a. EDURURAL data are for 1983.
b. EDURURAL is calculated on the basis of grades 1–4.
Source: EDURURAL research sample.

*Table 3-12. Mean Value of Community Characteristics by State
and Program Status for Sample Counties*

Characteristics	EDURURAL	OTHER
Agricultural productivity		
Average (for three states)	0.424	0.483
Piauí	0.136	0.137
Ceará	0.207	0.416[a]
Pernambuco	0.928	0.896
Socioeconomic status		
Average (for three states)	0.162	0.180
Piauí	0.089	0.061
Ceará	0.192	0.150
Pernambuco	0.205	0.330

Note: The agricultural productivity variable is constructed from information on the cruzeiro value of production per hectare. The socioeconomic status indicator is a complex variable incorporating information on the value of output per worker, the proportion of the labor force outside agriculture, the proportion of the population receiving income above the poverty line, the proportion literate, and the prevalence of houses with electricity and of medical doctors. See appendix B for a complete description of data construction.
a. Difference between EDURURAL and OTHER is significant at 5 percent level.
Source: EDURURAL research sample.

in which our research took place are a reasonable reflection of the relative levels of development of the three states: Piaui is the poorest, Pernambuco is by far the most developed, and Ceará is in between. Differences between EDURURAL and OTHER counties are not great.[68]

Our sample of schools from sixty counties in three states was not intended to replicate in miniature the essential features of education in northeastern Brazil. Most important, ours was a truly rural sample that excludes even small village schools in the county seats (*sede de municipio*).

Consider the information on all schools outside county seats, and their student enrollments in the four lower primary grades, for EDURURAL and OTHER areas. These data, displayed in table 3-13, come from the official county-level statistics collected annually by the state secretariats of education in conjunction with the federal ministry of education. The data indicate the volatility of schools. Ceará in particular stands out, with the total number of schools in the EDURURAL areas falling from 1,932 in 1981 to 1,662 in 1983. This suggests that schools are not being built more in EDURURAL than in OTHER areas.

With respect to the numbers of students enrolled, the overall trend is upward, but only in Ceará is there a suggestion that access in EDURURAL areas may be increasing faster than in OTHER areas. The startling proportion of enrollments concentrated in first grade (which includes the ano de alfabetização) is a reflection both of the large proportion of rural schools in the northeast that do not offer even the first four grades and of high repetition rates.

Table 3-14 shows the distributions of students by grade for the schools in our sample. Compared with table 3-13, it is evident that our sample schools have a significantly lower proportion of students in the first two grades. The explanation lies in the sampling methodology. In contrast to the population of schools, our sample includes only those schools (selected randomly from the county lists) that offered fourth-grade instruction in 1981; in subsequent years, schools that disappeared were replaced only with schools also offering fourth grade. But even in schools that offer fourth grade (all schools in our sample), 50 to 60 percent of all students are in first grade. Depending upon the state, between one-third and two-thirds of these first graders are actually in the preliminary ano de alfabetização, which does not figure in the official characterization of lower primary schooling.

Table 3-15 provides further information on students drawn from our surveys. Students in second grade are, on average, more than twelve years old; the "proper" age for this grade is eight or nine years. The difference is a reflection of late age at entry and very slow progression through the grades. Our second graders typically entered school more than one year late and then needed three to four years to attain their second-grade

Table 3-13. Primary Schools outside County Seats and Lower Primary Enrollments by State and Program Status in the Sixty Sample Counties, 1981, 1983, and 1985

Enrollment	Piauí			Ceará			Pernambuco		
	1981	1983	1985	1981	1983	1985	1981	1983	1985
Schools									
EDURURAL	1,082	1,063	985	1,932	1,662	1,535	526	534	493
OTHER	564	655	684	555	519	455	730	818	752
Total	1,646	1,718	1,669	2,487	2,181	1,990	1,256	1,352	1,245
Students in grades 1–4									
EDURURAL	47,746	49,290	47,890	53,501	53,058	58,440	24,397	27,744	25,221
OTHER	23,882	26,155	26,184	23,001	22,306	20,987	34,549	40,288	38,445
Total	71,628	75,445	74,074	76,502	75,364	79,427	58,946	68,032	63,666
Percentage of students in grade 1									
EDURURAL	69	64	55	77	75	79	66	64	50
OTHER	74	71	64	69	70	67	55	57	52
Total	71	66	58	75	76	76	59	60	51

Note: Data elaborated by the EDURURAL research team at Universidade Federal do Ceará, Fortaleza, from the yearly educational statistics collection of the state education secretariats.

Source: Fundação Cearense de Pesquisas e Cultura (various years).

Table 3-14. *Proportion of Students Enrolled in First Grade and Number of Students Enrolled in Second and Fourth Grades, Sample Schools, by Year, State, and Program Status, 1981, 1983, and 1985*

Enrollment	Piauí			Ceará			Pernambuco			Total		
	1981	1983	1985	1981	1983	1985	1981	1983	1985	1981	1983	1985
All sampled schools												
Percent enrolled in grade 1	58	56	49	58	64	61	48	49	46	56	57	53
Grade 2 enrollments	3,141	3,455	4,087	2,134	2,319	2,878	2,496	2,488	2,863	7,771	8,262	9,828
Grade 4 enrollments	1,413	1,738	1,828	786	947	1,533	1,104	1,278	1,555	3,303	3,963	4,916
Enrollments, all grades	16,204	16,688	16,737	10,526	12,976	16,873	9,242	10,715	11,930	35,972	40,379	45,540
EDURURAL												
Percent enrolled in grade 1	60	55	47	61	68	64	45	53	47	57	59	53
Grade 2 enrollments	2,362	2,673	3,312	1,256	1,325	1,747	1,605	1,377	1,757	5,223	5,375	6,816
Grade 4 enrollments	1,052	1,248	1,390	397	411	881	695	691	960	2,144	2,350	3,231
Enrollments, all grades	10,461	12,439	12,774	6,243	8,121	10,890	5,385	6,347	7,321	22,089	26,907	30,985
OTHER												
Percent enrolled in grade 1	54	59	55	55	55	55	52	44	46	54	52	52
Grade 2 enrollments	779	782	775	878	994	1,131	891	1,111	1,106	2,548	2,887	3,012
Grade 4 enrollments	361	490	438	389	536	652	409	587	595	1,159	1,613	1,685
Enrollments, all grades	5,743	4,249	3,963	4,283	4,855	5,983	3,857	4,368	4,609	13,883	13,472	14,555

Source: EDURURAL research sample.

Table 3-15. Mean Values of Selected Student Characteristics by Grade, State, Year, and Program Status, 1981, 1983, and 1985

Characteristic	1981		1983		1985	
	EDURURAL	OTHER	EDURURAL	OTHER	EDURURAL	OTHER
Age						
Second grade						
Piauí	12.33	12.58	12.27	12.51	11.69[a]	12.32
Ceará	13.08[a]	12.12	13.54[a]	11.50	13.16[a]	11.84
Pernambuco	12.09	11.74	12.19[a]	11.40	11.20[a]	11.23
Total	12.44[a]	12.05	12.65[a]	11.73	12.05	11.75
Fourth grade						
Piauí	14.45[a]	14.92	14.50	14.71	14.10	14.09
Ceará	15.28[a]	13.96	15.33[a]	14.37	14.75[a]	13.71
Pernambuco	14.54[a]	13.81	14.36	14.04	14.01[a]	13.77
Total	14.64[a]	14.11	14.61	14.35	14.26[a]	13.84
Age at entry to school						
Second grade						
Piauí	8.10	8.16	7.86	8.02	7.41	7.53
Ceará	8.19	7.99	8.14[a]	7.27	7.71[a]	7.16
Pernambuco	8.34[a]	8.01	8.08[a]	7.61	7.55[a]	7.30
Total	8.22[a]	8.04	8.01[a]	7.59	7.55[a]	7.30
Fourth grade						
Piauí	8.26	8.21	7.83[a]	8.28	7.48	7.37
Ceará	8.25[a]	7.64	7.88	7.50	7.58[a]	7.12
Pernambuco	8.25[a]	7.67	7.98	7.63	7.64[a]	7.35
Total	8.25[a]	7.79	7.88	7.80	7.56[a]	7.30
Years exposure to school[b]						
Second grade						
Piauí	4.10	3.91	4.23	4.13	4.18[a]	4.50
Ceará	4.38[a]	3.88	4.78[a]	4.03	4.89[a]	4.44
Pernambuco	3.51	3.45	3.78[a]	3.55	3.47	3.66
Total	3.88[a]	3.73	4.27[a]	3.89	4.23	4.18
Fourth grade						
Piauí	5.83[a]	6.36	6.34	5.83	6.53	6.39
Ceará	6.44	6.12	6.78	6.33	6.69[a]	6.26
Pernambuco	5.95	5.82	5.96	5.90	6.09	6.07
Total	5.99	5.98	6.30[a]	6.01	6.43[a]	6.23
Sex (percentage female)						
Second grade						
Piauí	56.3	61.2	55.9	55.9	57.2	53.8
Ceará	62.0[a]	55.7	63.7	61.8	63.3[a]	55.9
Pernambuco	58.1	60.5	60.8	65.4	58.0[a]	64.4
Total	58.6	59.3	61.1	59.9	59.4	58.3
Fourth grade						
Piauí	65.3	67.8	62.0	69.2	61.8	63.0
Ceará	71.2	73.4	70.4	69.3	74.6[a]	63.1
Pernambuco	68.4	69.9	75.5[a]	60.7	72.6	66.5
Total	68.9	68.8	68.0	65.9	69.0[a]	64.3

a. Indicates difference between EDURURAL and OTHER is significant at the 5 percent level.

b. Defined as age less age at entry to school less years since entry reported as not having attended school at all.

Source: EDURURAL research sample.

*Table 3-16. Mean Values of Selected Family Characteristics
by Grade, State, Year, and Program Status, 1981, 1983, and 1985*

Characteristic	1981 EDURURAL	1981 OTHER	1983 EDURURAL	1983 OTHER	1985 EDURURAL	1985 OTHER
Father's education						
(years)						
Second grade						
Piauí	1.88	1.83	1.83[a]	1.41	1.53[a]	1.07
Ceará	1.60	1.78	1.28[a]	1.48	1.16[a]	1.38
Pernambuco	1.59[a]	1.88	1.30[a]	1.74	1.40	1.44
Total	1.69[a]	1.82	1.50	1.55	1.37	1.32
Fourth grade						
Piauí	2.13	2.18	2.06[a]	1.37	1.65[a]	1.22
Ceará	2.06	1.93	1.69	1.65	1.05[a]	1.71
Pernambuco	1.87	2.08	1.70	1.74	1.34[a]	1.66
Total	2.00	2.07	1.87[a]	1.59	1.38	1.55
Mother's education						
(years)						
Second grade						
Piauí	2.13	2.01	2.01	1.95	1.72	1.73
Ceará	2.02[a]	2.35	1.67[a]	2.42	1.66[a]	2.31
Pernambuco	1.89[a]	2.15	1.83[a]	2.36	1.84	1.94
Total	2.00[a]	2.18	1.85	2.27	1.73[a]	2.03
Fourth grade						
Piauí	2.60	2.56	2.65[a]	1.56	1.85	1.91
Ceará	2.32[a]	2.79	2.50	2.33	1.88[a]	2.58
Pernambuco	2.13	2.33	1.93[a]	2.32	2.05	2.19
Total	2.33	2.48	2.36[a]	2.13	1.92[a]	2.24
Fathers are literate						
(percentage)						
Second grade						
Piauí	65	69	69	68	60	58
Ceará	59[a]	67	58[a]	64	55	57
Pernambuco	54	57	55	61	53	57
Total	59[a]	62	61	64	56	57
Fourth grade						
Piauí	69	66	70	72	62	64
Ceará	68	70	64	65	56	62
Pernambuco	59	65	63	58	48[a]	61
Total	64	66	67	65	56[a]	62
Mothers are literate						
(percentage)						
Second grade						
Piauí	69	69	67	73	62	62
Ceará	67[a]	73	65[a]	77	62[a]	68
Pernambuco	60	62	59[a]	70	58[a]	64
Total	65	67	64[a]	73	61[a]	65
Fourth grade						
Piauí	73	71	78	72	66	66
Ceará	79	83	78	81	68[a]	77
Pernambuco	64	67	66	72	59[a]	69
Total	70	71	74	75	64[a]	71

a. Indicates difference between EDURURAL and OTHER is significant at the 5 percent level.
Source: EDURURAL research sample.

status. There is a hint that average age at entry may have declined over the 1981–85 period, which would be consistent with a slight improvement in initial access to schooling. But the data on years' exposure to schooling suggest that progression rates after initial entry may even have declined.

Another unusual characteristic of education in rural northeast Brazil is evident in the sex composition of our sample. Contrary to the situation in a majority of developing countries, girls consistently outnumber boys, and the disparity uniformly increases with grade. The proportions are reasonably constant over the 1981–85 period. Fewer boys enter school and fewer are retained by school. This probably reflects the higher opportunity cost in lost production of sending boys to school, especially after age twelve. Girls, whose economic contribution is more often in sibling care and other domestic chores, can more easily be spared, especially in large peasant families with several sisters.

Finally, table 3-16 reveals that the parents of our sample children on average report having fewer than two years of schooling; typically only 60 to 65 percent are literate. Because of the importance of parents, both in setting educational standards and in helping directly in the educational process, this picture is especially bleak. Improvements in the overall education levels in northeast Brazil cannot realistically come from small incremental changes in schooling over generations. If attempted in that manner, northeast Brazil will clearly be doomed to its absolute and relative educational deficit for centuries, not just decades.

The Agenda

The previous sections make a very simple point. Rural northeast Brazil is perhaps unique in the world. It faces educational (and economic) poverty equal to the worst in the world but does so within a country that also has rich and technologically advanced areas approaching the educational (and economic) standards of the most developed groups of countries. Of course, the educational situation in the northeast is neither new nor unnoticed. The Brazilian government has undertaken a variety of policies and programs designed to remedy the situation. Among the most important, and perhaps the largest, of these in the 1980s was the EDURURAL program. The remainder of this book is devoted to answering the question, "Did it work?" and to using the evidence generated by the investigation to query, "Can anything work?"

PART II

Research Findings

4

Quantity: The Determinants of Continuation in School

THE DISMAL LEVELS OF SCHOOL COMPLETION in northeast Brazil—rivaling the levels found in the world's poorest countries—are a clear and pressing problem. Readily available measures of education for the adult population such as schooling completed and literacy rates all paint a picture of relative and absolute deprivation for this region. The area is unlikely to experience self-sustained development without significant improvements in its level of human capital, which will require focusing much more attention on the schooling of its youth. The evidence unambiguously suggests that aggressive interventions are warranted.

In this chapter we examine the traditional quantitative aspects of human capital formation: access to schooling and promotion through the grades. The next chapter then considers the more qualitative aspects of human capital formation: differences in educational performance, or achievement, of students.

The quantitative aspects of human capital formation—access and promotion—have been the central focus of most previous development policy discussions in the educational sector. They present a number of challenges to the policymaker. For example, while governmental policy in Brazil may declare that school attendance is mandatory between the ages of seven and fourteen, that is clearly insufficient to ensure effective human capital formation. Enforcing compulsory attendance is often not possible, particularly in rural areas where students can perform productive activities on farms. Moreover, presence in school does not guarantee that students progress through the grades or even that they learn anything while there. In fact, mandatory attendance can lead to extensive grade repetition with little gain in knowledge.[69]

Further, the quality implications of compulsory schooling policies are potentially serious. Resources for education are constrained everywhere, particularly in those developing countries that are furthest from universal

schooling. Expanding enrollments without commensurately expanding
the resources devoted to schooling would imply that other measures are
being taken to reduce per pupil expenditure. The options include allowing class sizes to rise, teacher salaries (and presumably their qualifications) to fall, or availability of textbooks and other materials to decline.
The possible sacrifice of quality inherent in such measures is clear
enough. More perversely, a portion of the students so enrolled may be
uninterested and not learning. If so, the funds used for such students are
effectively diverted from the provision of higher quality schooling for
those who are appropriately prepared and motivated to take advantage
of the school experience.

The budgetary tradeoffs between quantity and quality of schooling
have been frequently noted (for example, Solmon 1986). But these
discussions do not include any significant direct empirical investigation
of the relationship between the two.[70] The pure budgetary discussions
suggest that a more or less mechanical accounting exercise will provide
information about the tradeoffs. This approach, however, ignores at least
two central issues. First, the links between quantity and quality that arise
from the underlying behavior of students and teachers in the educational
process are nowhere considered.[71] Second, too much is assumed about
the relationships between quality and costs. (See chapters 5 and 6 for a
fuller discussion of this subject.)

The data generated by the EDURURAL evaluation research provide an
unique opportunity to address some of these gaps in the policy discussions. The longitudinal structure of the data allows inferences about the
relationships among school continuation, promotion, and student performance. Moreover, the rich observations about families and schools
permit investigation of the underlying determinants of promotion.

Student Flows and the Structure of the Data

Many students in rural northeast Brazil never finish the first four grades,
let alone attend secondary school or higher education. Students must
contend with poor schools, pressing poverty that realistically can be
alleviated only by taking advantage of opportunities for immediate employment in the agricultural sector, and frequent lack of support from
home. In such circumstances, students tend to progress slowly through
the grades and to drop out of school, often long before the prescribed
period of compulsory attendance is completed. The consequences—low
completion rates and excessive repetition in primary grades—were
chronicled in chapter 3 and are well known to policymakers in Brazil.
What is not understood is how this situation can be improved. This in
turn reflects the overall lack of knowledge about the underlying behavior
of students and families.

The primary difficulty in analyzing school completion and promotion patterns has been a general lack of detailed data describing the paths of students through school and measuring the factors that influence students' decisions. In simplest terms, neither aggregate data nor data about a cross-section of students can support the kind of analyses that are required for policy purposes. The EDURURAL data set, although not explicitly designed for this purpose, goes some distance toward remedying previous data inadequacies.

The EDURURAL data collection was based upon repeated sampling from the student bodies in a set of schools drawn randomly within EDURURAL and control (OTHER) counties. The schools were observed at four different times (1981, 1983, 1985, and 1987), and during each observation a random sample of second and fourth graders was surveyed and tested.[72] This data collection design, in which interviewers returned to the same school every two years, offered an opportunity to observe individual students repeatedly. Most important, there was a group of students—initially in the second grade—who were progressing at the expected pace so that they were in the fourth grade in the follow-up sampling.[73] Whether or not a student was actually observed in subsequent data collection was a function of many intervening factors including purely random sampling chances.

The ability to use the EDURURAL samples to analyze questions about the quantity of schooling depends crucially on understanding the dynamics of the samples and utilizing the panel data on both schools and students. For analytical purposes, it is convenient to think in terms of probability models and to link the conditional probabilities of a series of basic events to their determinants. The difficulty in this analysis is that the observations of events are incomplete.

Two important linkages of the data across years can be identified. First, from the repeated sampling of the same schools, it is possible to identify whether or not a given school continues to serve its students over time. Contrasting schools that survive with those that do not offers insight into the prevalence of schools in the research area. Second, for those schools that survive for the two-year period and also have a fourth grade, it is possible to find some second-grade students who are promoted to the fourth grade by the subsequent data collection. Comparing promoted students with others allows some insights into the determinants of progression in school.

Figure 4-1 presents a schematic diagram of the various paths a student initially observed in the second grade can follow, either to the fourth grade or to other possible outcomes.[74] The focus of our attention is on *time promotions* from the second to the fourth grade because this is what is observed through the alternating-years sampling scheme. Paths identified in the figure by heavy lines can be observed in our 1983 and

Figure 4-1. Possible Paths for a Student Initially Observed in Second Grade.

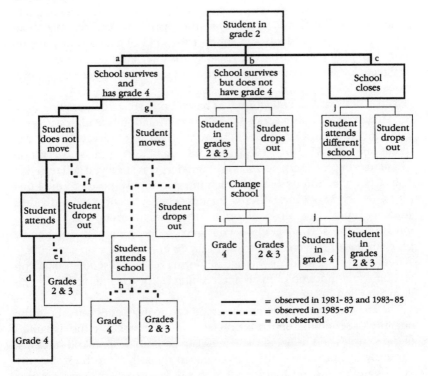

Note: Heavy boxes indicate students in sample.
Source: EDURURAL research samples.

1985 samples, and the flow probabilities can be estimated. Paths identified by thin lines are not observed in the samples, but those identified by broken lines on figure 4-1 can be found for the special subset of Ceará students surveyed in both 1985 and 1987. (This latter group is the subject of a special analysis.)

Understanding the flow of students is important for interpreting the subsequent analysis. The first analysis considers what determines whether a student's school survives with a fourth grade over the two-year period from initial to follow-up sampling. This is equivalent to the probability of being on path *a* as opposed to *b* or *c* in figure 4-1. The second analysis concentrates on the student's promotion chances, given that the student's school survives and has a fourth grade. This analysis compares path *d* with paths *e*, *f*, and *g*—the alternative routes for a student that include remaining in the second or third grade, dropping out of school, or moving away. In this analysis, it is not possible to distinguish among these latter outcomes; students are observed either to have been promoted on time or not. The special 1985–87 sample can distinguish among these outcomes, but cannot be used to analyze school survival.

The potential flows indicate three important points about the promotion modeling. First, the analysis is restricted to on-time promotions. A student still in grade 2 or 3 is treated the same as one who has dropped out; neither has progressed through school at the expected pace. Second, some students who have progressed to the fourth grade are not identified because they have changed schools between the two survey years; they are depicted in paths *h*, *i*, and *j* in the figure. Although the students on these paths are almost certainly few, this measurement problem could influence subsequent analysis.[75] Third, the sampling of students did not capture all of the fourth graders in those schools with a large (more than ten pupils) fourth grade. Moreover, except in 1987, there was no explicit attempt to resurvey those tested two years earlier in the second grade. This sampling does not cause much of an analytical problem, however, because the random selection eliminates bias in the subsequent behavioral estimation. Nevertheless, the mean promotion rates observed in the sample will understate the true overall on-time promotion rates.

Figures 4-2 and 4-3 present the overall division of the sampled second graders for 1981 and 1983, collapsing the flow patterns into those that can be identified within the data. For the first sample, the schools of 59

Figure 4-2. Analytical Samples for 1981 Student Flows.

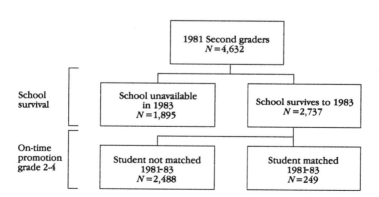

Source: EDURURAL research sample.

Figure 4-3. Analytical Samples for 1983 Student Flows.

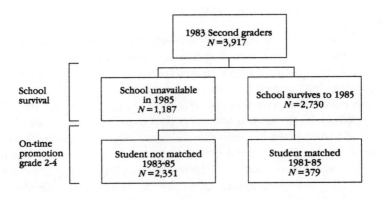

percent of the 1981 second graders (2,737 students) survive to 1983. Of these students who could potentially be matched with data for 1983, only 9 percent (249 students) are found in the fourth grade in the follow-up survey. The corresponding numbers for 1983 are 2,730 students in surviving schools and 14 percent (379) of these students found in the fourth grade in 1985.

The central task with respect to both school survival and student promotion is to determine what governs the outcomes that we observe. In each case, the outcome is viewed as the end result of a probabilistic process in which a number of exogenous factors affect the conditional probabilities of the outcome. By using the information from the initial surveys (1981 or 1983), statistical probability models are estimated to capture the different outcomes in the follow-up surveys (1983 or 1985). Our analysis begins with models of school survival and then turns to student promotion probabilities.

School Survival

In rural areas, the availability of a school is not assured. Yet, obviously, a prerequisite for school attendance is the existence of a school within a reasonable distance. In addition, schooling in rural areas is frequently disrupted because of schools closing down or not providing grades for further progress.

The sampling scheme of the EDURURAL project does not allow investigation of the general question of what determines whether or not a school exists for any individual student, but it does allow tracing the history and analyzing the survival of individual schools. As shown earlier (table 3-7), fully one-third of the schools originally sampled in 1981 no longer existed by 1983. Of those sampled in 1983, 17 percent disappeared by 1985. Only 49 percent of the schools sampled in 1981 both survived and offered a fourth grade in 1983; of those sampled in 1983, only 65 percent both survived and offered a fourth grade in 1985.

The simple question asked here is whether there are systematic differences between schools that survive during each of the two-year periods and those that do not. The approach is to estimate probit models that provide information about how various factors affect the probability of survival.[76] We hypothesize that this probability is affected by three general sets of factors that include the following: the economic conditions in the area, the quality of the existing school facilities, and the governmental support for the school. Schools in economically stronger areas are presumed to be more likely to survive since the locality can better support schooling investments. Additionally, schools that are more established and have better facilities are more likely to be continued.

The following tables convert the results of the probit estimation into estimated marginal effects on survival probabilities evaluated at the means for each of the variables.[77] Estimates based on probit coefficients that are not significantly different from zero at the 5 percent level are enclosed in parentheses.[78] Separate estimates are performed for each of the two sample periods: 1981 schools surviving to 1983, and 1983 schools surviving to 1985. Additionally, two variants are considered for each period: one with disaggregated physical characteristics of schools and one with an index of school facilities.

Economic Conditions

As demonstrated in table 4-1, the evidence that school survival is positively related to the wealth of the surrounding county is not very strong. For both 1981 and 1983, two variables were used as proxies for the wealth of the area: a measure of agricultural productivity (output per hectare at the county level about 1980) and the percentage of farmers in the county who sold crops in the market (as aggregated from data in the family questionnaires of our surveys). Selling crops proved not to be statistically significant in either year. The productivity index had an unexpected effect on survivability. For the 1983–85 time period, schools in the more productive counties had a lower probability of surviving than those in counties with poorer agricultural conditions, and this estimated effect was statistically different from zero (at the 5 percent level).

*Table 4-1. Effects of County Economic Conditions on School
Survival Probabilities, 1981–83 and 1983–85*

Variable	1981–83	1983–85
Agricultural productivity index	(0.001)	− 0.174
Percent selling crops	(− 0.001)	(− 0.000)
Participation in Emergência	—	− 0.003

— = Not available. (Program not in existence.)
Note: Estimated marginal probabilities are calculated at means of variables and holding
constant other factors contained in probit equations that include disaggregated school
facility measures. For full results, see appendix table C4-1. Estimates that are not significantly
different from zero at the 5 percent level are reported in parentheses.
Source: Appendix table C4-1.

We can offer no really convincing explanation for this counterintuitive
result.[79]

Short-term economic conditions, on the other hand, proved to be more
important for school survival. The drought that hit the northeast in the
early 1980s seriously affected farming and agriculture, producing significant out-migration in some areas and general economic hardship. To
provide some relief, the government in 1983 instituted the *Programma
de Emergência*, a public works employment program that used federal
funds to pay people for labor on road maintenance, water reservoirs,
irrigation canals, and other public works. Though we have no direct
measure of the severity of the drought in different areas, we use the
percentage of the population enrolled in the *Emergência* program to
proxy the severity of the drought. (This measure is unavailable for the
1981–83 period because the program was not operating then.) The estimates indicate that participation in Emergência is negatively related to
school survival, as we had hypothesized. Evaluated at the means for each
of the variables, the probit estimates indicate that if an additional 10
percent of the population is in the program, the chances of school survival
fall by about 3.5 percentage points, everything else being equal.

We investigated various other measures related to the wealth and income in the different counties, including our overall index of socioeconomic status (SES) at the county level[80] and school averages of agricultural employment data constructed from our sample surveys of schools.
None of these crude measures of economic conditions, however, provided any added insights into school survival probabilities and are not
included in the reported models.

While it may seem strange that variations in short-term economic conditions are important but that long-term economic conditions, or wealth,
are not, it must be remembered that we are looking at school survival.
In other words, given that a school once existed, how likely is it that it

exists two years later? It could well be that wealth has a more important effect on the original existence of schools—something that we cannot analyze. Alternatively, our measures of wealth may simply be too crude to capture true differences that do enter into survival.

School Characteristics

The effects of characteristics of the schools, estimated in two different ways, are summarized in table 4-2. The two most important school characteristics affecting school survival are size of the school and whether or not it is found in the teacher's house. Larger schools, measured simply by number of students in grades one through four, are more likely to continue; an addition of ten students to a school increases its chances of survival by 1 to 2 percent. The estimated effect of enrollment on survival is slightly higher in the 1983–85 period, but the overall effects are quite consistent. School size could operate in two ways. First, larger schools simply are more established and more integral to the total community. Second, larger schools provide a higher probability of having sufficient numbers of fourth graders to provide fourth-grade instruction.

Schools in the teachers' houses are for the most part marginal schools. They have not received high levels of support from the government, and their continued existence depends largely upon the continued good will of the teacher and upon the teacher's remaining in the good graces of the mayor. Not surprisingly then, schools in teachers' houses tend to go out of existence at fairly high rates, especially during local elections. The

Table 4-2. Effects of School Characteristics on School Survival Probabilities, 1981–83 and 1983–85

Variable	1981–83		1983–85	
	Disaggregated characteristics	Aggregated characteristics	Disaggregated characteristics	Aggregated characteristics
Number of students	0.0012	0.0014	0.0015	0.0018
Teacher's house	−0.1962	−0.2513	−0.0762	−0.1370
School facilities index		0.0010		0.0553
Buildings	(0.029)		0.1908	
Furnishings	0.0892		0.1438	
Electricity	0.0569		0.0632	
Water	−0.1025		(−0.034)	
OME	—		−0.0845	(−0.072)

— = Not available because OMEs did not exist in 1981.

Note: Estimated marginal probabilities are calculated at means of variables and holding constant other factors contained in probit equations. For full results, see appendix table C4-1. Estimates that are not significantly different from zero at the 5 percent level are reported in parentheses.

Blank cells indicate variables not included in regression.

Source: Appendix table C4-1.

estimates suggest that survival chances go down by 20 to 25 percentage points in 1981–83 and by 8–14 percentage points in 1983–85 if the school is located in the teacher's house.

Part of the difference between the periods may result from the drought and elections in 1983. But part also undoubtedly reflects the development of the school samples. The initial sample of schools attempted to be representative within the sample counties. As schools disappeared, they were replaced by nearby schools offering fourth grade. From the 1981 and 1983 means, we see that students attending schools in teachers' houses declined from 17 percent to 12 percent. Moreover, by keeping survivors in the sample, the 1983 sample includes more resilient schools—ones that have already been observed to survive the previous two years. Therefore, the 1981–83 estimates are probably better estimates of the marginal survival probabilities for these schools operating without appropriate facilities.

Since individual students are not traced, it is impossible to determine what happens to the students in these disappearing schools. Possibly, schools in teachers' houses simply move around more than those in regular facilities, so that individual students are not without schools as frequently as these estimates might suggest. Nevertheless, attending minimally supported schools is clearly risky in the sense that the schooling opportunity is much less permanent.

The physical characteristics of the schools are included in the analysis in two forms: as separate factors or as an index that combines them. While the precise effects of the separate factors vary across years and between each other, the general conclusion is simply that schools with more complete facilities are more likely to survive. In other words, communities that make larger investments in schools apparently work to ensure that their schools continue.

The one puzzling characteristic is the existence of water at the school, which is associated with significantly lower probabilities of survival, at least in the 1981–83 period. While we would expect schools with water to have higher survival rates (other things equal), the estimated negative effect could reflect unmeasured factors.[81]

Government Support

Beyond paying for buildings, teacher salaries, and instructional equipment, governmental support for schooling typically involves both routine managerial control, inspection, pedagogical supervision, and technical assistance. The *orgão municipal de educação* (OME) is the specialized county-level government agency established to systematize and institutionalize these functions of education administration. Prior to the advent of OMES in rural northeast Brazil in the early 1980s, these functions were usually neglected. Schools were administered on an ad hoc basis directly by the county executive (*prefeito*) without fixed rules and regulations and very much according to his whim. Establishment of OMES was thus deemed a necessary although not sufficient condition for improvement in educational performance. As shown in table 4-2, schools in counties with better OMES also tend to go out of existence more frequently.[82] An optimistic interpretation is that this may reflect quality control by the OME. With more and better personnel in the OME, schools can be evaluated better. Small unstable schools in the teacher's house are more readily consolidated into larger premises built for the purpose. An alternative, malevolent interpretation is that OMES operate to extend and systematize the effective influence through patronage of the county prefeito, which is exactly what their establishment was meant to diminish.

School survival probabilities also differ by state. Table 4-3 summarizes the differences in probabilities by state and by program status evaluated at the means for the county and school variables. The probabilities in the OTHER columns for Piaui and Ceará provide comparisons between the OTHER schools in those states and the OTHER schools in Pernambuco. The probabilities in the EDURURAL columns for all three states compare survival probabilities between the EDURURAL and OTHER schools within that state. The two sets of probabilities are additive.

From table 4-3, we see a simple ordering of survival probabilities by state for counties not included in the EDURURAL project. Other things being equal, in 1981–83 the chance of an OTHER school surviving in Piaui was 4.9 percent higher than in Pernambuco, and such schools in Per-

Table 4-3. Comparisons of Marginal Survival Probabilities by State and Program Status, 1981–83 and 1983–85

State	1981–83		1983–85	
	OTHER	*EDURURAL*	*OTHER*	*EDURURAL*
Pernambuco	n.a.[a]	(0.038)	n.a.[a]	(0.011)
Piaui	0.049	−0.076	0.169	−0.159
Ceará	−0.186	−0.258	−0.202	−0.260

n.a. = Not applicable.

Note: In OTHER columns, schools not in EDURURAL counties in Piaui and Ceará are compared to the survival probabilities of schools not in EDURURAL counties in Pernambuco. In the EDURURAL column, the comparison is to OTHER schools in the same state. Estimates are based on the probit models that include disaggregated facility characteristics. For complete specifications, see appendix table C4-1, columns 1 and 3 for the two sample periods. Estimates that are not significantly different from zero at the 5 percent level are reported in parentheses.

a. Reference group (see note).

Source: Appendix table C-1.

nambuco were 18.6 percent more likely to survive than those in Ceará. For 1983–85, the difference between Pernambuco and Ceará is approximately the same, but the added survival probabilities in Piaui have grown to 16.9 percent above Pernambuco.

The estimated probabilities for the EDURURAL columns indicate the differences in survival probabilities between program and nonprogram schools within each state. Within Pernambuco, the survival chances for schools are essentially the same in EDURURAL counties as they are in OTHER counties. In Piaui and Ceará, however, survival probabilities in EDURURAL counties are significantly lower than in OTHER counties.

The EDURURAL differences are perhaps not surprising for the early time period, as these counties were chosen for the EDURURAL program because they were thought to manifest the worst educational conditions and because the program could have lags in its effects. However, the lack of survival gets worse in Piaui by the second period, falling from 7.6 percent more likely to go out of existence to 15.9 percent. Ceará EDURURAL schools have the lowest overall chance of surviving, with 26 percent lower survival probabilities than the OTHER Ceará schools (which themselves had the lowest survival probabilities of the three states).[83]

There is not much evidence that school survival is related to the type of administrative control of the school. Each of the estimated probabilities displayed in table 4-4 is a comparison to the survival probability of an otherwise similar school under administrative control of the county (*municipio*) government—the dominant supplier of schools in rural northeast Brazil. Survival probabilities of state schools do not differ from those of the municipios. The samples of federal and private schools are very small, and therefore the results tend to be quite unreliable. There is a significantly lower probability of survival for private schools in the later period.

Table 4-4. Effects of Administrative Control of Schools on School Survival Probabilities, 1981–83 and 1983–85
(comparisons with county schools)

Administrative control	1981–83	1983–85
State	(–0.033)	(–0.011)
Federal	n.a.[a]	(0.381)
Private	(0.026)	–0.265

n.a. = Not applicable.

Note: Estimated marginal probabilities are calculated at means of variables and holding constant other factors contained in probit equations that include disaggregated school facility measures. See appendix table C4-1, columns 1 and 3. Estimates that are not significantly different from zero at the 5 percent level are reported in parentheses.

a. All federal schools in the sample survived during this period.

Source: Appendix table C4-1.

The complete effect of nonsurvival by schools cannot be determined from these data, because students could have switched to different schools after they were observed in the second grade (see figure 4-1). Nevertheless, we can safely assume that the chances of a student's continuing in school decline dramatically when a school closes. The probabilities of school survival are lowest in places where the drought hit hardest, the schools have poorer facilities, and the concentrations of students are smaller. Students attending schools in the teacher's house are also clearly in greater danger of losing their school. There are also significant differences across states and program counties. Schools in Ceará, both EDURURAL and OTHER, tend not to survive, although the reasons for this are unclear.

On-Time Promotion Probabilities

We now turn to the probability that a student is promoted to the fourth grade, given that his school survives and has a fourth grade. In terms of figure 4-1, this is a comparison of path d (on-time promotion) with paths e (retention in either second or third grade), f (dropping out), and g (migrating). While dropping out and retention in earlier grades are qualitatively different in ways that are important for policies, they cannot be distinguished within the 1981–83 and 1983–85 samples. The analysis here therefore considers only on-time promotions compared with all other possibilities. We conclude that promotion probabilities are affected both by the characteristics of the individual student and family and by characteristics of the school.

Whether individual student performance is related to promotion probabilities is a central issue in our analysis. This is extremely important for policy purposes, because it offers insight into how to assess different proposals for dealing with dropout and retention rates and their mirror image, promotion rates. Specifically, if promotion is only slightly related to actual student performance—that is, the people being left behind or dropping out are about as good academically as those being promoted— then high repetition rates and high dropout rates indeed represent wasted resources. Direct, regulatory efforts to lower this wastage and increase promotions—by, for example, a policy of automatic promotion—might well be called for. On other hand, if promotions are highly related to student quality, increasing the rates of promotion to reduce wastage continues students with lower performance. The benefits of an external intervention program of lowering wastage then would be much less.

The promotion probability models—like the previous school survival models—are estimated by probit techniques.[84] For exposition, the results of this estimation are again translated into estimates of marginal probabilities evaluated at the means of the separate variables.[85]

Because of the random sampling of students in the schools in each year, it is possible for an individual to be promoted on time but not to be included in the promotion sample. To deal directly with this, the probit models include the number of students in the schools, since the probabilities of individuals being missed by the sampling are directly related to the number of students in the school. The school size measure is significantly negative in the probit models, reflecting this sampling within schools.[86]

Student Characteristics

Table 4-5 summarizes the marginal probabilities associated with the various student and family characteristics employed in the promotion models. Other things being equal, females are over 3 percent more likely than males to stay in school and be promoted on time. Since the models incorporate differences in abilities, this reflects a lower opportunity cost of school attendance for girls; their value on the farms is less, so they are less likely to quit school to work. Not surprisingly, promotion probabilities dip with age. The older a student is when sampled in the second grade, the more likely the student has already repeated grades or dropped out for some period. Therefore, it is less likely that the student will be promoted to the fourth grade on time. In the earlier period, each additional year of age lowers the probability of promotion by 0.7 percent; in the later period this estimate rises to 1.7 percent. Since the mean promotion probabilities are respectively about 9 percent and 14 percent for the two periods, this effect of age is substantial.

The most interesting part of the model is the relationship between second grade test scores and promotion probabilities. (The criterion-

Table 4-5. Effects of Student and Family Characteristics on Promotion Probabilities, 1981–83 and 1983–85

Variable	1981–83	1983–85
Female	0.0319	0.0360
Age	−0.0067	−0.0170
Portuguese test score	0.0014	0.0026
Mathematics test score	(0.0003)	0.0009
Mother's education	(0.0037)	0.0070
Years residing in county	0.0009	0.0014

Note: Estimated marginal probabilities are calculated at means of variables and holding constant other factors contained in probit equations that exclude school control measures. For complete results, see appendix table C4-2, columns 1 and 3. Estimates that are not significantly different from zero at the 5 percent level are reported in parentheses.

Source: Appendix table C4-2.

referenced tests in Portuguese and mathematics were designed to measure performance on the schools' curricular objectives by each student. (See the descriptions in chapter 5 and appendix A.) As displayed in table 4-5, higher test scores consistently lead to greater promotion probabilities; this suggests that promotion has some basis in merit. Each 10 points on the Portuguese test, which has a standard deviation of approximately 25 points, increases promotion probabilities by about 1.5 to 2.5 percent for the average student in the sample. Across the full distribution, this implies that a student going from the 25th percentile to the 75th percentile on the test has 5 to 9 percent higher promotion probabilities. Between the 10th and 90th percentile, promotion probabilities rise by 9 to 17 percent. Again, since the mean observed promotion rate in the sample is only 9 percent in 1983 and 14 percent in 1985, these are significant differences due to merit. Performance on the mathematics test does not have as strong an influence on promotion. It is statistically insignificant in the 1981–83 period and has about one-third the effect of the Portuguese test in 1983–85. (The standard deviation of the mathematics test score is approximately equal to that for the Portuguese test.)

The education level of a student's mother is positively related to promotion. This reflects both family tastes for education and direct aid in education at the home. The education level of the father was tested in the models, but had no additional independent effect, perhaps reflecting the conventional wisdom that the mother, not the father, is the strongest educational influence on the child. The lasting effect of low education levels is seen from the intergenerational nature of the transmission of human capital from mothers to children; low attainment of this generation hurts not just this generation but also future generations.

Finally, students whose families have resided longer in the county are more likely to be promoted on time. We take this as indirect support for the hypothesis that migration has a negative effect on promotion.

Governmental Support

There are distinct differences in promotion probabilities across states and by program status, as shown in table 4-6. We take these to be indirectly indicative of varying overall levels of governmental support for primary schools. The promotion probabilities in Piaui are clearly greater than those in Pernambuco by 7.5 percent in 1981–83 and by 3 percent in 1983–85. Ceará also has 3 percent higher promotion rates than Pernambuco in 1981–83, but the differences become insignificant in the later period. Again, we cannot offer any explanations for these differences, which hold over and above any of the other factors in the models. Promotion rates in EDURURAL counties are initially lower than in OTHER counties, but any difference disappears by the later period.[87]

*Table 4-6. Marginal Effects of State and Program Status
on Promotion Probabilities, 1981–83 and 1983–85*

	1981–83	1983–85
Piaui	0.075	0.031
Ceará	0.032	(−0.002)
EDURURAL	−0.020	(−0.009)

Note: Estimated marginal probabilities are compared to Pernambuco calculated at means of variables and holding constant other factors contained in probit equations that exclude school control measures. See appendix table C4-2, columns 1 and 3. Estimates that are not significantly different from zero at the 5 percent level are reported in parentheses.
Source: Appendix table C4-2.

Migration, Dropping Out, and Promotion: The 1987 Survey

While the 1981 through 1985 surveys provided a broad view of the availability of schools and the chances of on-time primary school promotion, they do not allow a complete picture of the range of possible paths taken by students. The 1987 survey, which was restricted to a subset of Ceará schools, supplements this picture in important ways. The design was to create a sample of follow-ups to students surveyed in 1985. As such, it was not designed to provide a general view of available schools or of representative students. Further, because of limitations on funding and time for data collection, the sample was concentrated in those schools in Ceará that had larger numbers of 1985 second graders.

Armed with rosters of previously sampled second graders, the survey teams were instructed to locate as many as possible. When students were located, they were surveyed and tested. Students did not have to be in the fourth grade—as had been the case in previous surveys—to be interviewed. In fact, they did not still have to be in school. If the students could not be located, teachers and school officials were asked to supply as much information as possible about them.

From this approach, a much more complete picture of students is available than that previously depicted. But it is not without costs. This is not a representative survey of schools or students. Nor is it possible to say anything about school survival.

Figure 4-4 displays the information available in 1987, beginning with all second graders in the 1985 data collection in the state of Ceará. Because of the selection of a subset of schools, data could be obtained for slightly fewer than half (706 out of 1,516) of the 1985 second graders. Approximately one-quarter of these students moved away from the school by 1987. For students who did not move, reasonably complete information about their school status was obtained.[88] From the cohort of

Figure 4-4. Sample Outcomes for 1985 Second Graders in Ceará

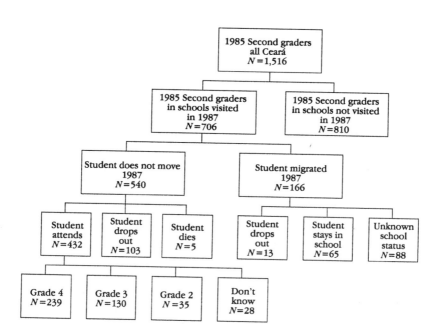

Source: EDURURAL research sample.

nonmigrants we see that fewer than half (44 percent) are promoted on time, but another 36 percent are still in school. A fifth have dropped out.

These 1987 data are primarily useful for separately analyzing the various reasons why individuals disappear from the matched samples previously used. In particular, they enable us to delve into the systematic determinants of migration and the differences between on-time promotion, retention at lower grades, and school dropout behavior. The previous analyses aggregated all of the various reasons for not being promoted within a given school. The behavioral modeling included factors characterizing the overall differences between promotion and the conglomerate of those alternative paths. Here we show the contribution of the separate underlying events—migration, retention, dropout—to the probability of being observed as promoted on time.

Before investigating these underlying behavioral relationships, however, we compare the picture of observed on-time promotion in 1985–87 to that in the two previous periods. This comparison indicates how the specialized sample in Ceará compares with the more representative samples in the previous periods. The estimated marginal probabilities

*Table 4-7. Comparison of Estimated Marginal Probabilities
of On-Time Promotion, 1983–85 and 1985–87*

Variable	1983–85	1985–87
Female	0.0360	(0.0045)
Age	−0.0170	−0.0233
Portuguese test	0.0026	0.0027
Mathematics test	0.0009	(0.0008)
Mother's education	0.0070	0.0134
Years residing in county	0.0014	0.0015
Number of students in school	−0.0008	0.0007
EDURURAL	(−0.0093)[a]	−0.1123

Note: Estimated marginal probabilities are calculated at means of variables and holding constant other factors contained in probit equations. See appendix tables C4-2, column 3, and C4-3, column 1, for on-time promotion. Estimates that are not significantly different from zero at the 5 percent level are reported in parentheses.

a. Appendix table C4-2, column 4, reports specific estimates for EDURURAL in Ceará, which, in terms of marginal probabilities, is −0.0027 but statistically insignificant.

Source: Appendix tables C4-2 and C4-3.

are presented in table 4-7 along with the comparable estimates for 1983–85. The complete probit estimates are set out in appendix table C4-3.

The on-time promotion models are strikingly similar across samples. The only occurrence of a change in the sign of an estimated parameter comes where it is expected—number of students in the school. In both periods, number of students is a measure of sampling probabilities of students. The sampling chances in 1983–85 are lower in a large school because a random selection of students within the school is taken. The sampling chances in 1985–87 are higher because schools in Ceará were chosen partially on the basis of their size. The remaining parameter estimates are quite close, with two exceptions. The later sample finds no difference between boys and girls in promotion probabilities, while the earlier samples found the on-time promotion probabilities of girls to be higher. Also, promotion in EDURURAL counties is estimated to be 11 percent less likely than in the OTHER counties in the later period; in 1983–85 those probabilities were about the same. However, the fundamental determinants of promotion probabilities—age, Portuguese achievement, mother's education, and years in the county—remain remarkably consistent.

This consistency across years of the overall model suggests that the special Ceará sample is in fact useful in decomposing the underlying behavior that adds up to observed on-time promotion. The variations in factors affecting behavior are easy to see. For example, while agricultural conditions in an area might affect migration behavior, they should not affect a student's progression through the primary grades. Therefore, a measure of agricultural productivity will appear in the overall on-time promotion model and in the disaggregated migration model, but not in the dropout and grade promotion models. (The complete probit models are set out in appendix table C4-3 and C4-4) In each case, conditional probability estimates are presented: for students attending sampled schools, whether or not they migrate; for those who did not migrate, whether or not they drop out of school; and for those still in school, whether they are retained in grade two, promoted to grade three, or promoted to grade four.[89] In the three disaggregated models, while an attempt has been made to replicate the overall on-time promotion models, the emphasis is placed on a specification tailored to the specific behavior.

Migration Behavior

Slightly under one-quarter of the second graders in the sampled schools moved away between 1985 and 1987, and the systematic determinants of this migration behavior are summarized in table 4-8. There is some systematic migration by students scoring higher on the Portuguese test; each point higher on the test increases migration probabilities by two-tenths of a percent. The exact reason for this is unclear. It could reflect an active searching for high-quality schools. But it is difficult to jump to such a conclusion on just this evidence, particularly since the estimated effect of mathematics achievement, while positive, is not statistically significant. Skepticism about this "search for quality" hypothesis is especially appropriate since none of the measured characteristics of schools and teachers appears to affect migration directly.

Migration behavior is clearly affected by costs and potential benefits

Table 4-8. Estimated Marginal Probabilities of Factors Affecting Migration in Ceará, 1985–87

Variable	Marginal probability
Portuguese test	0.0019
Mathematics test	(0.0006)
Years in county	(−0.0016)
Family size	−0.0136
Agricultural productivity	−0.4531
SES of county	(−0.1691)

Note: Estimated marginal probabilities are calculated at means of variables and holding constant other factors contained in the probit equation of migration. See appendix table C4-3, column 4. Estimates that are not significantly different from zero at the 5 percent level are reported in parentheses.

Source: Appendix table C4-3.

from moving. Larger families are noticeably less likely to move: each additional family member lowers the migration probability by 1.4 percent. Additionally, families residing in more productive areas stay, while those in less productive areas have a higher probability of moving.

Dropping Out

The pattern of dropouts suggested by the estimated probit models summarized in table 4-9 is particularly interesting. Nineteen percent of those second-grade students remaining in the same local area dropped out within the two-year observation period. The most important factor is whether the student's father is a farmer. If he is, the student is 23 percent more likely to drop out. This reflects the opportunity cost of children's attending school when they can be easily occupied in farming. It is also reinforced by the increasing dropout rate as the student ages: the chances of dropping out rise 5 percent with each year of age. Finally, in terms of statistically significant determinants of dropping out, more educated mothers tend to keep their children in school longer, although the magnitude of this relationship is small.

Both sex and achievement in school, factors commonly believed to be important in dropout behavior, are not significantly related to dropping out, although they do have the expected sign. Moreover, although not shown in table 4-9, the characteristics of the schools themselves have no discernible effect on dropouts.

The purely short-term economic motivation of dropout behavior coming from employment demand is both surprising and important. The problems of the depressed rural areas clearly place a lasting imprint on the population.

Table 4-9. Estimated Marginal Probabilities of Factors Affecting Dropout Behavior in Ceará, 1985–87

Variable	Marginal probability
Age	0.0532
Mother's education	−0.0021
Father not a farmer	−0.2273
Portuguese test	(−0.0017)
Mathematics test	(−0.0011)
Female	(−0.0233)

Note: Estimated marginal probabilities are calculated at means of variables and holding constant other factors contained in the probit equation of dropout. See appendix table C4-3, column 2 of Dropout Behavior. Estimates that are not significantly different from zero at the 5 percent level are reported in parentheses.

Source: Appendix table C4-3.

Promotion

Finally, table 4-10 provides information about the determinants of grade promotion. These estimates indicate how the probabilities of promotion vary *given that the student stays in school.* Overall, 9 percent of the students remain in the second grade for the two years, while 32 percent move into the third grade and 59 percent are promoted to the fourth grade. The ordered probit estimation assumes that the factors affecting promotion to the third and fourth grades are the same.

Each four points more on the second-grade Portuguese achievement test increases the probability of grade promotion by 1 percent. Thus a one standard deviation difference in test scores (20 points) translates into a 5 percent higher probability of promotion. Mathematics performance in the second grade appears unrelated to promotion. This may reflect the greater difficulty experienced by the teachers in recognizing high achievement in mathematics at the second grade. They often make promotion decisions based on informal and unsystematic assessment procedures.

Additionally, promotion probabilities improve if the mother has more education. A mother with six years of schooling will improve her child's promotion probabilities by 4.5 percent over a mother who never attended school.

Last, in our consideration of student and family characteristics, older students are less likely to be promoted. With each year of age, promotion probabilities fall by 1 percent. The precise reason for this relationship is, however, uncertain. It could reflect the fact that older students had not previously applied themselves to school—attending infrequently, not

Table 4-10. *Estimated Marginal Probabilities of Factors Affecting Grade Promotion in Ceará, 1985–87*

Variable	Marginal probability
Portuguese test	0.0027
Mathematics test	(0.0001)
Age	−0.0120
Sex	(−0.0040)
Mother's education	0.0073
Years in county	(0.0003)
EDURURAL	−0.0494

Note: Estimated marginal probabilities are calculated at means of variables and holding constant other factors contained in the probit equation of promotion. See appendix table C4-4. Estimates that are not significantly different from zero at the 5 percent level are reported in parentheses.

Source: Appendix table C4-4.

being motivated to do the work, and so forth. If this is the underlying cause, a variety of policies can be introduced to improve promotions. On the other hand, it could reflect simply lower ability; those who are older are simply those who have shown that they cannot get much out of school. If this is the underlying cause, the policy options are much more limited.

The only remaining factor that significantly affects promotion probabilities is attending an EDURURAL school. The promotion probabilities are 5 percent less in these schools than in OTHER schools, other things being equal. Again, the exact reason for this difference cannot be ascertained. Since a variety of explicit measures of school characteristics exhibit no independent effect on promotion (above that already reflected in Portuguese performance), this finding does not seem to reflect the easily measured characteristics of schools. Moreover, caution is required at this point because the analyses of on-time promotion for the previous periods show no consistent EDURURAL difference, while the special Ceará sample used here does. It is thus possible that the strong Ceará result simply reflects a peculiarity of the 1987 sampling of schools.

Summary

The school survival models and the promotion models together provide insight into the determinants of access and retention in rural northeast Brazil. By using information generated by the repeated sampling of schools and students in the EDURURAL and OTHER counties, it is possible to begin piecing together an important part of any school policy discussion.

The first noteworthy observation is the fragility of schools in this region. Even when economic conditions are reasonably normal (1983–85), 17 percent of the schools disappear over a two-year period; the figure is twice as high in a period of economic crisis (1981–83). The figures are much worse if survival with a fourth grade is the criterion. With these disappearance rates, developing a coherent educational program that retains students in schools is extremely difficult.

The survival chances of schools have some systematic components. As a general rule, places with a history of low support levels are most at risk. If the existing schools have poor facilities or, worse, if they are operated out of the teacher's house, they are much more likely to disappear. The drought also had its effects. Areas hardest hit by the drought simply found it more difficult to maintain schools, perhaps because this led to more migration out of the area.

This evidence suggests something commonly observed elsewhere. The evolution of schooling tends to reinforce existing inequities. Poor areas are most at risk of losing their primary schools.

There are also systematic differences in school survival across the states studied. Schools in Ceará are least likely to survive, particularly those in the EDURURAL counties. Schools in Piaui on the other hand are most likely to continue operating. The reasons are unclear, but the notorious role of patronage politics in rural Ceará—and the consequent difficulty of establishing stable administrative systems at the county level—may be part of the explanation.

From a policy viewpoint, the implications are clear. If these poverty-ridden rural areas are to improve their conditions, a minimum goal is to ensure that students have a local fourth grade.

From the viewpoint of the individual student, progress through school requires promotion. This region has very low promotion rates, and considerable attention has been given to policies that might increase promotions. Previous discussions have, however, suffered from lack of information about the underlying determinants of promotion and about the relationship between student performance and promotion probabilities. Such information is key to thinking about policies to deal with wastage.

The evidence presented here provides detailed information about on-time promotion rates. What leads students in the second grade to get to the fourth grade two years later? The most important factor is the student's performance. Demonstrated academic skills, particularly in Portuguese, are very important in determining success. In addition, girls are more likely than boys to progress to the fourth grade. This reflects lower opportunity costs of schooling for girls. More educated mothers also aid in the schooling and promotion chances of children, again suggesting that there is some reinforcement of previous inequality across generations.

The disaggregation of on-time promotion that is possible for 1985–87 provides additional insights into the underlying flows of students through schools. In broad terms, costs of moving for a family are most important in determining migration behavior; work opportunities for the student determine dropout behavior; and school performance and learning determine promotion probabilities.

These insights about student progress and completion (schooling quantity) are relevant for two reasons. First, they provide evidence for the evaluation of the EDURURAL program (chapter 7) and the evaluation of various potential policies (chapters 6 and 8). Second, they are immediately useful in understanding the achievement of students, as discussed in chapter 5.

5

Quality: The Determinants
of Achievement

MANY STUDIES HAVE delved into the operations of schools, attempting to discern which features account for differences in performance by students. But, few of these studies have relied on data specifically designed to address questions of scholastic performance, and many analytical compromises have been necessary. These undertakings—and the policy conclusions that should flow from them—have thus been severely constrained.

The EDURURAL data collection had a single purpose—to evaluate the performance of rural schools. A key element in this was to assess the effect on performance of the special inputs to schooling provided through the EDURURAL program. Special attention focused on three categories of inputs: (i) "hardware" such as classrooms, sanitary facilities, water and electrical service, and furniture for students and teachers; (ii) "software" such as textbooks and teacher's guides, audiovisual aids, notebooks, pencils, and other writing materials; and (iii) teachers who had completed specified inservice upgrading programs or preservice academic training. As described previously, numerous challenging measurement and data collection issues were encountered. They included the following: the testing of low-performing primary students; the mechanics of survey collection in sparsely populated, difficult-to-reach areas; and the management of complicated data bases involving the merging of information from several levels of aggregation and disparate sources, to name but a few. The result, nevertheless, is a data set uniquely capable of supporting analysis of school performance and evaluation of programmatic interventions.

Even with data specifically collected for the purposes of evaluation, however, challenging analytical issues remain. Because of our limited knowledge about the educational process, particularly in depressed settings such as the rural areas of northeast Brazil, uncertainty persists about exactly how to specify the empirical models. This chapter begins with discussions of the measurement of scholastic achievement and general issues of empirical specification and estimation. The subsequent sections present a systematic analysis of the determinants of scholastic performance.

The Measurement of Quality

The central focus of this entire study is the improvement of the educational performance of rural students. Our ability to analyze the situation and suggest improvements depends, of course, on our ability to measure performance accurately and reliably.

The fundamental measuring sticks employed here are a series of specially designed tests of achievement in Portuguese and mathematics. Ultimate success of the schools is probably better defined by other things—the ability of educated people to compete in the labor market, to increase the productivity of their farms, to participate in democratic society, to care for and nurture children. These ultimate goals of schooling are, however, virtually impossible to measure at the time of schooling and can be observed only after a substantial period of time has passed. Therefore, when assessing the character and determinants of successful schooling, proxies for these true goals must be employed. This leads us to standardized tests of the subject matter contained in the school curriculum.

Employing standardized tests of school performance assumes that mastering the school curriculum leads to success in the more fundamental dimensions of societal performance. As reviewed in chapter 2, the direct evidence on this is substantial. Increased quantity of schooling is highly related to incomes, agricultural productivity, and the like. The relationship between test performance and subsequent student outcomes is more difficult to determine, although reasonably consistent evidence does exist. Moreover, if mastering a larger portion of the curriculum results in completing more schooling,[90] tests of student achievement will be appropriate proxies for subsequent success and thus school quality.

Indeed, a major strength of this study is that it does not concentrate solely on quantity of schooling obtained by students but recognizes that there are qualitative differences among students at the same level of schooling. Grade levels and quantity of schooling provide crude differentiation among students but miss substantial differences both within given schools and across schools.

The Portuguese and mathematics tests employed here were developed specifically for the EDURURAL project. A team of psychometricians from the Fundação Carlos Chagas (FCC), a leading educational research institute located in São Paulo, constructed and validated the tests. FCC determined that existing standardized tests used in Brazil's urban areas of the south would be too difficult for the students in the rural northeast.[91] The tests given to the students in the EDURURAL sample were developed in 1981 and marginal improvements were made in later years. This section provides an overview of the tests, the students' performance on them, and the reliability of the specific instruments used in 1981, 1983, and 1985.[92] A more detailed discussion of the form of the tests and a presentation of basic test data are found in appendix A.

The tests were criterion-referenced to minimally acceptable levels of performance in second- and fourth-grade mathematics and Portuguese. (These performance levels were noticeably lower than those expected in the south.) The judgments about curricular materials for each grade came from teachers, technical staff, and administrators in the various educational organizations of the northeast. The Portuguese tests cover reading comprehension, writing, grammar, and (in the fourth grade) composition; the mathematics tests cover basic numeracy items.[93] The 1983 and 1985 tests were constructed to be parallel forms of the original 1981 test; that is, new questions were developed to examine the same concepts and to maintain the same level of difficulty.

The internal consistency of the tests is ascertained by constructing reliability measures for the tests. Specifically, for 1983 and 1985, Cronbach's Alpha coefficients were calculated.[94] These coefficients can be interpreted as indicating how the scores from these tests would compare with scores from other possible tests of the same conceptual domain. An Alpha of 1.0 indicates that the scores on these tests would be the same as on any other test of the concepts. Table 5-1 shows that the reliability coefficients tend to be 0.9 or better with the exception of the fourth-grade Portuguese scores; those lower reliabilities dip down to 0.83. All of these reliabilities, however, are acceptable by traditional standards for this type of work. Moreover, the test reliabilities tend to be stable over time and across states.

The means on the Portuguese and mathematics tests for the two grade levels are displayed in table 5-2. The statistics, based on the full test

Table 5-1. Portuguese and Mathematics Test Reliabilities as Indicated by Cronbach's Alpha, 1983 and 1985

	Portuguese		Mathematics	
Grade level	*1983*	*1985*	*1983*	*1985*
Second grade	0.90	0.91	0.94	0.94
Fourth grade	0.83	0.83	0.91	0.91

Source: Appendix table C-3.

Table 5-2. Mean Test Performance by State, 1981, 1983, and 1985

	Total			Pernambuco			Ceará			Piauí		
Grade/test	1981	1983	1985	1981	1983	1985	1981	1983	1985	1981	1983	1985
Second grade												
Portuguese	49.0	58.7	59.5	42.9	50.0	50.7	62.8	65.8	69.6	44.7	59.6	57.0
Mathematics	45.9	51.1	49.2	42.9	46.5	42.1	57.9	57.0	56.4	38.6	49.5	47.9
Fourth grade												
Portuguese	51.5	52.2	48.4	50.0	48.7	43.4	60.5	59.0	55.5	48.5	51.6	47.0
Mathematics	48.5	48.2	50.1	49.1	44.6	44.6	59.9	55.0	55.3	40.7	47.7	50.7

Source: Appendix table C-12.

samples in each year, provide some startling evidence about the overall level of performance. The average scores for the region as a whole fall between 45 and 60 points out of a possible 100. In other words, the actual performance is not even close to the minimal standards set by the local educators who constructed the tests.

The scores also show two interesting aggregate facts. First, students' performance, presumably measured on a consistent basis, showed general improvement over time only for Portuguese achievement in the second grade. The other scores do not indicate much change in the level of aggregate performance. Second, there are distinct differences in performance across states. Scores in Ceará are consistently above those in both Pernambuco and Piauí.

These aggregate scores do not, however, provide much guidance for policy. Certainly the low absolute performance levels warrant concern, but it was known before the start of the EDURURAL program that strong remedial action was required. The key to policy changes is understanding what factors contribute to individual performance levels, and then altering those factors. The aggregate data do not provide the basis for such understanding. Therefore, in the remainder of this chapter, we turn our attention to understanding in some detail the determinants of differences in individual student performance.

Specification of the Achievement Models

The overall framework for analysis follows a quite standard input-output specification for the educational process. The achievement of a given student at time t (A_t) is assumed to be related to current and past educational inputs from a variety of sources—the home, the school, and the community. To highlight some of the important features, we use a general conceptual model such as the following:

$$A_t = f(F(t), S(t), O(t), \epsilon_t),$$

where $F(t)$ = a vector of the student's family background and family educational inputs cumulative to time t;

$S(t)$ = a vector of the student's teacher and school inputs cumulative to time t;

$O(t)$ = a vector of other relevant inputs such as community factors, friends, and so forth cumulative to time t; and

ϵ_t = unmeasured factors that contribute to achievement at time t.

The approach is to measure the different possible inputs into education and to estimate their influence on student achievement. As described earlier, this emulates the approach adopted in the Coleman Report (Coleman and others 1966) and most follow-on studies in the United States (see Hanushek 1986) and developing countries (see Fuller 1985).

This conceptual model explicitly incorporates a stochastic, or random, error term—ϵ_t—to reflect the fact that we can never observe all of the factors affecting achievement. (Indeed, the distribution of this error term, as discussed below, has important implications for the estimation and interpretation of the effects of the other factors in the model).

To the extent that the vector of various school factors, denoted by $S(t)$, includes the pertinent instruments of policy, the relative effectiveness of possible educational strategies can be compared both with each other and, potentially, with the costs. Within the context of the EDURURAL project, effectiveness could be ascertained in two different ways using standard regression techniques. First, in a classic experimental evaluation, it would be possible to estimate overall mean achievement differences between EDURURAL and OTHER schools after accounting for measurable resource and family differences.[95] Second, it would be possible to measure explicitly the specific school resources provided by the project and to include these factors in estimates of student achievement relationships. This would provide coefficients, or *learning weights*, that can be used in assessing changes in performance induced by the specific inputs provided under the project.

The most serious drawback to these approaches is the likelihood of obtaining biased statistical estimates of the effectiveness of the EDURURAL program and of different school resources. In the equation, the source of such bias is centered on the error term, ϵ_t, which includes all unmeasured influences on achievement. It is natural to expect many things to be unmeasured in the case of individual student data. The key issue is whether the collection of these factors is unrelated to the observed family, school, and other influences on achievement that are measured and included in the analysis. If unrelated, standard regression analysis provides unbiased estimates of the achievement relationships. If they are systematically related, however, the parameter estimates will be biased, and their use for evaluation or policy analysis will tend to be misleading.

In a wide range of educational settings, it is difficult to accept that these error terms are uncorrelated with the measured inputs to achievement. These error terms are likely to contain a variety of unmeasured factors that are, nonetheless, systematic. First, since education is a cumulative process, the entire past history of inputs is needed to characterize achievement at any point in time. This implies an enormous data collection requirement—one that is seldom if ever accomplished. In fact, for practical reasons, measurements are usually limited to a single point, neglecting any variations in previous educational inputs. Second, most survey designs limit the range and character of the observed data. Even with the specially designed surveys here, for example, it is difficult to record any qualitative differences in teacher's behavior. Thus many contemporaneous factors escape measurement. Third, some factors nearly defy measurement. For example, most people believe that differences in innate abilities of students are important in determining achievement differences. But there is little consensus on how innate ability might be measured, and available instruments are not easy to administer efficiently to large numbers of children even if they are considered reliable. Similarly, the motivation and aspirations of students are extraordinarily difficult to measure even though they are very apt to be important.

All these unmeasured factors are likely to be correlated with observed family and school variables. Past school situations tend to be related both to family characteristics and to contemporaneous school inputs; qualitative differences in inputs often correspond to quantity and to family choices; innate abilities, motivations, and aspirations tend to be correlated with observed family characteristics. The risk of biased parameter estimates—and unreliable policy conclusions—is thus substantial.

One approach to dealing with this problem is to reformulate the basic achievement model to look at gains in achievement over time. If, for example, one can observe achievement at the end of an earlier time t^*, it is possible to analyze $(A_t - A_{t^*})$, or how much achievement changed between time t^* and t. Intuitively, the increase in performance in, say, a single grade would depend most upon the teacher, school, and family inputs in that year. Thus, if it is possible to collect information on gains in performance, it is less risky to concentrate on just the contemporaneous values of inputs. Further, to the extent that innate abilities more affect the absolute level of performance and less the rate of growth of achievement, this formulation gets around the lack of measurement.[97] But this formulation, which is often called a value-added specification, requires repeated sampling of the same individuals.

In the actual estimation, prior achievement, A_{t^*}, is frequently included as one of the explanatory variables in the regression (instead of analyzing the simple change in achievement). This has two advantages. First, it allows for differential growth in achievement based upon initial score.

If, for example, high achievers are able to extract more than low achievers from subsequent instruction, the simple differencing procedure will be inappropriate. Second, the modified specification also permits measurement of achievement using yardsticks with different units of measure over time, that is, it allows different tests to be used in the two years.

One other aspect of analysis is highlighted by the value-added formulation. The statistical properties of the estimated regression model depend upon the distribution of the error terms, ϵ_t.[98] When achievement in later grades is analyzed, the sample of observed children may not be representative of the entire population. Specifically, since children tend to drop out of school as time goes on, only children who have stayed in school and who have been promoted will be observed. Moreover, since students who perform better in school tend to be the ones who stay in school, the sample is selected in a specific way that relates directly to the achievement of students. This problem of sample selection bias has been discussed extensively in different contexts (see Heckman 1979 or Maddala 1983).

The intuition behind sample selection bias is clear. Assume that only the best students stay in school until they are observed in the sampling of schools. These are students who tend to have high unmeasured abilities, attitudes, or other advantages; that is, students who have $\epsilon_t > 0$. If the statistical analyses do not take this into account, the school and family inputs are likely to be confused with high abilities of the observed students, yielding biased estimates of what would happen if, say, a set of school inputs was changed.

The most straightforward corrective procedure involves estimating the probability that an individual will appear in the sample. If this can be done, consistent estimates of the underlying achievement parameters can be obtained by including sample selection probabilities directly into the model of achievement. The probit analyses in the previous chapter provide the needed information about selection probabilities for correcting the achievement models explored here.

The potential problems of sample selection are most severe when there is only a single cross-section of data on schooling. For example, if data are only available for fourth graders in a given year and many students do not make it to the fourth grade, correcting the achievement models is very difficult. One needs information about the determinants of fourth grade attendance, and this would not be directly available in the sampled data. These considerations pinpoint one of the unique and most valuable features of the sample design in the EDURURAL program.

Finally, note that in a value-added form the potential selection problems would be further reduced. If the probability of promotion to the fourth grade was determined completely by the measured performance in the prior grade and if that prior performance was included in a value-added model, the sample selection problems would not appear.[99] Nevertheless, because of peculiarities in the sample design for the EDURURAL research, potential biases remain even in the value-added versions.

The value-added formulation does, however, introduce some of its own problems. Specifically, prior achievement is itself measured with error, because of peculiarities of the test instrument, random circumstances related to the time of measurement or test-taking, and other similar factors that lower test reliability. This was demonstrated earlier when the reliability coefficients were found to be less than one. Such test measurement errors introduce another reason for correlation of the error term in the equation, ϵ_t, with the explanatory variables and must be corrected.[100] The severity of such problems increases with the size of the error variance relative to the variance in true prior performance.

The most commonly used corrective procedure employs instrumental variables techniques.[101] If one can find a variable that is correlated with the true prior achievement of the student but is uncorrelated with the measurement errors, the estimation can be adjusted to eliminate the problems introduced by the measurement errors. As discussed below, applying instrumental variable techniques is straightforward in this case.

Implications of Modeling and Estimation Choices

Typically, a researcher has little opportunity to choose among alternative ways of formulating and estimating the achievement models since the availability of data constrains the analytical approach. Nevertheless, the approach followed will color the interpretation of results and the conclusions that are drawn. Before discussing our specific empirical results, therefore, we first consider the implications of our modeling choices.

Within the EDURURAL evaluation, the full range of analytical approaches is available because the basic data set is so rich. While a standard cross-sectional model can be estimated for second and fourth grades in three different years, the panel data of the EDURURAL data make it possible, in addition, to estimate value-added models and models corrected for selection bias. More important, since each of these approaches can be pursued consistently within the same set of data, the potential effects of each on the results can be isolated and assessed.

As discussed, the conceptually preferred approach to modeling performance is to consider value-added models that correct for any sample selection biases. Such formulations minimize the potential for statistical bias. Especially in our data, however, they do so at a cost, because they require samples of matched students across two years of the study. This reduces the cross-sectional observations available in any year by 90 percent or more—a significant loss of data about scholastic performance. Moreover, the preferred approach is available here only for the analysis of fourth-grade performance in 1983 and 1985. Any analysis of second-grade performance must rely on purely cross-sectional estimation.

The EDURURAL data allow four basic "experiments" in empirical specification of the achievement models. These are value-added and level, or cross-sectional, models, each estimated with and without sample correction. Fourth-grade Portuguese and mathematics achievement can be analyzed in both 1983 and 1985 to ascertain the effects of alternative approaches. These are relatively small samples—227 students in 1983 and 349 in 1985—so that imprecision of parameter estimates complicates the evaluation. Nevertheless, some general patterns appear in the results. In addition to these basic experiments, the effects of instrumental variable correction for prior achievement scores can be investigated. In each of the experiments a basic production relationship is estimated. The specific models include a series of pupil characteristics, of teacher and school characteristics, of administrative and state information, and of program measures.

We will thus report on the five variants of estimation of this standard model defined above: longitudinal value-added with and without sample selection correction, cross-sectional level form with and without sample selection correction, and value-added with instrumental variables and sample selection. In four of the variants, precisely the same sample of students was used in the estimation. Because of missing data in constructing the instrumental variables, the samples for that estimation were slightly smaller.

The sample selection correction takes the results from the previous chapter to obtain consistent estimates of the probability that individuals will appear in the fourth-grade matched samples. Specifically, the coefficients derived from the full sample of second graders for the determinants of school survival[102] and on-time promotion are applied to the actual characteristics, as measured at second grade, of the students appearing in our fourth-grade samples. The data on school survival and on-time promotion yield separate estimates of the probability that each student attends a school that survives over the two-year observation periods and of the probability that each is promoted on time. These probabilities are used in estimating the two selection factors, which are then entered directly into the achievement estimation.[103]

Here we attempt to summarize the major implications of the alternative estimation approaches. (The full statistical results are available in appendix tables C5-1 through C5-4.) Subsequent sections will consider the substantive implications of specific parameter estimates.

The first result is that correcting for sample selection in the value-added models has virtually no effect on the estimated models. In each case (two selection factors and four separate estimating models), it is not possible to reject the hypothesis that selection has no effect at the

5 percent level. In fact, only one of the eight individual t-statistics on the selection coefficients is even greater than 1.0. Further, F-tests on the joint hypothesis that both are equal to zero are never significant at the 5 percent level. Finally, inclusion or exclusion of the selection terms from the estimates has small, almost imperceptible, effects on the estimated coefficients and standard errors for the remaining parameters in the model. For these reasons, for selection effects we concentrate exclusively on a three-way comparison: value-added models with selection corrections versus level models with and without selection corrections.

The value-added models of fourth-grade achievement include second-grade performance on both Portuguese and mathematics scores; the level models exclude these terms. As one might expect, knowing earlier performance levels contributes substantially to our ability to explain fourth-grade performance. The explained variance in performance, R^2, increases 70 to 150 percent when initial achievement is added to the pure level models (rising to about one-half in the 1985 models and to between one-third and two-fifths in the 1983 models). Everything else being equal, this reduction in overall error variance helps in obtaining more precise estimates of the remaining coefficients.

The fundamental question to be asked is whether or not the choice of analytical methods will lead to large changes in our understanding of the educational process and, consequently, to differences in derivative policy recommendations. This possibility can be assessed in tables 5-3 and 5-4, which compare the conceptually superior models (value-added without and then with selection correction) to the most commonly used models (level, or cross-sectional, without and then with sample selection correction). In these tables, the results for the separate Portuguese and mathematics models are aggregated together, but the different years are separated.

Table 5-3 summarizes the estimated statistical significance and the relative magnitudes of the parameters derived from the two different analytical methods while ignoring sample selection correction. The models for 1985 are probably superior to those for 1983, both because of better measurement of teacher differences and because of slightly larger sample sizes. Therefore, we concentrate on the results from the 1985 estimation.

In terms of statistical significance of the coefficients, the two estimation methods give a very different overall picture. While twenty-eight coefficients in the 1985 value-added models would be judged to be statistically different from zero at the 10 percent level, only seventeen of these twenty-eight would pass a similar test in the level models. While the comparisons are better in 1983 (twelve out of twelve), the dominant feature of the 1983 models is the imprecision and lack of significance of all of the estimates. When both estimation methods yield significant

Table 5-3. Comparison of Estimated Parameters: Value-added Versus Level Models without Sample Correction, 1983 and 1985

Parameter	*1983*	*1985*
Number of common parameters estimated	48	52
Coefficients statistically significant at 0.10 level in value-added models	12	28
Statistically significant in level form	12	17
With the same sign in two versions	12	17
And with less than 50 percent difference	12	16
Statistically insignificant in level form	0	11
With the same sign in two versions	0	8
And with less than 50 percent difference	0	4
Coefficients statistically insignificant at 0.10 level in value-added models	36	24
Statistically significant in level form	2	0
With the same sign in two versions	2	0
And with less than 50 percent difference	1	0
Statistically insignificant in level form	34	24
With the same sign in two versions	22	22
And with less than 50 percent difference	9	13

Note: Estimated intercepts and coefficients on prior achievement and selection probability terms are excluded from comparisons. Portuguese and mathematics models are combined.

Source: Appendix tables C5-1 to C5-4.

coefficients, it is encouraging that they always have the same sign and that they are generally close to each other in magnitude—most are estimated within 50 percent of each other.

The other major deviation between the two models would occur when the value-added coefficient is estimated as insignificantly different from zero but the level model is judged to be significant. As shown in the bottom portion of table 5-3, this is not a very common occurrence. Only two out of thirty-six possible times was this found in 1983, and it was never found in 1985.

If one or both of the coefficients is statistically insignificant, there is a greater tendency for the estimated coefficients to differ in sign. Further, the quantitative estimates of the parameters will be further apart. These findings are, of course, not very surprising because the coefficients are simply estimated imprecisely or the specific factor has no real influence on achievement.

These results suggest quite serious potential problems in the estimation of achievement models from simple cross-sectional data. Even with the extensive data on schools, teachers, and individual families that are available here, errors from historical inaccuracies in the measurement of inputs, from lack of knowledge of individual ability differences, and

from sample selection yield substantial differences in the estimated results—and in the conclusions that would likely be drawn from them.

The sources of the differences can be partially separated from each
other with the EDURURAL data. Specifically, since the previous chapter
provides estimates of the probability of selection into the matched fourth-
grade sample, the level models can be corrected for sample selection
biases. One of the sources of sample selection is, of course, prior achievement, so the correction for sample selection is partially a correction for
individual differences in ability and historical schooling factors.

Table 5-4 presents the summary results for the comparison of the value-
added models with the level models, when each is corrected for sample
selection. Compared with table 5-3, the most noticeable feature of this
table is the lack of substantial improvement in congruence of statistically
significant coefficient estimates. In 1985, the comparative pattern is exactly the same. In 1983, the estimates continue to be quite unreliable,
and are even less in agreement with the preferred estimates than those
in the simpler level models.

The selection term related to student promotion in the level models
is statistically significant for both Portuguese and mathematics in 1985.
However, all remaining selection terms are statistically insignificant. Se-

*Table 5-4. Comparison of Estimated Parameters: Value-added Versus
Level Models with Sample Correction, 1983 and 1985*

Parameter	1983	1985
Number of common parameters estimated	48	52
Coefficients statistically significant at 0.10 level in value-added		
models	12	28
Statistically significant in level form	9	17
Level form with the same sign in two versions	9	17
And with less than 50 percent difference	9	16
Statistically insignificant in level form	3	11
Level form with same sign in two versions	2	8
And with less than 50 percent difference	2	4
Coefficients statistically insignificant at 0.10 level in value-		
added models	36	24
Statistically significant in level form	1	0
With the same sign in two versions	1	0
And with less than 50 percent difference	0	0
Statistically insignificant in level form	35	24
With same sign in two versions	26	22
And with less than 50 percent difference	15	13

Note: Estimated intercepts and coefficients on prior achievement and selection probability terms are excluded from comparisons. Portuguese and mathematics models are combined.
Source: Appendix table C5-1.

lection due to nonsurvival of schools appears unimportant. In none of the four separate cases is this selection term significantly different from zero at the 5 percent level, indicating that school survival is not systematically related to unmeasured factors affecting individual achievement gains.

The exact character of the selection effects is important for the achievement analyses reported here. For the fourth-grade achievement relationships, we rely exclusively on the value-added estimations (with sample selection correction). For the second grade, however, it is impossible either to estimate value-added models or to correct for sample selection, because there are no prior observations on the second-grade students. Any influence of sample selection is almost certainly not as important at the second grade as it is for on-time promotion to the fourth grade. The biases that are introduced through differences in student promotion will probably be much less important for the second grade. Further, because the nonsurvival of schools appears random with respect to individual students and their achievement, biases in basic sample design are not likely to have much effect.

The largest problem with the second-grade cross-sectional estimates is lack of measurement of individual ability differences. Because the history of schooling is less, there is a considerably reduced problem of bad measurement of past resources. And, as discussed, selection is sure to be a less important problem.

There are two possible effects of lack of measurement of prior achievement in the second grade. First, and most important, if ability differences are correlated with the various school and family factors included in the level regressions, the estimated parameters will be biased. Second, as seen previously, knowledge of variations in earlier scores helps to improve the overall estimates because it reduces the amount of unexplained variation. This second problem is, however, compensated for by using the much larger samples available in the cross-sectional analysis of the second grade.

The evidence thus suggests that caution must be used in interpreting the second-grade level cross-sectional results—because of the potential for bias resulting from unmeasured ability differences of students. However, the potential damage of using level models is considerably less at the second grade than at the fourth grade.

Finally, the alternative estimation experiments included the use of instrumental variable techniques to correct for errors in measurement of second-grade achievement in the value-added models. Because we have second-grade achievement models, we can easily produce instruments for these variables. (See appendix tables C5-1 to C5-4.) They yield only inconsequential changes in either the parameter estimates or the estimated standard errors of the coefficients. Therefore, we ignore this potential complication in the subsequent analyses.

What Makes a Difference?

We are now in a position to analyze the determinants of scholastic achievement, our definition of the quality of schooling received by the students in rural northeast Brazil. We actually have several snapshots of student achievement and are able to provide several parallel analyses of educational performance. Specifically, we can examine the achievement in both mathematics and Portuguese of fourth graders in 1983 and 1985 in a value-added framework as well as the achievement in the same subjects of second graders in 1981, 1983, and 1985 in a cross-sectional framework. In addition we can examine special aspects of achievement in both subjects of second, third, and fourth graders in Ceará in 1987, again in a value-added model. These analyses quite clearly are not independent of each other—they involve overlapping sets of students and schools. Nevertheless, the ability to consider several analyses of the underlying relationships provides extra information about the consistency and reliability of any specific findings.

The following sections review the estimation results obtained in the different years, different grades, and different areas of performance (Portuguese and mathematics). Appendix tables C5-5 through C5-17 give complete results.

Each section below extracts the relevant results for major sets of inputs—families, students, peers, schools, teachers, and administrative control. Although the results for a given factor—say the influence of student work behavior on achievement—are compared across grades and years, *they are always the marginal effects of the specific factor after allowing for variations in the other factors included in the full models.* Estimated coefficients, presented in the tables and described in the test, are all stated in terms of points on the achievement tests, which were scored from 0 to 100 points.

The results that are obtained in several different models pertaining to a specific factor are combined, but the most weight should be placed on the results from the fourth-grade value-added models for 1985. These are the most accurate and reliable results.

How the variables are specified and how accurately they are measured must color all interpretation of results. As already discussed, measurement of academic achievement in the lower primary grades among young and often semiliterate children is a particular challenge. Other variables also posed methodological difficulties, noted below whenever essential to understand the results. Details of the performance measurement issues and variable specifications are contained, respectively, in appendixes A and B.

Families

Studies of educational performance, particularly in developed countries, invariably indicate that learning that occurs in the home is extremely important, perhaps even dominant. But the educational environment in the home in developed countries is dramatically different from that in northeast Brazil. In the United States the average parent has a high school education; in rural northeast Brazil, the average parent has two years of schooling. The absolute levels of schooling can be misleading, however, because the real issue is whether variations in parental education lead to varying performance of their children.

The quality of the educational environment at home is typically prox-ied by the educational levels of the parents, by the income levels of the parents, or other indicators of the socioeconomic status of the family. In addition, many have hypothesized that the family structure as captured by the absence of one or more parents, by the family size, or by the distribution of school-age children is important in home education.

Our data set allows us to investigate each of these hypotheses in con-siderable detail. The richness of information about family education and economic position permits us to replicate most other studies of specific family inputs. Even so, of course, many family attributes that might well contribute to the scholastic performance of children have not been in-cluded in this study. It is never possible to identify all such attributes, let alone to measure them properly. This complication, as discussed pre-viously, is, however, mitigated in the fourth-grade value-added specifi-cations, at least as it pertains to the unbiased estimation of relevant school factors.

A notable feature of these fourth-grade models is that no explicit mea-sure of parental or family inputs to education enters directly. This is a consequence of the value-added specification. These models provide in-sights into how achievement changes or grows during the third and fourth grade. This depends, of course, on achievement levels at the end of the second grade. Therefore, family inputs that are steady over time, influencing second-grade performance as well as fourth-grade perfor-mance, will already have been largely taken into account in the earlier achievement measures included in the models.[104]

The import of early family effects can be observed in table 5-5. The level of both the mother's education and the father's education exerts a positive and generally significant influence on second-grade achieve-ment. Nevertheless, while the precise estimates vary by year and test, the quantitative magnitude of the effects is relatively small. The estimated

*Table 5-5. Effects of Family Characteristics on Second-Grade
Achievement, 1981, 1983, and 1985*

	Mother's education		Father's education		Family size	
Year	Portuguese	Mathematics	Portuguese	Mathematics	Portuguese	Mathematics
1985	0.68	0.56	(0.22)	0.60	−0.38	(−0.10)
1983	0.62	0.56	0.68	0.91	−0.29	(0.02)
1981	(0.34)	(0.33)	0.78	0.78	−0.04	(0.10)

Note: Extract of regression coefficients from level form in appendix tables C5-11 and C5-12, both
columns 3; and table C5-13, both columns 3t. Coefficients in parentheses are not significantly different
from zero at the 5 percent level.
Source: Appendix tables C5-11, C5-12, and C5-13.

effect of one year of either mother's education or father's education is
(with one exception) between 0.3 and 1.0 points of Portuguese and
mathematics achievement. If both the mother and the father had an additional four years of schooling, their child's second-grade Portuguese
and mathematics achievement would be 3 to 6 points higher—equivalent
to less than a third of a standard deviation. At the fourth-grade level,
achievement would then be only 2 to 4 points higher (compared to a
standard deviation of roughly 18 points for Portuguese or 24 points for
mathematics).[105]

The final family factor displayed in table 5-5 is family size. Increased
family size generally has the expected negative effect on achievement
(because of the children's competition for parents' time), even though
it is never statistically significant in the mathematics equations. Again,
the estimated effects of varying family size are quite small in absolute
terms.

Direct measures of the economic status of the family and of parental
literacy had no independent effect on student performance (in either
the second- or the fourth-grade models).[106] Clearly, however, it is difficult to measure income and economic status in rural economies where
there is less reliance on market transactions than in more developed
sectors.

On balance, these results do not support the hypothesis that families
have an overwhelming importance in the educational performance of
their children in the depressed rural environment of northeast Brazil.
Rather, the results are consistent with the proposition that family background exerts less of a force on student achievement in developing countries than in developed countries. This idea was first suggested in Heyneman and Loxley (1983); see chapter 2 in this volume. But it must be
remembered that the results also depend crucially on the specific measures of differences in family background. There is also less empirical
evidence from developing countries than developed countries about how

to measure important family differences. Moreover, as indicated in chapter 4, family factors do enter directly into school continuation and the quantity of schooling any student receives.

Students

Individual students perform differently because of a wide variety of factors. At the top of the list would undoubtedly be differences in individual abilities and motivation, though these concepts have proved very difficult to measure. Estimation in value-added form circumvents this problem, however, at least to the extent that ability and motivation are constant over time and can be implicitly taken into account by examining growth in achievement.[107]

Schools in rural northeast Brazil are characterized by huge variations in the age and attendance patterns of students. Many students continue on-and-off attendance over extended periods of time, leading in part to their being stuck in given grades for long periods of time. Unfortunately, no reliable direct measures of attendance patterns are available.[108] However, indirect measures, such as age and work behavior, are available and are employed.

Table 5-6 shows the effects of student age and work behavior on achievement. At the fourth grade, older students do noticeably worse (although this is statistically insignificant in the early sample period). In contrast, older students appear to do better in the second grade.

Table 5-6. Effects of Student Age and Work on Achievement, 1981, 1983, and 1985

	Age		Work	
Grade/year	*Portuguese*	*Mathematics*	*Portuguese*	*Mathematics*
Fourth-grade value-added models[a]				
1985	−1.37	−1.43	(−5.72)	(−6.87)
1983	(−0.40)	(−1.70)	−12.71	(−7.58)
Second-grade level models[b]				
1985	0.73	1.20	(−0.50)	(2.08)
1983	0.43	0.93	(−0.90)	(0.58)
1981	0.77	1.19	(−0.60)	(−2.24)

Note: Coefficients in parentheses are not significantly different from zero at the 5 percent level.

a. Extract of regression coefficients from value-added form in appendix tables C5-5 to C5-8, columns 1.

b. Extract of regression coefficients from level form in appendix tables C5-11 and C5-12, both columns 3; and table C5-13, both columns 3t.

Source: Appendix tables C5-5 to C5-8 and C5-11 to C5-13.

The difference in direction of effect across grades is not as inconsistent as it might appear at first sight. The second-grade effect combines several factors. Older second graders will on average have repeated the second grade one or more times and may as well have entered school at a later age. They would be expected to master the second-grade material more readily than second graders who had spent less time with the material or who entered with one or more years less maturity. Once age of entry is taken into account, however, older students will tend to be less able and less motivated, otherwise they would have already been promoted. The positive second-grade effects indicate that the learning dividend from repetition, and possibly from more mature entry to school, is more important than the negative factors that are proxied by age. At the fourth grade, where prior ability is measured and where repetition can never be observed,[109] age reflects just the negative influences of low motivation or increasingly sporadic attendance at school as claims grow on the student from family and community (other than from actually working).

Not surprisingly, if a student works, performance appears to be lower. While the effect of work behavior is generally not statistically significant in the estimation, the consistency of estimated magnitudes at the fourth grade suggests important effects.[110] Specifically, growth in performance appears to be 5 to 13 points lower if a student works than if the student does not work.

The effects of working on second-grade performance are always small and insignificant. The work by second graders typically involves lesser time commitments and therefore is less intrusive on schooling. Because it is necessary to separate normal household chores from more substantial activities and because this division is less clear with younger students, even the measurement of work commitments at the second-grade level is more difficult.

Another factor influencing individual performance could be the sex of students. Boys and girls in developing countries clearly have different opportunity costs outside of schools, have been given different expectations that may also affect motivations, and perhaps have different kinds of skills and abilities. Additionally, particularly in developing countries, there is a question about how students interact with teachers of the same and opposite sex.

Table 5-7 displays the evidence from the EDURURAL program related to student sex and to the students' sex match with their teachers. As the first column shows, girls tend to do better at Portuguese than boys do. The growth in fourth-grade achievement is 5 to 8 points higher for girls than boys. At the same time, the results for math performance are generally consistent with the stereotype that girls do not perform as well in mathematics.

The right-hand portions of the table display the effects of student-

Table 5-7. Effects of Relationship between Student and Teacher Gender on Achievement, 1981, 1983, and 1985

Grade/year	Student female		Student and teacher male		Student and teacher female	
	Portuguese	Mathematics	Portuguese	Mathematics	Portuguese	Mathematics
Fourth-grade value-added models[a]						
1985	(4.70)	−13.58	8.91	9.92	(−0.85)	(5.83)
1983	(7.89)	(7.92)	(1.03)	(2.91)	(−5.43)	(−6.49)
Second-grade level models[b]						
1985	7.17	(−5.58)	7.99	5.28	(−3.22)	(−0.78)
1983	(0.79)	−8.91	(0.64)	(2.09)	(1.42)	(1.05)
1981	(−5.11)	−11.62	(−3.79)	−5.15	4.93	4.55

Note: Coefficients in parentheses are not significantly different from zero at the 5 percent level.

a. Extract of regression coefficients from value-added form in appendix tables C5-5 and C5-8, column 1.

b. Extract of regression coefficients from level form in appendix tables C5-11 and C5-12, both columns 3; and table C5-13, both columns 3t.

Source: Appendix tables C5-5, C5-8 and C5-11 to C5-13.

*Table 5-8. Relative Effects of Student and Teacher Gender
on Fourth-Grade Achievement, 1985*
(compared with male student in class with female teacher)

| Student gender | Teacher gender | | | |
| | Male | | Female | |
	Portuguese	Mathematics	Portuguese	Mathematics
Male	8.9	9.9	0.0	0.0
Female	4.7	− 13.6	3.8	− 7.8

Source: Calculations from table 5-7.

teacher gender match. In 1985, a fourth-grade male student will score 9 points higher in Portuguese and 10 points higher in mathematics if he has a male teacher rather than a female teacher. The female fourth grader in 1985 is estimated to achieve about the same in Portuguese regardless of the sex of the teacher and will perform 6 points higher in mathematics with a female teacher, although both estimates are very imprecise.

Table 5-8 summarizes how fourth-grade performance of students in 1985 varies relative to a boy with a female teacher. Having a teacher of the same sex is uniformly more important for boys than for girls, and may even hurt girls according to the estimates for Portuguese achievement. This is particularly interesting because organization of single-sex schools—a policy designed in part to ensure that girls also have female teachers—has been proposed as a means of improving the performance of girls.

The 1985 fourth-grade results are clouded by the imprecision of the estimates: the male-male result is significant at the 95 percent level for Portuguese and mathematics, but the female-female relationship is significant at only the 80 percent level for mathematics and the 20 percent level for Portuguese. Further, the results in the second grade and in 1983 are quite unreliable. Part of the uncertainty results from the small number of students with male teachers (8 percent), and part results from incomplete measurement of the past history of all teachers. On balance, it is best to think of the identified interactions between students and teachers of the same or opposite sex as being suggestive rather than conclusive.

School Peers

Education comes not only from parents and teachers but from other children in the school. When these other children are positive about school, when they aspire to complete higher grades, and when they are generally engaged in the learning process, the individual student would be expected to perform better than when other students hold more negative attitudes. Moreover, when the other students speak better Portuguese and when they better understand the mathematical concepts being presented, they can actively help in the teaching process.

Our data do not directly capture the interactions among students in the school. Nevertheless, within each school the background, attitudes, and achievement of other students in the classroom are observed. We use three broad measures of peer characteristics to test the influence of other students on the educational process: income and wealth of other families, sex composition of the classroom, and achievement of fellow students. The socioeconomic status (SES) measures of families attempt to capture the attitudes and direct inputs of other parents. The separate inquiry into effects of the sex composition of the classroom follows directly from the issues introduced in the previous section. Any sex discrimination against girls in schools could lead to the learning environment of the class being colored by its composition. Finally, the measurement of achievement of fellow students allows direct testing of the contribution of smart friends.

Table 5-9 displays the effects of two measures of the SES of other families

Table 5-9. Effects of Classroom Income and Wealth on Achievement, 1981, 1983, and 1985

Grade/year	Proportion families not farming		Proportion families on large farms	
	Portuguese	Mathematics	Portuguese	Mathematics
Fourth-grade value-added models[a]				
1985	10.12	6.74	(0.19)	(−0.41)
1983	13.97	15.47	(7.37)	16.74
Second-grade level models[b]				
1985	10.59	(1.84)	(0.07)	(0.10)
1983	(−3.38)	(0.02)	(4.11)	(−0.32)
1981	(−5.20)	−6.64	12.06	11.92

Note: Coefficients in parentheses are not significantly different from zero at the 5 percent level.

a. Extract of regression coefficients from value-added form in appendix tables C5-5 to C5-8, column 1.

b. Extract of regression coefficients from level form in appendix tables C5-11 and C5-12, both columns 3; and table C5-13, both columns 3t.

Source: Appendix tables C5-5 to C5-8 and C5-11 to C5-13.

of the child's grade. First, the higher the proportion of families not in farming the better the individual student did. On average, only about 10 percent of families are not in agriculture, and these people are employed in all of the commercial and service occupations. This peer measure is interpreted simply as a crude indicator of the better living standards of the average person who was not dependent on agriculture for a living. An increase of 10 percentage points in families outside agriculture will boost each student's achievement by 0.7 to 1.5 percentage points in the fourth grade. The findings for the second-grade cross-sections are, however, quite unreliable.

Second, the proportion of families working on (but not necessarily owning) "large" farms[111] tends to be positively associated with performance, although few of the estimates are statistically significant. This further positive effect of higher SES does give additional support to the idea that the character of the student body influences individual achievement.

Our investigation does not, however, support the common presumption that the sex composition of the school has an influence. The results of this analysis are displayed in table 5-10. The primary question is whether or not the proportion of female students in the class affects individual performance. A related question is: Does it have a specific

Table 5-10. Effects of Female Composition of Classroom on Achievement, 1981, 1983, and 1985

Grade/year	Proportion female classmates		Proportion female classmates for females	
	Portuguese	Mathematics	Portuguese	Mathematics
Fourth-grade value-added models[a]				
1985	(−0.48)	(−4.66)	(2.60)	(7.41)
1983	(8.45)	27.09	(0.27)	(−17.89)
Second-grade level models[b]				
1985	(2.92)	(2.80)	(3.62)	(2.52)
1983	(−3.38)	(0.02)	(4.12)	(−0.32)
1981	−7.27	(0.71)	10.79	(1.29)

Note: Coefficients in parentheses are not significantly different from zero at the 5 percent level.

a. Extract of regression coefficients from value-added form in appendix tables C5-5 to C5-8, column 1.

b. Extract of regression coefficients from level form in appendix tables C5-11 and C5-12, both columns 3; and table C5-13, both columns 3t.

Source: Appendix tables C5-5 to C5-8 and C5-11 to C5-13.

effect for girls that is different from that for boys? Our data show that the proportion of females has no consistent effect on achievement for either boys or girls.[112] Within these data, therefore, there is little support for any proposal to move toward single-sex schools. This could possibly be modified if one believes that the impact of sex composition of the classroom is very nonlinear; that is, that it is only important at or very close to complete sex segregation.[113]

Additionally, in the value-added models it was possible to investigate how the achievement composition of the class affects learning.[114] Previous educational discussions have debated the pros and cons of ability grouping of students. Our data allow direct investigation of the effects of various groupings.[115] We calculated the average second-grade achievement of the class, the variance in achievement, the proportion of students more than one standard deviation below the mean, and the proportion more than one standard deviation above the mean.[116] These measures capture, we believe, all of the different aspects of class composition that people have hypothesized to be important. There is no evidence that any of these factors is important. While we do not present the results separately, none of these variables had a statistically significant relationship to achievement in the 1983 or 1985 value-added models. We conclude that in rural northeast Brazil the mixing or segregating of students by achievement levels has little systematically to do with how teaching is done or what is learned.

Physical Facilities and Learning Materials

Understanding the effects of the school facilities and materials available to the students is particularly important, because they are readily adjusted through governmental policies and are thus frequently the preferred instruments of educational development programs. They are also inputs that have entered significantly into previous investigations of the educational process in developing countries. We consider two broad categories of factors, school facilities (hardware) and writing materials and textbooks (software). Table 5-11 shows how measures of these factors are related to performance.

Improved facilities are systematically beneficial to student learning.[117] The index takes on values between 0 (for a school having none of the measured facilities) and 1 (for a school with all the measured facilities). The results for fourth grade indicate that supplying all components of the facilities index to a school that previously had none of them could increase student achievement by 9 to 13 percentage points. The effect at the second grade is somewhat less certain, particularly given the imprecision of the estimates in 1985. Nevertheless, the overall picture is

Table 5-11. Effects of School Resources on Achievement 1981, 1983, and 1985

Grade/year	Facilities		Writing materials		Texts[a]	
	Portuguese	Mathematics	Portuguese	Mathematics	Portuguese	Mathematics
Fourth-grade value-added models[b]						
1985	9.47	13.21	7.82	12.65	(2.15)	(3.49)
1983	11.85	(10.85)	(−1.43)	(6.38)	(−1.66)	(−7.99)
Second-grade level models[c]						
1985	(−2.32)	(0.37)	3.59	6.13	6.26	(1.88)
1983	8.97	6.31	4.70	3.27	6.40	4.23
1981	8.91	11.96	(0.75)	(−2.07)	5.52	5.64

Note: Coefficients in parentheses are not significantly different from zero at the 5 percent level.
a. Text coefficients refer to "high" level of provision in each year. Note, however, that questionnaire items differ across years.
b. Extract of regression coefficients from value-added form in appendix tables C5-5 and C5-8, column 2.
c. Extract of regression coefficients from level form in appendix tables C5-12, columns 3 and 4 for both Portuguese and mathematics and table C5-13, columns 3t and 4t for both Portuguese and mathematics.
Source: Appendix tables C5-5 to C5-8, and C5-11 to C5-13.

that quality of the physical plant is positively related to student performance.

Past research, as reviewed in chapter 2, has generally found that the availability of writing materials and texts is important in schooling for developing countries. The results here reinforce that view, although again the results, particularly for textbooks, are more imprecise (less statistically significant) than one would like for policy purposes. The 1985 fourth-grade value-added findings and the second-grade results for 1983 and 1985 support the importance of adequate writing materials for the students.[118] The size of the coefficients suggests that achievement gains of roughly a third to one-half of a standard deviation may be acquired by supplying a package of writing materials to all students. The results for the second grade consistently support the importance of textbooks, but the results in the value-added models are estimated with large errors and have the wrong sign in 1983.[119] We do, nevertheless, give weight to these overall findings, especially when combined with the strength of findings in previous studies.

Table 5-12 reports on two more aspects of schools—homework and the use of graded classrooms, two factors that receive elevated attention because of how they have fit into policy discussions in Brazil and elsewhere. Homework is in reality an interaction between the school and

Table 5-12. Effects of Homework and School Organization on Achievement, 1981, 1983, and 1985

	Homework		Graded classrooms	
Grade/year	Portuguese	Mathematics	Portuguese	Mathematics
Fourth-grade value-added models[a]				
1985	(1.93)	(3.75)	(−3.87)	−6.19
1983	4.52	(5.62)	(−1.68)	(4.81)
Second-grade level models[b]				
1985	3.56	2.21	(0.55)	(−0.94)
1983	3.53	2.72	−3.94	−1.98
1981	—	—	(−1.15)	(−0.07)

— = Not available.

Note: Coefficients in parentheses are not significantly different from zero at the 5 percent level.

a. Extract of regression coefficients from value-added form in appendix tables C5-5 to C5-8.

b. Extract of regression coefficients from level form in appendix tables C5-11 and C5-12, both columns 3; and table C5-13, both columns 3t.

Source: Appendix tables C5-5 to C5-8 and C5-11 to C5-13.

the student. As measured, it represents both whether or not it is assigned and whether or not it is actually accomplished.[120] While academic performance is positively related to more homework, the estimated effect is usually not statistically significant in the value-added models for the fourth grade. This pattern of results is somewhat surprising because one would expect homework to become increasingly important as the student advances in grade level. We speculate that larger sample sizes, which would improve the precision of the estimates, might confirm that the quantitative importance of assigning homework approaches that of providing texts or writing materials to students.[121]

The use of graded classrooms is an obviously important aspect of the organization of the school, especially where dispersed rural populations constrain school size. In rural northeast Brazil where class sizes are typically small, providing individual teachers for small single-grade classes rather than fewer teachers managing larger ungraded classes or multigrade classrooms has enormous economic implications. As table 5-12 indicates, the use of single-grade classrooms, rather than ungraded or multigrade classes, actually appears to affect performance negatively. The results are not overly strong, however, with several of the coefficients being insignificant.[122]

These findings cast doubt upon the common presumption that moving to all graded classrooms is desirable. At the very least, the suggestion is strong that the one-room school with students at various levels being attended to simultaneously by one teacher is not detrimental to learning. For the context of rural northeast Brazil, mixed-grade classrooms may in fact offer advantages. In a pedagogical environment dominated by rote memorization of material presented verbally or on the blackboard by the teacher, a student may profit from repeated hearing and seeing of the same material and from the peer teaching typical of the multigrade classroom. Another possibility is that in an environment where pupil absences are frequent because of sickness or the need for children to work, the repetition offered in a multigrade classroom saves many children from being entirely lost upon return from school after an absence. Finally, in some infrequent circumstances graded classes in schools too small to accord each grade a classroom may reduce effective time on task.[123] Confronted with more than one grade in a classroom, the teacher may send the pupils not currently being taught outside for recreation or otherwise allow them to remain idle as attention is given to a single grade.

Teachers

Though quality of teaching is an elusive concept for researchers, it has some common characteristics in the minds of the public and of policymakers. These characteristics are thus often found in research. The intensity of teacher interaction with the student is typically proxied in the pupil-teacher ratio. Teacher quality is normally proxied by such variables as experience in the profession and type and duration of both preemployment education and inservice training. Less frequently, direct measurement of the teacher's actual cognitive mastery of the subject matter is substituted for the normal quality indicators. Finally, teacher salary is often, if rather uncritically, used as a proxy for teacher quality, on the presumption that teachers command higher pay in direct proportion to their quality.

Our data permit us to examine, in an environment of stunning educational and economic deprivation, the validity of these presumptions about teacher quality and its measurement. Specifically we can ask three important questions. Is achievement influenced by the following: the standard measure of quantity of teacher input to an educational process, the pupil-teacher ratio; the standard indirect summary measure of teacher quality, teacher salary; or by more direct indicators of teacher quality?

Pupil-teacher ratios. The arguments favoring altering, or, more specifically, reducing, class sizes are well known. In fact, policy proposals to reduce class sizes are among the most popular ones throughout the world, even though they are extremely costly. As the number of students who share the time of a teacher decreases, each student potentially receives more direct attention from the teacher. To the extent individualized attention from the teacher is an important learning determinant, student achievement would be expected to benefit. On the other hand, as catalogued in chapter 2, there is no consistent evidence from past studies—in either developed or developing countries—to support policies of reduced class sizes.

The evidence from northeast Brazil, presented in table 5-13, lends little new support to proposals for reducing class sizes. In the fourth-grade value-added specifications, the pupil-teacher ratio has the expected (negative) sign in 1985, but it is not statistically significant. In 1983, however, the sign on this variable is uniformly positive, intuitively suggesting that student performance improves as class size grows.[124] Even if we take these statistically insignificant estimates at face value, the estimated coefficients are very small, so that substantial changes in class size would be required to produce a discernible effect on achievement. For example, changing class size by ten pupils in either direction—around sample means between 25 and 30—would alter achievement gains from second to fourth grade by at most one point, even though it would have a tremendous effect on educational costs.

The results at second grade do not appreciably alter the conclusions. The only statistically significant negative estimate is for Portuguese achievement in 1983, and this is counterbalanced by two statistically

Table 5-13. Effects of Pupil-Teacher Ratio on Achievement, 1981, 1983, and 1985

Grade/year	Portuguese	Mathematics
Fourth-grade value-added models[a]		
1985	(−0.11)	(−0.06)
1983	(0.12)	(0.20)
Second-grade level models[b]		
1985	0.08	(0.00)
1983	−0.07	(−0.04)
1981	0.07	(0.03)

Note: Coefficients in parentheses are not significantly different from zero at the 5 percent level.

a. Extract of regression coefficients from value-added form in appendix tables C5-5 to C5-8, column 1.

b. Extract of regression coefficients from level form in appendix tables C5-11 and C5-12, both columns 3; and table C5-13, both columns 3t.

Source: Appendix tables C5-5 to C5-8 and C5-11 to C5-13.

significant positive estimates, which suggest that larger classes improve student performance. Indeed, it is safe to conclude that enrollments could expand in the rural schools of northeast Brazil without paying a price in terms of student achievement.

Teacher salaries. In analyzing the impact of teacher quality, salaries are a natural place to focus attention for several reasons. First, standard economic analysis suggests that, when hiring inputs, relative costs should be proportional to the marginal contribution of each separate input. Turned around, this implies that salary can be used as a proxy for quality—at least if schools are operating efficiently and are paying teachers relative to their productivity in teaching. Second, teacher salaries are attractive policy instruments because they are easily measured and because they are amenable to manipulation by policymakers. Third, many who bemoan the perceived low quality of the teacher force (whether in Brazil, in other developing countries, or in developed countries) also point to the relatively low pay of teachers. For example, in our rural sample, mean teacher salary is less than 60 percent of the minimum wage.[125] Therefore, these people often turn to salary policies as a way of improving schools; by increasing salaries they would hope to attract new and better people into the teaching profession.

Table 5-14 summarizes the effects of teacher salary (measured as a percentage of the minimum wage) on student achievement.[126] These effects are estimated in two fundamental ways. First, complete models including the family and individual effects are estimated with salary as

Table 5-14. Effects of Teacher Salary on Student Achievement, 1981, 1983, and 1985

Grade/year	Portuguese	Mathematics
Fourth-grade value-added models[a]		
1985	(0.01)	0.04
1983	(0.02)	(0.02)
Second-grade level models[b]		
1985	0.05	0.04
1983	0.05	0.06
1981	0.03	0.03

Note: Coefficients in parentheses are not significantly different from zero at the 5 percent level.

a. Extract of regression coefficients from appendix tables C5-9 to C5-10, columns 1 and 3.

b. Extract of regression coefficients from level form appendix tables C5-11, C5-12 and table C5-13, both columns 1.

Source: Appendix tables C5-9 to C5-13.

the sole descriptor of teachers. If salaries are set according to teaching productivity, this single measure will capture all of the systematic differences among teachers. Second, separate salary estimates are made for each of the three states, allowing for both differences in cost of living and differences in labor market conditions. Because the separate state estimates provide little additional information, we concentrate on the overall estimates.

In all cases, the estimated salary coefficient has the expected positive sign: as salary increases as a proportion of minimum wage, achievement is enhanced. The coefficients are, however, exceedingly small and, with the exception of 1985 mathematics performance, not significantly different from zero in the value-added models. In practical terms, the impact on achievement is very small. An increase in salary from the sample mean of about 65 percent of the minimum wage to 100 percent is associated with an achievement gain in mathematics in 1985 of fewer than 1.5 points.

The results at second grade reveal a broadly similar pattern. In all three years and for both subjects, the effect of salary on achievement is positive and statistically significant. However, the effects remain small. These results do not lend very strong support to the idea that teacher salaries are a good measure of teacher quality. While related to teaching performance, salaries themselves apparently ignore considerable variation in teacher quality. Further, it is evident that increasing teachers' pay indiscriminately, by itself and without regard to their other characteristics, will not meaningfully enhance student achievement.

The situation is, of course, more complex than this simple statement. First, this conclusion is predicated on the existing institutional structure behind salaries, which tends to reward background factors, such as experience or education levels, instead of actual teaching performance (see chapter 6). If this pay structure were altered, changes in pay could have a much larger impact on achievement. Second, if pay schedules were raised significantly, an entirely different group of people could be attracted into teaching. This possibility can only partially be analyzed from the current regression information.[127]

Explicit indicators of teacher quality.   When attempting to delve into the specific teacher characteristics that are related to performance, researchers and policymakers typically turn to a standard list that includes years of teaching experience, level of formal preservice education, and inservice training.[128] We investigate these factors along with two other qualitative measures developed specifically for the EDURURAL survey. First, several survey items were developed to characterize the classroom activities of the teacher and the teacher's use of materials. Second, in 1985 teachers were given the same Portuguese and mathematics achievement tests as those administered to fourth-grade students, thus providing a direct comparison of how much the teacher could contribute to the learning of the students.

Table 5-15 describes the relationship of teachers' preservice educational attainment and on-the-job experience, both expressed in years, to student achievement. At the fourth-grade level, teachers with more formal education are apparently no better than those with less education. In models of both Portuguese and mathematics learning, the estimated effect of teacher education is not significantly different from zero. In fact, three of the four estimates are negative, suggesting implausibly that more schooling for teachers actually lowers students' performance. The positive and frequently statistically significant relationship between teacher education and achievement for the second-grade cross-sections does offer conflicting evidence. However, even in the second-grade cross-sections, whose specification is methodologically less rigorous (and whose results, therefore, are more questionable), the predicted effect of an additional year of teacher education is typically only a fraction of a point on tests with mean scores in the 45–60 percentage point range.

The unimportance of teacher education is somewhat surprising. Within our sample, the mean schooling of teachers is between seven and eight years with a standard deviation of three years. Further, more than 20 percent of the sampled teachers themselves have *four or fewer years of schooling*. Given both the level and the variation in schooling of teachers, it seemed plausible that this would be an important indicator of quality differences among teachers.[129] Apparently, differences in the quality of

Table 5-15. Effects of Teacher Education and Experience on Student Achievement, 1981, 1983, and 1985

	Teacher education		Teacher experience	
Grade/year	Portuguese	Mathematics	Portuguese	Mathematics
Fourth-grade value-added models[a]				
1985	(−0.13)	(−0.08)	(0.06)	(0.26)
1983	(−0.33)	(0.46)	(0.20)	(0.23)
Second-grade level models[b]				
1985	(0.01)	0.54	(−0.01)	(0.05)
1983	0.79	1.22	(0.00)	(0.10)
1981	(0.56)	0.59	(0.02)	0.19

Note: Coefficients in parentheses are not significantly different from zero at the 5 percent level.

a. Extract of regression coefficients from value-added form in appendix tables C5-5 to C5-8.

b. Extract of regression coefficients from level form in appendix tables C5-11 and C5-12, both columns 3; and table C5-13, both columns 3t.

Source: Appendix tables C5-5 to C5-8 and C5-11 to C5-13.

schooling of teachers are sufficiently large to obscure any possible effects of quantity differences.

None of our models suggest that teacher experience is a statistically significant determinant of Portuguese achievement of students, although the sign on the estimated coefficients suggests, with one exception, a positive relationship. The evidence from students' mathematics achievement is only slightly more supportive of conventional wisdom. Disregarding statistical significance, the conclusion again is that the effects are small. An additional year of experience amounts to about one-quarter of an additional point of mathematics achievement gain. This implies that an increase of one standard deviation in experience (seven years) corresponds to less than two points in achievement gain.

Overall, the results so far call into question the broadly held view that simply providing more educated and more experienced teachers to rural schools in northeast Brazil will by itself noticeably improve the learning performance of students.

Table 5-16 characterizes the effect of the two inservice teacher training programs associated with the EDURURAL project intervention. Each is specified as a dummy variable to separate teachers who are participating in the programs from those who are not at the time of our surveys.[130]

The Logos program seeks to provide teachers who have already completed the eight years of primary education with a qualification equivalent

Table 5-16. Effects of Participation in Teacher Training Programs on Student Achievement, 1981, 1983, and 1985

Grade/year	Logos program		Qualificação program	
	Portuguese	Mathematics	Portuguese	Mathematics
Fourth-grade value-added models[a]				
1985	(−0.22)	(0.65)	(−2.21)	−5.94
1983	(2.00)	(0.72)	(1.02)	(2.96)
Second-grade level models[b]				
1985	(1.86)	(1.80)	(0.60)	(1.43)
1983	3.59	2.62	(−0.16)	−3.62
1981	(−0.88)	(0.26)	n.a.	n.a.

n.a. = Not applicable.

Note: Coefficients in parentheses are not significantly different from zero at the 5 percent level.

a. Extract of regression coefficients from value-added form in appendix tables C5-5 to C5-8.

b. Extract of regression coefficients from level form in appendix tables C5-11 and C5-12, both columns 3; and table C5-13, both columns 3t.

Source: Appendix tables C5-5 to C5-8, and C5-11 to C5-13.

to three years of secondary school. On balance, any evidence of success of Logos is not very compelling; there is no consistency of results, and specifically there is no evidence that the program accomplished its objective in the late survey years when it would presumably have been having a measurable impact. On the other hand, it is admittedly early to evaluate an on-going training program.

The evidence is even less compelling with respect to the success of the *Curso de Qualificação* program, a remedial effort whose objective is to provide the equivalent of an eighth-grade education to teachers who have not completed the full primary cycle. The statistically significant negative coefficients on the Qualificação program variable for fourth-grade mathematics achievement in 1985 and second-grade mathematics achievement in 1983 are disconcerting at first glance.

There is, however, a plausible alternative interpretation of the estimated negative effects of these inservice programs. In equations that include more direct measures of preservice formal education and of teacher cognitive competency, the Qualificação variable could simply be isolating those teachers who, precisely because of their low levels of formal educational attainment and measured subject matter mastery, are judged most in need of upgrading and are therefore encouraged to participate in the inservice Qualificação program. In this interpretation a negative and significant coefficient is the expected result—the right teachers have been targeted—but it does not then provide direct evidence about the efficacy of the teacher upgrade program.

Teacher subject matter knowledge. The survey effort also included attempts to specify and measure qualitative differences among teachers—differences that showed up in what they know or how they teach classes as opposed to how much school and experience they have had.

The investigations of the classroom activities of teachers and of their use of materials proved unfruitful. These measures employed teacher survey data to construct indexes of techniques thought to be good by professional educators. Neither show even a consistently positive effect on achievement.[131] The failure of these measures to identify good teaching could reflect either a misguided view of what classroom techniques are important or simply the fact that how well they are executed (which is not measured) is the dominant factor.

The most interesting findings on teacher quality concern the competency of the teachers themselves on the same tests of Portuguese and mathematics that were administered to the fourth-grade students.[132] The absolute level of teacher performance is itself interesting. As shown in table 5-17, teachers of fourth graders did better than their students on the criterion-referenced tests of the fourth-grade curriculum, but their performance was far from spectacular.[133] Our expectation was that teachers, for whom the mean level of educational attainment is about eight years, would easily and consistently register perfect scores on tests carefully constructed to measure performance against the specific learning objectives of the fourth grade. They do not. The average fourth-grade teacher misses one-fifth of the questions on the test of fourth-grade Portuguese and still half that many on the test of fourth-grade mathematics.

Table 5-17. Mean Achievement Scores of Teachers and Students on Fourth-Grade Tests, 1985
(standard deviations in parentheses)

	Portuguese		*Mathematics*	
Sample	*Students*	*Their teachers*	*Students*	*Their teachers*
1985 Fourth-grade cross-section (1,789 students)	48.5 (18.3)	78.3 (13.8)	50.1 (23.5)	87.3 (12.6)
1985 Fourth-grade matched sample (349 students)	47.2 (17.8)	79.3 (11.8)	48.2 (24.2)	87.8 (9.6)

Source: Appendix B.

Table 5-18. Effects of Teacher Test Scores on Student Achievement, 1985

	Teacher's Portuguese score		Teacher's mathematics score	
Grade/year	Portuguese	Mathematics	Portuguese	Mathematics
Fourth-grade value-added models[a] 1985	0.17	−0.18	0.18	0.52
Second-grade level models[b] 1985	−0.08	−0.16	0.13	0.12

Note: All coefficients are not significantly different from zero at the 5 percent level.

a. Extract of regression coefficients from value-added form in appendix tables C5-5 to C5-8.

b. Extract of regression coefficients from level form in appendix table C5-13, both columns 3t.

Source: Appendix tables C5-5 to C5-8, and C5-13.

Table 5-18 demonstrates the value of subject matter knowledge, as measured by teacher test scores (on fourth-grade achievement tests), for student learning in second and fourth grades in 1985. The teacher's command over the mathematics subject matter she is expected to teach is unambiguously important in fostering student achievement in mathematics. At fourth grade, a ten-point improvement in the mean teacher's command of her mathematics subject matter (which would still leave the mean somewhat below 100 percent) would engender a five-point increase in student achievement; this is equivalent to a 10 percent improvement over the mean score of fourth graders. The effect of mathematics knowledge in the second grade, although about one-quarter the size in the second-grade cross-section, is also significant. The teacher's command of Portuguese subject matter is also shown to be a significant predictor of fourth-grade student achievement in that subject, although the size of the coefficients is less impressive than for mathematics. The sign of the second-grade effect is, however, inexplicable.

The evidence on the cross-subject effects of the teacher's command of these two subjects on student achievement in them is inconsistent. On the one hand, the teacher's knowledge of mathematics may marginally enhance student achievement in Portuguese; here there is reinforcement across subjects. On the other hand, there is no mechanism to explain, and it is counterintuitive to conclude, that more developed command of Portuguese by teachers is actually detrimental to mathematics achievement of students. We cannot find a reasonable interpretation of this and and so are reduced to discounting it as an anomaly in our sample data.

Conclusions about teacher effects. The overall conclusions on teacher characteristics and student achievement in rural northeast Brazil are very similar to those found elsewhere in the world. A teacher's knowledge of the subject matter makes a noticeable difference to student learning of that subject, especially in mathematics. On balance, however, the policy instruments traditionally relied upon—class size, teacher education, inservice training, and teacher experience—are not systematically and importantly related to student performance.

One simple explanation of the findings is that qualitative differences in the explicit teacher measures—say, in the quality of the teacher's schooling or the specific character of the inservice training of each teacher—along with differences in "teaching skill" that are unrelated to the measured attributes are much more important than the readily identified dimensions employed here and elsewhere. Failure adequately to measure these deeper aspects of teachers makes detection of other systematic relationships impossible. Selecting the commonly used but crude quantitative indicators of teacher characteristics is then a hit-or-miss proposition: sometimes a good teacher is found, but just as frequently a less good teacher turns up.

If this is the case, education decisionmaking must be more sophisticated. Especially when the general levels of teacher education, training, and subject matter knowledge are so low, policymakers cannot rely on simple traditional indicators of school quality. Rather, when selecting teachers, policymakers should pay closest attention to what teachers can demonstrate they actually know about what they will teach. However, our analysis does not uncover simple rules about selecting specific teacher characteristics that are consistently related to performance. This indicates that if there is to be a noticeable change in the performance of the school system fundamental changes may be required in the selection and evaluation system for teachers.

State, Program Status, and Administrative Support

Having described how specific characteristics of students, schools, and teachers enter into the educational process and how they influence the level of student performance, we turn to other differences in schools that are hard to pinpoint and measure but that also influence performance. Most specifically, the education system does differentially well across states and across the EDURURAL and OTHER counties. In these cases, we can note the overall mean differences (after allowing for any differences in the measured factors included in the models). We cannot be sure, however, of the source of these differences, or whether they can be altered by policies.

Table 5-19 provides comparisons of macrodifferences in performance

Table 5-19. Effects of State Differences on Student Achievement in
OTHER *Counties (Relative to Pernambuco Schools), 1981, 1983, and*
1985

Grade/year	Ceará		Piaui	
	Portuguese	Mathematics	Portuguese	Mathematics
Fourth-grade value-added models[a]				
1985	18.67	23.77	16.58	(9.78)
1983	19.22	(11.22)	(11.98)	(18.38)
Second-grade level models[b]				
1985	14.13	6.19	(−0.12)	−12.59
1983	14.43	7.45	11.77	(−3.39)
1981	18.50	8.96	4.16	−4.44

Note: Coefficients in parentheses are not significantly different from zero at the 5 percent level.

a. Extract of regression coefficients from value-added form in appendix tables C5-5 to C5-8, column 1.

b. Extract of regression coefficients from level form in appendix tables C5-11 and C5-12, both columns 3; and table C5-13, both columns 3t.

Source: Appendix tables C5-5 to C5-8, and C5-11 to C5-13.

across the states. In each instance, the estimated state effects refer only to education in OTHER (that is, non-EDURURAL) counties; schools located in the OTHER counties in Ceará and Piaui are compared with those in Pernambuco. The overall finding is that, other things being equal, students in Pernambuco tend to perform worst. Students in Ceará outperform those in Pernambuco across grades and years. Similarly, students in Piaui tend to outperform those in Pernambuco, with the possible exceptions of the second-grade Portuguese in 1985 and second-grade mathematics in all years. These differences, however, are not very precisely measured and are frequently statistically insignificant.

Table 5-20 pinpoints mean differences for EDURURAL counties compared with the OTHER counties within each state. With one exception (Pernambuco in 1985) the differences in the value-added models are all statistically insignificant. The results for the second grade are not consistent over time and across states, but that is not particularly surprising because the program has been implemented in very different ways across the northeast. There is little support here for the proposition that the EDURURAL counties benefited differentially from the program. The evaluation hypothesis is explored more rigorously in chapter 7.

Finally, this table also includes information about the effects of the county educational organizations (OMES) on education. OMES began to

Table 5-20. *Effects of Program Status and Administrative Support on Student Achievement, 1981, 1983, and 1985*

Grade/year	Ceará EDURURAL[a]		Pernambuco EDURURAL[a]		Piauí EDURURAL[a]		OME	
	Portuguese	Mathematics	Portuguese	Mathematics	Portuguese	Mathematics	Portuguese	Mathematics
Fourth-grade value-added models[b]								
1985	(−6.69)	(−4.00)	11.88	8.96	(−4.29)	(4.32)	8.04	7.44
1983	(−4.30)	(1.63)	(−1.12)	(4.99)	(−0.56)	(0.56)	(−6.40)	(−5.12)
Second-grade level models[c]								
1985	(0.02)	(−0.82)	−4.07	−9.13	(0.84)	11.09	(−2.04)	−9.00
1983	11.15	11.38	(2.40)	(−0.72)	(−1.76)	5.38	(−1.68)	−6.78
1981	7.45	11.29	6.35	2.49	(−1.17)	(0.79)	n.a.	n.a.

n.a. = Not applicable.

Note: Coefficients in parentheses are not significantly different from zero at the 5 percent level.

a. The coefficients compare performance in EDURURAL and OTHER schools *within* each state.

b. Extract of regression coefficients from value-added form in appendix tables C5-5 to C5-8, column 1.

c. Extract of regression coefficients from level form in appendix tables C5-11 and C5-12, both columns 3; and table C5-13, both columns 3t.

Source: Appendix tables C5-5 to C5-8, and C5-11 to C5-13.

be established in 1982 as a means for providing administrative and pedagogical support for county schools. They are designed to coordinate
state and federal programs, to provide teacher training, to perform a
variety of administrative tasks, and to supervise the instructional process.
The specific measure of OMES is an index including both quantity and
quality of staff. The value-added specifications for 1985 indicate that
better OMES do indeed have a significant and strong influence on local
education. Going from the worst to the best OME implies about an eight-
point gain in both Portuguese and mathematics scores.

Not surprisingly, the OMES in 1983, when they were still very new, did
not show the same positive effect. On the other hand, the second-grade
level models indicate a negative effect of OMES. We have no explanation for this and in fact question whether or not this is a true effect.

Schools and Teachers: Aggregate Quality Differences

The analysis until now of "what makes a difference to achievement" has
examined the separate influences attributable to a variety of specific
factors. For some important inputs to schooling—for example, facilities,
learning materials, and the subject matter knowledge of the teachers—
these effects are seen to be substantial. For others—for example, the
more usually tracked characteristics of teachers such as their education,
experience, and inservice training, and the attributes of classroom organization—the discernible effect on student achievement is much less.
The conclusion is *not*, however, that differences among teachers and
schools are unimportant. This evidence reveals only that differences in
the *measured inputs*, specified in a particular way in the achievement
models, do not appear important. It is valuable to know this, because
these measured inputs are frequently the subject of policy interventions.
Nevertheless, there are two reasons to stop short of generalizing about
the effect of teachers from this finding about common measures.

First, and most important, extensive prior evidence (as reviewed in
chapter 2) indicates that we have a very imperfect understanding of the
fundamental characteristics and behaviors of teachers that signal good
teaching performance. In simplest terms, from previous work we have
not fully identified nor do we know how to measure many specific attributes that are important. This is exactly what was discovered in the
analysis reported earlier in this chapter. Attempts to isolate the effect of
specific educational inputs was largely a failure.

Second, even if there is a set of specific factors that is important, there
must be a strong suspicion that their separate effects are somewhat idiosyncratic, depending upon the way that they are bundled together in
individual teachers and schools. For example, it might be that intensive
study of Brazilian literature in combination with a teacher's appreciation

of language skills leads to good teaching performance but that the study of literature by a teacher who is more mathematically oriented has no effect on performance. Unless these detailed interactions are faithfully modeled in the analysis, it is impossible to detect any influence of the more fundamental characteristics. Our understanding of such complex interactions is very primitive, and this reinforces the first problem of not knowing what characteristics to measure and to include in our modeling activities.

We will refer to differences in the package of performance-enhancing characteristics of teachers as skill differences.[134] A more skilled teacher is one who can produce higher student performance than another, less-skilled teacher. As with the skilled craftsman or the skilled artist, it is often easier to judge the quality of performance by examining the final result than it is to identify the characteristics of the individual or the techniques that blend together in producing the output.

In this section we estimate total school differences, of which we believe skill differences among teachers are the most important component. This is a direct attempt to circumvent the troublesome measurement problems described above. We do not ask, "What specific inputs to schooling make a difference to student achievement?" Rather, we ask, "Does the specific classroom or school in which the student is placed differentiate his or her academic performance from that of children in other classrooms or schools?" Assuming appropriate controls are in place for nonschool factors that influence achievement, an affirmative answer provides important information about the scope of skill differences among teachers along with systematic school-level inputs.

The data from the special 1987 survey in Ceará permit examination of the extent to which achievement-enhancing inputs to schooling exert their influence jointly within the classroom environment common to all students in it. As discussed in chapters 3 and 4, the 1987 data collection was qualitatively different from that in earlier years. An attempt was made to track all students in a subset of larger schools in Ceará who had been sampled in the second grade during 1985. These students were tracked even if they had dropped out of school or had not been promoted to the fourth grade. Data on specific characteristics of the students' schools and teachers were not collected in 1987. (A special collection of health-related information was included, and the analysis of these data is presented in the following section.) These school data permit an analysis of total school and teacher effects, one similar to those discussed in the review of developed country research in chapter 2.

Students who were subsequently interviewed in 1987 (30 percent of the relevant 1985 second graders) were given the second-grade achievement tests. The means and standard deviations, respectively, for the tests administered in 1987 were 85 and 15 for Portuguese and 73 and 20 for mathematics.[135]

The empirical specification of achievement models employed here follows directly from the previous modeling efforts except for the specification of school and teacher factors. We estimate basic value-added models with adjustments for specific characteristics. A student's achievement in 1987 is related to age, to sex, and to achievement two years earlier (this time on exactly the same test). Because students in different grades are included in the analysis, we add a measure of how far the student has progressed through school grades in the intervening two years.[136] To control for the possibility that between 1985 and 1987 the EDURURAL program in Ceará had been particularly successful in raising achievement, a program status variable signifying an EDURURAL county is also included.

The regression of achievement in 1987 on these background variables accounts for most important learning determinants except those that are related to classroom(s) or school(s) in which the student passed the intervening two years. School and teacher quality differences are then measured implicitly by including in the regression equation a series of dummy variables identifying the specific schools.[137] These dummy variables will capture the joint influence of all school-specific quality variables. The estimated coefficient for any given school dummy variable is interpreted simply as the mean gain in achievement after adjusting for individual differences in ability and other characteristics of the students. Those schools with the largest positive achievement effects are clearly the "best" and those with the largest negative coefficients are the "worst."

This formulation is superior to previous specifications because it does not require direct measurement of the individual characteristics of schools and teachers that are important.[138] Moreover, it gives direct information about the variation among teachers and schools in aggregate effectiveness.[139] This approach has obvious advantages given the imprecision of our knowledge of what affects performance and the difficulties of measurement in any event.

A rigorous statistical test unequivocally indicates that some schools are in fact better than others. Differences in performance of schools are assessed by calculating the F-statistic for the variance reduction from inclusion of the set of school-specific dummy variables. For both Portuguese and mathematics, the F-statistics were well above the critical value at the 5 percent level, indicating highly significant differences in achievement results of children according to the school they attend.[140]

The school a child attends clearly makes an enormous difference to achievement outcomes. Table 5-21 displays the estimated achievement advantages and deficits accruing to children in the highest and lowest performing schools in the 1987 Ceará sample. Children attended fifty-

Table 5-21. Achievement Differences between Schools in Ceará, 1987

	Portuguese	*Mathematics*
Number of "good" schools[a]	4	18
Average achievement advantage of students in "good" schools[b]	16.2	18.4
Average achievement advantage of students in four "best" schools[c]	16.2	28.9
Number of "bad" schools[a]	7	6
Average achievement advantage of students in "bad" schools[b]	− 13.5	− 16.9
Average achievement advantage of students in four "worst" schools[c]	− 18.9	− 18.4

Note: "good" and "bad" are defined as statistically significant positive or negative school coefficients; "best" and "worst" are defined as four schools with largest estimated positive or negative achievement gains.

a. Schools' dummy coefficient positive (negative) at 5 percent level.

b. Mean of positive (negative) and significant school dummy coefficients.

c. Mean of highest (lowest) four school dummy coefficients.

Source: Full regression results underlying model specified in appendix tables C5-15 and C5-16, columns showing bottom 40 percent of model 2.

nine different schools, and performance comparisons were made with a reference school found in the midrange of school performance.[141] Children attending "good" schools (defined as being significantly above the reference school at the 5 percent level of statistical significance) enjoy a 16 to 18 point achievement advantage depending upon the subject tested.[142] Students attending 'bad" schools (significantly below the reference school at the 5 percent level) are penalized 13 to 17 points. We further define the "best" and "worst" schools in an absolute sense: the bottom four or top four schools in terms of estimated value-added, or school performance. Students in the four best schools have a 16 to 29 point advantage over the reference school; those in the four worst schools have about an 18 point deficit. In the context of standard deviations of, respectively, 14 and 20 points for Portuguese and mathematics achievement scores in 1987, these are enormous differences.

By any standard, schools and teachers have a powerful effect on student performance. Holding constant the ability and characteristics of the student, moving from the worst school to the best would change the student's expected achievement by over two standard deviations. At the center of the achievement distribution, this amounts to a change of *over 60 percentile ranks* in the two-year span considered here. Alternatively, if we thought of moving a student from an average school in our sample to one of the best, we could expect an improvement in achievement of over 30 percentile ranks during this period of schooling.

The estimated differences among schools include all systematic resource differences, both in facilities and other physical attributes (such
as instructional materials) and in teachers. The previous analysis in this
chapter pinpointed the potential effects of differences in specific hardware and software provided by the schools, and these factors almost
certainly contribute to the estimated differences. Nevertheless, on the
basis of analysis of our Brazilian data and of other analyses, *we believe
that the largest differences are found in the skill levels of the teachers.*
The estimated school differences based on facilities, materials, and the
like appear small relative to the differences uncovered in this analysis.
The evidence, however, is subject to varying interpretations.

Two major problems limit our ability to disaggregate the total differences with any precision. First, there is real uncertainty about the specific
resource or teacher characteristics that may be important, implying that
any quantitative analysis will be constrained by the particular specifications employed. Second, even if we wished to pursue such an analysis,
we are confined to the available data, which are extremely scarce for
1987. The 1987 survey did not attempt to collect new teacher or school
data, implying that investigation of specific factors must rely on 1985
data. For certain attributes, however, analysis of 1985 data is reasonable,
given the special nature of the schools and survey.

Because the 1987 survey went to precisely the same school buildings
as the 1985 survey, the physical characteristics of the schools in 1985
provide some evidence about the difference between the best and worst
schools. Table 5-22 presents organizational, hardware, and software differences between these schools. The hardware differences, which are
the most expensive to alter, are almost certainly better indicators of
school inputs between 1985 and 1987 than the organizational and software inputs. The organizational and software features of the schools are
more likely to have changed between 1985 and 1987 than are the hardware inputs. Overall, the best schools have better hardware than the
worst schools. The differences, however, are relatively small, and the
differences are not seen for all of the components that go into the hardware index. The pattern of these differences between the best and worst
schools lends support to our previous analysis that indicates quality of
the facilities is systematically related to student performance. The magnitude of these differences (coupled with the prior estimates of the importance of hardware in affecting achievement) also shows, however,
that hardware is unlikely to be the primary component of the estimated
total aggregate differences.[143] The software differences, which are small
and somewhat inconsistent, do not appear to contribute to the achievement variation between best and worst schools, although this might simply reflect errors arising from the use of 1985 data. Finally, the previous
finding that ungraded classrooms are superior is reinforced in these data,

Table 5-22. Input Provision in the "Best" and "Worst" Schools in Ceará, 1985

	Portuguese		Mathematics	
Resource	Four best schools	Four worst schools	Four best schools	Four worst schools
School organization and support				
Graded classroom (percent)	0.57	1.0[a]	0.68	0.78
Homework (percent)	0.21	0.62[a]	0.48	0.48
OME index	0.45	0.42	0.46	0.42
Hardware				
Furniture index	0.78	0.69	0.79	0.68
Facilities index	0.89	0.68[a]	0.79	0.60
Water (percent)	0.47	0.54	0.48	0.78[a]
Electricity (percent)	0.79	1.0	0.84	0.56[a]
Software				
Writing materials index	0.88	0.95	0.84	0.90
Textbook used, school and home (percent)	1.0	0.96[a]	1.0	0.96
Teacher inputs				
Pupil/teacher ratio	16.1	25.8[a]	17.7	26.4[a]
Salary (percent minimum wage)	18.8	14.4	23.4	11.2[a]
Portuguese test score	82.1	79.1	84.3	72.9[a]
Mathematics test score	84.0	88.3	89.2	75.3[a]
Education (years)	5.26	8.25[a]	5.6	5.7
Experience (years)	5.95	9.67[a]	4.9	5.5
Logos	0.0	0.0	0.36	0.0

Note: "Best" and "worst" are defined on the basis of mean achievement of students in 1987. The resource differences between best and worst schools, however, refer to 1985; data on input provision were not collected in 1987.

a. Indicates difference between best and worst is significant at the 5 percent level.

Source: EDURURAL research sample.

even though the potential magnitude of the effect again cannot explain the overall differences.

Reliance on the 1985 data to analyze teacher differences is especially error prone. For schools operated in teachers' houses in 1985 and 1987, it is reasonable to assume that the teacher is the same in both years and that her characteristics have changed very little, if at all. But this is only 5 percent of schools in the 1987 sample. For students in regular schools, however, this is much less likely to be true, although the probability of having different teachers in the two intervening years is not so large as might be expected. In small rural schools, especially those not using graded classrooms, a student quite often will have the same teacher for two or more years.

We did not expect the comparison of specific teacher factors to provide a very definitive view of performance differences, and indeed it does
not. Again, however, this simply reinforces our previous finding that it
is difficult to disentangle the underlying characteristics of teachers that
account for skill differences. The differences in effectiveness among
schools—which, we believe, are largely attributable to skill differences
among teachers—remain, and the fundamental issue is how to use this
information of quality differences to improve the overall levels of
achievement. We return to this subject in chapter 8, where the policy
implications are pursued.

Health Status of Children

As is typical of areas of extreme poverty elsewhere in the world, malnutrition and poor health are prevalent in northeast Brazil. School-age
children as well as their younger siblings are among the most severely
affected. The school is thus a logical point of intervention in a strategy
to enhance nutritional and health status. Like many other countries, Brazil
operates a feeding program in schools, targeted on the poorest areas and
especially on schools in the rural northeast.[144] In our surveys, children
receiving lunch through this school feeding program during all months
of the year increased from 24 to 36 percent between 1983 and 1985;
during the same period, an additional 69 percent of students received a
school lunch during some months in 1983 and 63 percent in 1985.[145]
By 1985, then, essentially every child in our sample was receiving food
at school for some part of the year.

The official rationale for the school feeding program in Brazil has two
elements. First and most immediately, availability of food at school was
expected to increase the attractiveness of school attendance for children
and their parents alike. In areas where physical capacity of the schools
is not the binding constraint, access to education would increase. Second
and ultimately perhaps more important, provision of food at school was
expected to improve academic performance by enhancing the overall
health status of the children. Several mechanisms drive this hypothesis.
Malnourished children are known to be less resistant to disease than
their adequately nourished peers. Because of more absences from school,
they are likely to have more limited exposure to the learning opportunities of the school. Even in school, malnourished children are likely to
have lower attention spans, energy levels, and motivation; all of these
have negative effects on mental development and ability to learn. Finally,
children with a history of severe malnutrition from birth (or before) may
have suffered lasting, even irremediable, brain lesions, which impair ability to learn.[146]

To investigate whether the school feeding program did indeed affect achievement, data on the nutritional and health status of sampled children were collected within the survey conducted in Ceará in 1987.[147] Each child's height, weight, age, and triceps skinfold thickness were expressed as percentages of commonly used norms.[148] Chronic or persistent malnutrition, sometimes called stunting, is reflected in substandard height-for-age. Current or acute malnutrition, often termed wasting, is reflected in substandard weight-for-height; this indicator has the advantage of being independent of age, which may suffer from greater measurement error than the anthropometric characteristics. An alternative indicator of current nutritional status, more sensitive to sudden change in food intake, is triceps skinfold thickness-for-age. Weight-for-age is an overall indicator of nutritional status reflecting stunting, wasting, or both.

Visual acuity, as measured using the Sneller Chart, was also obtained for each student. We hypothesized that students with uncorrected visual deficiency would be at a learning disadvantage.[149]

Table 5-23 contains the mean values for health status measures[150] for two samples of students: 352 students in the 1987 sample of children in Ceará and the subset whose achievement level in 1985 placed them in the bottom 40 percent of the distribution (133 children in Portuguese and 139 children in mathematics). It is evident that, despite full coverage of the school feeding program by 1985, malnutrition and poor health status remain pressing concerns in 1987. Stunting appears somewhat less a problem than wasting. In general, the nutritional deficiency is greatest on the measures most susceptible to change over relatively short time periods. Skinfold thickness-for-age among our children was only 85 percent of the norm; and fully 12 percent of the sample registered 50 percent or less of the norm for this measure. Only 56 percent of these school children have fully normal vision, and over 7 percent of them, with visual acuity 60 percent or less of normal, are severely disadvantaged. While differences are often not very large, EDURURAL students are significantly less well nourished than their OTHER peers in Ceará in 1987. In general, students who performed poorly on the Portuguese and mathematics tests in 1985 exhibit slightly greater nutritional deficits than their peers; curiously, this difference is less noticeable for mathematics.

To examine the general effect of nutritional and health status on achievement, we employed regression models designed to take advantage of the unique character of the 1985–87 matched Ceará sample. But focusing attention on achievement gains could complicate the isolation of effects on achievement that start early in life and persist thereafter. The preferred value-added specification was thus checked for consistency against cross-section specifications estimated on exactly the same samples.

Specifically, the Portuguese and mathematics test scores of children in 1987 are regressed upon age, sex, achievement two years earlier, grade

Table 5-23. Descriptive Statistics for Health Status of Students in Ceará, 1987

Health indicator	Entire sample			Bottom 40 percent in 1985 on	
	Total (N = 352)	EDURURAL (N = 196)	OTHER (N = 156)	Portuguese (N = 133)	Mathematics (N = 139)
Weight-for-age: overall indicator					
Mean value (percentage of norm)	85.7	84.1[a]	87.7	83.8	84.5
Proportion below 70 percent of normal	11.9	14.3	9.0	13.5	10.8
Height-for-age: stunting					
Mean value (percentage of norm)	94.8	94.6	94.9	94.1	94.7
Proportion below 88 percent of normal	7.4	8.7	5.8	9.8	7.9
Weight-for-height-for-age: wasting					
Mean value (percentage of norm)	90.0	88.5[a]	92.1	89.0	89.0
Proportion below 75 percent of normal	9.4	12.8[a]	5.1	11.3	10.8
Skinfold thickness-for-age: short-term wasting					
Mean value (percentage of norm)	84.8	77.9[a]	93.4	90.8	84.9
Proportion below 50 percent of normal	12.5	14.3	10.3	11.3	10.8
Visual acuity					
Mean value (percentage of norm)	56.1	56.2	55.9	53.5	56.8
Proportion below 60 percent of normal	7.4	7.1	7.7	9.8	10.1

a. Indicates difference between EDURURAL and OTHER is significant at the 5 percent level.
Source: EDURURAL research sample.

level in 1987, and the EDURURAL program dummy. Once achievement scores are in effect adjusted (controlled) for these variables, any independent influence of the several indicators of health and nutritional status can be readily discerned.[151]

We report results for the two samples described earlier: all students that provided test information and low achievers (bottom 40 percent) in 1985. The low-achieving sample was employed because of possible interactions with health and nutrition factors.[152] The 1987 findings on the control variables (not displayed here) are generally consistent with those based on earlier data; they are also quite insensitive to stratification of the sample according to 1985 achievement scores. This suggests that the underlying behavioral models are quite similar across surveys.[153] For both subjects, performance two years earlier is the most important determinant of achievement. The girls remain at a disadvantage in mathematics, although their earlier superior performance in Portuguese does not reappear. The negative influence of age comes through strongly. Only the effect of program status is radically different in these models. School attendance in an EDURURAL county produces a consistently significant and large achievement advantage over schools in OTHER areas.[154]

Table 5-24 extracts the coefficients on the nutrition and health indicators from the value-added models. The initial impression is that health and nutritional indicators have little if any consistent effect on achievement after the influence of other variables in the equations has been taken into account. Height-for-age, weight-for-age, and weight-for-height are never statistically significant and vary in sign. Surprisingly, visual capacity appears never to make a difference either in these value-added specifications.[155]

Quite possibly these negative findings reflect the fact that the influence of poor health and nutritional status on achievement begins early in life and is cumulative. Poor health and nutrition are more likely an explanation for the generally low achievement results that students already registered by second grade in 1985 than for the changes in those scores between 1985 and 1987, or even for the absolute levels in 1987.

Skinfold thickness-for-age, the measure of nutritional status most quickly responsive to changes in feeding patterns, reveals somewhat different results. Its sign is consistently negative, signaling an achievement disadvantage for malnourished children by comparison with their normal peers. More important, the coefficients are often statistically significant and larger for those most malnourished. This suggests some potential for a school feeding program, since skinfold thickness-for-age would be sensitive to immediate changes in nutrition. The remainder of this section pursues this possibility further.

Because the 1987 Ceará survey did not gather new data on the availability of learning resources (as had the three previous surveys), we have

Table 5-24. Marginal Effects on Fourth-Grade Achievement of Nutrition and Health Status Indicators in Ceará, 1987

	Portuguese Value-added specifications		Mathematics Value-added specifications	
Health indicator	Full sample	Bottom 40 percent[a]	Full sample	Bottom 40 percent[a]
Skinfold-for-age:				
50–60 percent of normal	(−3.224)[b]	−8.199	−6.316	(−7.344)
Below 50 percent of normal	(−3.640)	−15.099	−6.064	−14.89
Height-for-age: percent of normal	(−0.316)	(−0.772)	(0.149)	(0.206)
Weight-for-age:				
below 80 percent of normal	(−0.807)	(−6.510)	(1.961)	(3.372)
Weight-for-height:				
below 75 percent of normal	(0.902)	(0.192)	(−0.471)	(1.796)
Visual capacity: 60 percent of normal	(−0.857)	(0.767)	(−3.942)	(−9.046)

a. Bottom 40 percent of 1985 distribution on respective achievement test in 1985.
b. Coefficients in parentheses are not significantly different from zero at the 5 percent level.
Source: Appendix table C5-14.

Table 5-25. Independent Effects of Acute Malnutrition on Fourth-Grade Achievement Using Value-added Models for Ceará, 1987

	Skinfold thickness-for-age	
Model form/achievement measure	50–60 percent of normal	Below 50 percent of normal
Without school quality dummies for:		
Portuguese		
Full sample	(−2.57)	(−2.65)
Bottom 40 percent	(−6.58)	−12.63
Mathematics		
Full sample	−6.40	−6.40
Bottom 40 percent	−6.84	−14.75
With school quality dummies for:		
Portuguese		
Full sample	(−1.01)	(−1.01)
Bottom 40 percent	(−0.13)	(−7.95)
Mathematics		
Full sample	(−3.92)	(−3.98)
Bottom 40 percent	(−3.43)	(−6.64)

Note: Coefficients in parentheses are not statistically different from zero at the 5 percent level.
Source: Appendix tables C5-15 and C5-16.

no direct indicators of the quantity or quality of available schooling inputs of the sort included in the analyses of achievement discussed earlier in this chapter. However, as discussed in the previous section, a reasonable statistical control of the overall joint effect of these inputs on achievement is obtainable by including in the regressions dummy variables identifying each school.

Table 5-25 allows a more systematic examination of the possible effect of skinfold thickness-for-age on achievement gains between second and fourth grades. These results refer to models where skinfold measures are the only health dimension included and compare estimates with and without school dummy variables. Complete results can be found in appendix tables C5-15 and C5-16.

For the sample of low initial achievers, table 5-25 makes clear that the achievement disadvantage of being severely malnourished (skinfold thickness-for-age less than half the norm) is considerable for both Portuguese and mathematics, at roughly 0.85 and 0.75 standard deviations respectively. For the somewhat less malnourished, the achievement penalty reduces to half for Portuguese (though the coefficient is no longer significant) and to somewhat less than half for mathematics. Clearly, the effect of malnutrition on academic performance varies with the extent, not just the fact, of nutritional deprivation.

For the full sample of students, the evidence is mixed. Malnutrition has a significant negative effect on achievement gains in mathematics (about 0.33 standard deviations), although the effect is not sensitive to the degree of nutritional deprivation. The evidence that malnutrition jeopardizes achievement gains in Portuguese, however, is less compelling (the coefficients have the correct negative signs but are statistically insignificant and small).

These coefficients with no school dummies in table 5-25 compare closely in sign, statistical significance, and even size to those of table 5-24, where the equations included other indicators of health and nutritional status. The achievement effect of skinfold thickness-for-age is apparently independent of any influence exerted by other indicators of nutrition and health status.

At this point, it appears that acute malnutrition most severely penalizes precisely those children whose academic performance in prior years was weakest. Those worst off are most hurt. It is likely that some portion of the learning deficit of these children at second grade resulted from malnutrition in earlier years—perhaps including stunting as well as wasting. Failure to provide adequate food to children has an insidious and cumulative negative effect on their school performance.

When the school dummies are included in the equations to measure school quality, an important change occurs.[156] As shown in table 5-25, none of the nutritional status coefficients is any longer statistically significant.[157] This suggests that the mechanism by which nutritional status affects achievement operates through factors delivered at the school level. One such factor is the feeding program. There are, nonetheless, other explanations of these results, and the findings must be taken as suggestive rather than definitive.

Overall, the estimated effect on achievement of differential health status is not very large. Moreover, the fact that our examination of health effects was limited to the specially selected 1987 Ceará sample tempers any conclusions. Nevertheless, the one revealed effect—the detriment owing to short-run nutritional deficiencies—is the health factor most amenable to policy.

The Value of Knowledge of the Educational Production Process

The previous sections have taken a tour through the extensive empirical investigations of the educational production process, but they touch only tangentially on why such information is valuable. While understanding more about the educational process has its own scientific purposes, the central focus here is on developing the requisite ingredients for the development of more informed educational policies.

Knowledge of the effects of various inputs on students' performance is an essential component of standard policy deliberations that involve adjusting the resources available to schools. This knowledge allows prediction of the outcomes that will result from policy choices. Frequently, however, because precise empirical information is unavailable, policy-makers or educators simply rely upon their guesses about the effects of different resources. Unfortunately, as we have documented, the conventional wisdom about the effectiveness of a wide variety of potential policies is simply wrong.

The results of our various statistical modeling efforts are complicated, but there are a number of straightforward conclusions about the educational process that emerge. These are summarized in the first sections of chapter 8. Before moving to that summary, however, we use the detailed information developed so far to reach a series of parallel conclusions about educational policy and evaluation.

The previous estimates form the empirical basis for these policy and evaluation efforts. Combined in the next chapter with cost information, the results are used to analyze the propriety of many central policy ideas. Combined with programmatic information in chapter 7, they are used to evaluate the EDURURAL program as such.

6

Costs and Benefits of Alternative Policies

THE FUNDAMENTAL QUESTION for the educational policymaker is which specific school inputs are most efficient in raising student achievement scores, given an available level of resources. Often, policy is made solely on the basis of analyses like that reported in chapter 5. That work provides direct estimates of the benefits of altering the different inputs to the educational process. It thus allows the inputs to be ranked on the basis of their effectiveness. Yet, while this is better than having no empirical basis at all for policy determination, it is perilous. Specifically, it does not incorporate anything about the costs of such alterations. This chapter integrates the previous analysis of marginal educational effects with estimates of the costs of making different input adjustments. Efficiency rather than effectiveness becomes the focus of analysis.

Efficiency calculations—the appropriate basis for assessing different policies to educate a given student population—involve the joint consideration of outputs and the costs of inputs required to implement any policy. In the best of all situations, the outputs can be valued in monetary terms so that costs of inputs can be compared directly to the resulting outputs, that is, cost-benefit analysis. In our situation, output is measured in terms of academic achievement, which cannot be readily translated into monetary terms. Therefore, we concentrate on the closely related approach of cost-effectiveness analysis (see Lockheed and Hanushek 1988, 1991).

The first section provides a traditional static cost-effectiveness analysis for major input categories. Directly estimated effects of inputs, provided in the previous chapter, are combined with estimates of the marginal costs of these inputs. This offers a means for comparing alternative policies, since they can be ranked on achievement gains per dollar invested in each specific input. (All costs are translated into 1983 U.S. dollars, so as to eliminate problems caused by the high Brazilian inflation rate of the time.)

The second section considers teacher salary policies in Brazil's northeast. By relating the salaries paid to teachers to certain characteristics of these teachers, we can infer which characteristics are implicitly being rewarded. This information can then be compared with the previous analysis of the educational advantages of having teachers with specific attributes. If the characteristics that are implicitly being rewarded are not the same as those that in fact produce learning gains, changes in teacher pay policies are indicated.

Finally, and most important, policy determination is put into a dynamic context. The static calculation of cost-effectiveness of specific inputs employs the gross costs of different inputs. The net costs will differ from these because improving student academic performance also entails dynamic efficiency gains.

The dynamic gains are conceptually straightforward, even if seldom empirically demonstrated. When students learn more because of more or better inputs to their schooling experience, they are more likely to be promoted at each point in time (as demonstrated in chapter 4). This reduces the total time they spend in the system in order to reach any given grade level. Increasing the flow through the system implies cost savings, since fewer student-years of schooling services have to be provided on average for a student to reach the given level. These savings offset the costs of instituting the original policy change.

The cost reductions attributable to improving flow through schools can be quite substantial. The levels of repetition displayed previously imply that the average student arriving in the fourth grade in rural northeast Brazil will already have spent 7.6 years in school, instead of the 3 required by steady on-time progression.[158] Of course, this vastly understates the overall economic cost of attaining that level of schooling, since it ignores the resources expended on students who enter school but never reach fourth grade. In fact, in rural northeast Brazil an average of 15.2 student-years of schooling services is provided for each student who reaches fourth grade. In other words, repetition and dropout multiply the cost of a graduate fivefold compared with the conceptual norm of steady progression through the primary grades.[159] Since wastage is so high, even small improvements in promotion probabilities (which, of course, imply decreases in rates of repetition or dropout) can result in significant savings.

Thus, the final analytical section calculates the offsets to gross program costs arising from improved student flows. The result is estimates of net cost effectiveness. While this is the appropriate criterion for considering policies, we are aware of only one other attempt to consider such feedback effects (Jamison 1978).

The results of this exercise are extraordinary. A wide range of investments made to improve educational quality can actually be thought of as making money. In other words, the savings from improved flow efficiency are often larger than the original costs of providing improved inputs in the schooling process. The finding of net cost gains through improved efficiency generally holds even when allowance is made for uncertainty in the estimates. The normally postulated trade-off between quality and quantity of schooling appears to be quite the opposite in circumstances of severe educational deprivation. Instead, there is a positive interaction wherein enhanced quality engenders increased quantity.

Static Cost-Effectiveness of Investments in Quality

Cost-effectiveness analysis provides a method for directly comparing alternative policies to raise achievement. The approach focuses on the least cost—that is, most efficient—way to produce an additional unit of output. For each input the dollar amount required to purchase enough of that input to raise achievement scores by one point is calculated. Alternatively, the inverse may be used to rank inputs in terms of their efficiency—that is, the achievement gain per dollar invested in the input. Because it simplifies some calculations later in the chapter, we use this second specification.

Three principal steps are required in such an analysis. First, the regression coefficients from the education production functions estimated in chapter 5 are used as estimates of the marginal achievement gains attributable to the different inputs. Second, the total economic costs per student of the individual inputs are calculated. Third, alternative inputs are ranked in terms of their contribution to improving scores relative to their costs. Those alternatives with the largest achievement gains relative to costs are the most cost-effective. Typically, policymakers should give them highest priority in allocating educational expenditure.

Cost Estimation for Inputs Purchased by EDURURAL[160]

Table 6-1 shows the per student economic costs of the various inputs. These are the result of somewhat tedious calculations, detailed elsewhere,[161] which use extensive information on a wide variety of inputs. Most of the basic information used in costing the inputs was obtained from Ceará State Secretariat of Education.

The "ingredients" method is used to calculate the costs of each input (Levin 1975, 1983). First, all the ingredients for replicating an input or program are specified in detail. For example, a remedial reading program might involve separate elements of specialized teacher time, of new textbooks, and of workbooks and materials. Second, an annual cost is placed

Table 6-1. Annual Cost per Student of Key Educational Inputs

Infrastructure inputs	U.S. dollars
Hardware inputs	
Water	1.81
School furniture	5.45
Bookcase	0.60
Teacher table	0.33
Pupil chair	2.20
Pupil desk	2.32
School facilities	8.80
Two classrooms	2.94
Large room	2.48
Director's room	0.83
Kitchen	0.86
Toilet	1.41
Store cupboard	0.28
Total hardware	16.06
Software inputs	
Writing material	1.76
Chalk	0.03
Notebook	0.51
Pencil	0.34
Eraser	0.15
Crayons	0.73
Textbook usage—grades 2–4 package	1.65
Total software	3.41
Alternative teacher education strategies	
Inservice teacher education	
Curso de qualificação	2.50
Logos	1.84
Education within formal school system	
4 years primary education	2.21
3 years secondary education	5.55

Source: Armitage and others, 1986.

upon each ingredient. The sum of these costs provides an estimated total annual cost for each intervention. Third, these costs are translated into costs per student.

Capital costs are converted into effective annual costs based on estimates of the lifetime of the capital good and an interest rate that reflects the social cost of capital. Economic lives for capital goods in this region are judgmental, and the estimates were reached after discussions with teachers and personnel from the state secretariats of education. The interest rate should reflect the productivity of the resources used in their best alternative social use. There is considerable theoretical controversy surrounding the correct social discount rates, and there is even larger uncertainty about the correct empirical calculation of this. Here we simply use 10 percent, a common choice in applied work.[162]

We estimated the replication cost of each input—that is, how much it would cost to reproduce the input or program in a new setting. This cost corresponds closely to the marginal cost of an input. The costs associated with initial development or evaluation activities of the input were not included. Nor was an attempt made to allocate the overhead cost of the central administration of the education system to the various inputs. However, considerable effort was spent to make sure that all the economic resources—not only the explicit direct expenditure by the state secretariats—were included. This involved, for example, estimating the opportunity costs of resources such as training facilities provided free by the local county executive (preféito) and of the time spent in training by teachers.

The cost analysis required special care, because of the extremely high and volatile rates of inflation prevailing in Brazil throughout the study period. The relevant month and year were specified for the quoted price of each ingredient. These were then converted into dollar prices by dividing the Brazilian prices by the official exchange rate prevailing in the pertinent month and year to obtain a uniform basis for comparison. Movements in the exchange rate during the period were largely to maintain purchasing power parity, with very little real depreciation or appreciation.

Finally, because the achievement gains associated with each input were calculated on a per student basis, it was necessary to calculate the costs per student of each input. This translation relied on standardized input ratios and utilization rates reflecting average current practice. While the true marginal costs of providing student inputs might differ from these average costs, depending on specific local circumstances, it is unlikely that long-run costs of major changes will differ substantially from the costs calculated here.[163]

The calculation of the costs of teacher training and teacher education programs also involves amortizing this training over a typical teaching career. The calculations in table 6-1 include the two teacher training programs employed in the northeast (Logos and Curso de Qualificação). They also include additional formal education of teachers, calculated as providing an additional four years of primary schooling or three years of secondary schooling. These latter policies either complete primary schooling (eight years) or secondary schooling (eleven years) for teachers who lack such preparation. Logos was meant to provide nonformal inservice training equivalent to the former and the Curso de Qualificação to the latter.

As shown in table 6-1, costs of different input packages vary dramatically. Complete software packages cost less than a quarter of complete

Table 6-2. *Cost-Effectiveness Ratios, 1981, 1983, and 1985*
(achievement gain per U.S. dollar spent)

Grade/input	1981		1983		1985		Average[a]	
	Portu-guese	Mathe-matics	Portu-guese	Mathe-matics	Portu-guese	Mathe-matics	Portu-guese	Mathe-matics
Second grade								
Infrastructure inputs								
Hardware	0.55	0.74	0.56	0.39	?	(0.03)	0.37	0.39
Material inputs								
Textbook usage	3.34	3.42	3.88	2.56	3.96	1.52	3.73	2.50
Writing materials	?	?	2.67	1.86	(1.24)	2.70	1.30	1.52
Software	1.73	1.41	1.43	(0.74)	3.23	2.26	2.13	1.47
Alternative teacher education strategies								
Curso de Qualificação	n.a.	n.a.	?	?	(0.27)	(0.55)	0.13	0.27
Logos	?	(0.14)	1.95	1.42	(0.79)	(0.69)	0.91	0.75
4 years primary school	1.02	1.06	1.44	2.21	(0.33)	1.07	0.93	1.45
3 years secondary school	0.30	0.32	0.43	0.66	(0.10)	0.32	0.28	0.43
Teacher salary	0.07	0.08	0.14	0.16	0.12	0.10	0.11	0.11

Fourth grade

Infrastructure inputs						
Hardware	0.73	(0.52)	0.55	0.77	0.64	0.65
Material inputs						
Textbook usage	?	?	(1.15)	?	0.58	0.00
Writing materials	?	(1.60)	4.70	7.23	2.35	4.42
Software	?	?	(1.96)	3.23	0.98	1.62
Alternative teacher education strategies						
Curso de Qualificação	(0.41)	(1.81)	?	?	0.20	0.90
Logos	(1.09)	(0.39)	?	(0.36)	0.54	0.37
4 years primary school	?	(0.83)	?	?	0.00	0.42
3 years secondary school	?	(0.25)	?	?	0.00	0.12
Teacher salary	(0.06)	(0.06)	(0.03)	0.11	0.04	0.08

n.a. = Not applicable

Note: Ratios in parentheses reflect statistically insignificant coefficients in the underlying regression models; question marks reflect negative coefficients.

a. Average cost-effectiveness ratios are calculated across years without regard for statistical significance. Negative estimates are entered as zero.

Source: Appendix tables C6-1 and C6-2.

hardware packages (on a per student basis). The teacher training programs, on an annual per student basis, are also relatively inexpensive.

One final note about the cost analysis—and the limits on cost-effectiveness considerations—is important. Much of educational policy revolves around characteristics of teachers and the effect of teachers with certain backgrounds and abilities on student learning. For example, we previously considered teacher experience and teacher knowledge of Portuguese and mathematics. Unfortunately, we do not know much about the cost of supplying these separate inputs. Teachers are paid as bundles of characteristics; separate payments for specific characteristics are not explicitly made. Therefore, we have difficulty estimating the marginal cost of separate attributes, at least by the methods employed here. This precludes consideration of many explicit policy options related to teachers.

We know that teachers are extremely important, and their absence from these discussions should not imply otherwise.

We will return to additional policies directly related to teachers in chapter 8. We will also provide some insights into the effective pay for different characteristics under current institutions in the analysis of salaries found later in this chapter. Ultimately, however, further analysis of the costs of supplying teacher characteristics will be required for any policies related to teacher inputs.

We do consider a few teacher training options. This is possible because we can consider the actual production costs explicitly. Other potential policies are not amenable to such an approach.

Gross Effects per Dollar of Investment in Inputs

Table 6-2 contains the end results of the cost-effectiveness analysis.(For more detailed information on the derivation of these figures see appendix tables C6-1 and C6-2.) The cost-effectiveness ratio is the quotient of the achievement gain per student attributable to the provision of the input divided by the annual cost per student of providing the designated input—that is, achievement gain per dollar spent. Therefore, the higher the ratio, the greater the policy priority associated with that input.[164]

As discussed earlier, the regression coefficients that provide the best estimates of the marginal productivity of the various inputs are not completely stable. They vary between 1981, 1983, and 1985, and between second and fourth grades, in size, significance, and sometimes even in sign. Therefore, due caution is required when formulating recommendations for educational policy and practice upon these findings. Because of the variations in estimates over time, we present averages for each of the tests, and concentrate on these combined estimates when we examine the policy implications.

The most uniform finding is that software expenditure leads to the largest achievement gains. The fourth-grade estimates, the ones on which we place most weight, indicate that a one-dollar expenditure will yield a 1.0–1.6 point achievement gain, depending on whether we are considering Portuguese or mathematics. The second-grade results provide even stronger support for such investments with the estimated gains exceeding 2 points per dollar for Portuguese. The precise interpretation of the underlying source of this effect is unclear, because the fourth-grade estimates point most strongly to the availability of writing materials while the second-grade results point to textbook policies. Without doubt, however, provision of a standard package of writing materials (pencils, erasers, notebooks, and chalk) is a very cost-effective policy.

The provision of quality facilities (hardware) is also an attractive policy, although less effective per dollar than the provision of software items. The fourth-grade estimates suggest that a dollar expenditure on hardware yields two-thirds of an achievement point in both Portuguese and mathematics. The second-grade results are slightly below four-tenths of a point. If hardware is disaggregated into its components, the results suggest that providing water is most cost-effective, and providing furniture is least cost-effective. This disaggregation, however, is subject to considerable uncertainty in terms of both costs and marginal effectiveness.

These calculations indicate that policy should first be directed at providing a full complement of software items, and, once this has been accomplished, attention should switch to improving facilities.

The achievement models, particularly for the fourth grade, do not indicate that either inservice teacher training or general preservice training is very effective. The estimated marginal effects are generally statistically insignificant and frequently of the wrong sign for the fourth grade. If, however, some training strategies are considered, the evidence in table 6-2 provides guidance for which choices to make. First, bringing all teachers up to complete primary schooling (eight years) should be undertaken before any secondary schooling is contemplated. This chiefly reflects the fact that providing primary schooling is a less expensive option. Second, if any training is to be provided at secondary-school level, something like the Logos program—an inservice approach—is preferred. The evidence on the Curso de Qualificação program—an inservice approach to primary training—is meager because the program was not fully operational by the end of our observational period. The second-grade estimates are generally more supportive of teacher training programs, but even those estimates are quite unstable, and we believe that they are less reliable.

The salary paid to teachers is often viewed as a proxy for their quality under the assumption that more highly paid teachers produce greater academic achievement in their students. In our data, teachers with higher salaries are indeed associated with improved student achievement in both Portuguese and mathematics (see table 5-14). But simply buying more highly paid teachers would be one of the least cost-effective strategies for increasing academic performance. The other measured inputs consistently produce more gain for the same money. Further, any policy that uncritically relied on raising the salaries of current teachers as a device for improving student performance would rest on the exceedingly dubious assumption that higher pay by itself motivates teacher behavior conducive to higher achievement.

This analysis considers only the achievement payoff from differences in salaries, and says nothing about the absolute level of salaries, which appears appallingly low in rural northeast Brazil. For a variety of reasons, many have been concerned with the overall level of salaries. Perhaps most relevant for the work here is the possibility that higher salaries will attract better people into teaching in these rural areas. Within our data, it is not possible to investigate directly changes in the overall level of salaries, but it is possible to investigate how salaries are distributed across teachers. From this, we can infer something about how future salaries might be meted out. This is the subject of the next section.

Teacher Salaries: Are Teachers Efficiently Compensated?

We have seen on the one hand that, though teacher salary is related to student achievement, its effects are both quantitatively small and costly per unit of achievement gain compared with other quality-enhancing inputs. On the other hand, we have also seen that certain teacher characteristics do, in fact, produce improved student achievement. An obvious question now arises: to what extent are teachers remunerated for possessing characteristics that are in fact important determinants of student achievement, rather than for characteristics that are not germane to learning outcomes?

To investigate this question, we regressed teacher pay (specified as a percentage of the minimum wage) on a number of characteristics of teachers and their schools in 1981, 1983, and 1985. The results are summarized in table 6-3.[165] These models account for substantial proportions of the variation in teacher salaries. They are remarkably consistent across the three survey years and for the pooled data.[166] Findings must therefore be considered unusually robust, and we concentrate on the estimates that combine the data from all years.

Personal and institutional factors enter the salary picture quite apart from the indicators of teacher quality discussed above. Given their intrinsic interest, they merit brief mention as control variables in the examination of the relationship between teacher remuneration and achievement-enhancing teacher characteristics.

Table 6-3. Determinants of Teacher Salary

(*t*-statistics underneath coefficients)

Input	Raw form[a]	Log form[b]
Teacher's gender	−12.921	−0.164
	−4.20	−2.95
Teacher's experience	0.758	0.146
	6.20	7.07
Teacher's education	4.153	0.509
	14.33	14.29
Logos	4.268	0.094
	1.90	2.33
Qualificação	−3.150	−0.057
	−1.32	−1.32
Benefits	3.729	0.031
	0.88	0.94
Portuguese test score	0.229	0.228
	2.06	1.77
Mathematics test score	0.046	0.139
	0.46	1.45
Contract status	19.300	0.279
	8.08	6.35
Regular status	8.271	0.179
	2.82	3.34
Fourth-grade teacher	4.535	0.123
	2.71	4.08
Graded classroom	7.121	0.227
	3.99	7.01
Pupil/teacher ratio	0.140	0.144
	3.62	5.68
Federal school	136.691	1.176
	7.55	3.59
State school	53.374	0.723
	18.50	13.84
Private school	5.321	0.085
	0.86	0.76
SES of municipio	28.350	0.101
	7.07	6.22
EDURURAL	−4.144	−0.265
	−2.49	−8.78
Piauí	10.792	0.071
	4.42	1.58
Ceará	−29.474	−1.071
	−13.79	−27.71
Federal school, 1981	−111.549	−0.560
	−4.38	−1.21
Federal school, 1983	−75.098	−0.572
	−2.41	−1.01
Constant	−21.668	0.630
	−2.33	1.20
Year 1981	24.610	1.624
	2.87	3.12
Year 1983	27.165	1.664
	3.23	3.21
Adjusted R squared	0.54	0.62
Number of observations	2,216	2,216

a. Dependent variable is teacher's salary expressed as a percentage of regional minimum wage.
b. Dependent variable is log of teacher salary expressed as a percentage of regional minimum wage.
Source: Appendix tables C6-3 and C6-4.

Female teachers are systematically paid less than males. Teachers on regular (permanent) appointments and on fixed-term contracts are better paid than teachers who have no legalized employment relationship and are entirely at the whim of the local authorities, a situation afflicting over 75 percent of the teachers in our sample. Schools under the administrative control of federal or state governments, or privately owned and operated, pay teachers significantly more than do schools operated by county (municipio) authorities. Schools in comparatively rich counties pay teachers better than schools in poor counties. All of this accords with the conventional wisdom on schooling in rural northeast Brazil.

More surprising is the fact that, after taking account of the level of development of the counties, Piaui (the poorest state) has salary levels at least equal to Pernambuco (the richest state). Notorious for low public sector pay, Ceará lags far behind both. When data are pooled for all three years, it is clear that teacher salaries as a proportion of minimum wage, already scandalously low in 1981, were still lower in 1983 and 1985. Teachers of our fourth-grade students enjoyed a salary advantage over those of our second graders, at least in 1983 and 1985. Although we are aware of no specific rules and regulations that should make this so, it is likely that the younger and newer teachers are disproportionately assigned to the lower grades. And finally, other things equal, teachers in the EDURURAL counties were consistently less well paid than their colleagues in the OTHER counties, again for reasons obscure to us.

Teachers operating in graded classrooms (those accommodating either a single grade or two or more firmly grade-delineated groups of students) were paid more than those functioning in undifferentiated multigrade environments. This is interesting, since the earlier analysis of achievement determinants revealed that children in those graded classrooms performed no better, and often worse, than their peers in multigraded environments. Teacher pay consistently increases with the size of the class (the pupil-teacher ratio), which is similarly interesting since we concluded that this variable has little if any impact on achievement.

Here then are two examples of teachers being rewarded with increased salaries for performing in specific environments that do not discernibly benefit student achievement. While we are unaware of explicit salary rules that mandate higher pay in graded classrooms and for larger classes, it is certainly possible that the salary process implicitly takes both of these circumstances into account on the assumption that they entail harder work for the teacher.

More serious inconsistencies emerge with respect to the teacher quality variables. There is no evidence that teacher pay increases with teacher knowledge of mathematics, and only a weak suggestion that a greater knowledge of Portuguese commands higher pay. Yet we saw earlier (table 5-15) that the teacher's subject matter knowledge has an important influence on student achievement. Conversely, teacher pay does consistently increase with experience and education, especially education. But again, as we saw earlier (table 5-14) neither characteristic is strongly related to achievement. Indeed, teacher education was a significant determinant of student achievement only in the second-grade cross-section specifications, and teacher experience was essentially never significantly related to achievement in our models. Once again, we see that teachers are evidently rewarded with higher salaries for possession of characteristics that have little or no impact on achievement, and are not rewarded for an obviously important determinant of student achievement, subject matter knowledge.

Of the two teacher training variables, the sign on the Qualificação program is uniformly negative but never significantly different from zero. The salary relationship most likely simply reflects the fact that teachers deemed most in need are enrolled in the Qualificação program and are paid comparatively little. This was supported by the data in table 5-16, which indicated that the effect of the Qualificação program on achievement is never positive and significant. Participation in the Logos program appears to be weakly rewarded in salary terms, although the findings are hardly robust. But Logos participation did not consistently produce a discernible positive achievement differential.

In general, then, the teacher characteristics that produce improved student performance do not command higher pay for teachers, whereas other characteristics that have no discernible learning benefits for the students do indeed have salary payoffs for the teachers. The policy implications of this are evident. As a general rule, efforts to systematize and institutionalize the teacher selection and salary determination process should eschew relating salaries to years of formal education, teaching experience, and even participation in inservice training programs. Past that, however, the situation gets very complicated, in large part because we do not know what the teacher supply function looks like. We return to these issues later.

A Dynamic View: Net Cost-Effectiveness and Partial Benefit-Cost Analysis[167]

The static cost-effectiveness analysis presented earlier in this chapter misrepresents the true effect of changing any of the educational inputs. Specifically, since improvements in student learning increase the chances that a student is promoted, any general improvements to schools will increase the flow of students through the system. Increased flow implies reduced resources to obtain a graduate of any grade and quality level, since fewer resources will be consumed by repeaters and dropouts.

The previous analyses provide a basis for correcting the cost-effectiveness calculations to take into account the increased flow efficiency of the primary school system resulting from quality improvements. One approach would be to recalculate the gross cost figures to reflect the offsetting efficiency gains. That is, cost savings could be subtracted from original investment costs to arrive at net costs of any policy. In some cases, however, the efficiency gains could be so dramatic as to reduce total educational costs by more than the original investment. The subtraction of gains from gross costs would then provide a negative net cost figure—that is, a benefit. Dividing achievement gains by these net costs would no longer make any sense.

As an alternative, we calculate *partial benefit-cost ratios*.[168] We directly compare our estimated gains (in dollars) from improved student flows to the costs (in dollars) of any potential change in school inputs. It is, nonetheless, important to understand the partial nature of these calculations. Only one aspect of the benefits of an investment is considered, namely, the lessened total schooling costs arising from improving the pace of schooling. The estimates thus produced seriously underestimate the true total value of quality-enhancing investments in two important ways. First, they stop with the effects observed in the fourth grade, ignoring any effects later in the schooling process. Second, since the offset to costs accrues solely from the increased flow efficiency, the value of having higher achieving graduates is likewise ignored. As amply demonstrated elsewhere, these payoffs are both likely to be substantial, and policy conclusions should incorporate both of these obviously important benefits of any change. Indeed, many educational investments are completely justified solely on the basis of long-run enhancements to individual skills and productivity; that is, through standard calculations of internal rates of return to investments.

The partial benefit-cost ratios can, however, provide strong policy guidance. If this ratio is greater than one, efficiency savings outweigh costs, and the intervention would be clearly beneficial without even considering the spillover effects beyond fourth grade or how the achievement gains of students should be valued. A ratio between zero and one implies that net costs are lower than gross costs, but that any investment will still involve a net outlay of funds. Therefore, ascertaining whether or not a specific investment would be warranted requires added information about the parts of the analysis that are omitted: the effects on later grades and the valuation of students' higher academic achievement. Finally, a ratio of zero implies that the gross and net cost effectiveness calculations are the same—that is, that there are no efficiency savings associated with the specific inputs. In this case, nothing is added to the information already obtained from the traditional static cost-effectiveness calculations.

Calculation Methodology

The conceptual steps involved in calculating partial benefit-cost ratios are straightforward, although the actual application requires making a variety of judgments and assumptions. This section describes the overall approach along with the sources of the data needed for the calculations. The next sections display the results of the basic estimation along with a variety of sensitivity analyses based on alternative assumptions about key parameters of the educational process.

There are five major steps in the estimation:

• Calculate the expected achievement gains (in both Portuguese and mathematics) that would come from a one dollar expenditure on each purchased input to be considered.

• Estimate how much the probability of being promoted to the next grade will increase with an added point of Portuguese or mathematics achievement.

• Chain the results of the previous two steps together to obtain an estimate of the increased promotion probability that accrues from a one dollar investment in each input.[169]

• Compare the average number of student-years required for promotion before any investment to the number after the investment, yielding the savings in student school-years that are directly attributable to the initial dollar invested.

• On the basis of the estimate of the marginal cost of a student-year of schooling, convert these time savings into dollars—that is, calculate the dollar benefits of efficiency savings flowing from the initial dollar of cost.

The previously produced analyses provide all of the necessary ingredients for conducting these partial benefit-cost analyses. Indeed, they provide more than one estimate of each of the key parameters that are inputs to such a calculation, and so facilitate a check on the reliability and stability of results.

The expected achievement gains per dollar of expenditure on given inputs are simply the output of the static cost-effectiveness analysis and are available for models of second- and fourth-grade achievement in both Portuguese and mathematics in the different years. For our purposes, we consider the different sets of parameter estimates of the achievement models for each subject, by year and grade, to be alternative estimates of the same fundamental underlying relationships of the educational process. Similarly, the promotion probabilities associated with different achievement levels are available for 1981, 1983, and 1985 from the on-time probit promotion models presented in chapter 4.[170]

The expected number of student-years that accumulate before a person reaches any given grade level are directly related to the promotion and dropout probabilities at each grade. The lower the promotion probability, the slower students will progress through the system and thus the larger will be the number of years that go into producing a primary school graduate. For evaluation purposes, we base our calculation on estimated transition probabilities derived from the experience in various regions of Brazil in 1982.[171]

Finally, any savings in student-years must be transformed into dollar values. Using information obtained directly from our survey data on teacher salaries and the data in table 6-1, we obtained US$29.57 as our estimate of the cost per student-year of primary schools in the rural northeast.[172] The analogous figure from the best available Brazilian study is US$31.50;[173] for rural schools in the interior of the center-west states, the figure calculated by the same authors is US$33. Given the consistency of these three separate estimates, we have used a round figure of US$30 as the cost per student-year when evaluating the value of time saved.[174]

The "Money Machine"

Table 6-4 displays both the years saved and the dollars saved per dollar invested in six key quality-enhancing inputs to schooling. These calculations rely on promotion and dropout probabilities for "low-income, rural northeast Brazil," the combination of geography and income status that most nearly approximates the areas in which our surveys were conducted.[175] The six inputs were selected for analysis because they are often—and were in the EDURURAL project—the chosen instruments of public policy aiming to improve the quality of primary schooling.[176] The figures in table 6-4 are the mean and maximum of the estimates from the alternative models of promotion in chapter 4 and achievement in chapter 5. For more extensive results, disaggregated by grade and year, see appendix tables C6-5 and C6-6. In the calculations underlying the mean benefit-cost ratios, the point estimates of all positive coefficients were employed without regard for statistical significance; all negative coefficients were treated as zero, or as having no relationship. We return later to the possible bias this introduces in the results.

Since the underlying achievement models are so different in analytical perspective, we report second- and fourth-grade results separately. Because the second-grade models have not eliminated various potential sources of bias that could contaminate results, we rely most heavily on the fourth-grade results and tend to treat the second-grade results as simply reasonably plausible upper bounds. For purposes of this discussion, we assume that the methodologically stronger estimates at fourth grade are proxies for what would have been obtained by a similarly

Table 6-4. Flow Improvements and Partial Benefit-Cost Ratios for Selected Investments in Low-income Rural Northeast Brazil

	Mean estimates		
Saving	Second grade	Fourth grade	Maximum estimates
Student-years saved per dollar invested in:			
Software	0.2316	0.1342	0.4206
Hardware	0.0465	0.0796	0.1011
Teacher salary	0.0141	0.0069	0.0224
Teacher training strategies			
Logos inservice training	0.1002	0.0626	0.2651
4 years more primary schooling	0.1277	0.0113	0.2412
3 years secondary education	0.0389	0.0034	0.0745
Dollars saved per dollar invested in:[a]			
Software	6.95	4.03	12.62
Hardware	1.39	2.39	3.03
Teacher salary	0.42	0.21	0.67
Teacher training strategies			
Logos inservice training	3.00	1.88	7.95
4 years more primary schooling	3.83	0.34	7.24
3 years secondary education	1.17	0.10	2.23

a. Years saved valued at US$30 per student-year.
Source: Appendix tables C6-5 and C6-6.

rigorous approach at second grade. In other words, the apparently exaggerated second-grade findings are attributable to the methodological deficiencies of those estimates rather than to any underlying differences in the educational production process between second and fourth grades.

The results are stunning. The direct material inputs—hardware and software—produce much more than the original investment in dollars saved from increased flow efficiency. In other words, by investing in known quality-enhancing resources, it is possible to produce the same number of fourth graders, although fourth graders of higher quality, with *no* true additional costs, just savings.

Further, the magnitude of these net benefits can be breathtaking. The partial benefit-cost ratios can be greater than 2.0, signifying that twice the original cost of the investment is returned quickly in savings resulting from increased flow efficiency brought about by investing in inputs that engender achievement gains. At least in the severely deprived environment of rural northeast Brazil, investment in school quality is a real money machine.

We also look at selected teacher attributes, but we place much less emphasis on these analyses. Teacher salary, as described below, cannot be interpreted as indicating what would happen with a general change in salary schedules. Instead, it says more about differentiation among individuals within the current stock of teachers. The teacher training and educational programs, while not subject to those criticisms, simply have huge uncertainties attached. As described in chapter 5, there is not strong or reliable evidence about the effectiveness of these, independent of any cost considerations. We return to the issues of uncertainties below.

Differences among the several inputs mirror the previously discussed static cost-effectiveness estimates. Investments in educational software— in our study defined as textbooks and writing materials—produce enormous benefits. These benefits exceed costs by a multiple of four, and in the most reliable fourth-grade equations they are nearly twice as high as those accruing to investments in hardware, the next most attractive input. Hardware itself also returns a handsome premium over costs. The training results suggest that even Logos inservice training could be an attractive strategy to enhance student achievement by upgrading the quality of teachers, although these results are subject to much greater estimation uncertainty. Teacher salary consistently fails to deliver in savings more than its initial cost.

These most general conclusions hold up without regard to the underlying achievement model. However, reliance on the second-grade models would decrease somewhat the relative priority of investments in hardware and increase priority for investments in software and in at least two of the three strategies for teacher training.

Sensitivity Analysis: Can This Really Be True?

While these startling results are reasonably robust across the several achievement and promotion models and data years (not shown), they could be challenged as a basis for policy determination because of uncertainties arising from three primary sources. The reliability of the findings depends centrally upon the accuracy of: (1) the underlying parameter estimates of the effect of the specific inputs on Portuguese and mathematics achievement, (2) the estimated marginal effect of achievement gains on promotion probabilities; and (3) the figure used for cost per student-year of schooling. If the general conclusions were to change radically with only slight alterations in any of these, the utility of the findings for framing policy would be questionable. Therefore, we investigate the sensitivity of these results to the underlying data on schooling.

The last of these possible challenges—erroneous evaluation of the cost per student-year—is the easiest to set aside. Three different calculation methods converged on our figure of US$30, suggesting that it warrants unusual confidence.[177]

The first two possible challenges cannot be dismissed so easily. While we attempted to ensure the best possible underlying parameter estimates, imprecision in point estimates remains. So it is important to test for the sensitivity of the results to possible bias in the achievement and promotion models that underlie the benefit-cost ratios.

Five separate estimates of the achievement effects of each input are available (by grade and sample year). Inspection of the separate underlying models, originally presented in chapter 5, does reveal substantial differences in quantitative results, depending upon which underlying achievement model is used. Averaging results (albeit separately for the second- and fourth-grade models) provides some protection against excess reliance on a possibly inaccurate individual parameter estimate. (This is in addition to the unusual efforts to eliminate the most frequent sources of difficulty through the value-added specification, the correction for sample selection bias, and the test for the effect of errors in measurement of second-grade achievement in the fourth-grade value-added models.) Nevertheless, the partial benefit-cost calculations underlying table 6-4 utilized all positive point coefficient estimates, without regard to their statistical significance. Especially for the relatively small samples of the fourth-grade value-added achievement models, this introduces a positive bias to the results.

Bias in the estimates of the determinants of on-time promotion, derived from our three independent probit estimates, also could potentially be quite serious. Years saved in the schooling process is a direct function of the estimated increase in promotion probabilities due to achievement gains.

To assess the possible joint impact of ignoring the statistical significance of the point estimates in the achievement models and of having only three point estimates of the impact of Portuguese and mathematics achievement on promotion, *lower-bound* partial benefit-cost ratios were developed. The intent was to construct a stringent test of the robustness of the findings of partial benefit-cost ratios greater than one. For these lower-bound ratios, two simultaneous alterations were made in the calculations. First, all statistically insignificant and negative coefficients in the achievement models were set to zero—that is, inputs were treated as having no effect unless we were quite confident that there was a positive relationship with achievement (significant at the 5 percent level). Second, the coefficients on Portuguese and mathematics achievement in the probit models of on-time promotion were set at the lower bound of the 90 percent confidence interval for each.[178]

Naturally, as shown in table 6-5, the partial benefit-cost ratios calculated with these rather extreme lower bounds are all smaller than before.

*Table 6-5. Lower-Bound Estimates of Flow Improvements
and Partial Benefit-Cost Ratios for Selected Investments
in Low-Income Rural Northeast Brazil*

Saving	Mean lower-bound estimates		Maximum lower-bound estimates
	Second grade	Fourth grade	
Student-years saved per dollar invested in:			
Software	0.1468	0.0101	0.3013
Hardware	0.0273	0.0452	0.0616
Teacher salary	0.0082	0.0003	0.0150
Teacher training strategies			
Logos inservice training	0.0460	0.0000	0.1879
4 years more primary schooling	0.0633	0.0000	0.1593
3 years secondary education	0.0192	0.0000	0.0487
Dollars saved per dollar invested in:[a]			
Software	4.40	0.30	9.04
Hardware	0.82	1.36	1.85
Teacher salary	0.25	0.01	0.45
Teacher training strategies			
Logos inservice training	1.38	0.00	5.64
4 years more primary schooling	1.90	0.00	4.78
3 years secondary education	0.58	0.00	1.46

Note: Lower-bound means: (a) all positive but statistically significant coefficients in the achievement models are assumed to be zero; and (b) coefficients on Portuguese and mathematics achievement in the probit models of on-time promotion are set at the lower bound of their 90 percent confidence interval.
a. Years saved valued at US$30 per student-year.
Source: Appendix tables C6-7 and C6-8.

The attenuation of results is particularly noticeable in the value-added fourth-grade models. Only hardware investments remain "money makers." Software returns are reduced to US$0.30 on the dollar invested in the form of a cost offset. The other inputs are no longer seen to produce any offset to the original cost of the investment in the fourth-grade estimates. The small sample sizes of the value-added models, which unavoidably imply relatively great imprecision in the estimates and therefore fewer statistically significant estimates, are probably largely responsible.

The indelible point remains, however, that, even under these extreme estimation procedures, there is strong evidence of significant offsets to costs of investments in properly selected inputs to primary schooling. Indeed, even these very cautious estimates suggest that investments in school quality can still dramatically improve school efficiency through accelerating the flow of students.

This conclusion is reinforced in the cross-sectional second-grade models, where imprecision in the estimates of the achievement effect of schooling inputs arises not from small sample sizes but from failure to control for prior achievement and ability and for sample selection bias. Even at the lower bound of the 90 percent confidence interval for the achievement coefficients in the probit models, investments in software, and to a lesser extent in four years more primary education for teachers and in Logos inservice teacher training, still return substantially more dollars in efficiency savings than their initial cost.[179]

Levels of Wastage and Potential Efficiency Gains

Another type of sensitivity of results relates to different levels of educational development and, specifically, different amounts of wastage. Are these estimates important only in the extreme conditions of the rural northeast? What do the results say about investments outside the low-income areas of the rural northeast?

As one might expect, the partial benefit-cost ratios are highly sensitive to the underlying transition matrices for movements from grade to grade. The benchmark, repeated in table 6-6, is that an investment in software in low-income rural northeast Brazil will return about US$4.00 for each dollar it costs (US$6.95 if the second-grade cross-section models are used rather than the fourth-grade value-added specification). But if the level of educational wastage began at that prevailing in low-income Brazil generally, the payoff would be only about US$2.90. While the decline is substantial, this is still a remarkable figure. If the sample areas of the rural northeast started at the further reduced repetition and dropout levels prevailing in the most advantaged areas of the country (that is, high-income, urban southeast), the offset to investment costs, while still a considerable US$0.52 per dollar of investment, would no longer exceed initial costs.

An alternative interpretation of the data of table 6-6 puts these calculations into an overall development perspective. Suppose it is assumed that the underlying education production function is roughly the same in all primary schools (with variations in the quantity and quality of inputs explaining the known differences in outcomes) and that relative costs of inputs are the same throughout the country. Although it could be argued that these are strong assumptions if comparing the very worst areas with the very best, it is much more plausible when not dealing with the polar extremes. In these circumstances, the partial benefit-cost ratios broken down by geographical area are reasonable indicators of the results to be had from investments in quality-enhancing inputs outside

Table 6-6. Partial Benefit-Cost Ratios for Selected Investments in Various Regions of Brazil

| | Mean estimates | | | | | | | |
| | Brazil | | Rural northeast | | Urban southeast | | | |
Investment	All	Low-income	All	Low-income	All	High-income
Second-grade estimates						
Software	1.40	4.93	5.38	6.95	1.03	0.90
Hardware	0.28	0.99	1.08	1.39	0.20	0.18
Teacher training strategies						
Logos inservice training	0.60	2.13	2.32	3.00	0.44	0.38
4 years more primary schooling	0.76	2.71	2.96	3.83	0.56	0.49
Fourth-grade estimates						
Software	0.81	2.86	3.12	4.02	0.60	0.52
Hardware	0.47	1.69	1.84	2.39	0.35	0.30
Teacher training strategies						
Logos inservice training	0.37	1.33	1.45	1.88	0.27	0.24
4 years more primary schooling	0.07	0.24	0.26	0.34	0.05	0.04

Note: Years saved valued at US$30 per student-year.
Source: Appendix table C6-9.

the rural northeast. Given these assumptions, the data demonstrate that, for most combinations of geography and income in Brazil, educational wastage remains high enough that investments in at least some, and often several, quality-enhancing inputs have partial benefit-cost ratios greater than one—that is, they pay back in monetary savings more than the cost of the investment. This conclusion, again, ignores the value of higher achieving students and cumulative effects higher up in the educational pyramid.

These results effectively rank-order the efficiency gains to be had in educational investments in various parts of the country. We return to this issue later.

Consideration of Personnel and Salary Practices

The previous discussion concentrated on material inputs to the educational process, but the analysis of achievement suggested that differences in student performance related to differences among teachers were likely to dwarf those arising from material inputs. Unfortunately, the methodology developed here for partial benefit-cost considerations cannot readily accommodate consideration of alternative teacher salary policies. The reason is simple: we do not know what the supply function for teachers with specific characteristics looks like.

The teacher salary models describe the implicit payment to existing teachers with various measured characteristics and represent the confluence of current supply and demand for teachers. They do not, however, indicate what would happen if an attempt were made to alter the schedule completely—for example, by offering a sizable bounty to individuals with a deep knowledge of mathematics and Portuguese or, even more extreme, by paying teachers according to student achievement.[180] Such policies would be designed to bring a different group of people into teaching, and we do not observe these people (who are not currently within teaching) in our sample.

The previously presented calculations—based on specific, observable inputs—are possible because of direct observation of data on the costs of providing the resource. Specific characteristics of teachers, such as their mode of classroom instruction or their ability to maintain classroom order, are not directly purchased. Without experience with different salary schedules, payment schemes, incentives, and the like, we cannot be sure of how much a different teacher attribute might cost. Thus, we cannot readily translate any estimates of effectiveness into the cost-effectiveness terms relevant for policy deliberations.

On the other hand, we ought not overdo this argument. First, we know that the current policies are inefficiently discriminating among teachers on the basis of unproductive characteristics. We clearly should not continue these policies.[181] Second, we know that the differences among teachers in teaching skill are extremely large, implying that there is considerable latitude in salary policies that could replicate the "money machine" effect previously described for material inputs—that is, within the fairly narrow bounds of effectiveness of school material policies, investment costs could be more than fully offset. With teachers, where the range of effectiveness is much greater, it seems plausible to expect that there are many different salary policies that could lead to self-financing results. Third, other inefficiencies, say, those arising from possible political factors in teacher hiring, also suggest considerable room for improvement. For example, regulatory procedures, such as requiring all teachers to pass subject matter examinations, may be appropriate if teacher hiring is too heavily based on patronage.[182] Again, such procedures will interact with the supply of teachers, but it is plausible to presume that redirection of incentives will have desirable (efficiency-enhancing) results.

The discussion of teacher practices is simply an extension of the policy recommendations with regard to facilities and other material inputs. The conclusion of the previous section was that the inefficiency in the current system is so large that a variety of quality improving actions are likely to return very large dividends. With teachers, the potential for gain is larger—because teachers have more leverage on student achievement—but the policy uncertainty is also larger—because the determinants of teacher supply are imprecisely understood. Nevertheless, available evidence and knowledge of the current organizational structure suggest that we pursue teacher related alternatives, both to gain immediate improvements and to produce new information on which to base future policies.

A *Summary of Benefit-Cost Considerations*

Under a wide variety of Brazilian conditions, investments in some quality-enhancing inputs to schooling cost substantially less than the savings they ultimately generate through increased flow efficiency. The results clearly are sensitive to the context in which they were developed, and, specifically, sensitive to the underlying educational parameters employed. But even substantial changes to allow for parameter uncertainty fail to wipe out entirely the partial benefit-cost ratios greater than one, indicating investments in some inputs return more than their costs.

Further, the relative priority of investments in different inputs is unaltered even when the absolute payoff amounts are attenuated. Investments in texts and writing materials and in quality hardware items are essentially safe bets for returning more than they cost. The evidence is much more mixed for investments in teacher training, but even they might be money makers in some circumstances. And, there is little evidence to support a simple salary enhancement policy that did not attempt to alter the current salary structure and to expand the present pool of teachers.[183]

The lower the flow efficiency of a system before an investment in quality-enhancing inputs, the greater the potential offset to the initial costs of the investment and the greater the priority that ought to be accorded to such investments. Put crudely from a national perspective, the policy prescription is: attack the worst first, because that is how the most resources are generated. Resources so generated can then be used for further educational (or other) investments. There is a highly important positive interaction—no trade-off at all—between efficiency and equity objectives. In other words, efficiency dictates improving the quality of schools in general but beginning with the worst. Further, this conclusion does not rely on any notions of distributional effect or equity.

Finally, new light is thrown on the policy debate about automatic promotion as a device to enhance flow efficiency in primary schools, and thereby to free resources for educational investments in other children. Automatic promotion can certainly unclog constipated school systems. But it does so at some likely sacrifice of average academic achievement of students, or at least without necessarily enhancing student achievement. The alternate route to the same end, delineated above, generates resources for increased investment while simultaneously increasing achievement.

Conclusions: Investment Strategy for Educational Development

This chapter moves the discussion beyond effectiveness of alternative inputs to their efficiency in improving schooling. Costs, which should always be a central part of policy decisions in real life, are here injected into the world of research on determinants of achievement and access in Brazilian primary schools. The result is a series of suggestions for educational development strategy in impoverished rural areas.

The firmest of our conclusions are negative and concern the blind alleys to educational development that ought to be avoided. For example, indiscriminate lowering of class sizes suggests increased costs with no expectation of achievement gains. Similarly, selecting and compensating teachers on the basis of their education, thought to be important to their classroom performance, is costly and in some instances counterproductive. Likewise, payment for teacher experience per se has little appeal based on the existing evidence.[184]

Good teachers are very important, and indeed the most leverage on student performance appears to come from selection of good teachers. Efficient resource allocation to teachers almost certainly requires basing decisions on measured performance of their students and not on input indicators. Nevertheless, it is difficult to go beyond the previous admonitions with any precision, because of uncertainties about teacher supply (and costs) and the alternative mechanisms that could be employed.

There are also a number of very precise recommendations outside the area of teacher personnel policies. Successful educational development strategies in conditions of extreme rural poverty should focus attention on carefully selected improvements to physical facilities in schools and on instructional software. These are among the most important tools that teachers use to foster student learning. Moreover, these are concrete targets for public policy and are easily obtained and delivered to schools. Especially when initiated in the worst performing schools and areas, such strategies will not only improve academic achievement and promotion, but by doing so will generate savings that exceed the cost of the initial investment. This in turn releases resources for educational development efforts elsewhere, or for reallocation to needs in other sectors.

Our focus has been efficiency, and our analysis does not address issues of overall spending very directly. Therefore, whether or not any resources released through efficiency improvements are returned to the educational sector is generally not a subject of this work. On the other hand, to the extent that the use of funds affects the incentives of school administrators and decisionmakers, this issue may be relevant. For example, if school administrators believe that all funds generated by efficiency improvements will leave the sector, they may not look for efficiency improvements, and may even resist efficiency improvements. The overall incentives are, in other words, important to the implementation of efficient policies.

7

The Effect of EDURURAL

EDURURAL SOUGHT improved educational performance through attainment of three objectives presumed to be causally connected. Initially, student achievement was to be improved. This was valued by itself because fundamental literacy and numeracy would positively affect labor productivity and other aspects of welfare. Moreover, it was assumed that heightened academic achievement would increase promotion rates and reduce dropouts (reduce wastage). This in turn would enable the existing schools to serve more children (expand access).[185] The mechanism for achieving these goals was to be a quantum jump in the availability of learning resources in the schools, which would improve the education process by increasing achievement. More and better learning resources would also directly and positively influence wastage and access, independent of their indirect role in increasing achievement.

Such was the theory. But did it work in practice? The material presented in chapters 4 to 6 certainly suggests that key links in the hypothesized causal chain do in fact operate. In general, better learning resources were shown to increase achievement. Higher achievement was shown to reduce wastage. Further, the cost of achievement enhancing inputs (most notably the software items) was substantially less than the savings in educational resources attributable to increased promotion rates.

But these results are general ones, unconnected to the particular intervention program called EDURURAL. They address the questions of effectiveness of overarching policies, not the specific question of whether a given policy intervention, *as actually implemented* through the EDURURAL program, had the expected effect.

The answer to the overall program evaluation question must be approached in two stages. If the resources do not get to the classrooms, they can have no effect on achievement, repetition and dropout, or access. Even if resources are infused, there can be no assurance that achievement will improve because the wrong resources might be delivered.

159

First, we confront the implementation issue. Did the EDURURAL project actually succeed in delivering quality-enhancing inputs to schools any more effectively than other educational improvement efforts that were simultaneously implemented elsewhere? Then, we deal with the issue of effectiveness. If learning resources were indeed delivered, did they make the difference—to achievement, to wastage, and to access—that our analysis suggests should have materialized?

In a classic experimental design, the educational systems and socio-economic characteristics of EDURURAL and OTHER counties would have been identical at the start of the program. Assignment of counties to program status (EDURURAL or OTHER) would have been random. The educational intervention would have been applied consistently in all its aspects across all the EDURURAL counties, and in none of its aspects in any of the OTHER counties. Nothing else that might influence attainment of the program objectives (such as economic circumstances) would change while the program was implemented; if some things did change, randomizations would prevent biases.

If all these conditions had obtained, answers to both evaluation questions could be had through simple comparison between EDURURAL and OTHER counties of means on empirical measurements of the stated program objectives: learning achievement, promotion, access. Quite often, evaluations of social programs proceed on this basis, on the (usually unfounded) assumption that the previously identified conditions are fulfilled.

The real world, of course, is not so simple. The descriptive information in chapter 3 and the analyses in chapters 4 and 5 make clear that none of the ideal conditions was fulfilled. Thus, reliable assessment of program effect requires indirect evaluations based upon complicated statistical analyses, some of which were presented in previous chapters.

The conclusions we shall ultimately draw about program effectiveness are sobering. Despite the optimistic analytical findings of chapters 4 to 6, strong support for the policy theories driving the EDURURAL program are hard to find in our data about the specific effect of the program.

Three unavoidable limitations of the findings must, nonetheless, always be kept in mind. First, EDURURAL was implemented in 218 counties in nine states, but our empirical information comes from only thirty EDURURAL and thirty OTHER counties in three states. We have no way of ascertaining whether the story in other states and counties is the same. There may have been unique characteristics associated with the other states and/or counties that produced quite different results. In fact, our earlier results give some indication of such differences, because coefficients on state dummy variables in the analytical equations were often significant. A second possibility is that factors that we did not even try to measure, or measured only poorly, are nevertheless central to the attainment of achievement, promotion and retention, and access goals. An example might be school-level pedagogical assistance supplied through OME (county educational organization) supervisors. The teacher's style of classroom interaction with the pupils might be another. If such factors are also important aspects of the EDURURAL program intervention not generally available in OTHER counties, our conclusions would have to be tempered. Finally, many of our yardsticks, even of the most important school quality inputs, are necessarily crude proxies for the real-world phenomena. Such is the case, for example, with the measures of textbook use, which we know from elsewhere is a powerful component of educational performance. In short, caution is definitely in order when interpreting our findings.

EDURURAL and the Availability of Learning Resources

From an operational perspective, it is enormously important to determine whether massive financial inputs to a central ministry actually obtained tangible improvements in the availability of learning resources in a multitude of distant and desperately disadvantaged rural classrooms. Only if this implementation question can be answered affirmatively will governments and donor agencies feel confident—even when armed with analytical findings about potential policies—that investments in learning resources can in fact be effective instruments for enhancing educational performance among the rural poor.

The EDURURAL surveys in 1981, 1983, and 1985 collected extensive data at the school level on the availability of learning resources thought to be potentially important determinants of achievement. Special attention was accorded the inputs that were supplied by the EDURURAL program. Those inputs correspond to commonly identified school quality indicators and are not necessarily those derived from our previously presented modeling efforts. While we make such a linkage later, it is useful to begin the discussion of project evaluation with a broad overview of the EDURURAL implementation effort.

Table 7-1 lists twenty-four separate indicators of the quality of school inputs that are available in strictly comparable form for all three years. Experience in the 1981 survey suggested that more precision would be desirable in measuring certain inputs. Thus table 7-2 lists sixteen additional indicators that are available in strictly comparable form only for 1983 and 1985.

A parsimonious approach to analyzing the wealth of resource data is obviously needed to judge whether the availability of learning resources increased across time and location. The basic summary approach begins by establishing a criterion for deciding whether the change in an indicator from one period to another represented an improvement, a de-

Table 7-1. Strictly Comparable School Quality Indicators for 1981, 1983, and 1985

Teachers with 1–4 years of formal schooling
Teachers with 5–8 years of formal schooling
Teachers with more than complete primary education
Teachers with salary less than 25 percent minimum regional wage
Teachers with salary 25–75 percent minimum regional wage
Teachers with salary greater than 75 percent minimum regional wage
Teachers operating graded classrooms
Teachers assigning homework every day
Mean years of teacher experience
Index of instructional materials used by the teacher
Index of teacher's classroom activities
Teachers who have participated in secondary school equivalency inservice
    program (Logos)
Schools with drinking water on premises
Schools with electricity on premises
Schools with a bookcase
Schools with a table for the teacher
Schools in which all students have a chair or bench on which to sit
Schools in which all students have a desk or table on which to write
Schools with two or more classrooms
Schools with a multipurpose room
Schools with an office
Schools with kitchen facilities
Schools with sanitary facilities
Schools with a locked storage cabinet

Source: EDURURAL research sample.

terioration, or no significant change. The criterion employed is based on
the proposition that an increase in average availability of learning resources among a group of children is generally an improvement (assuming no change in the variability of provision). Similarly, an increase in
the variability of provision—in the standard deviation—is generally a
deterioration of the schools (assuming no change in the overall average).

More specifically, any indicator whose mean value grew from one
period to another *and* whose proportional change was greater than any
proportional positive change in its standard deviation is deemed to have
improved. This criterion allows for some deterioration in the variability
of provision, as long as it is proportionately less than the improvement
in average availability. By contrast, any indicator whose mean value declined from one period to another *and* for which the absolute value of
its proportional decline was greater than any proportional negative
change in the standard deviation is deemed to have deteriorated. This
allows for some improvement in the variability of provision as long as
it is less than the proportionate decline in average availability. Quality

Table 7-2. Strictly Comparable School Quality Indicators Available Only for 1983 and 1985

Schools with chalk
Schools providing notebooks for students
Schools providing pencils for students
Schools providing erasers for students
Schools providing colored pencils for students
Schools providing students use of textbook some days at the school
Schools providing students use of textbook every day at school and allowing book to go home
Schools receiving a reading book for all students
Schools receiving the teacher's guide to the reading book
Schools receiving a first-grade textbook for all students
Schools receiving the teacher's guide to the first-grade textbook
School receiving a curriculum guide for second grade
Schools receiving a curriculum guide for fourth grade
Teachers currently enrolled in upper primary school equivalency inservice program (Qualificação)
Teachers currently enrolled in secondary school equivalency inservice program (Logos)
Teachers currently enrolled in postsecondary teacher training program

Source: EDURURAL research sample.

indicators falling outside these two groups are deemed to have manifested no significant change.

This criterion is arbitrary, but the intent is to provide a conservative, stringent criterion of change, up or down. For improvement to occur, not only must the mean increase, but it must increase proportionately more than any increase in the standard deviation that may also have occurred, thereby more than counterbalancing any increase in the variability of provision that accompanied the increase in the mean. Deterioration involves not only a decrease in the mean but also a proportionately larger decrease in the mean than any decrease (improvement) in the standard deviation that may have occurred.

In short, the measure of improvement (or deterioration) balances changes in mean characteristics with changes in the distribution across students. No effort is made at this point to weight the individual factors differently (such as by educational effectiveness or cost); this is done in the next section. Further, since the various specific measures are not always or all independent of each other, different ways of capturing the same conceptual inputs could lead to somewhat different quantitative results. Nevertheless, it is clear that the estimates here do in fact capture the most significant changes in the sampled educational environments.[186]

Table 7-3 summarizes the situation for the twenty-four indicators of learning resource availability for which we have comparable data in each

Table 7-3. *Distribution of Twenty-Four School Quality Indicators by Direction of Change from 1981 to 1985, by Project Status within States, and Overall—Full Sample*
(percentages)

Direction of change	Piaui			Ceará			Pernambuco			Overall	
	EDURURAL	OTHER	Total	EDURURAL	OTHER	Total	EDURURAL	OTHER	Total	Total	Overall
1983 > 1981	63	67	75	46	58	42	67	63	58	58	67
1983 = 1981	8	13	0	8	8	17	13	4	4	4	4
1983 < 1981	29	21	25	46	33	42	21	33	38	38	29
	100	100	100	100	100	100	100	100	100	100	100
1985 > 1983	67	71	67	75	63	83	63	54	63	63	75
1985 = 1983	13	13	17	8	0	4	17	4	13	13	13
1985 < 1983	21	17	17	17	38	13	21	42	25	25	13
	100	100	100	100	100	100	100	100	100	100	100
1985 > 1981	71	75	71	63	58	67	75	67	79	79	79
1985 = 1981	8	8	17	21	8	21	8	8	4	4	4
1985 < 1981	21	17	13	17	33	13	17	25	17	17	17
	100	100	100	100	100	100	100	100	100	100	100

Note: Percentages may not sum to 100 percent because of rounding. Criteria for improvement [>], no change [=], and deterioration [<] as explained in text. Includes twenty-four indicators available for 1981, 1983, and 1985; full sample of schools.

Source: Data summarizing the availability of learning resources to children in the sample of schools in which data were collected in the three survey years are available from the authors on request; two sets of five tables.

of the three survey years. Without distinguishing among states or between EDURURAL and OTHER areas within states, the table shows that there
was indeed a significant overall improvement in the availability of learning resources between 1981 and 1985. While there are differences among
the states, 79 percent of the measured school quality indicators increased
between 1981 and 1985, while only 17 percent declined. Put differently,
fewer than one-quarter of the indicators remained constant or declined.

Pernambuco, the wealthiest of the three states, perhaps fared a little
better on the whole than the other two. A larger proportion of its indicators increased, but, because a slightly larger proportion also declined,
the difference between Pernambuco and the other two states was less
than the advantage shown in improving indicators.

Table 7-3 also contains hints of a generally upward trend over time in
the availability of learning resources. In Ceará and Pernambuco, the proportion of improving indicators was noticeably higher, and the proportion of deteriorating indicators somewhat lower, for the second two-year
period (1983–85) than for the first (1981–83). In Piaui, the proportion
of deteriorating indicators also declined between the first and second
periods.

The question of differential change within each state in learning resource availability between EDURURAL and OTHER areas is intriguing. For
the full four-year period (1981–85), the proportion of improving indicators is larger, and of deteriorating indicators smaller, for EDURURAL than
for OTHER areas in Ceará and Pernambuco, although the reverse is true
for Piaui. Only in Pernambuco does this pattern of better delivery of
learning resources to schools in EDURURAL areas hold up for each of the
two-year periods. In Ceará, better EDURURAL performance in this respect
is evident only for the 1983–85 period. Indeed in Ceará, the reversal is
striking from 1981–83 to 1983–85 in the relative performance in
EDURURAL and OTHER areas. The cautious conclusion is that the EDURURAL
project succeeded in the final two years in improving delivery of the
desired inputs, at least in two of the three states.

In Piaui, however, the conclusion on implementation is not so sanguine, at least on the basis of data available for all three years. While it
is clear that learning resource availability increased throughout the state,
the data suggest that, if anything, this occurred to a greater extent in
OTHER areas. There is no evidence from these data that implementation
of the EDURURAL project in Piaui improved learning resource delivery.

Table 7-4, however, shows the changes between 1983 and 1985 for
the sixteen additional indicators for which data are available only in those
years. The data reconfirm and strengthen the positive findings of better
delivery in EDURURAL than in OTHER areas in Pernambuco and Ceará. More
important, for Piaui, there is also unmistakable evidence that EDURURAL
was successfully implemented, even though for EDURURAL areas the pro-

Table 7-4. Distribution of Sixteen School Quality Indicators by Direction of Change from 1983 to 1985, by Project Status within States, and Overall—Full Sample
(percentages)

Direction of change	Piaui			Ceara			Pernambuco			Overall
	EDURURAL	OTHER	Total	EDURURAL	OTHER	Total	EDURURAL	OTHER	Total	
1985 > 1983	75	38	50	88	69	69	81	75	81	75
1985 = 1983	0	19	19	6	6	6	6	6	6	6
1985 < 1983	25	44	31	6	25	25	13	19	13	19
	100	100	100	100	100	100	100	100	100	100

Note: Percentages may not sum to 100 percent because of rounding. Criteria for improvement [>], no change [=], and deterioration [<] as explained in text. Includes sixteen indicators available only for 1983 and 1985; the full sample of schools was used.

Source: Data summarizing the availability of learning resources to children in the sample of schools in which data were collected in the three survey years are available from the authors on request; two sets of five tables.

portions of increasing indicators is still smaller, and of deteriorating indicators is still larger, than in the other two states.

It is thus reasonable to conclude that, in the full sample of schools included in the three cross-section surveys in 1981, 1983, and 1985, the availability of learning resources increased in all states but did so to a greater extent in Pernambuco and Ceará than in Piaui, in EDURURAL than in OTHER areas, and in the 1983–85 period than in the first two years of implementation.

Now the question arises whether this generally positive finding on the implementation question is affected by the fact that the schools appearing in the three sample surveys are not all the same from year to year. Does the disappearance of schools from the sample, and their replacement by hitherto unsurveyed schools, appreciably alter the conclusion on implementation?

Data in tables 7-5 and 7-6, which summarize the changes in learning resources in the matched schools (those schools that appeared in the sample at both dates in each comparison), confirm and strengthen the finding that the EDURURAL project was successfully implemented. In terms of differential delivery of learning resources to schools in EDURURAL areas, especially in Pernambuco and Ceará, the effect was more pronounced in the second two years than in the first, as one would expect because of implementation lags in the program.

But there is bad news as well in all this information on the changes in availability of learning resources. The actual values of many of the school quality indicators are eloquent testimony both of the continuing overall poverty of the learning environment in the rural primary schools of northeast Brazil and of the modest nature of the changes that even sizable and concentrated effort such as the EDURURAL project can achieve. For example, the proportion of children in our samples whose teachers had four or fewer years of formal education declined from 30 percent to 21 percent over the four-year period. The proportion whose teachers assigned homework increased from 59 percent to 69 percent. The proportion whose schools had a bookcase rose from 23 percent to 36 percent. Even the increase in the proportion of pupils using a textbook from 47 percent in 1983 to 82 percent in 1985 means that nearly one-fifth of the pupils still did not have access to that most fundamental of learning resources. There is still a very great deal to be done.

That brings us to the question of effectiveness. Did the demonstrated greater availability of learning resources have any discernible effect on the three dimensions of educational performance that EDURURAL was designed to improve: achievement, promotion, and access? The evidence discussed in chapters 4 to 6 could reasonably lead to an optimistic expectation in this respect.

Table 7-5. Distribution of Twenty-Four School Quality Indicators by Direction of Change from 1981 to 1985, by Project Status within States, and Overall—Matched School Sample
(percent)

Direction of change	Piauí			Ceará			Pernambuco			Overall
	EDURURAL	OTHER	Total	EDURURAL	OTHER	Total	EDURURAL	OTHER	Total	Total
1983 > 1981	75	58	79	54	54	50	58	63	58	63
1983 = 1981	8	13	17	8	17	17	17	8	17	13
1983 < 1981	17	29	4	38	29	33	25	29	25	25
	100	100	100	100	100	100	100	100	100	100
1985 > 1983	67	67	71	63	54	67	63	58	67	71
1985 = 1983	17	8	17	13	0	0	8	4	4	13
1985 < 1983	17	25	13	25	46	33	29	38	29	17
	100	100	100	100	100	100	100	100	100	100

Note: Percentages may not sum to 100 percent because of rounding. Criteria for improvement [>], no change [=], and deterioration [<] as explained in text. Includes twenty-four indicators available for 1981, 1983, and 1985; only those schools in sample in both years indicated are used for each comparison.

Source: Data summarizing the availability of learning resources to children in the sample of schools in which data were collected in the three survey years are available from the authors on request; two sets of five tables.

Table 7-6. *Distribution of Sixteen School Quality Indicators by Direction of Change from 1983 to 1985, by Project Status within States, and Overall—Matched School Sample*
(percent)

Direction of change	Piaui			Ceará			Pernambuco			Overall
	EDURURAL	OTHER	Total	EDURURAL	OTHER	Total	EDURURAL	OTHER	Total	
1985 > 1983	75	38	50	69	69	69	81	75	81	81
1985 = 1983	0	19	19	6	6	6	6	6	6	6
1985 < 1983	25	44	31	25	25	25	13	19	13	13
	100	100	100	100	100	100	100	100	100	100

Note: Percentages may not sum to 100 percent because of rounding error. Criteria for improvement [>], no change [=], and deterioration [<] as explained in text. Includes sixteen indicators available only for 1983 and 1985; only those schools in sample in both years indicated are used for each comparison.

Source: Data summarizing the availability of learning resources to children in the sample of schools in which data were collected are available from the authors on request; two sets of five tables.

EDURURAL's Effect on Student Achievement

Two basic analytical strategies are employed to investigate the effects of the EDURURAL program. First, following the tenets of a quasi-experimental design, mean differences in achievement across intervention and control counties are traced over the evaluation period. Second, however, there is an explicit consideration of how the various input differences previously identified interact with student achievement. This is achieved through aggregating observed differences according to their previously estimated relationship to student achievement.

A Univariate Approach—Unadjusted Achievement Differentials

As a first rough approximation, table 7-7 contains a measure of the achievement differential of EDURURAL over OTHER areas for our three sample years by state and grade. Somber conclusions emerge.

Achievement in EDURURAL areas in all states, in both grades and subjects, was clearly higher than that in OTHER areas in 1981 when the program began. The relative achievement measures indicate that the performance in EDURURAL counties started 5 to 15 percent above OTHER counties. At least with respect to measured academic achievement, EDURURAL counties were not the most disadvantaged areas of the three states. In fact, they started out ahead in student performance.

Overall, for the three states combined, the data strongly suggest that EDURURAL's initial achievement advantage was somewhat diluted over the period. This finding is inconsistent with the hypothesis that EDURURAL has made a significant contribution to achievement, and disturbing in light of the general success of the project in delivering learning resources.

Examining performance for the states individually, it is evident that in Ceará and especially Pernambuco (the two states with the best performance in implementing resource changes), academic performance deteriorated sharply in EDURURAL areas as compared with OTHER counties during the project implementation period. Only in Piaui (where implementation performance was least impressive) did the EDURURAL advantage get wider rather than narrower, and even there Portuguese achievement in the fourth grade barely held its own. The inference is that EDURURAL succeeded in boosting achievement, if at all, only in Piaui. Furthermore, it did so in spite of mediocre performance, relative to the other states, in providing the learning resources hypothesized to be associated with achievement gains.

In 1981, the achievement advantage enjoyed by EDURURAL students over their peers in OTHER counties was generally much higher in mathematics than in Portuguese. In Piaui, where the data suggest more successful implementation of the program, the relative advantage of math-

Table 7-7. Mean EDURURAL Achievement as Proportion of Mean Achievement in OTHER Areas, by State, 1981, 1983, and 1985

State/achievement	1981	1983	1985
All states			
Second grade			
Portuguese	1.09	1.08	1.04
Mathematics	1.10	1.10	1.09
Fourth grade			
Portuguese	1.05	0.99	1.02
Mathematics	1.15	1.07	1.07
Pernambuco			
Second grade			
Portuguese	1.09	1.03	0.94
Mathematics	1.03	0.94	0.90
Fourth grade			
Portuguese	1.05	0.98	1.02
Mathematics	1.16	0.93	0.97
Ceará			
Second grade			
Portuguese	1.13	1.21	1.05
Mathematics	1.21	1.29	1.05
Fourth grade			
Portuguese	1.12	1.04	1.01
Mathematics	1.31	1.20	1.04
Piaui			
Second grade			
Portuguese	1.06	0.96	1.15
Mathematics	1.17	1.08	1.48
Fourth grade			
Portuguese	1.06	0.98	1.06
Mathematics	1.11	1.17	1.21

Source: EDURURAL research sample.

ematics over Portuguese expanded significantly, possibly suggesting that the effect of the program was greater on the mathematics curriculum and teaching. In the two other states, where the trend is downward, the initial advantage enjoyed by mathematics (except in Pernambuco for second grade) almost entirely disappeared by 1985. The suggestion is that mathematics is the more sensitive of the two curricular areas to the EDURURAL intervention.

The reliability of these first evaluation results, of course, is subject to multiple challenges. One is that they take no account of the movement of students in and out of our three cross-sectional surveys. In other words, the means of achievement in each year refer to different groups of students. Taking advantage of the longitudinal nature of some of our data,

Table 7-8. Mean EDURURAL *Achievement as Proportion of Mean Achievement in* OTHER *Areas, by State—Matched Samples for 1981–83 and 1983–85*

	Follow-up year	
State/achievement	1983 Fourth graders	1985 Fourth graders
All states		
Second grade initial test		
Portuguese	1.04	0.93
Mathematics	1.11	1.00
Fourth grade follow-up		
Portuguese	0.94	0.93
Mathematics	1.11	0.96
Pernambuco		
Second grade initial test		
Portuguese	1.11	0.82
Mathematics	0.98	0.85
Fourth grade follow-up		
Portuguese	0.87	0.96
Mathematics	0.92	0.87
Ceará		
Second grade initial test		
Portuguese	1.17	1.00
Mathematics	1.27	1.05
Fourth grade follow-up		
Portuguese	1.00	0.91
Mathematics	1.22	0.84
Piaui		
Second grade initial test		
Portuguese	1.02	0.98
Mathematics	1.22	1.15
Fourth grade follow-up		
Portuguese	1.01	0.96
Mathematics	1.23	1.15

Source: EDURURAL research sample.

tables 7-8 and 7-9 contain analogous indicators of comparative performance for the children who appeared in more than one survey.

Even with this less-contaminated criterion, the conclusions change little. Table 7-8 shows that matched children in EDURURAL counties uniformly performed better at the outset in 1981 than did their peers in OTHER counties, except for mathematics in Pernambuco. The initial EDURURAL advantage was generally dissipated over the four-year period,

Table 7-9. Mean EDURURAL *Achievement as Proportion of Mean Achievement in* OTHER *areas—Matched Sample for Ceará, 1985–87*

	1987 student placement			
Achievement	4th grade	3rd grade	2nd grade	Not in school
1985 initial test				
Portuguese	0.98	1.17	1.11	0.95
Mathematics	1.02	1.07	1.17	0.92
1987 follow-up test				
Portuguese	1.03	1.08	1.20	0.89
Mathematics	1.16	1.18	1.28	1.00

Source: EDURURAL research sample.

and indeed more often than not turned into an EDURURAL disadvantage. The earlier suggestion that the program performed comparatively well in Piaui must be modified to one of having performed least badly in Piaui. The finding of especially disappointing performance in Ceará and Pernambuco is strengthened. Except in Piaui, and Pernambuco fourth graders in 1985, the trend over time is unforgivingly downward. This is revealed in the table by examinination of the vertical differences in each state between second and fourth grade (as well as the horizontal differences in each state across the two years). EDURURAL looks more and more like a loser.

The only glimmer of optimism is provided by the reduced 1985–87 matched sample from Ceará. In table 7-9, not only were the same children tested in the two years, but exactly the same test (designed for second graders) was administered in both years. For the student who progresses normally—in two years—from second to fourth grade, EDURURAL seems to have some positive differential effect, especially in mathematics. Curiously, the same pattern holds for children who have been stuck in second grade. For children whose progression was only one year delayed—those in third grade in 1987—the pattern holds for mathematics, but is reversed for Portuguese. In light of the pessimistic conclusions emerging from the 1981–83 and 1983–85 matched samples, an unqualified conclusion from these 1985–87 results that the program had positive impact in Ceará is unwarranted.[187] At the very best, there may be a hint here of the EDURURAL program beginning to show a positive achievement effect some six years after its launching.

A *Multivariate Approach to Achievement Differentials*

The intervention-specific effectiveness story, so far, is based on a crude examination of achievement differentials between children in EDURURAL and OTHER areas over time. If the EDURURAL program had satisfied true experimental conditions, this examination of mean differences in achievement between EDURURAL and OTHER children would be compelling. But EDURURAL was obviously not a scientific experiment. It was rather, an ambitious social program with all the contamination of experimental purity that this implies.

In this context, the appropriate way to deal with the effectiveness question makes use of both (1) the results presented earlier from the regression of achievement on school quality inputs and home, community, and individual characteristics; and (2) the measured differences between EDURURAL and OTHER areas in mean provision of learning resources.[188] Specifically, the coefficients on the school quality variables in the regressions are consistent estimates of the effect of each variable on achievement, after accounting for the influence of other variables in the equation.[189] Multiplying those estimated effects by the mean differences between EDURURAL and OTHER areas in measured availability of the learning resources in question provides a direct approximation of the true effect on achievement of the EDURURAL program for each variable. The total of those individual estimates is a measure of the overall impact on achievement of the greater supply of learning resources in EDURURAL than in OTHER areas.

Of course, this evaluation methodology relies upon what may be a rather heroic assumption—that changes in learning resources were attributable to the EDURURAL program. Our research, however, does not trace the delivery to specific schools of learning resources actually procured by EDURURAL managers. Our surveys instead took an inventory of the learning resources available in the sampled schools in both EDURURAL and OTHER counties. To the extent that the inventoried items in EDURURAL schools were not supplied through the program but rather by some other mechanism, or that the inventoried items in OTHER schools were supplied by the EDURURAL program rather than by other means, the proposed methodology would not give an accurate picture of the true effect of EDURURAL.

As to the first possibility, we believe EDURURAL was the overwhelmingly dominant source of incremental learning resources in project areas. So, for practical purposes we discount the likelihood of upward bias in our overall assessment from this source. Regarding the second possibility, we know that similar inputs were supplied to OTHER areas, in part thanks to the politically powerful demonstration effect of implementing EDURURAL in some areas and not others. And, of course, since money is fungible, it is possible that World Bank–financed inputs in EDURURAL areas, rather than increasing resources, simply substituted for resources that otherwise would have been provided, thereby freeing money for use in OTHER areas. Thus, we cannot rule out the possibility of such leakage leading to a downward bias in our estimates of program impact. On balance, however, given the overall penury of learning resources available for distribution in the region, we judge that leakages directly attributable to EDURURAL were not large overall, and were in any event relatively unimportant in the OTHER municipalities, which tended to be geographically distant from EDURURAL counties.

Also, we have included dummy variables in the regression equations to capture the effect of program-status-within-state. The coefficients on these dummies can best be interpreted as the differential effect (of EDURURAL schools compared to OTHER schools) on achievement test scores of school characteristics that were either entirely left out of the equations or were imperfectly measured. These effects of unmeasured influences are over and above any associated with individually measured learning resources.

Combining the estimates of achievement effect of measured and non-measured learning determinants produces an overall summary indicator of EDURURAL's impact as an education improvement program. The results of such calculations, for each of the three states, are summarized in table 7-10. The detailed data are contained in appendix tables C7-1 to C7-3.

Table 7-10. Program Efficacy: Net Effect on Achievement Scores of Program Resource Differences (EDURURAL versus OTHER Schools)

Achievement	Piaui	Ceará	Pernambuco
Second grade—Portuguese			
1981	−0.3	6.4	5.7
1983	−1.3	11.7	2.3
1985	3.5	0.0	−2.3
Second grade—mathematics			
1981	2.1	10.4	1.6
1983	5.7	12.2	−1.0
1985	13.1	−0.5	−7.3
Fourth grade—Portuguese			
1983	0.4	−4.6	−3.9
1985	−3.9	−8.4	10.4
Fourth grade—mathematics			
1983	1.4	−4.3	−1.9
1985	5.1	−6.6	6.6

Note: Net program effects are calculated by evaluating the educational effects of school resource differences according to estimated regression parameters.
Source: Appendix tables C7-1 to C7-3.

For the second grade, a now quite familiar pattern emerges of generally deteriorating performance in EDURURAL schools except in Piaui. In both Portuguese and mathematics, EDURURAL schools had an achievement advantage in 1981, except in Portuguese in Piaui. In Ceará and Pernambuco, this had entirely dissipated by 1985 or had clearly been reversed so that the calculated achievement effect of the EDURURAL program was negative. In Piaui, by contrast, EDURURAL shows a positive impact on achievement, and the effect is much bigger for 1983–85 than for 1981–83, and for mathematics than for Portuguese.

For the fourth grade, where the conclusions are derived from the more rigorous value-added regression equations for a much reduced sample of children, the findings are less uniform. With respect to Portuguese achievement, the EDURURAL program had a negative effect on what children in Ceará and Pernambuco learned between 1981 and 1983, and only a negligible positive effect in Piaui. For the succeeding two years, the story in Pernambuco changed, but in the other two states the negative effect of the program enlarged. For mathematics, EDURURAL boosted achievement a bit in the 1981–83 period in Piaui, and then contributed to a more substantial improvement in the next two years in both Piaui and Pernambuco. Ceará by contrast shows deterioration from modest negative EDURURAL effect in 1983 to more heavily negative effect by 1985. The evidence that EDURURAL as an education improvement program was more effective in mathematics than in Portuguese is somewhat weaker at fourth grade than second for Ceará, but the overall hypothesis of a stronger effect on mathematics finds added support in Pernambuco in fourth grade toward the end of the period.

These more refined estimates of the impact of EDURURAL resources do not provide very strong support for its efficacy. At least if we consider EDURURAL to be a uniform and homogeneous program, as opposed to a wide variety of county- or school-level experiments, there is no clear and decisive evidence that it resulted in general improvement in school performance.

When the constituent elements of these overall findings on effect are examined, there is additional reason to be cautious about education improvement strategies that seek to raise achievement by providing standard packages of incremental learning resources to a large number of schools. In many instances, the preponderant influence on achievement is not from the measured learning resources presumably supplied by the project but rather from the unmeasured attributes of EDURURAL schools that affect achievement.[190] This finding offers little comfort to the education planner whose common sense and professional credo both indicate that increasing the supply of learning resources will translate reliably into higher achievement. The "black box" of the school is too complicated for such simple approaches.

One important caveat is needed, however. We have backed away from the classical experimental design position to one where we analyze net program differences. This accepts the changes in resources in OTHER areas as a measure of what would have happened in EDURURAL counties in the absence of the program. This might not be the appropriate comparison, since existence of the program might have induced OTHER counties to work harder or, more likely, might have induced the government to redirect some resources to counties not receiving EDURURAL inputs.

EDURURAL's Effect on Pupil Flows

An important EDURURAL objective was to increase promotion and decrease dropout rates in rural schools afflicted with perhaps the highest documented educational wastage of any major region of the world. Did it succeed in doing so?

A first, admittedly crude, measure of educational wastage is the proportion of children bottled up in first grade (including the ano de alfabetização). A *flow-perfect* school, with neither dropouts nor repeaters, would have enrollments distributed fairly evenly over the four lower primary years.[191] The higher the proportion of children in grade one, the lower the flow-through rates and the higher the wastage. Declining proportions in first grade from 1981 to 1985 indicate increasing flow rates, acquired through increased promotion up through the early grades of lower primary school.

Table 7-11 provides a first approximation to the evaluation question of whether EDURURAL had a discernible effect on educational wastage. The top half of the table tells an interesting story for all the schools outside the county seats in our sixty-county study area. The underlying data here come from official county-level educational statistics, not from our surveys. In Piaui, where our proxy for wastage improved unambiguously between 1981 and 1985 in both EDURURAL and OTHER areas, the gain for EDURURAL (a 14-point decline in the proportion enrolled in first grade) was greater than for OTHER areas (a 10-point decline). In Pernambuco, where overall educational wastage declined only modestly from 1981 to 1985, schools in the EDURURAL areas showed a marked improvement while pupil flows in OTHER areas changed very little. In Ceará, the changes in both areas were small, with a slight deterioration in pupil flows in EDURURAL counties being just about offset by a small gain in OTHER areas. This pattern suggests weak positive program impact in Piaui and Pernambuco, and none in Ceará, at least with respect to promotion in the earliest grades.

The bottom half of table 7-11 contains analogous information from the same sixty counties for the schools that were actually sampled. The underlying data here are from our own school-level surveys. Overall, for

Table 7-11. Percentage of Total Enrollments in First Grade in Sixty-County Study Area, 1981, 1983, and 1985
(percent)

	Piauí			Ceará			Pernambuco		
Schools	*1981*	*1983*	*1985*	*1981*	*1983*	*1985*	*1981*	*1983*	*1985*
All schools in 60-county study area									
EDURURAL	69	64	55	77	75	79	66	64	50
OTHER	74	71	64	69	70	67	55	57	52
Total	71	66	58	75	76	76	59	60	51
Sampled schools in 60-county study area									
EDURURAL	60	55	47	61	68	64	45	53	47
OTHER	54	59	55	55	55	55	52	54	46
Total	58	56	49	58	64	61	48	49	46

Source: Table 3-13 for all schools in sixty-county study area; table 3-14 for sampled schools in sixty-county study area.

the three states taken together, the proportion of students enrolled in first grade declined four points in EDURURAL areas from 1981 to 1985, and two points in OTHER areas. But this most meager of hints that educational wastage declined faster in EDURURAL than in OTHER areas masks important differences by state. The evidence of substantially greater progress in reducing wastage in EDURURAL areas is clearest once again for Piaui. The hint above that EDURURAL areas in Ceará suffered an increase in wastage while OTHER areas did not is strengthened, although the differences remain small. In Pernambuco, EDURURAL certainly had no positive impact on pupil flows.

The conclusion so far must be that EDURURAL attained its pupil flow objective only in Piaui, clearly failed in Ceará, and at best produced ambiguous results in Pernambuco.

Also evident is the time sequence of changes in pupil flows. Except in Piaui, the situation generally deteriorated from 1981 to 1983, with any gains being registered only thereafter. Indeed, if 1983 and 1985 are used as endpoints in the comparison, rather than 1981 and 1985, EDURURAL is seen to have a distinctly positive impact on pupil flows in all three states. This may suggest how much time education improvement programs take to make their mark.

The proportion of children bottled up in first grade is a crude and somewhat indirect proxy for educational wastage. Years-behind-grade would be a much more reliable, direct, and informative measure of the joint effect of dropout and repetition on pupil flows.[192] What can our data tell us about EDURURAL's impact on this indicator of wastage?

The overall magnitude of the pupil flow problem is evident from table 7-12, which contains summary information on years-behind-grade by state for our several years and samples. On average, pupils are more than two years behind grade by the time they reach the end of second grade.[193] This figure does not increase much between second and fourth grade, which simply strengthens common knowledge that in northeast Brazil the pupil flow problem is concentrated in the lower grades.

Differences among states are substantial. Ceará is uniformly above and Pernambuco below the overall averages. Surprisingly, the average retardation in progress up through the grades is not radically different for students in the matched samples.[194] By comparison with their fourth-grade peers, the matched children have been relatively successful in that, except for Ceará in 1985–87, all have proceeded on time in two years from second to fourth grade. Consequently, the expectation is that these fourth graders would have experienced substantially less retardation in the schooling process. But the data show that this is clearly not so in 1985; in 1983 the differences are in the expected direction but are meaningful in size only for Ceará and Pernambuco.

The benchmark data in table 7-12 provide few grounds for asserting

Table 7-12. Years-behind-grade, by State and Grade, 1981, 1983, and 1985

For full cross-section samples	1981	1983	1985
All states			
Second grade	2.14	2.46	2.45
Fourth grade	2.35	2.63	2.63
Piaui			
Second grade	2.28	2.42	2.39
Fourth grade	2.35	2.55	2.64
Ceará			
Second grade	2.56	2.96	3.14
Fourth grade	2.71	3.20	2.93
Pernambuco			
Second grade	1.74	1.99	1.70
Fourth grade	2.22	2.37	2.36
For matched longitudinal samples, fourth grade only	*1981–83*	*1983–85*	*1985–87*
All states	2.25	2.66	—
Piaui	2.43	2.72	—
Ceará	2.24	2.98	3.39
Pernambuco	2.01	2.37	—

— = Not available.
Source: EDURURAL research sample.

that the pupil flow problem abated over the years of our study. If anything, the situation seems generally to have deteriorated slightly.

For evaluation purposes, the real interest centers on differences between EDURURAL and OTHER schools. Table 7-13 shows years-behind-grade in EDURURAL schools expressed as a proportion of years-behind-grade in OTHER schools. Numbers greater than one thus indicate that EDURURAL schools are characterized by more severe pupil flow problems than OTHER schools; similarly, a decline over time in the proportion indicates an improvement in EDURURAL schools relative to OTHER schools.

There are evidently very few occasions when wastage problems in EDURURAL schools are less severe than in OTHER schools; Piaui is remarkable in this respect. This stands in contrast to the academic performance data, which indicated that students in EDURURAL schools started with higher achievement.

More encouragingly, except for Piaui in fourth grade, the trend in grade retardation is downward over time. During the implementation of the program, EDURURAL schools recuperated somewhat from their years-behind-grade disadvantage with respect to OTHER schools. On balance,

*Table 7-13. Years-behind-grade—EDURURAL as a Proportion of OTHER,
1981, 1983, and 1985*

For full cross-section samples	1981	1983	1985
All states			
Second grade	1.116	1.223	1.025
Fourth grade	1.030	1.093	1.076
Piaui			
Second grade	0.929	0.988	0.819
Fourth grade	0.812	1.172	0.978
Ceará			
Second grade	1.371	1.496	1.291
Fourth grade	1.302	1.182	1.245
Pernambuco			
Second grade	1.012	1.160	0.832
Fourth grade	1.070	1.008	1.004
For matched longitudinal samples, fourth grade only	*1981–83*	*1983–85*	*1985–87*
All states	1.286	1.148	—
Piaui	1.663	1.081	—
Ceará	1.116	1.576	1.397
Pernambuco	1.010	0.959	—

— = Not available
Source: Appendix table C7-4.

years-behind-grade data show that wastage declined more rapidly in EDURURAL than in OTHER schools, even if it remained higher in EDURURAL areas throughout the period. This suggests, although it certainly does not prove, that the EDURURAL project may in fact have achieved some reduced educational wastage.

An even better measure of educational wastage would be actual promotion rates from second to fourth grade. Chapter 4 reported on an investigation into the determinants of on-time progression up through the grades. Table 7-14 contains the coefficients from a probit estimation, for 1981 and 1983, of a second-grade student being found in fourth grade two years later, given that the student's school survived the two-year period and offered a fourth grade two years later. The alternate specifications of the underlying probit models use dummy variables on program status (EDURURAL vs. OTHER) both aggregated and separated by state. The EDURURAL coefficients provide a measure of the general effect of the project across all three states. The three state-specific EDURURAL variables provide measures of the project effect within the given state. In both cases, the effect on promotion of the characteristics of the student, his

Table 7-14. Marginal Effects of Program Status on Promotion, 1981, 1983, and 1985 in Ceará

Effect	1981	1983	Ceará 1985
Overall effect	−0.1473	(−0.0503)	−0.5247
Within-state effects			
Piaui	(−0.2181)	(−0.1684)	n.a.
Ceará	(−0.2828)	(−0.0146)	n.a.
Pernambuco	(−0.0310)	(0.0518)	n.a.

n.a. = Not applicable.
Note: Coefficients not significantly different from zero at the 5 percent level are in parentheses.
Source: Appendix tables C4-2 and C4-3. These are raw coefficients from the probit equations, not conditional probabilities derived from these models.

family, and his school, and the overall differences among the three states, has already been taken into account.

Inspection of the coefficients in table 7-14 reveals that, except for the overall effect in Ceará in 1985 and in 1981 when the program started, they are never significantly different from zero. In a rigorous technical sense the conclusion must be that the EDURURAL program had no discernible impact, positive or negative, on timely promotion from second to fourth grade in any of the three states. However, the signs of the coefficients—with only one exception, they are uniformly negative—suggest that promotion in EDURURAL schools might actually have been somewhat slower than in OTHER counties. There is no support here for the hypothesis, consistent with the findings from analysis of years-behind-grade, that the EDURURAL project improved pupil flows.

Finally, we tested various specifications of the school promotion models that included the quality-enhancing instructional variables that the EDURURAL project was designed to deliver, such as textbooks and writing materials and improved physical facilities. To no avail: none of the coefficients was ever significant. School quality variables play no direct role in reducing educational wastage. Whatever effect improved quality of instruction has on pupil flows is indirect, exercised through its role in producing achievement gain, which does indeed accelerate progression up through the grades. If the achievement effects of EDURURAL described in the previous section (that is, relative deterioration) are taken at face value, one might even project net deterioration in student flows. (See appendix table C4-2 and the discussion in chapter 4.)

This more rigorous method for assessing project impact on educational wastage leads to a somber general conclusion. Nowhere, at least during the first four years of its implementation and with respect to promotion

after second grade, did EDURURAL achieve its objective of increasing promotion rates.

EDURURAL's Effect on Access

Access is customarily measured by enrollment rates, which relate students actually in school to the overall number of children in the relevant
age group in a particular geographic area. Unfortunately, we are not able,
for the study areas, to calculate enrollment rates. Accurate age-specific
population data are not available either for the sixty study counties or
for their areas outside the county seats. Nor can we use the numbers of
students actually enrolled in sample schools as an indicator of access,
because the number and identity of schools in the sample changes from
one year to the next. While direct assessment of access in its most usual
meaning is thus not feasible, alternative approaches are available.

The Ministry of Education's records of EDURURAL implementation show
that between 1981 and 1987 the program was directly responsible for
the construction of 1,561 new primary schools, of which 651 were in
the states of Pernambuco, Ceará, and Piaui. These schools had 37,345
total student places, of which 32,760 were in new schools providing only
the first four grades. Moreover, 175 primary schools in the three states
were provided with additional classrooms accommodating 6,125 students. From our own surveys, we know that 38 of the 447 schools sampled in EDURURAL counties in 1985 had been constructed by the project.
Of course, if these new schools were substitutes for previously existing
ones rather than a net addition to the stock of school places, EDURURAL's
effect on access could be questioned. But there is no evidence that this
was the case. So in that limited sense, EDURURAL's impact on access cannot
be questioned.

Table 7-15 provides another perspective on access. At least with respect to the proper school buildings in our sample (that is, schools not
in the home of the teacher), EDURURAL areas in Ceará do not appear to
have built more new schools, or enlarged more existing ones than OTHER

Table 7-15. Physical Status of Sampled School Buildings, 1985
(percent of schools not located in teachers' homes)

School building	Piaui		Ceará		Pernambuco	
	EDURURAL	OTHER	EDURURAL	OTHER	EDURURAL	OTHER
Built in 1981 or after	18.9	4.5	27.9	26.5	23.5	15.9
Enlarged in 1981 or after	14.2	38.6	23.3	27.9	15.1	22.2

Source: EDURURAL research samples.

areas. In Piaui and Pernambuco, the proportions of schools built since 1981 is higher in EDURURAL than in OTHER areas, but the proportion of schools enlarged is smaller. Overall, these data do not support a conclusion of significant differential EDURURAL effect on access. The method for adding new schools to the samples in 1983 and 1985 does not, however, ensure that these are rigorously representative samples.

In rural northeast Brazil, since schools are something less than permanent phenomena, there is another facet to access. From one year to the next, some schools close and others open. Certainly, when a school closes, access of the children in the catchment area is compromised. Similarly, if a school does not offer the grade level for which the child is ready, access is restricted. In an environment where the supply of schooling places is so volatile, a program seeking to increase educational opportunity should be expected to enhance school survival from one year to the next. This effect on access would be over and above any increment achieved through construction of new schools. The question thus arises: did the EDURURAL intervention reduce the propensity of schools to close?

The investigation into the determinants of school survival, reported in chapter 4, provides an answer. Table 7-16 recapitulates the results on program status from the probit models of school survival. Dummy variables were included that measure the effect, within each state, of location in an EDURURAL county as compared with an OTHER county. The effect on school survival of the three dummies is, of course, net of the influence of other county and school characteristics and general differences among states included in the models.

Examination of the coefficients on the dummy variables identifying the EDURURAL schools in each state reveals that, in Piaui and Ceará, the EDURURAL schools are much less likely to survive and offer a fourth grade two years hence than are schools in OTHER areas. In Pernambuco, the sign is at least positive, but the estimated coefficients are not statistically

Table 7-16. *Marginal Effects of Program Status on School Survival by State, 1981–83 and 1983–85*

State	1981–83	1983–85
Piaui	− 0.1963	− 0.5154
Ceará	− 0.6663	− 0.7754
Pernambuco	(0.0991)	(0.0353)

Note: Coefficients not significantly different from zero at the 5 percent level are in parentheses.

Source: Appendix table C4-1. These are raw coefficients from the probit equations, not conditional probabilities derived from these models such as appear in table 4-3.

significant; school survival in Pernambuco is not demonstrably different in EDURURAL and OTHER areas. These findings suggest that EDURURAL did not achieve its objectives of increased access, at least not through its effect on the survival of schools and their propensity to offer fourth grade.

These pessimistic conclusions, however, should not be accepted too readily. The school survival probit models also included among the estimators a number of learning resources to be delivered through EDURURAL. As noted in chapter 4, it stands to reason that the indicators of higher quality physical facilities should all be important determinants of school survival. And indeed, this is the case (see table 4-2), because the estimated coefficients on the "hardware" inputs are generally positive and often significant. To the extent that EDURURAL schools enjoyed higher mean levels of such inputs than OTHER schools, school survival in EDURURAL counties would be higher than in OTHER counties. If any such difference in mean inputs could plausibly be attributed to the action of the project, it would be reasonable to conclude that the program had a positive effect on school survival.

We already know that hardware inputs are uniformly less available in EDURURAL than in OTHER schools in Pernambuco and more available in EDURURAL schools in Piauí.[195] In Ceará the situation is mixed, with variations across grades and years.[196] At best the negative finding above for Piaui is moderated slightly. On balance overall, there is little evidence that EDURURAL contributed directly or indirectly to school survival.

Summary and Conclusions about Evaluation

These evaluation results on availability of learning resources, and on learning achievements, wastage, and access are sobering. Of course, it is never possible to prove a negative. Moreover, we noted at the outset potentially important general limitations to the conclusiveness of our judgments as well as the possibility of leakages between EDURURAL and OTHER areas, which could significantly contaminate results. So it is not legitimate to assert flatly that EDURURAL failed to meet its stated objectives. But, despite the generally positive implications of the findings of chapters 4 to 6 and a rigorous search for program-specific effect on several fronts, there is no compelling evidence even four years after it was launched that EDURURAL in fact had begun systematically to achieve its ultimate objectives.

The purposes of this chapter, however, go beyond simply documenting the overall effects of the EDURURAL program. Certainly such documentation is important, since a history of similar evaluations might lead to general conclusions about how to run major educational interventions. Moreover, program evaluation was the raison d'être for the underlying data collection behind this research project. Nevertheless, the lasting message that we wish to impart from this has more to do with evaluation methodology than with evaluation results.

In simplest terms, we find little appeal to a simple quasi-experimental design methodology. Major projects that run over a period of time will always be confounded by outside factors and purposeful behavior of participants. It is difficult to imagine being able to collect sufficiently large and randomly drawn samples to allow uncomplicated comparisons of mean differences.

Moreover, simply collecting readily available data on basic resources does not allow assessment of effects. It is necessary to know how to weight any differences in resources. And for this, there is no substitute for investigations into the fundamental educational relationships that lie behind student performance.

Finally, as seen from the previous analyses, accounting for changes in samples of students and schools over time can have important effects on the interpretation of any data. As projects evolve, both schools and students disappear, sometimes to be replaced by new observations. Unless sampling is perfect, these changes can lead to misleading evaluations.

PART III

Significance

8

Education Amidst Poverty:
Implications for Policy

ANALYSIS OF THE EDURURAL DATA has revealed much about a set of schools in the impoverished rural areas of northeast Brazil. We believe that the analysis provides lessons that can be generalized to wider settings— impoverished rural areas elsewhere in Brazil and in other developing countries, and probably even further. Such generalizations of course must be made cautiously. We identify here what we believe the analytical findings have to say about these broader concerns of educational policy, while pointing out open questions and concerns.

The lessons are not restricted to the operations of schools and the selection of teachers. The research grew out of the development of a (then) novel loan from the World Bank and its associated implementation in Brazil. In the course of research into schools, we have gained insights into the operation of large-scale educational programs, both those linked to outside resources and those that are designed and administered exclusively by state and local governments. We have also learned about the conduct of educational research activities in developing countries and, especially, in their rural areas. While our research has gone beyond what has been possible in other studies, it still has limitations and shortcomings. A number of these are avoidable or correctable.

This chapter pulls together the findings of the entire study, converting them directly into policy terms whenever possible. It also sets an agenda for future research. Its organization is simple. Research findings are presented and translated into lessons for educational policy. Within this context, the evaluation results for the EDURURAL program are presented and then also translated into lessons for program design and program evaluation. Finally, we sketch some of the lessons for educational research.

When there is a specific part of the text that presents the evidence on a topic, the initial page reference is provided in parentheses.

189

The laboratory for our analysis is rural schooling in the northeast of Brazil. The observations of students and schools span seven years (1981–87) and record a variety of schooling circumstances and direct policy interventions. The entire analysis is concerned with lower primary schooling, with special emphasis on the experiences between second and fourth grades.

The analysis of primary schooling has two important facets: the attendance patterns of students and the subsequent performance of students. Attendance patterns encompass access, promotion, and dropout behavior of students; we refer to these as the quantity of schooling. Student performance refers to scholastic accomplishment in two fundamental domains of all school curricula: language (Portuguese) and mathematics; this is the quality of schooling. The various aspects of the quantity of schooling are intimately related to student performance (and, indeed, to subsequent success in the labor market and society). This study is unique in its ability to delve into the interrelationships between quantity and quality of schooling and into the underlying determinants of each.

The Imperative of Educational Improvement

Before reviewing the major findings, it is useful to reiterate the basic facts of schooling in rural northeast Brazil and, by extension, in similarly deprived rural environments elsewhere. Schools are available for a substantial fraction of the children (p. 31). But most lack many or all of the attributes of primary schools taken for granted in more prosperous settings. There is not even a guarantee of a building, however modest and minimally maintained, built to serve as a school. Existing buildings are often missing water service and sanitary facilities or desks and chairs for the students and teachers. Direct educational inputs such as a blackboard, chalk, and other instructional materials for use by the teacher, or texts and exercise books and library holdings for student use, similarly can be missing or inadequate. As a simple example, fewer than 70 percent of students have a desk and chair. Coupled with this, too many of the teachers are untrained and unprepared for teaching (p. 161). The result is students who make little progress through the schools (pp. 31, 45). Their progression through grades at least partially reflects their achievement. On specially constructed tests designed to measure the minimally acceptable curricular objectives for each grade, second and fourth graders had mastered only half by the end of the school year (p. 82). When they finish their formal schooling, many are still unprepared in terms of basic literacy and numeracy.

The contrast is stark between, on the one hand, the realities of schooling in northeast Brazil and, on the other, either what exists elsewhere in Brazil or what might be thought of as necessary to fulfill minimum basic human needs. The discrepancy is partly due to a long history of inadequate national commitment to the region. Partly, however, the challenge in Brazil and elsewhere is to know what to do.

The arguments for providing universal high-quality primary education are well known. But controversy surrounds the appropriate policies to pursue when resources are constrained. Virtually every study of the labor market results of primary schooling suggests that schools are an exceptionally good investment. For example, Psacharopoulos (1981, 1985, 1989) presents evidence from around the world that social internal rates of return to primary schooling are typically in the range of 20–30 percent, making schooling a much better investment than most alternative places to put funds.

These paybacks are, however, calculated without reference to school quality. Behrman and Wolfe (1984) and Behrman and Birdsall (1983, 1987) argue that measures of quantity of schooling alone misstate the true rewards for schooling by neglecting student differences and quality aspects of schools, reflected ultimately in variations in academic achievement. They suggest that returns to quantity by themselves are likely to be much less, and that the real source of elevated returns is high-quality schooling. Boissiere, Knight, and Sabot (1985), Schiefelbein and Farrell (1982), and Knight and Sabot (1990) carry this argument further by demonstrating the market returns to cognitive knowledge actually acquired in school.

On the basis of such evidence that what matters is what is learned and not mere attendance, some scholars argue for rethinking strategies focused on simple expansion of the educational system. Alternative programs to develop quality schools might be superior. This is the position taken also by Lockheed and Verspoor (1991) after their thorough analysis of potential policies toward primary education. The focus of educational development efforts shifts from simple expansion of access, including reduction of wastage (repetition and dropout), to increasing the academic achievement of children in school. The policy debate thereby becomes much more embroiled because, while the means to increase access are well known and comparatively easy to implement, the same cannot so surely be said for how to increase learning.

Of course, both expanding and improving schooling requires resources, which are always in limited supply. So the central issue quickly becomes which to select from among the many possible combinations of schooling quantity and quality that can be obtained for the available budget. The tradeoff between children's access to the educational system and their scholastic performance within it is seen to be at the heart of the discussion.

We address the presumed tradeoff between school quantity and quality directly, based on unique data about the relationship between student flows and student achievement. We demonstrate empirically that in a wide variety of circumstances, and especially in situations of extreme poverty, *there is no tradeoff.* Quantity does not have to be sacrificed to improve quality. Instead, a determined concentration on quality will generate the resources needed to address quantity concerns as well.[197] Where primary schooling is both quantitatively and qualitatively deficient—as is typically the situation in poor rural areas of developing countries—properly targeted strategies to improve educational performance not only involve economically sound investments but also, ultimately, can be self-financing. In such circumstances, the imperatives for educational improvement should be irresistible. That is the overarching lesson of this research, which, with its various subsidiary elements, is examined in detail below.

Fundamental Research Findings

The next two major sections recapitulate what we have learned. This section concentrates on the major new research findings about the educational process—what determines the availability of schools, the progress of students through schools, and the achievement of students. The following section translates these empirical results into potential governmental policies.

The Fragility of Schools

One of the most striking aspects of the rural schooling environment is the rate of demise of entire schools. Fully one-third of our original sample of schools in 1981 no longer existed by 1983 (p. 37). The experiences in 1983 may have been atypical because of the severe drought that hit the northeast and caused substantial economic dislocation. Nevertheless, another 17 percent of sampled schools disappeared between 1983 and 1985, suggesting that the stability of the schooling system in these rural areas is open to serious question.[198]

The demise of schools is a problem if the closing of a school means lowered access for rural students or a break in the schooling of individual students. It may, however, be perfectly efficient to close individual schools that are uneconomically small or have unacceptable facilities, provided they are replaced with larger consolidated schools with more adequate facilities that also are within reach of the children. Our data do not provide direct evidence about what happens to students if their local school closes. Nevertheless, we conclude that typically the closing of a school will have adverse consequences for the students served by the school, given the highly dispersed nature of the rural population and the generally low commitment to schooling by students and parents.

Primary schooling in these rural areas suffers from an additional problem of restricted grade offerings. While the school offering first- and second-grade instruction may continue, it may not offer instruction in the later grades. Of the sampled schools, 18 percent of those with second graders in either 1981 or 1983 did not have fourth-grade instruction two years later (p. 37). Again, while these data do not by themselves reveal the range of options available, the lack of continuous opportunities through the primary grades indicates access problems that will inhibit the completion of further levels of schooling, by currently enrolled students as well as by future cohorts.

Our research shows that *having stable and available schools is most simply a matter of direct governmental commitment.* Schools continue to survive largely because of past investments. If a school has better facilities and if it serves a larger population of students, it is much more likely to continue operating over time (p. 62). Schools in the teacher's house represent perhaps the lowest commitment to schooling, and their survival rates reflect this.

In some places, the selection of teachers and the placement and support of schools are subject to political patronage. Although there is no direct data on this from our study, one interpretation of the high turnover of schools in the teacher's house is that these are most vulnerable to the changing whims of the local political system. The noticeably lower survival rates for such schools in 1981–83 (compared to 1983–85) may reflect the effects of local elections in the earlier period.

Our analysis also indicates that regions suffering temporary economic setbacks (here, those hit hardest by drought) will have a tendency to let their schools close (p. 62).[199] This suggests that extra care for schooling—a central welfare determinant in the long-run future of an area—is needed when there are significant temporary pressures on an area. By extension, policymakers are well advised to protect resources destined for education when other policies, such as the imposition of harsh measures for macroeconomic adjustment, have short-term welfare costs.

Within the northeast of Brazil, state and local support for schools varies dramatically. In terms of pure survival probabilities, schools in Ceará are much less likely to survive than those in the other states, even after allowing for other differences in the schools (p. 37, 45, 62). The cause of these differences across states is, however, unknown, and by itself this finding does not lead to obvious policies (other than those about providing appropriate levels of resources).

The analysis of school survival, at least in its specifics, applies to the sampled region in northeast Brazil. Because these findings result from the organizational and environmental realities of the area, they are not easily translated to other settings. This research does, however, have two implications for research and policy elsewhere. First, the issue of school availability per se cannot be ignored. Indeed, there are likely to be systematic factors entering into this. Second, for technical analytical reasons these relationships must generally be considered in the course of understanding the determinants of achievement (p. 88).

Quantity-Quality Interactions: The Key Role of Quality

The central focus of most educational planning activities in developing countries is the quantitative aspect of schooling. How many years of school are attained by students? What is the effect on costs of repetition of grades or students' dropping out of school before completion? How can enrollments be expanded? Indeed, a tradeoff between quality and quantity is often postulated. Within any overall budget, if money is spent on improving and upgrading existing schools, so it is argued, the number of schooling slots must necessarily be restricted, and fewer students can go through the system. We find that this is a mistaken perspective when considering primary education in low-income and educationally disadvantaged areas.

The rural schools in northeast Brazil illustrate vividly the costs of running a low-quality system. Students in this setting make slow, at times almost imperceptible, progress through the curriculum. On average in the rural northeast, only 22 percent of students will be promoted out of the first grade in any given year (p. 31). When this is combined with a 5 percent dropout rate in first grade, the result is that some 4.5 student-years of schooling go into producing each student who makes it to the second grade.[200] Because of continuing low promotion rates and high dropout rates in subsequent grades, the cumulative student-years required to produce one entrant into the fourth grade reaches eighteen. These dismal statistics are extreme; the rest of Brazil and many rural areas elsewhere in the developing countries achieve better performance. Nevertheless, throughout most of the developing world, repeaters and dropouts produce an enormous drain on the system, either pushing up overall costs of the schooling system or limiting the numbers that can attend, or both.

Our research employs detailed longitudinal data on individual students to study the determinants of student progression in school. Our analysis demonstrates that academic performance is an extremely important determinant of student progress (p. 69). As a student's achievement in Portuguese and mathematics rises, the probability of being promoted rises. On the face of it, this seems tautological. But in the schools of rural northeast Brazil and in similar areas of other developing countries, promotion decisions are made by individual teachers, whose own command of the subject matter in the curriculum is often tenuous. Further, teachers make those decisions without any necessary reliance on reliable measures of academic performance. So it is perfectly plausible to hypothesize that promotion has little if anything to do with a child's actual command of the curriculum. We are able firmly to reject this hypothesis, which often forms part of the rationale for introducing automatic promotion in developing countries.

The observed relationship between promotion and academic performance implies that *improving the quality of schooling will also improve the flow efficiency of the schools.* In other words, if policies are implemented that increase student achievement, promotions will rise. There will then be savings in the amount of instruction (student-years) needed to produce graduates of any given level. The increased flow through schools will free resources, perhaps even permitting improvements in overall access.

Progress through primary schooling is also directly related to the level of mother's education, reflecting both parental views on the importance of schooling and the ability of the family to aid the student with schoolwork (p. 69). This link suggests a long term effect of expanded and improved education. Investments today in schooling will not only affect the current students but will also have a continued effect on future generations through education from parents.

The analysis of student schooling choices further indicates that higher opportunity costs for students reduce levels of schooling attainment. Specifically, even though we are looking at lower primary schooling, the attractiveness of farming opportunities affects migration and dropout behavior (p. 62).[201] In areas where the employment opportunities are higher for students, the schools are less able to hold the students. Moreover, when students work while attending school, which a majority do, their performance suffers (p. 97). Out-migration is also higher in bad agricultural areas, suggesting another inhibiting factor to schooling.[202] Thus, policies toward school attendance should take into account opportunities outside schools. Keeping students in school will require additional efforts when opportunities are rife for them to enter into productive employment.

There is reason to believe that these general findings are relevant for other parts of the developing world. The influence of economic factors and the opportunity cost of being in school involves fundamental behavioral relationships that are likely to be found in other areas. The influence of quality on progress simply provides empirical support for the underlying mechanism that is presumed almost universally. The strength of this latter relationship has important policy implications, and further research is required to ascertain the stability of the precise quantitative relationships.

The Educational Value of School Resources and School Organization

The focal point of our empirical analysis is understanding the determinants of student performance, as measured by specially developed criterion-referenced tests of Portuguese and mathematics. This analysis, which follows a long tradition of research (pp. 14, 22), employed the best data ever available for these purposes in developing countries (and equal to the best in developed countries). The quality of the data base and overall sampling scheme permits estimation of models that are much more reliable than commonly used.[203] This, in turn, strengthens the generalizations that are possible and provides a sound base for policy considerations.

Our research indicates that providing quality basic facilities and adequate writing materials and textbooks improves student performance (p. 103).[204] Previous analyses of the provision of such instructional inputs in developing countries have tended to support these findings of effectiveness, although with quite varied results across studies (p. 28). The results here, based on more reliable statistical analyses, lend strong support to the efficacy of improving overall achievement by ensuring minimally adequate material resources.

The rural areas in northeast Brazil do not now insure that full facilities or adequate books and supplies are uniformly available (p. 161). In terms of facilities, schools located in the teacher's house (which accommodated some 17 percent of the sampled second graders in 1981) are noticeably more poorly equipped.[205] But, regular schools also suffer shortcomings in both facilities (hardware) and materials (software).

The decision to improve on the provision of these resources should not, however, be made solely on the basis of effectiveness—that is, whether or not the resources increase achievement. Efficiency should be the key criterion—that is, the effectiveness of providing increased inputs relative to the costs of doing so. Therefore, the policy implications of these research findings are postponed until the section on "Self-Financing Educational Investments" (below), when resource costs are brought into the picture.

The EDURURAL program also demonstrates benefits from improved educational administration through the development of strengthened county administrative apparatuses—municipal education organizations (OMES). These organizations are designed to provide administrative and pedagogical support to local schools. Our research suggests that this is a productive device and that better OMES help local schools produce higher achievement (p. 115).[206] Again, however, decisions about use of such organizations depend upon the resources that must be devoted to them. Unfortunately, we cannot analyze this question, because we do not have reliable cost information for the OMES. As is the case for many aspects of schooling, developing accurate estimates of per student costs of providing the input is a complex and tedious task.

The Importance of Highly Skilled Teachers

The evidence is unequivocal:

Having good teachers is extremely important for student achievement.

Variations in performance across teachers were directly estimated with the special subset of data collected in 1987, and, it is important to note, these estimates do not rely on identifying specific characteristics of teachers—such as experience or education—(p. 118). The results suggest that the difference between an average teacher and one of the best can be sufficient to move a student more than 30 percentile ranks in the achievement distribution over just a two-year period.[207]

The observed variations in teacher effectiveness, or teacher skill, indicate a potential for policy interventions. In the past, some have been led to believe that there is little scope for teacher and school policies, largely because of the difficulty of discerning large achievement differences that are directly linked to measures of teachers and schools. The evidence here, which is also supported by analyses in other settings (pp. 14, 22), provides a very different sense of the possibilities and promises. The estimated effects of a good teacher are substantial by any measuring stick, and an overall improvement in the stock of teachers—increasing the proportion of highly skilled teachers—could bring about revolutionary changes in student performance.[208]

The Impossibility of Measuring Inputs of Specific Teachers

The quandary encountered in most past research concerns whether or not the differences among teachers that occasion the performance differentials among their students can be identified and measured. Past work has shown that simple proxies of teacher quality such as the level of teacher education or the amount of teacher experience are not consistent indicators of teachers' quality (pp. 14, 28). Our work leads to similar conclusions.

Neither differences in teacher schooling levels nor differences in teacher experience are systematically related to student performance (p. 106).

The finding with respect to teacher's education is particularly surprising, given the variations in teacher preparation.[209] The average amount of teacher's education for our primary school teachers is eight years, but a full 30 percent of the second-grade teachers have four or fewer years of schooling. Apparently, however, variations in the quality of education for teachers are more important than just the grade level that they reach. This would explain why we do not observe a reliable relationship between the teacher's training and the performance of her students. We interpret the findings with respect to teacher experience similarly. Any gains in ability accruing to more experience are difficult to unravel from variations in underlying skill and ability of the teacher.

Two teacher training programs have been used in Brazil to substitute for other forms of teacher education, but their effectiveness is uncertain. The Logos program provides instruction to teachers who have completed the full eight years of primary schooling; it is designed to be equivalent to three years of secondary school training. There is a suggestion, although the evidence is mixed, that the program might lead to some upgrading of teacher performance (p. 106). A second program, *Curso de Qualificação*, was instituted to substitute for lack of complete primary school training by many of the rural teachers. There are, however, insufficient data (no teachers had completed the instruction during our sampling) to provide clear guidance on its effectiveness.

The intensity of teacher input as measured by pupil-teacher ratios is also not systematically related to students' performance (p. 106). This finding is no longer a particular surprise, at least to researchers (pp. 14, 28). But it does go against the stated objectives and observed actions of many governments and educational authorities that work to reduce class sizes.

These negative findings about the relationship of common characteristics of teachers and classes to achievement of their students are quite at odds with conventional wisdom. Coupled with the previous research, however, these findings appear sufficiently strong to be incorporated into school policy decisions. They reveal blind alleys for policy that ought to be avoided.

In contrast, there is strong evidence that specific knowledge on the part of the teacher is important.

Teachers who know their subject matter perform better than those who do not (p. 106).

In 1985, the teachers in our sampled classrooms took exactly the same fourth-grade Portuguese and mathematics tests that the students took. While the teachers performed better than their students on average, they did not uniformly demonstrate mastery of the subject matter they were teaching.[210] Measured by the results of their students, teachers who had higher achievement systematically did better at teaching the subject matter than those who had lower achievement. While this may appear obvious, there is little evidence that teachers are consciously chosen for their subject matter knowledge.

Variation in performance due to subject matter knowledge is, however, only a small portion of the total variation in teacher skill. In other words, while such differences in teachers are significant, there are other important dimensions to effective teacher performance beyond subject matter knowledge.

The investigation of schooling attempted to go deeper into teacher behaviors by ascertaining the types of activities in the classroom and the range of materials used, but to no avail.[211] No systematic differences in student performance were related to these measures, even though they reflected differences thought to be important by Brazilian educators (p. 106). While this could reflect just bad measurement of factors known to be important, it more likely reflects our general inability to recognize a simple set of characteristics that identify a better, or more skilled, teacher.

Unfortunately, overall findings such as these are frequently misunderstood. They should not be interpreted as implying that differences in teachers are unimportant. To the contrary, we have strong evidence that teachers vary widely in their teaching abilities. Rather, the findings about specific teacher characteristics simply indicate that conventional measures of good teachers are not very accurate. Also apparent is the fact that there are many other aspects of good teaching that were not measured. Others may not even be known. Teaching may simply be more art than science. Skill in the classroom has been only crudely captured by subject matter tests and other measures of the teacher's background and preparation. The conclusion is only that it is foolish to choose among prospective teachers solely on the basis of credentials and experience.

The Role of Gender

The systematic discrimination against females in schooling is a matter of concern in much of the developing world. But our research in rural northeast Brazil paints a different picture of gender differences. In the aggregate, Brazil does not exhibit the large gender differences in schooling attainment found elsewhere; in our sample, for example, mothers tend to have more schooling than fathers. In school, direct estimates of promotion probabilities also indicate that, other things being equal, girls are more likely to be promoted than boys. The difference on average amounts to a 3–3.5 percent higher probability of being promoted from second to fourth grade, a noticeable amount given the low promotion rates in this area.[212] In terms of achievement, while there is some imprecision in the estimates, the basic answer is the stereotypical one: girls perform better in Portuguese and worse in mathematics.

Gender-based school policies appear unlikely to have much effect on students' achievement and, specifically, on that of females. Such policies address the general concern about the difficulties that girls face in developing country schools. Common proposals include single-sex schools, matching the sex of student and teacher, and the like. The relationship between the achievement of boys and girls on the one hand, and teacher assignment policies and the gender mix of schools on the other, speaks to these issues. In our data, male students tend to do better with a male teacher than with a female teacher. For females, however, teacher sex has little effect one way or the other. In no case does sex composition of the classroom appear to exert any systematic effect on student performance.[213]

Health, Nutrition, and Learning

People in the rural regions of northeast Brazil, like those in other economically depressed areas, face multiple deprivations, of which poor health and nutrition frequently rank high. Furthermore, there has long been the suspicion that poor health status interacts negatively with schooling. Using the limited special sample of students in Ceará in 1987, a direct investigation of the role of health status in educational performance was conducted.

Malnutrition and poor health status indeed remained as pressing concerns to the children of this region in 1987, despite the full coverage of school feeding programs by 1985. On a wide range of health and anthropometric measurements—including measures of chronic and acute malnutrition and visual acuity—the sampled students were found on average to be noticeably below established norms.

When the interaction of health status and student achievement was investigated, however, the effects of various deficiencies were ambiguous. The most consistent finding was that short-term malnutrition, measured by skinfold thickness-for-age, was associated with poorer school performance. Moreover, the lowest-achieving strata of students had the largest nutritional deficits.

Direct Policy Ramifications

The research in this project was motivated by the possibility of improving educational performance through altered public policies. The extensive statistical investigations of Part II clearly point the way to changes that hold the potential for dramatic improvement in the performance of schools. The specifics apply most directly to rural northeast Brazil, but there is little doubt that many of the findings are also applicable to a much wider set of schools.

The Improvement of Student Flows: Quality Enhancement

Grade repetition and student dropouts are generally considered a drag on the system. If students could be moved through the system more quickly, it would be cheaper to produce graduates at any specified level, and more students could be accommodated within the current school system. The previous results provide immediate guidance about overall approaches.

Pursuing quality improvements is a much more attractive way to in-crease access than actions aimed directly at reducing dropout and rep-etition rates. Direct interventions that are frequently contemplated for this purpose include mandatory attendance laws and automatic grade promotion. Brazil and many other developing and developed countries already have attendance laws, but they are seldom enforced. Automatic promotion is generally equivalent to redefining the level of learning that characterizes students at a given grade. By not enforcing achievement standards, the meaning of being, say, a fourth grader is devalued. Quality improvements, on the other hand, achieve the objectives of increased flow efficiency without having the same negative effects.

The Economics of Resource Policies: Wasteful Decisions

Schooling in developing countries always confronts issues of scarcity. Even if education is valuable and even if it can be demonstrated to be a very profitable investment for society, schools will probably be funded at lower levels than teachers, administrators, and policymakers desire. The simple fact is that there are many needs and desires, many ways in which the citizens and the government can spend the available resources. Schooling, like every other use of resources, must compete for support. This is especially true in developing economies where incomes are largely devoted to the necessities of life.

Given perpetual scarcity, schools ought to spend their resources in the most productive way possible. This implies simply that school policy must take into account both the effectiveness of various educational in-puts and their costs. The previous sections reviewed the educational effectiveness of different common inputs to schools. We now turn to policy recommendations, a subject that necessarily involves costs of in-puts.

Throughout this analysis, we concentrate entirely on allocation poli-cies within the educational sector. We do not consider whether more money should be spent on education, a decision that must incorporate information about other possible places to put expenditure. Moreover, we do not consider distributional issues such as who should receive schooling or what should be spent on primary education as opposed to other levels of education. Instead, we stick to questions of how best to provide schooling for the students currently enrolled in primary education. Of course, if money is freed up by improvements in the efficiency of operation, it would be possible to expand the entire education system or to reallocate resources to noneducational uses.

There are some easy and straightforward policies that follow immediately from consideration of costs and effectiveness. Specifically:

If an input costs money to provide and does not lead to higher achievement, its use should not be expanded.

We have already seen some examples of policies that violate this rule. For example, there is almost constant pressure to consider policies that reduce class size. Such policies are among the most expensive ones that can be considered, yet the evidence is that smaller classes do not typically lead to higher student achievement. Moreover, some classes might actually be increased in size. The average pupil-teacher ratios in our samples fall between twenty-five and thirty students, but this balances a number of quite small classes against fewer large ones. Roughly half of the second-grade classes have twenty or fewer students. Where possible, some consolidation of classes (or adding students to the classes) appears appropriate.[214] The resources saved by such policies could then be used to improve overall school quality or to expand access to the educational system.

A policy may, of course, be pursued without regard to effectiveness or costs for political or other reasons. For example, mayors may pay teachers with certain characteristics—ones that do not imply higher student achievement—because the patronage aspects allow them to meet other objectives. Or, as another example, teachers may push for smaller classes, possibly because they mean less work or perhaps because they lead to higher levels of satisfaction. Such inefficient policies simply drain resources in a system that is very resource-constrained.

Another straightforward example of supposedly obvious policies relates to the push toward graded classrooms. Because of the small scale of many rural schools, students are frequently grouped together in multigrade classrooms. Arguments against this practice are made on pedagogical grounds, and a common policy objective in many developing-country school systems is the elimination of multigrade instruction.[215] But our analysis provides no support for the effectiveness of such policies. If anything, achievement appears to be higher in multigrade settings than in graded classrooms (p. 103). Since there appears to be no gain from having graded classes, there is little argument for incurring the additional expense involved in splitting a multigrade class into smaller graded classes, especially since the smaller classes per se offer no apparent achievement gains.

The hiring and pay policies for teachers present a variant on this theme. The study of teacher effectiveness suggests that teacher experience and teacher education have little consistent payoff in terms of achievement levels of students. On the other hand, examination of the implicit pay policies for teachers reveals that teachers with more experience or with higher education levels are systematically paid more (p. 142). This is not an efficient way to hire or compensate teachers, since these characteristics are not systematically associated with higher student achievement.[216] Of course, this does not imply that the overall teacher salary bill can be reduced, say by paying all teachers regardless of experience or education the salary of a new entrant. If that were done, the expected earnings for teachers would be lowered, thus affecting adversely the supply of people willing to enter teaching. Instead, the finding implies that alternative ways of setting salaries for individual teachers could possibly lead to significant efficiency gains. The efficiency gains would come from improving the overall quality of the teacher stock that is hired for any given total budget.

Self-Financing Educational Investments

The standard decision rule for selecting a set of inputs in which to invest is conceptually straightforward, though sometimes difficult to apply precisely. The achievement gains expected from a one dollar expenditure on each input are compared, and those inputs with the highest achievement gain are selected. The estimated achievement models in chapter 5 provide the expected achievement gains associated with each input. A separate cost analysis is needed to indicate how much of each input can be purchased for a given expenditure.

The derivation of the costs of supplying inputs is never easy. At best, it is a complex and tedious process requiring large amounts of data and a variety of assumptions to which the results may be sensitive (p. 135). For some inputs, the unit costs of providing them to each child are, for practical purposes, not possible to calculate at all. A good example is the cost of providing teachers with greater subject matter knowledge, which cannot be estimated without exhaustive information about the supply function for teachers with different levels of cognitive achievement.

Even when costs can be derived, the standard decision rule must be modified when considering educational investments because of the feedback effects of higher quality schooling. Specifically, a productive input to schools will increase student performance. This increase in performance will increase student promotion rates. The increase in promotion rates will improve the flow of students through the system. This increase in flow will reduce the cost of producing students at any given grade level. These reduced costs of operating the system offset the initial in-vestment in quality-enhancing inputs.

A number of schooling investments will reduce schooling costs by more than the cost of the investment, making them not only completely self-financing but also revenue-generating.

In other words, the amount of repetition in these rural schools is so substantial that quality improvements lead to enormous savings through more efficient flow through the grades (p. 148). As shown by our purely monetary calculations (called *partial benefit-cost ratios*), investments in some quality-enhancing inputs effectively release funds that can be used for other purposes.[217] They can be used to purchase additional quality-enhancing inputs, to expand the availability of schools, to improve other levels of the education system, or to release money currently spent on schools for uses outside the educational system. These findings are all the more extraordinary because the actual calculation methodology considers only part of the gains in flow efficiency (those that accrue between the second and fourth grades) and neglects any valuation what-soever of the achievement gains to students.

Our calculations suggest that the clearest savings would result from investment in hardware (facilities and equipment) and software (writing materials and texts) items. A one dollar investment in improving school furnishings and facilities would yield direct cost savings of $1.39 to $2.39. In other words, the investment would more than completely pay for itself. Similarly, a one dollar investment in upgrading writing materials or textbooks would return $4.03 to $6.95 through improved flow effi-ciency.[218] Even alternative, more conservative estimates reflecting the uncertainty about the true effects of inputs on achievement and of achievements on promotion lead to similar conclusions.[219]

In rural Brazil, it is difficult to argue against aggressive pursuit of such quality improvements. The efficiency gains available are sufficient to pay completely for the improvements; no additional funds are needed in the educational system in order to undertake the investments.[220] In fact, many of these investments will actually entail such large savings over time as to release substantial sums to alternative uses after paying the full cost of the investments themselves.

Most educational investments are justified on the basis of long-run returns through increased productivity of workers in the labor market, but this finding provides a more immediate justification. Any returns from the labor market to quality investments simply reinforce the startling conclusion that some investments are immediately paid off by cost savings.

The extent to which these results can be generalized depends on the overall state of the schooling system. As the level of educational wastage declines, say to the point of schools in the urban southeast of Brazil, the efficiency gains from added investment decline (p. 157). Whenever there is substantial repetition, however, it is possible to offset at least part of the investment costs for quality-improving items.

Some investments, of course, do not yield totally offsetting cost savings, but they may still be justified. The previous calculations use the example of resource policies for which the estimates are reliable and the net benefits are large. Other of our results are more uncertain, implying more analysis is needed. For example, the Logos teacher training program has quite uncertain effects (p. 106), but it is also relatively cheap—suggesting that it is possibly a good investment (p. 148). It is important, however, to calculate costs properly so that savings through improved flow efficiencies are netted out.

Teachers and Output Incentives

Educational authorities can viably intervene with policies directed at tangible educational inputs such as the physical plant, textbooks, and writing materials. An education ministry or the county administration can, for example, readily supply the inputs and can expect to see improvements in achievement. The situation is quite different, however, with respect to policies toward teachers, the most important and most expensive input to the educational process. We have not been able to identify well the characteristics of teachers that are systematically related to good performance. Many of them are presumably intangible. The central problem highlighted by the research is that teacher personnel policies based on the usual readily identifiable teacher characteristics are prone to substantial error when educational effectiveness is the criterion. Moreover, if we are forced to rely only upon such policies, we are unlikely to be able to improve the schools very much. Because teachers are so important in the educational process, this is a truly unfortunate situation.

Policies toward improving teachers almost certainly must involve institutional changes that emphasize teacher performance.

There is too much uncertainty about the characteristics of teachers and the behavioral patterns that lead to good student performance to rely on external policy prescriptions for these inputs to schooling. Instead, rewards for good teaching must be instituted. These rewards would relate the continued hiring of teachers and their compensation to how much students learn.

Such policies clearly are difficult to develop and to institute. In fact, because there is so little experience with such approaches, we discuss this topic below under the general heading of uncertain policies. Nevertheless, the corollary to the general statement must be emphasized:

There is little reason to believe that input-oriented teacher policies will improve student performance.

The one exception might be the case of teacher knowledge of subject matter. Hiring teachers with extensive subject matter knowledge does improve student performance (p. 106). We do not, however, know what it would cost to hire teachers who have more subject matter knowledge. Moreover, subject matter knowledge is just one part of the underlying skill differences among teachers. As a temporary solution, nevertheless, this research is probably sufficient to justify more sophisticated selection and pay policies that take teacher knowledge into account. If part of the problems with inadequate teachers arises from the patronage nature of teacher selection, the institution of a national teacher examination may be an effective regulatory way to improve the quality of the teacher force.[221]

Areas of Uncertainty: Key Unanswered Questions

This analysis, though it provides many insights into the educational process in rural areas and developing countries in general, clearly leaves unanswered questions. Heading the list of unresolved issues is the design of personnel systems based on notions of performance. While things like merit pay for teachers and school administrators have been often mentioned, there are few examples of operational systems.[222] Such systems face opposition by teachers' groups or unions. They also face difficult measurement questions about the rating of teacher performance. Teachers are not only "inputs" into the educational process but also decision-makers with almost complete control of what happens in the classroom. Therefore, they must be centrally involved in the design and operation of any achievement-related system.

The supply function for highly skilled teachers is also unknown. The data demonstrate that the current group of teachers contains some surprisingly ill-prepared teachers. This may frequently reflect the fact that they were the best available given the pay. We have no direct information on the range of teachers that would become available at different salaries. Also, we have little information about how teachers would respond to different payment schedules. This accounts for the inability to cost out teacher inputs of different qualities. The situation is especially complicated because teacher skill—the ability to elicit high student performance—is not readily identified through review of a teacher's background or characteristics. This makes investigations of the supply of skilled teachers very difficult unless experimental methods are employed.

Whether these findings can be generalized to other schooling situations must also be considered. This analysis has focused exclusively on performance in the first four grades of primary school. While we would expect many of the findings to carry over to higher levels of general education, the details and magnitudes of effects will change. Development of explicit policies for those other levels would require additional work.

The Surprising Similarity of Policy Regimes

Schooling in rural northeast Brazil looks to be as far from what exists in the United States and other developed countries as is possible. Nowhere in the United States or other OECD countries, for example, is schooling conducted in mud shacks or with teachers who are themselves barely literate. The average expenditure per student in the United States is literally more than one hundred times that in rural Brazil.

Yet in many fundamental aspects, the substantial differences notwithstanding, the conclusions about the current state of school policy are the same in Brazil and the United States. Consider the following statements. Teachers are very important, and a student's achievement can be dramatically different depending upon the specific teacher the student draws. The characteristics of teachers and schools that are important, however, are not the ones conventionally identified or rewarded. Levels of teacher education and of teacher experience and size of class are not systematically related to performance, even though these are important determinants of the costs of schooling. Teacher salaries are not closely linked to teaching performance, and there is no institutional structure to link teacher personnel policies to teaching performance. Remarkably, in no case is it necessary to distinguish between a statement about schooling in northeast Brazil and schooling in the United States. Each of these statements applies equally to these very disparate conditions.

Differences exist, of course. Family background appears to have a much more powerful direct effect on student achievement in the United States than in Brazil, although part of the difference could simply be measurement problems in the Brazilian data (p. 95).[223] It may be that family backgrounds differ widely but that the available measures do not adequately capture the differences. Perhaps more important in this analysis, however, is the relatively limited range of family backgrounds observed in our samples. If we enlarged the sample to include wealthier regions, we might see more importance attributed to family background factors.

The cardinal importance of repetition and flow efficiency pertains only to the discussion of Brazil and other developing countries. The overall findings about the large discrepancy between gross investment costs and net investment costs (obtained after feedback from flow efficiencies) apply little, if at all, to OECD countries. And the near universal availability in those privileged environments of both reasonable facilities and acceptable textbooks and writing materials makes clear-cut educational development strategies involving material inputs much less obvious there.

We return, again, to one final similarity. Across different societies, bringing about substantial changes in the achievement of students will require attracting and retaining high-quality teachers. The current operations of schools, however, do nothing to ensure that the best teachers are selected or rewarded. Because of our broad ignorance about the specific characteristics or behaviors that define a good teacher, we must turn our attention instead to observing the actual performance of teachers. Implementing a scheme in which reward and promotion are based on teaching performance faces enormous difficulties in both rural Brazil and urban United States. Nevertheless, the chances for fundamental improvement in the performance of students rest on finding ways to implement performance-based schools.[224]

Project Implementation and Design

This book reports findings from two distinct activities—an intensive research effort to understand key underlying behavioral relationships in education and a program evaluation effort that delved into the EDURURAL project itself. However, these two facets of the work are quite closely connected. The evaluation is reliable, and thus an appropriate basis for policymaking, only to the extent that it integrates and builds upon the research findings.

The EDURURAL Outcomes

The apparently simple question, "Did EDURURAL work?" is actually quite difficult to answer. In the tradition of the commonly employed quasi-experimental design, we constructed a sample of schools in counties included under the EDURURAL program and a sample of schools in comparison counties (OTHER). The naive notion behind such an approach usually is that a simple comparison of overall differences in mean performance will indicate whether or not the program worked. However, accurate assessment of program effects requires more detailed analyses based on knowledge of both input differences and the effects of inputs on performance.

The EDURURAL program was designed to expand resources at local schools. It did this by making extra funds available to state education secretariats for the purchase of incremental learning resources. These agencies then distributed the extra resources to county education authorities, who in turn distributed resources to the local schools. This arrangement permits substantial leakage—resources that never reach their intended destinations. It also introduces the possibility of substituting project money for funds that would otherwise have gone to the project schools, freeing resources for other schools.

An in-depth analysis of resources available in EDURURAL schools indicates some relative improvement over the OTHER schools. School resources generally improved in both project and nonproject counties, but the improvement was greater in the project areas. Thus, the project was successfully implemented; it made a discernible difference in resource flows (p. 161).

The findings with respect to performance, however, are quite different. Performance of EDURURAL and OTHER schools was analyzed in a simple achievement growth format and in a multivariate framework that utilized the estimated models of educational performance. When the relative gains of students in EDURURAL and in OTHER areas are analyzed over the years of the project, the evidence suggests slippage in performance in the EDURURAL schools (p. 170). In other words, output or achievement indicators do not support the efficacy of the program. There were also differences across states, with the EDURURAL project in Piaui doing comparatively better than those in Ceará and Pernambuco. This is surprising since implementation of the project in Piaui was worse—that is, fewer additional resources appeared to be actually delivered to its schools.

Alternative estimates of program performance based on the explicit models of educational performance provide little additional reason to be sanguine about the efficacy of the EDURURAL program. There is still some variation across states and time periods, with Piaui's program generally doing relatively better again than the others (p. 174). However, at this stage we cannot accurately describe how the programs differed across states and what aspects we might want to replicate.

From the evaluation exercise emerges an appreciation for the link between evaluation and more fundamental research into the educational process itself. Analysis only of implementation—changes in resources available—can provide misleading answers about the effectiveness of a program. Resource differences must be evaluated in terms of their effect on achievement, something that is seldom known without additional research. Additionally, detailed understanding of program differences is required to interpret the overall results. In our case, program effectiveness differed across the three states of our analysis. But despite massive amounts of data, we cannot pinpoint exactly why the performance differed.

Intervention and Evaluation

This project has provided considerable information about carrying out research and evaluation of schooling in developing countries. We should note immediately what is perhaps the study's greatest achievement. It was not clear at first that large-scale empirical research on schools in such remote, poverty ridden, rural areas was feasible at all. There is now no question that such analysis can be conducted.

However, this kind of evaluation involves a substantial commitment of time, energy, and money. A certain patience is needed to wait for results of longitudinal investigations. The managerial challenges of sustaining a complex research endeavor over several years are not trivial, and the requisite research competence is nowhere plentiful. In money terms, endeavors of the needed magnitude are not cheap; in total, the work reported here cost about US$1.4 million. Nevertheless, compared with the magnitude of overall educational expenditure on primary education, or even to World Bank lending in this area, these are small expenditures. Between 1982 and 1989, the World Bank approved about US$4.5 billion in new loans for education projects, while committing less than US$100 million to research components (Lockheed and Rodd 1990). Moreover, although this amounts to slightly over 2 percent of total loans, the proportion of funds allocated to research and evaluation has declined through the decade.

While much cheaper in every sense, the standard ex post facto assessment carried out on major educational interventions is quite different and much less satisfying. First, an audit ascertains whether or not the funds allocated were spent in the intended manner. Second, some attempt is usually made to verify that the inputs purchased with project funds actually reached the site of the intervention. Then the institutional and other weaknesses that might explain any observed shortfalls in implementation are enumerated. Finally, the project evaluation involves collecting a little aggregate data on the numbers of classrooms built, pupils affected, teachers trained, textbooks delivered, and the like. Sometimes, but not always, it may also involve interviewing actors in the system to determine their satisfaction with the intervention. World Bank completion reports, prepared on every project it finances, closely approximate this stereotype.

Though these standard program assessments are important, they do not substitute for serious analysis of programs and effects. In neglecting both effectiveness and efficiency, such assessments simply provide no new information on which to base the next educational program.

Proper evaluation must be built into programs at the very beginning. For example, without adequate baseline data, it is often impossible to ascertain whether anything happened. To slight the evaluation function, while continuing to reinvent programs or repeat past mistakes, is myopic, wasteful, and doomed to maintain the status quo.

If improvements are sought through new educational policies, learning about the efficacy of various interventions must be a standard aspect of innovations in education.

Of the research projects included in World Bank loans, only a minority was ever completed. And, for those completed, a very small percentage looked at effects on measures of educational performance (Lockheed and Rodd 1990). In addition, the experiences of the 1980s were similar to those of the 1970s (see Tan 1982).

Lessons for Research on Education

This study has contributed to a growing clarity about modeling the educational process. The strengths and shortcomings of the research design give new insights into components of the ideal study. This section is not intended, however, as a complete description of how research should proceed. Instead, it addresses a few key issues that we believe have not been fully appreciated in past work.

The Need for Longitudinal Designs

The performance of each student today depends not only on the activities of his current class but also on the student's preparedness for the curricular material. Preparedness depends in part on the activities of past classes. Education is a cumulative process, building on the inputs and experiences of the past. But, more than that, students differ in ability to absorb and retain material—which for simplicity we might label innate abilities. The cumulative nature of the process implies that one must consider the effect of the whole history of educational inputs, things that are not easily measured at a single point in time. Moreover, because such things as innate ability are difficult to measure at all, it is virtually impossible to record all of the various factors that go into determining student performance, much less to disentangle their separate effects.

These difficulties may be lessened by focusing on how achievement changes over a set period of time. This approach, often called the value-added model, requires longitudinal data on performance and the intervening inputs to the educational process. Such longitudinal modeling reduces considerably the data requirements while simultaneously dealing with some of the most serious and vexing estimation problems (p. 84). Moreover, the examination of alternative procedures for analysis, which in part compares value-added models with purely cross-sectional models, demonstrates the analytical importance of the longitudinal modeling strategy (p. 88).

On the basis of this and other modeling efforts, we conclude that:

Only longitudinal designs should be employed in analyzing educational performance.

Collecting longitudinal data is clearly more expensive and requires a longer commitment of time. However, there is simply no substitute, given our current knowledge of the educational process and of how to measure important components.

Alternative Sampling Designs

The EDURURAL sample was based on repeated sampling of schools with a random selection of students within the schools. This design permitted an investigation of school survival possibilities. It also supported estimation of value-added models for a subset of students who were selected in successive school samples. This was not, however, the only feasible sample design. Other designs would facilitate enquiries that were here possible only in part or not at all.

Any sampling design should ensure the availability of matched longitudinal data for individual students. Planning for this in the design phase can provide considerable cost savings. The sampling for this study was wasteful in the sense that many fourth graders could not be matched with their prior achievement, making these observations unusable in the desirable value-added achievement models. The inefficiency in the sampling came largely from the practice of continued random sampling of students in the second and third waves of the survey, instead of searching for the specific students previously sampled.

There are several advantages to moving to a student-based sampling design where individual students are followed over a period of time. This immediately provides the longitudinal structure. Further, depending upon the characteristics of the follow-up, it can provide new information completely unavailable in the EDURURAL samples. By locating, surveying, and testing students in whatever grade they are in subsequently, detailed analyses of promotion and achievement growth are possible.[225]

Fundamental options must be addressed in the sampling design, and the choices made will have important implications for both costs and the range of analyses that are possible. First, the search for students can be restricted to their initial schools. This will permit essentially the same analyses as in this volume (with the expansions mentioned above). It is also the cheapest of the options. Second, an attempt can be made to track students to different schools if they have changed (because of school closings, migration, or other reasons). This approach offers the possibility of new analyses because the implications of changing school for progression and achievement can now be directly studied. Such a design is clearly more expensive, and indeed the complete tracking of students is virtually impossible. Third, by also tracking students who have dropped out of school, even more significant analyses are possible. It would then be possible to model directly the determinants of dropout behavior and to study characteristics of their transition from school to work or other activities.[226] Again, there is an obvious increase in costs related to intensified searching and interview expense.

In whatever sample design is chosen, there are significant advantages to a cluster sampling that locates substantial numbers of students in the same classrooms. By doing this, the analysis can combine direct investigations of the characteristics of teachers and classrooms with the more general estimation of aggregate differences among classrooms (p. 118).[227] Though we cannot now identify specific teacher characteristics that enter into achievement, the more general analysis is useful. It provides a benchmark for how much of the differences in teachers is captured by specific characteristics.

Identifying Attendance Patterns

Schooling for individual students in developing countries frequently does not follow a regular pattern. Students attend school for a while but then are distracted by work demands, boredom, or whatever, leading them to drop out for a period. The actual attendance patterns through the school year and across different years have never been accurately recorded. Instead, descriptions are more anecdotal, thus defying inclusion in analyses of educational performance. This study is no different. Although considerable effort was made to devise ways to collect attendance information, in the end the Brazilian survey team could not be convinced to collect such information. Their primary concern was accuracy of information.

Various methods of collecting such data could be employed, even to deal with cases where regular attendance records are not kept by the schools. Random sampling of attendance over the year, for example, could provide sufficient attendance information for analysis of individual student performance.

Understanding the role of attendance would greatly enhance analyses of both promotion patterns and student performance. This is particularly true in rural areas where students are moving in and out of work even in the early grades. We believe that this is a priority for future research.

The Need for Cost Information

Any analysis of efficiency of school operations requires data on the costs of different inputs and policies. Yet costs are seldom analyzed in ways that are useful for policy purposes. We speculate that these data are not collected on the theory that they are easy to obtain and, moreover, that the real question is effectiveness, not cost.

But this standard view is wrong on both counts. The necessary information to make policy decisions is the added costs that would be incurred by adding specific resources. This is not what is generally available. At best, one has average costs of inputs, which might include a variety of fixed costs that would not necessarily be incurred over time. For example, if microcomputers were to be introduced for drill and practice work in mathematics, it would be important to distinguish among initial capital investments for the machines, initial programming costs to provide the basic materials, and operating and maintenance costs for the system. Knowledge of each element of total costs would be useful for some kinds of decisions, but almost any analysis requires that they be separated from each other. These disaggregated data are, however, seldom available.

The case of teachers is an even better example of both the difficulty and the importance of understanding costs. As noted above, we currently know extremely little about the supply of teachers and how teachers with different characteristics will respond to different salaries. Teachers vary dramatically in their characteristics and their performance in the classroom. Yet we do not understand how much it costs to get a teacher with different characteristics or performance. For example, if we wanted to hire teachers in rural Ceará with a high level of mathematics knowledge as we suggested earlier in this chapter, we do not know what salaries would be required.

But costs of inputs that are apparently more straightforward are also problematic. Writing materials and textbooks can be priced fairly simply in stores in urban areas, but this does not accurately reflect what it would cost to ensure textbook availability in some of the rural areas of our study.

Obtaining reliable and useful cost information requires a serious research effort. This is particularly true when input quality is an issue. Policy advice, however, cannot do without cost information. And, in the absence of good cost estimates, judgments based on inappropriate cost figures are likely to rule the day.

A Concluding Plea

Research documents typically end with a plea for further research, and ours is no exception. The case is simple. Education remains the largest governmental expenditure in most developing countries after the military. Moreover, conventional wisdom, common arguments by policymakers, and data suggest that developing countries are underinvesting in education. The problem, documented here and elsewhere, is that available funds for education are not being spent wisely: there is substantial inefficiency in the schools. And, new projects of the governments in developing countries, often in partnership with international agencies, do not show evidence of being significantly better or more efficient than existing programs. It is not a conspiracy. It is simply lack of knowledge about what to do.

Appendixes

A

Measuring Achievement: The Tests, Their Reliability, and Overall Results

CENTRAL TO THIS STUDY is the measurement of academic achievement in Portuguese and mathematics among primary school students in the most rural areas of Brazil's northeast region. This appendix describes the tests employed for this purpose, summarizes information about their reliability, and presents the overall test results for the several central sample subgroups. This section draws extensively on work by Donald Holsinger, who conducted the initial analysis of test reliability and results in 1985.

The tests were designed to measure basic capability in Portuguese and mathematics in the second and fourth grades. The nature of the sample, the selection of participating grade levels and classrooms, the selection and training of field workers, and other details pertaining to the actual data collection procedures are described elsewhere (Fundação Carlos Chagas 1987, listed under works by EDURURAL evaluation research team members). The tests were administered to 18,644 students, broken down as follows:

	1981	1983	1985	1987
Students	6,432	5,546	6,271	395
Second grade	4,718	3,969	4,368	35
Fourth grade	1,714	1,577	1,904	217
Third grade	n.a.	n.a.	n.a.	116
Not in school	n.a.	n.a.	n.a.	27
Schools	586	599	642	80

n.a. = Not applicable.
Source: EDURURAL research sample.

In 1987, the second-grade tests for 1985 in Portuguese and mathematics, identical item-for-item, were administered to all children in the differently drawn 1987 sample. In addition, the fourth-grade tests in Portuguese and mathematics for 1985 were administered to the teachers of the students in the 1985 sample.

Test construction and validation was the responsibility of a team headed by Bernadette Gatti at the Fundação Carlos Chagas (FCC), located in São Paulo. The FCC staff also scored all the tests. FCC is the preeminent Brazilian educational research organization. It has extensive expertise and experience in both psychometrics and educational evaluation.

Test Content

Organization of the Tests

The tests of Portuguese and mathematics used in 1983 and 1985 were constructed so as to be parallel forms of the tests that were used in 1981, with the same objectives and the same difficulty level. This was achieved in part through content validation and item matchings by specialists in tests and measurement. The tests are criterion-referenced using a minimally acceptable standard in certain competencies or skills. The determination of minimally acceptable levels of competency was made through the combined judgment of local school teachers and of the technical staff of the municipal education organizations (OME) of the sampled counties and staff from the state secretariats of education. The competency levels thus defined are significantly lower than those that would be expected in the south of Brazil. Indeed, tests originally developed by FCC for use in São Paulo were shown to be much too difficult for children in the northeast, as well as being inappropriate (particularly in Portuguese) because of regional differences in language usage. The construction of the tests in 1983 and 1985 was done with the objective of demonstrating the student's mastery of the identical skills considered to have been minimal and indispensable for the first (1981) evaluation. The same general structure of the test was preserved, and only the wording of the questions was changed. In drafting the new test items, the greatest caution was taken not to alter the degree of difficulty or otherwise to compromise the reasonableness of the comparative analysis of scores at the several dates.

Test Objectives and Structure

Tables A-1 and A-2 contain information on the general structure of the tests: the objectives of the tests of Portuguese and mathematics for the second and fourth grades, the total points each group of items received as a function of its importance in relation to the progress expected at various points in the curriculum, and the number of test items. Except

Table A-1. Objectives for the Portuguese Test for Second and Fourth Grades, 1981, 1983, and 1985

	Second grade						Fourth grade					
	1981		1983		1985		1981		1983		1985	
Objective	Number of items	Points	Number of items	Points	Number of items	Points	Number of items	Points	Number of items	Points	Number of items	Points
Reading comprehension	6	36	6	36	6	36	6	30	6	30	6	30
Writing	18	34	18	34	18	34	20	20	20	20	20	20
Grammar	15	30	15	30	15	30	21	34	21	34	21	34
Composition	n.a.	n.a.	n.a.	n.a.	n.a.	n.a.	5	16	5	16	5	16
Total	39	100	39	100	39	100	52	100	52	100	52	100

n.a. = Not applicable.
Source: Calculations from test instruments.

*Table A-2. Objectives for the Mathematics Test for Second
and Fourth Grades, 1981, 1983, and 1985*

	1981		1983		1985	
Objective	*Number of items*	*Points*	*Number of items*	*Points*	*Number of items*	*Points*
Second grade						
Number recognition	14	28	14	28	14	28
Concept of tens and hundreds	4	8	4	8	4	8
Concept of dozen	3	6	3	6	3	6
Numerical relations:						
twice, half, even, and odd	3	6	3	6	3	6
Addition and subtraction	6	6	6	6	6	6
Multiplication and division	7	7	7	7	7	7
Four operations	12	24	12	24	12	24
Story problems	3	15	3	15	3	15
Total	52	100	52	100	52	100
Fourth grade						
Number recognition	13	26	13	26	13	26
Measure of volume,						
lengths, and time	2	4	2	4	2	4
Multiplication and division	11	11	11	11	6	6
Rational numbers	1	2	1	2	1	2
Unit measures	5	10	5	10	5	10
Four operations	11	22	11	22	11	22
Story problems	5	25	5	25	5	25
Total	48	100	48	100	43	95

Note: Five items in the 1985 subtest of multiplication and division were discarded, due
to an undiscovered printing error on the test forms. For purposes of calculating the achievement scores, the points achieved on each subtest were multiplied by (100/95), such that
the maximum total score was 100.
Source: EDURURAL research sample.

for the minor complication introduced in the multiplication and division
objective on the fourth-grade mathematics test in 1985, the tests were
identical in the three years. They measured the same objectives, assigned
the same relative weight in the total test score to each objective, and
used the same number of items to measure each objective.

The second-grade Portuguese test. For the reading comprehension
objective, the test sought to reveal whether the student was capable of
answering questions about a text he had read, demonstrating comprehension of written language. Thus, items were considered to have been
correctly answered that displayed evidence of understanding, even when

the answer contained orthographic errors. In the writing and grammar sections, answers were marked incorrect that showed inadequate spelling. The ability of a student to compose original sentences was tested by adding points to two existing questions when the students' responses were judged to contain elements of originality or creativity that went beyond the simple correct answer.

The fourth-grade Portuguese test. The same reading comprehension and writing and grammar objectives were used as in the second-grade test. However, different criteria were employed for the composition objective. By requiring the student to write a simple letter, it was intended to discover whether the student could follow instructions to organize the letter by including the names of the sender and the receiver and could use simple punctuation. The exercise also sought to identify the number of orthographic errors committed as a proportion of words written.

The second- and fourth-grade mathematics tests. These tests were designed to eliminate the possibility of partially correct answers. All responses were considered correct if they presented the anticipated answer, even when the student failed to indicate the calculations required to arrive at the answer. The tests were designed to keep the numeric values of intermediate and final results small, thereby improving the chance of obtaining correct answers from mental rather than written calculations.

Test Reliability

The design of the EDURURAL evaluation research called for comparison of student achievement in Portuguese and mathematics across several years and important sample subgroups (especially for EDURURAL and OTHER areas, and for the three states). The legitimacy of such comparisons depends upon the yardstick employed for the measurements. In particular, it was important from one year to the next *both* that the technical reliability of the tests be high and relatively stable *and* that the difficulty level of the tests not be significantly different. Data presented below suggest confidence on both counts.

Technical reliability refers to the extent to which the selected items in a test truly reflect the universe of items that exhaustively describes the characteristic being measured. If the average correlation of items within a test (or the average covariance among items if the items are not all standardized to a standard deviation of one) is high, they are considered to be measuring a common underlying phenomenon. The test items are said to be internally consistent.

This study continues a long tradition in the testing literature of using Cronbach's alpha as its measure of internal consistency reliability. The discussion below follows closely the summary given in the manual describing the SPSSC/PC computer program employed to calculate internal consistency reliability coefficients.

Cronbach's alpha can be interpreted in two ways: (1) as the correlation between our tests of Portuguese and mathematics and all other possible tests of the same number of items in each subject that could have been constructed from an imaginary universe of Portuguese and mathematics test items; or (2) as the squared correlation between the score a student got on the Portuguese or mathematics test and what he would have gotten if the tests had included all of the possible items in each subject.

Tables A-3 and A-4 contain the calculated Cronbach alpha coefficients for, respectively, the full samples in 1983 and 1985 at second and fourth grades, and the samples broken down by program status and state. Unfortunately the item responses necessary to calculate Cronbach's alpha for 1981 were lost in Brazil prior to conduct of formal reliability analysis. The overall results in table A-3—Cronbach's alpha generally greater than 0.9—are well within the acceptable range for work of this sort and are reasonably stable across years and grade levels (except that the result for fourth-grade Portuguese are a little lower). Table A-4 reveals that the stability of these highly acceptable results is maintained for the key sample breakdowns by program status and state. There is reason to be confident that the measuring instruments employed were equally reliable for the several subgroups of children.

The generally high and stable Cronbach alpha internal consistency reliability coefficients are further documented in tables A-5 to A-8, in which the tests are analyzed in terms of the reliability of their component objectives. Intuitively it is clear that Cronbach's alpha is a positive function of the number of test items, it being much easier accurately to represent the full universe of items with a large rather than a small number of test items. When examining the reliability of subtests (objectives) comprising as few as three to five items, therefore, a noticeable decline in the calculated coefficients is to be expected. And indeed this occurs, particularly in the fourth-grade Portuguese test (table A-6), where most coefficients are below 0.8.

As noted above, care was taken in constructing the tests not to alter the difficulty level of the items. One way to gauge success in this endeavor is to examine the proportion of pupils in each year who scored above the midpoint of the possible total responses (answered correctly more than half of the items) comprising each test objective. Tables A-5 to A-8 also record this proportion for each subtest (objective) and grade and year. While there clearly are some variations, they tend to be small in the subtests with a substantial number of items. There is no compelling

Table A-3. Test Reliabilities, 1983 and 1985

Grade	Portuguese		Mathematics	
	1983	*1985*	*1983*	*1985*
Second grade				
Cronbach's alpha	0.897	0.909	0.935	0.938
Number of items	39	39	52	52
Number of cases	3,969	4,368	3,969	4,368
Fourth grade				
Cronbach's alpha	0.833	0.827	0.911	0.905
Number of items	52	52	48	43
Number of cases	1,577	1,904	1,577	1,904

Note: The computer tape with item responses for 1981 was inadvertently destroyed prior to conduct of formal reliability analysis. However, as explained in the text, the 1981 test was exactly analogous in content and level of difficulty to those of 1983 and 1985. So there is no reason to assume Cronbach's alpha for 1981 would be meaningfully different from those reported for 1983 and 1985 for this and subsequent tables.
Source: EDURURAL research sample.

Table A-4. Test Reliability: Stability of Cronbach's Alpha, 1983, 1985

Grade	1983		1985	
	EDURURAL	*OTHER*	*EDURURAL*	*OTHER*
Portuguese				
Second grade	0.898	0.896	0.911	0.905
Fourth grade	0.828	0.841	0.825	0.832
Mathematics				
Second grade	0.939	0.923	0.939	0.934
Fourth grade	0.913	0.907	0.907	0.898
Number of cases				
Second grade	2,619	1,350	2,950	1,418
Fourth grade	997	580	1,273	631

Grade	1983			1985		
	Pernambuco	*Ceará*	*Piaui*	*Pernambuco*	*Ceará*	*Piaui*
Portuguese						
Second grade	0.901	0.869	0.896	0.912	0.866	0.913
Fourth grade	0.850	0.824	0.803	0.839	0.797	0.811
Mathematics						
Second grade	0.925	0.934	0.939	0.931	0.923	0.946
Fourth grade	0.902	0.902	0.918	0.901	0.892	0.910
Number of cases						
Second grade	1,246	1,338	1,385	1,314	1,541	1,513
Fourth grade	556	352	669	645	588	671

Source: EDURURAL research sample.

Table A-5. Internal Consistency and Difficulty Level: Portuguese Achievement Subtests for Second Grade, 1981, 1983, and 1985

Subject	1981	1983	1985
Reading			
Cronbach's alpha	—	0.807	0.812
Number of items	6	6	6
Maximum points	36	36	36
Total number of cases	—	3,969	4,368
Above midpoint (percent)	63	64	63
Writing			
Cronbach's alpha	—	0.840	0.877
Number of items	18	18	18
Maximum points	34	34	34
Total number of cases	—	3,969	4,368
Above midpoint (percent)	60	68	72
Grammar			
Cronbach's alpha	—	0.834	0.846
Number of items	15	15	15
Maximum points	30	30	30
Total number of cases	—	3,969	4,368
Above midpoint (percent)	57	60	54

— = Not available (see table A-3 note).
Source: EDURURAL research sample.

evidence in these numbers that the difficulty level of the tests varied significantly or systematically from one year to the next. (The proportions of students scoring above the midpoint in 1983 and 1985 are substantially different for the composition subobjective in the fourth-grade Portuguese test. Prima facia, some variation in difficulty level cannot be excluded. However, the number of items on this segment of the test is small, and of all portions of the test this is the only one in which the possible subjectivity of test scorers enters the picture. This, combined with the almost identical wording of the items in both years, suggests to us that difficulty level probably was not the main cause of the discrepancy.

As noted above, in 1985 the fourth-grade versions of the tests were administered to teachers and in 1987 the second-grade tests for 1985 were administered to a differently chosen sample of children, all of whom had previously been tested in 1985. The universe of test items fully reflecting Portuguese and mathematics knowledge of teachers and of a composite group of second through fourth graders could plausibly differ from that of a universe reflecting the knowledge of discrete groups of second- and fourth-grade students. Thus, it is important to verify the

Table A-6. Internal Consistency and Difficulty Level: Portuguese Achievement Subtests for Fourth Grade, 1983 and 1985

Subject	1983	1985
Reading		
Cronbach's alpha	0.628	0.544
Number of items	6	6
Maximum points	30	30
Total number of cases	1,577	1,904
Above midpoint (percent)	40	41
Writing		
Cronbach's alpha	0.796	0.801
Number of items	20	20
Maximum points	20	20
Total number of cases	1,577	1,904
Above midpoint (percent)	78	74
Grammar		
Cronbach's alpha	0.761	0.738
Number of items	21	21
Maximum points	34	34
Total number of cases	1,577	1,904
Above midpoint (percent)	34	34
Composition		
Cronbach's alpha	0.775	0.795
Number of items	5	5
Maximum points	16	16
Total number of cases	1,577	1,904
Above midpoint (percent)	77	41

Source: EDURURAL research sample.

internal consistency reliability of the tests when administered to these special groups.

Table A-9 contains the pertinent data on internal consistency reliability of scores on the 1985 second-grade tests administered in 1987 to a sample of children in Ceará. These children were in second through fourth grade, but all had been in second grade and taken the tests two years previously. For students who were still in the second grade in 1987, as they had been in 1985, estimated reliability of both tests is comparable to the figures in table A-3. There is a decline in both subjects for students who in the two-year intervening period had progressed to third or fourth grade. The alpha coefficients decline, in the case of Portuguese in fourth grade, to a level (0.76) that could occasion some concern about measurement error. The decline, however, is quite logical. The universe of material that third and fourth graders are meant to master is naturally different from that of second graders. So a test constructed as a sample

Table A-7. Internal Consistency and Difficulty Level: Mathematics Achievement Subtests for Second Grade, 1983 and 1985

Curricular objective	1983	1985
Number recognition		
Cronbach's alpha	0.863	0.874
Number of items	14	14
Maximum points	28	28
Total number of cases	3,969	4,368
Above midpoint (percent)	53	53
Concepts[a]		
Cronbach's alpha	0.821	0.828
Number of items	10	10
Maximum points	20	20
Total number of cases	3,969	4,368
Above midpoint (percent)	57	57
Four operations[b]		
Cronbach's alpha	0.921	0.917
Number of items	25	25
Maximum points	37	37
Total number of cases	3,969	4,368
Above midpoint (percent)	43	41
Story problems		
Cronbach's alpha	0.661	0.674
Number of items	3	3
Maximum points	15	15
Total number of cases	3,969	4,368
Above midpoint (percent)	49	40

a. Concepts includes concepts of tens and hundreds, concept of dozen, and numerical relations as displayed in table A-2.

b. Four operations includes addition and subtraction, multiplication and division, and four operations as displayed in table A-2.

Source: EDURURAL research sample.

from the theoretical universe of second-grade items should be expected to be less internally consistent when administered to third and fourth graders who in the meantime had moved on from second grade.

Table A-10 contains the internal consistency reliability calculations for the tests administered to the teachers in 1985, which were identical to those used with the fourth-grade students in our sample for that year. The results are very close to those obtained for the fourth-grade students in 1985 (table A-3). The slight increase in alpha for mathematics is probably attributable to there being five more items. These were the items judged as possibly confusing to students and therefore dropped when calculating student results.

Table A-8. Internal Consistency and Difficulty Level: Mathematics Achievement Subtests for Fourth Grade, 1983 and 1985

Curricular objective	1983	1985
Number recognition		
Cronbach's alpha	0.819	0.820
Number of items	13	13
Maximum points	26	26
Total number of cases	1,577	1,904
Above midpoint (percent)	53	59
Concepts[a]		
Cronbach's alpha	0.660	0.682
Number of items	8	8
Maximum points	16	16
Total number of cases	1,577	1,904
Above midpoint (percent)	37	43
Four operations[b]		
Cronbach's alpha	0.897	0.862
Number of items	22	17
Maximum points	33	28
Total number of cases	1,577	1,904
Above midpoint (percent)	62	60
Story problems		
Cronbach's alpha	0.723	0.755
Number of items	5	5
Maximum points	25	25
Total number of cases	1,577	1,904
Above midpoint (percent)	34	37

a. Concepts includes measure of volume, length, and time, rational numbers, and unit measures shown in table A-2.

b. Four operations includes multiplication and division and four operations shown in table A-2.

Source: EDURURAL research sample.

Table A-9. 1987 Test Reliability (Ceará Sample)

Grade	Portuguese	Mathematics
Second grade		
Cronbach's alpha	0.928	0.949
Number of cases	35	35
Third grade		
Cronbach's alpha	0.844	0.916
Number of cases	116	116
Fourth grade		
Cronbach's alpha	0.763	0.877
Number of cases	217	217
Number of items[a]	39	52

a. All fourth graders answered one question correctly, leaving only thirty-eight items usable in the scale.

Source: EDURURAL research sample.

Table A-10. 1985 Teacher Test Reliability

	Portuguese	*Mathematics*
All teachers		
Cronbach's alpha	0.811	0.921
Number of cases	857	857
Number of items	52	48

Source: EDURURAL research sample.

Achievement of Students and Teachers

Tables A-11 to A-15 summarize the results obtained by our sample students on the Portuguese and mathematics tests. What general conclusions can be drawn from these data?

Turning first to tables A-11 and A-12, the most striking result is the generally low level of academic achievement. Given that the tests were referenced to a minimal criterion level, the expectation was that students would be able to answer correctly nearly all of the test questions. From that perspective, the observed levels of test performance fell far short of what was anticipated. It would not, of course, have been useful for evaluation purposes if the test had actually fulfilled its producer's purported objective of having all students answer all items correctly.

If the test is seen as a description of what local teachers and school administrators expect students to have mastered at each grade level, the scores obtained indicate how far students have come in relation to those expectations. In pondering these scores, it is worth remembering that the expectations placed on students are much more modest in the northeast than they are in São Paulo. This is revealed by FCC's experience in attempting first to use a test developed for São Paulo. In trial administrations the difficulty level was found to be so high as to make discrimination among rural northeast students impossible.

The median scores in table A-11 show that one-half of the second-grade students in our samples never achieved more than 66 points in Portuguese or more than 51 points in mathematics. In other words, half the second-grade students did not learn a full third of the minimally prescribed Portuguese curriculum or an entire half of the minimum mathematics curriculum. At fourth grade the corresponding figures are 54 points and 50 points (table A-11). Again, half the children are failing to master fully half the material.

While devastatingly bad everywhere, the situation is not identical in the three states. At both grade levels and in both subjects, students in Ceará uniformly do better on average than their peers elsewhere, and those in Pernambuco generally are the least successful academically,

Table A-11. Achievement of Second-Grade Students in Portuguese and Mathematics by State, 1981, 1983, and 1985

Subject	Pernambuco			Ceará			Piauí			Total		
	1981	1983	1985	1981	1983	1985	1981	1983	1985	1981	1983	1985
Portuguese												
Mean	42.9	50.0	50.7	62.8	65.8	69.6	44.7	59.6	57.0	49.0	58.7	59.5
Standard deviation	27.1	24.7	26.0	24.2	20.4	19.8	27.3	23.0	25.9	27.8	23.6	25.2
Median	46.0	54.0	54.0	68.0	72.0	75.0	50.0	66.0	62.0	53.0	64.0	66.0
Number of cases	2,020	1,246	1,314	1,317	1,338	1,541	1,381	1,385	1,513	4,718	3,969	4,368
Mathematics												
Mean	42.9	46.5	42.1	57.9	57.0	56.4	38.6	49.5	47.9	45.9	51.1	49.2
Standard deviation	26.8	23.4	23.2	24.3	24.4	22.9	24.8	25.6	26.7	26.6	24.9	25.0
Median	41.0	45.0	42.0	61.0	58.0	58.0	37.0	50.0	48.0	46.0	51.0	49.0
Number of cases	2,008	1,246	1,314	1,317	1,338	1,541	1,381	1,385	1,513	4,718	3,969	4,368

Note: The statistics for 1983 and 1985 are calculated from the data files employed in the reliability analysis; these include all children for which valid test scores were obtained during the field surveys. The statistics for 1981 are calculated from the cross-section master files for 1981; these also include all children for which valid test scores were obtained during the field survey in 1981.

Source: EDURURAL research sample.

Table A-12. Achievement of Fourth-Grade Students in Portuguese and Mathematics by State, 1981, 1983, and 1985

Subject	Pernambuco			Ceará			Piauí			Total		
	1981	1983	1985	1981	1983	1985	1981	1983	1985	1981	1983	1985
Portuguese												
Mean	50.0	48.7	43.4	60.5	59.0	55.5	48.5	51.6	47.0	51.5	52.2	48.4
Standard deviation	20.0	19.3	18.6	19.1	17.2	16.9	19.8	17.0	17.3	20.2	18.3	18.3
Median	51.0	49.9	42.9	63.0	62.9	57.0	50.0	52.1	47.0	53.0	53.8	48.9
Number of cases	859	556	645	323	352	588	532	669	671	1,714	1,577	1,904
Mathematics												
Mean	49.1	44.6	44.6	59.9	55.0	55.3	40.7	47.7	50.7	48.5	48.2	50.1
Standard deviation	23.1	21.8	22.6	23.5	22.4	22.3	24.6	24.1	24.2	24.6	23.3	23.5
Median	49.0	44.0	45.3	63.0	56.0	55.8	39.0	47.0	51.6	48.0	48.0	50.5
Number of cases	859	556	645	323	352	588	532	669	671	1,714	1,577	1,904

Note: The statistics for 1983 and 1985 are calculated from the data files employed in the reliability analysis; these include all children for which valid test scores were obtained during the field surveys. The statistics for 1981 are calculated from the cross-section master files for 1981; these also include all children for which valid test scores were obtained during the field survey in 1981.

Source: EDURURAL research sample.

232

Table A-13. *Achievement of Second-Grade Students in Portuguese and Mathematics by State and Project Status, 1981, 1983, and 1985*

| Subject | Pernambuco | | | | | | Ceará | | | | | | Piauí | | | | | |
| | EDURURAL | | | OTHER | | | EDURURAL | | | OTHER | | | EDURURAL | | | OTHER | | |
	1981	1983	1985	1981	1983	1985	1981	1983	1985	1981	1983	1985	1981	1983	1985	1981	1983	1985
Portuguese																		
Mean	44.4	50.6	49.4	40.6	48.9	52.8	65.6	70.5	70.9	58.1	58.2	67.3	45.4	59.0	58.8	43.0	61.4	51.0
Standard deviation	26.3	24.4	25.7	28.1	25.1	26.4	22.8	17.3	19.0	25.7	22.6	20.8	28.0	23.5	26.0	25.4	21.7	24.9
Median	46.0	56.0	50.0	43.0	50.0	56.0	70.0	74.0	76.0	63.0	64.0	72.0	50.0	66.0	66.0	43.0	67.5	56.0
Number of cases	1,219	764	819	801	482	495	829	828	977	488	510	564	989	1,027	1,154	392	358	359
Mathematics																		
Mean	43.6	45.4	40.4	42.5	48.4	45.0	61.8	62.3	57.4	51.2	48.4	54.6	40.2	50.5	51.9	34.3	46.7	35.1
Standard deviation	27.9	23.3	23.4	25.3	23.3	22.7	22.8	24.2	23.0	25.2	22.2	22.6	25.0	26.2	26.3	23.7	23.9	23.6
Median	43.0	44.0	39.0	41.0	47.0	45.0	65.0	66.0	59.0	54.0	49.0	56.0	39.0	52.0	53.0	31.0	45.0	33.0
Number of cases	1,219	764	819	801	482	495	829	828	977	488	510	564	989	1,027	1,154	392	358	359

Note: The statistics for 1983 and 1985 are calculated from the data files employed in the reliability analysis; these include all children for whom valid test scores were obtained during the field surveys. The statistics for 1981 are calculated from the cross-section master files for 1981; these also include all children for whom valid test scores were obtained during the field survey in 1981.

Source: EDURURAL research sample.

Table A-14. Achievement of Fourth-Grade Students in Portuguese and Mathematics by State and Project Status, 1981, 1983, and 1985

Subject	Pernambuco						Ceará						Piaui					
	EDURURAL			OTHER			EDURURAL			OTHER			EDURURAL			OTHER		
	1981	1983	1985	1981	1983	1985	1981	1983	1985	1981	1983	1985	1981	1983	1985	1981	1983	1985
Portuguese																		
Mean	51.0	48.2	43.7	48.7	49.3	42.9	63.5	60.1	55.6	56.5	57.7	55.2	49.3	51.4	47.7	46.3	52.3	45.2
Standard deviation	18.9	18.4	18.6	21.5	20.6	18.6	18.3	16.1	16.6	19.4	18.2	17.4	19.3	17.5	17.5	20.8	15.7	16.8
Median	51.0	49.0	43.0	51.0	51.4	41.9	67.0	63.0	57.0	59.0	62.2	57.8	51.0	52.3	47.1	46.0	52.0	45.2
Number of cases	511	327	409	348	229	236	184	186	374	139	166	214	380	484	490	152	185	181
Mathematics																		
Mean	52.0	43.2	44.1	44.9	46.5	45.5	66.8	59.8	56.0	50.9	49.7	54.0	41.9	49.7	53.2	37.6	42.3	44.0
Standard deviation	22.4	21.9	23.1	23.5	21.6	21.8	20.9	21.5	22.7	23.8	22.2	21.6	24.9	24.2	24.0	23.7	23.1	23.5
Median	52.0	42.0	43.2	44.0	46.0	46.3	70.5	62.0	56.8	50.0	48.5	54.7	41.0	49.0	55.8	35.0	41.0	42.1
Number of cases	511	327	409	348	229	236	184	186	374	139	166	214	380	484	490	152	185	181

Note: The statistics for 1983 and 1985 are calculated from the data files employed in the reliability analysis; these include all children for whom valid test scores were obtained during the field surveys. The statistics for 1981 are calculated from the cross-section master files for 1981; these also include all children for whom valid test scores were obtained during the field survey in 1981.

Source: EDURURAL research sample.

especially after 1981. Further, even with higher mean achievement, the standard deviations of test scores are almost always less in Ceará than elsewhere (although not always greatly so), indicating a more uniform result.

The time trends overall are not particularly striking. At fourth grade there is no evidence of improvement, and at second grade the progress is remarkable only in Portuguese. Looking at these trends disaggregated by state, a distinct improvement in second- and fourth-grade mathematics in Piaui is also clearly evident. Especially if the assertion of no significant change in difficulty level of the tests is accepted, the downward movement of some of the means over time is discouraging. Except in Portuguese at second grade and in Piaui generally, there is little evidence of improved overall levels of learning.

Tables A-13 and A-14 further disaggregate the data to allow the examination of results within each state by program status (counties participating in the EDURURAL program and OTHER counties, which are not). These tables are the source for the overview presented in chapter 7 (table 7-7).

Table A-15 contains similar descriptive statistics for the special group of children from the 1985 second-grade sample in Ceará who were traced and tested again in 1987. The instruments used, as noted earlier, were the 1985 tests, unaltered. The numbers are too small for very robust conclusions. But it is clear (from comparison with table A-11) that stu-

Table A-15. Achievement of Second-, Third-, and Fourth-Grade Students in Portuguese and Mathematics, 1987

Grade	Portuguese	Mathematics
Second-grade students		
Mean	74.8	67.9
Standard deviation	24.1	26.1
Median	80.0	79.0
Number of cases	35	35
Third-grade students		
Mean	81.6	68.0
Standard deviation	15.3	21.3
Median	84.5	73.0
Number of cases	116	116
Fourth-grade students		
Mean	89.3	77.2
Standard deviation	9.8	16.4
Median	92.0	80.0
Number of cases	217	217

Source: EDURURAL research sample.

dents who were found once again in second grade in 1987 had learned *something* during those extra years in second grade, especially in mathematics. In Portuguese their mean scores improved by about one-fifth of a standard deviation, while the corresponding figure for mathematics is about one-half a standard deviation. The median scores also moved upward, especially in mathematics. Grade repetition produces some, although surprisingly little, incremental achievement.

Advancement through the grades also increases mastery of the second-grade curriculum. For both subjects, means and medians increase between second and fourth grade, and the standard deviations decline. The proportional effect here is greater in Portuguese. Even so, half of the fourth-grade students in 1987 still had mastered less than 90 percent of the second-grade Portuguese and 80 percent of the second-grade mathematics curriculum. Further, at least in our results, students in third grade do not seem to receive much reinforcement of the second-grade curriculum, which suggests that an examination of sequencing of material by year might pay dividends.

Students who proceed on schedule from second to fourth grade in two years appear to show definite achievement gains. Mean scores of the fourth graders in 1987 (on the second-grade tests) were about 20 points (one standard deviation) higher in both subjects than the mean scores of the much larger peer group of second graders in 1985, and standard deviations were very much lower. But caution is required in

Table A-16. Achievement of Teachers on Fourth-Grade Tests of Portuguese and Mathematics, 1985

Grade	Portuguese	Mathematics
All teachers		
Mean	74.5	81.5
Standard deviation	16.0	19.3
Median	77.4	88.0
Number of cases	857	857
Second-grade teachers		
Mean	72.2	77.1
Standard deviation	16.5	21.7
Median	77.1	84.0
Number of cases	402	402
Fourth-grade teachers		
Mean	78.4	88.2
Standard deviation	14.3	11.2
Median	81.1	90.0
Number of cases	270	270

Source: EDURURAL research sample.

interpretation, since part of the difference must be attributed to sample selectivity. Only the best students advance on schedule through the grades. In fact, if the scores on the second-grade tests of the same 217 children are compared in 1985 and 1987, mean achievement in Portuguese has risen only 14 points (about 0.9 standard deviations) rather than about 20 points, and mean achievement in mathematics has risen only 16 points (about 0.7 standard deviations) rather than about 20 points.

Table A-16 contains descriptive statistics on achievement of teachers in 1985 on the fourth-grade tests administered to students. On the one hand, it is encouraging to see (comparing these results with those for fourth-grade students in table A-12) that teachers evidently know more of the subject matter that they impart than their students. Mean scores are 26–30 points higher, and standard deviations a little lower. Further, the teachers most knowledgeable about the subject matter are found in fourth grade rather than second. On the other hand, there is little comfort to be derived from the fact that half the teachers of fourth-grade students have failed to master 23 percent of the Portuguese and 12 percent of the mathematics curriculum they purport to teach.

B

Variable Definitions and Descriptive Statistics

THIS APPENDIX CONTAINS information on how all variables employed in the analytic models are measured. It also provides data on their means and standard deviations. Most data come directly from the surveys employed in the EDURURAL research project, but a few variables were defined on the basis of existing public data for Brazil. These variables were used to describe the environment of the schools. The two key variables of this type were the Agricultural Productivity Index and the County Socio-Economic Status (SES) Indicator. These are defined as follows:

- *Agricultural Productivity*
Production in 1,000 cruzeiros per hectare at the county level in 1980 (from data of the Brazilian Institute of Geography and Statistics, IGBE).

- *County Socioeconomic Status*
Constructed index representing the first principal component from six separate county measures: (a) mean productivity in agricultural, industrial, commercial, and service employment; (b) percentage of workforce outside agriculture; (c) percentage of workforce who are medical doctors; (d) percentage of houses with electricity; (e) percentage of population receiving at least one regional minimum wage; (f) percentage of population who are literate. For details, see Armitage and others (1986).

Other indexes were also created from the EDURURAL survey data. Most are straightforward and easily described in the tables that follow. One index, however, is more complicated. The EDURURAL project created an educational organization for each county, the *orgão municipal de educação* or OME. OMEs were designed to provide administrative and pedagogical coordination at the local level and had varying numbers of people with different background characteristics. For both 1983 and

1985, an index was created that combined the experience, education, and salary information of the director, the supervisors, and the technicians in each OME. A weighted average of characteristics was formed and then normalized to fall between 0 and 1. For details, see Armitage and others (1986).

Table B-1: Variables Used in at Least One of the Following Years: 1981, 1983, and 1985 (means with, where appropriate, standard deviations underneath)

Variable Description	Variable Definition	1981	1983	1985	1981-83	1983-85
Age	Student Age (in Years)	12.29 2.45	12.33 2.58	11.95 2.49	13.91 2.23	13.60 2.33
Agricultural productivity	Production (in 1000 cruzeiros) per hectare at the county level, in 1980. Data comes from IBGE.	0.50 0.40	0.43 0.39	0.42 0.38	0.42 0.37	0.42 0.38
Benefits (1)	The proportion of separate employment-related benefits the teacher receives.		0.49 0.24	0.55 0.56		
Ceara	1 If State is Ceara	0.28	0.34	0.35	0.19	0.24
Contract status (1)	1 if the teacher has a temporary contract	0.68	0.63	0.67		
Days absent last two months	Number of absences in the last two months (if the variable is missing, its value was set to the median, 5.3)	6.29 5.40				
EDURURAL - Pernambuco	1 if the county is in Pernambuco and it is in EDURURAL project	0.26	0.19	0.18	0.22	0.19
EDURURAL - Ceara	1 if the county is in Ceara and it is in EDURURAL project	0.18	0.21	0.23	0.07	0.13
EDURURAL - Piaui	1 if the county is in Piaui and it is in EDURURAL project	0.21	0.26	0.27	0.31	0.30
Electricity	1 if school has electricity	0.25	0.30	0.35	0.28	0.31
% Emergencia	Percentage of families whose head of the household work in the Emergencia Program		52.60 24.75		48.20 25.95	
Family size	Number of persons living in the household	7.51 2.67	7.92 2.76	7.76 2.77	8.14 2.83	7.65 2.70
Father's education	Level of father's formal education (For 1985, all responses greater than fourth grade were coded as fifth grade)	1.55 1.73	1.52 1.75	1.35 1.79	1.74 1.83	1.55 1.91
Federally operated	1 if it is a Federal School	0.00	0.00	0.00	0.00	0.00
Female classmates when female student	Proportion of female classmates if the student is female. Otherwise it is 0.	0.39 0.36	0.41 0.37	0.39 0.36	0.57 0.39	0.49 0.40
Female student	1 for female student	0.59	0.61	0.59	0.73	0.66
Female teacher/ female student	1 if the teacher and the student are both female	0.56	0.56	0.55	0.65	0.59
Fourth Grade	1 if the teacher teaches in the fourth grade	0.45	0.53	0.53		
Graded class	1 if it is a graded classroom	0.26	0.38	0.50	0.20	0.31
Hardware index	(FURN + FACIL + WATER + ELECT)/4	0.46 0.22	0.42 0.25	0.51 0.24	0.42 0.24	0.45 0.23
Homework	1 if the student does homework always		1.71	1.63	0.72	0.69

241

Table B-1 (Cont'd)

Variable Description	Variable Definition	1981	1983	1985	1981-83	1983-85
Logos teacher training	1 if teacher took Logos (in service training)	0.17	0.17	0.26	0.25	0.28
Male teacher/ male student	1 if the teacher and the student are both male	0.03	0.04	0.03	0.05	0.03
Mathematic test score in Second Grade	(See Annex 1)	45.73 26.58	51.18 24.94	49.19 25.04	50.06 24.55	51.06 24.68
Mathematics test score in Fourth Grade	(See Annex 1)				46.49 22.32	49.64 24.31
Mother's education	Level of mother's formal education (For 1985, all responses greater than fourth grade were coded as fifth grade)	1.94 2.04	2.00 2.15	1.83 2.08	2.29 2.36	2.10 2.21
Percent families not farming	Proportion of families not farming (measured at school level)	0.08 0.15	0.09 0.17	0.11 0.16	0.10 0.20	0.08 0.19
Number of students	Sum of the number of students in kindergarten through the fourth grade	76.51 61.61	79.73 63.94	83.39 66.51	87.53 60.83	72.71 50.07
OME	(See Note Below.)		0.42 0.21	0.40 0.23	0.44 0.22	0.41 0.27
On-time promotion	1 if the student is in second grade in the first sample year and has been promoted to fourth grade in the second sample year.	0.06	0.1			
Not farmer	1 if the head of the household doesn't work in agriculture	0.08	0.09	0.11	0.09	0.09
Percent female classmates	Proportion of female classmates	0.59 0.21	0.61 0.21	0.59 0.21	0.69 0.26	0.66 0.28
Piaui	1 if state is Piaui	0.29	0.35	0.35	0.47	0.43
Portuguese test score in Second Grade	(See appendix A)	48.81 27.71	58.69 23.64	59.59 25.19	58.53 22.18	60.49 23.29
Portuguese test score in Fourth Grade	(See appendix A)				51.73 17.87	50.70 19.85
Privately operated	1 if it is a private school	0.03	0.01	0.01	0.00	0.01
Pupil works	1 if student works (Wording of question varied slightly by year)	0.90	0.88	0.94	0.92	0.96
Pupil/ teacher ratio	Number of students divided by number of teachers in school	36.83 28.65	26.78 14.56	24.77 16.00	30.85 15.64	25.75 16.25
Qualificacao training	1983: 1 if teacher took Qualificacao training (inservice training)		0.15		0.13	

Table B-1 (Cont'd)

Variable Description	Variable Definition	1981	1983	1985	1981-83	1983-85
	1985: 1 if teacher took at least one "modulo" of Qualificacao training (inservice training)		0.24			0.22
Regular status (1)	1 if the teacher is a regular staff	0.18	0.23	0.16		
Relatively large landholders	Proportion of families own more than 35% of MODULO, a measure of minimum amount of land required to support a single family according to local land characteristics. MODULO is developed by IBGE	0.17 0.21	0.16 0.21	0.16 0.20	0.19 0.25	0.20 0.27
School facilities	(TWO OR MORE CLASSROOM + MULTIPURPOSE ROOM + PRINCIPAL OR SECRETARY OFFICE + KITCHEN + BATHROOM + STORAGE ROOM)/6 (1983), where each component of the index is a dummy variable.	0.36 0.23	0.42 0.28	0.59 0.25	0.41 0.27	0.46 0.28
School furniture	1981: (DESK FOR TEACHER + BOOKCASES + SEAT FOR ALL STUDENTS + PLACE TO WRITE FOR ALL STUDENTS)/4 , where each component of the index is a dummy variable.	0.54 0.32				
School lunch every day	1981: 1 if the school received lunch for all students	0.31				
	1983 and 1985: 1 if the school received lunch all year long		0.24	0.36	0.28	0.33
School lunch some days	1981: 1 if the school received lunch but not sufficient for all students	0.37				
	1983 and 1985: 1 if the school received lunch only some months these years.		0.69	0.63	0.69	0.66
School survival	1 if the school was operational in both sample years and there were second and fourth grade students in the base sample year.	0.58	0.69			
SES	(See Note Below)	0.21 0.24	0.19 0.21	0.19 0.21	0.19 0.21	0.20 0.25
% sold crops	Percentage of families who sell crops	21.31 14.56	10.75 11.59	43.71 23.89	11.41 12.37	42.87 23.14
Software index	1981: (TEXT + WRTMATA/2 + WRTMATB)/2	0.64 0.24				
	1983: (BOOKA/2 + BOOKB + WRMAT)/2		0.72 0.23		0.70 0.23	
	1985: (BOOKC/2 + BOOKD + WRMAT)/2			0.84 0.21		0.78 0.25
State operated	1 if state is a state school	0.12	0.13	0.12	0.16	0.16
Teacher activity index	(DRAMA + SINGING + MANUAL WORK + TELL STORIES + GAMES + TRIPS + GROUP STUDY + COMMEMORATIVES DAYS + CLEAN SCHOOL) / 10 , where each component of the index is a dummy variable.	0.44 0.22	0.52 0.22	0.48 0.23	0.54 0.21	0.50 0.23

243

Table B-1 (Cont'd)

Variable Description	Variable Definition	1981	1983	1985	1981-83	1983-85
Teacher materials index	(OTHER TEXTBOOK + MATERIAL WROTE BY TEACHER + MATERIAL WROTE BY STUDENTS + POSTER + MAPS) / 6 , where each component of the index is a dummy variable.	0.36 0.25	0.41 0.24	0.41 0.27	0.47 0.25	0.49 0.27
Teacher salary	Teacher salary as a percentage of the minimum wage	55.76 49.28	58.25 55.96	53.45 57.24	76.50 67.18	66.90 63.32
Teacher salary -- Pernambuco	Teacher salary as a percentage of the minimum wage if the state is Pernambuco. Otherwise it is 0	29.15 46.28	19.97 36.97	18.09 36.88	21.25 38.38	25.53 47.67
Teacher salary -- Ceara	Teacher salary as a percentage of the minimum wage if the state is Ceara. Otherwise it is 0	5.74 14.07	6.20 14.94	6.47 15.35	4.67 13.90	5.73 22.25
Teacher Salary -- Piaui	Teacher salary as a percentage of the minimum wage if the state is Piaui. Otherwise it is 0	20.88 43.36	32.08 58.89	28.89 57.74	50.57 75.35	35.64 61.38
Teacher's house	1 if the school is in the teacher's house	0.17	0.12	0.09	0.08	0.09
Teacher's mathematics test score	(See appendix A)		79.17	21.06	84.60	14.90
Teacher's Portuguese test score	(See appendix A)			73.28 16.36		76.44 13.94
Textbooks used in classroom	1 if teacher uses textbook in classroom	0.88				
Textbook used in classroom	1983: 1 if student uses the textbook some days a week		0.29		0.36	
	1985: 1 if student has book but uses it only at school			0.04		0.02
	1983: 1 if student uses textbook everyday		0.57		0.48	
	1985: 1 if student has book and uses it at school and at home			0.85		0.78
Water	1 if school has drinkable water	0.71	0.35	0.43	0.38	0.37
Writing materials index	(CHALK + (NOTEBOOK + PENCIL + ERASER + COLORED PENCIL)/2)/5, where the first component of the index is a dummy which is equal to 1 if the school received chalk, and the other one is 2 if the school received the material for everyone, 1 if the school received the material only for some students, and 0 if the school did not receive the material.	0.71 0.29	0.80 0.26	0.73 0.28	0.76 0.29	
Writing materials for all	1 if school received writing material for all the students	0.16				
Writing materials for some	1 if school received writing material only for some students	0.48				

244

Table B-1 (Cont'd)

Variable Description	Variable Definition	1981	1983	1985	1981-83	1983-85
Years behind grade	Student age - age started school - current grade	2.13 2.01	2.40 2.14	2.44 2.14	2.21 2.01	
Years in county	Number of years that the family has been living in the county	27.61 16.13	26.33 15.62	23.37 14.59	27.05 14.95	26.81 14.20
Years teachers education	Level of teacher's formal education	7.00 3.00	7.19 2.95	7.53 3.01	7.94 2.79	8.14 2.97
Years teachers experience	Year of teacher's experience as a teacher	7.67 6.88	8.02 6.63	8.60 7.30	9.73 8.27	9.28 7.64

Table B-2: Variables Used in the 1987 Sample
(means with standard deviations underneath)

Variable Description	Variable Definition	1985-87
Age	Student's age	14.02 2.18
Dropout Behavior (1)	1 if the student dropped out	0.18
EDURURAL	1 if the county is in the EDURURAL project	0.58 0.49
Fourth Grade in 1987	1 if students is in 4th grade in 1987	0.55 0.5
Height-for-age	Percentage of height-for-age according to the standard norm	94.71 4.62
Mathematics test 1985	(See appendix A)	57.31 22.82
Mathematics test 1987	(See appendix A)	72.65 20.05
Migration (1)	1 if the student migrated	0.22
Portuguese test 1985	(See appendix A)	69.96 20.29
Portuguese test 1987	(See appendix A)	85.15 14.44
Sex	Student's sex (1 for female)	0.63 0.48
Skinfold-for-age 50%-60% Norm	1 if the skinfold-for-age is in between 50% and 60% of the standard norm	0.15 0.36
Skinfold-for-age Lt 50% Norm	1 if the skinfold-for-age is less than 50% of the standard norm	0.13 0.33
Third grade in 1987	1 if students is in 3rd grade in 1987	0.29 0.46
Visual 60	1 if the visual accuity is equal or less than 60%	0.06 0.25
Weight-for-age 80% Norm	1 if the weight-for-age is between 75% and 80% of the standard norm	0.09 0.29
Weight-for-height < 75% Norm	1 if the weight-for-age is equal or less than 75% of the standard norm	0.12 0.32

(1) The mean was calculated on the full sample in 1987 (732 cases) whether the student was tested in 1987 or not.

C

Statistical Appendix

IN THE FOLLOWING TABLES, empty cells reporting results of multivariate statistical analysis indicate that the variable in question was not included in that particular equation.

Table C3-1: Sizes of Samples, by Year, State, Program Status, and Grade, 1981, 1983, and 1985

	1981				1983				1985			
	PI	CE	PE	Total	PI	CE	PE	Total	PI	CE	PE	Total
Schools												
EDURURAL	124	164	109	397	129	164	111	404	142	180	125	447
Old school									130	167	112	409
Newly built school									12	13	13	38
OTHER	47	77	65	189	48	80	67	195	48	80	67	195
Total	171	241	174	586	177	244	178	599	190	260	192	642
Teachers												
EDURURAL	163	191	109	463	180	183	136	499	206	224	176	606
Old school									190	205	160	555
Newly built school									16	19	16	51
OTHER	69	97	65	231	77	109	92	278	81	113	97	291
Total	232	288	174	694	257	292	228	777	287	337	273	897
Pupils												
2nd grade												
EDURURAL	989	829	1219	3037	1027	828	764	2619	1154	977	819	2950
Old school									1051	918	723	2692
Newly built school									103	59	96	258
OTHER	392	488	801	1681	358	510	482	1350	359	564	495	1418
Total	1381	1317	2020	4718	1385	1338	1246	3969	1513	1541	1314	4368
4th grade												
EDURURAL	380	184	511	1075	484	186	327	997	490	374	409	1273
Old school									454	340	379	1173
Newly built school									36	34	30	100
OTHER	152	139	348	639	185	166	229	580	181	214	236	631
Total	532	323	859	1714	669	352	556	1577	671	588	645	1904

Note: PI indicates Piaui, CE indicates Ceara, and PE indicates Pernambuco.

248

Table C3-2: Percentage Distribution of Samples, by Year, State, Program Status, and Grade, 1981, 1983, and 1985

	1981				1983				1985			
	PI	CE	PE	Total	PI	CE	PE	Total	PI	CE	PE	Total
Schools												
EDURURAL	21	28	19	68	22	27	19	67	22	28	19	70
Old school									20	26	17	64
Newly built school									2	2	2	6
OTHER	8	13	11	32	8	13	11	33	7	12	10	30
Total	29	41	30	100	30	41	30	100	30	40	30	100
Teachers												
EDURURAL	23	28	16	67	23	24	18	64	23	25	20	68
Old school									21	23	18	62
Newly built school									2	2	2	6
OTHER	10	14	9	33	10	14	12	36	9	13	11	32
Total	33	41	25	100	33	38	29	100	32	38	30	100
Pupils												
2nd grade												
EDURURAL	21	18	26	64	26	21	19	66	26	22	19	68
Old school									24	21	17	62
Newly built school									2	1	2	6
OTHER	8	10	17	36	9	13	12	34	8	13	11	32
Total	29	28	43	100	35	34	31	100	35	35	30	100
4th grade												
EDURURAL	22	11	30	63	31	12	21	63	26	20	21	67
Old school									24	18	20	62
Newly built school									2	2	2	5
OTHER	9	8	20	37	12	11	15	37	10	11	12	33
Total	31	19	50	100	42	22	35	100	35	31	34	100

Note: PI indicates Piaui, CE indicates Ceara, and PE indicates Pernambuco.

Table C3-3: Student Flows in Brazilian Primary Schools, 1982

	Brazil	Rest of Brazil (a)	Northeast	Urban northeast	Rural northeast	Rest of rural northeast (a)	Low-income rural northeast
Population (percent)	100.00%	66.50%	33.50%	16.90%	16.60%	2.40%	14.20%
As proportion of age cohort							
Grade 1							
Repeaters	1.044	0.814	1.500	1.225	1.819	1.807	1.821
Promotees	0.862	0.939	0.710	0.848	0.552	0.866	0.499
Dropouts	0.038	0.015	0.083	0.054	0.125	0.013	0.144
New entrants	0.900	0.954	0.792	0.901	0.677	0.878	0.643
Grade 2							
Repeaters	0.433	0.360	0.577	0.612	0.583	0.778	0.550
Promotees	0.806	0.897	0.625	0.789	0.418	0.785	0.356
Dropouts	0.056	0.042	0.084	0.058	0.134	0.081	0.143
Grade 3							
Repeaters	0.282	0.242	0.361	0.392	0.381	0.493	0.362
Promotees	0.729	0.827	0.534	0.723	0.291	0.664	0.228
Dropouts	0.078	0.071	0.091	0.066	0.127	0.121	0.128
Grade 4							
Repeaters	0.186	0.156	0.246	0.310	0.226	0.285	0.216
Promotees	0.561	0.639	0.406	0.609	0.142	0.432	0.093
Dropouts	0.168	0.188	0.128	0.114	0.149	0.232	0.135
As proportion of enrollment							
Grade 1							
Repeaters	0.537	0.461	0.654	0.576	0.729	0.673	0.739
Promotees	0.443	0.531	0.310	0.399	0.221	0.322	0.203
Dropouts	0.020	0.009	0.036	0.025	0.050	0.005	0.058
Grade 2							
Repeaters	0.334	0.277	0.449	0.419	0.514	0.473	0.524
Promotees	0.622	0.690	0.486	0.541	0.368	0.477	0.339
Dropouts	0.043	0.032	0.065	0.040	0.118	0.049	0.136
Grade 3							
Repeaters	0.259	0.212	0.366	0.332	0.477	0.386	0.504
Promotees	0.669	0.725	0.542	0.612	0.364	0.519	0.318
Dropouts	0.072	0.063	0.092	0.056	0.159	0.095	0.178
Grade 4							
Repeaters	0.203	0.158	0.315	0.300	0.437	0.301	0.486
Promotees	0.613	0.650	0.521	0.590	0.275	0.455	0.209
Dropouts	0.184	0.191	0.164	0.110	0.288	0.244	0.304

(a) Statistics for these two columns are calculated from the Profluxo material on the assumption that the grade-specific distribution of population by regions is the same as the distribution of the total population. Since this is clearly not precisely true, the data in these two columns must be considered approximate.

Source: PNAD82 as utilized in Philip R. Fletcher and Sergio Costa Ribeiro, "Profluxo: The Brazilian Education Reality", IPEA, Brasilia, 1986. Note that the PNAD82 sample excludes the rural north region entirely.

Table C3-4: Flow Efficiency of Brazilian Primary Schools, 1982

	Brazil	Rest of Brazil (a)	Urban Northeast	Rural northeast	Rest of rural northeast (a)	Low-income rural northeast
Years of schooling services required for: Entry of one student into: (b)						
Grade 2	2.3	1.9	3.2	2.5	4.5	3.1	5.0
Grade 3	4.1	3.4	5.9	4.6	9.4	5.8	10.7
Grade 4	6.1	5.1	9.2	6.9	18.0	9.3	22.6
Grade 5	9.6	8.2	14.7	10.2	45.7	17.2	70.7
Progression of one student from grade 2 to grade 4	3.3	3.0	4.3	3.7	6.6	4.4	7.8
Average years to attain grade 4 (c)	5.0	4.5	6.3	5.6	7.6	6.6	7.9

Note:
(a) See appendix table C3-3, note a.
(b) Calculations use promotion and dropout rates from table 3.3 and assume students leave after five years of repetition.
(c) Averages pertain to just those students actually reaching grade 4.

Table C4-1: Probit Models of School Survival, 1981 and 1983
(t-statistics underneath)

Variable	1981 (1)	1981 (2)	1983 (3)	1983 (4)	1981 Mean (a)	1983 Mean (a)
County Characteristics						
Agricultural Productivity	0.0015	-0.0407	-0.5656	-0.6298	0.497	0.4319
	0.0	-0.4	-3.8	-4.3	0.404	0.385
Percentage selling crops	-0.0027	-0.0020	-0.0001	0.0009	21.38	10.74
	-1.7	-1.2	0.0	0.3	14.59	11.60
Participation in Emergencia			-0.0111	-0.0118	n.a.	52.63
			-6.0	-6.4		24.74
School characteristics						
Number of students	0.0032	0.0037	0.0048	0.0058	77.197	79.78
	7.2	9.0	7.4	9.3	61.48	64.05
HARD		0.0026		0.1796	1.858	1.6629
		0.1		5.9	0.880	0.9990
Facilities	0.0747		0.6196		0.356	0.4176
	0.7		5.0		0.229	0.276
Furnishings	0.2306		0.4670		0.5395	0.5948
	3.2		4.2		0.317	0.273
Electricity	0.1472		0.2051		0.2498	0.2967
	2.8		3.2		0.433	0.457
Water	-0.2650		-0.1092		0.7124	0.3538
	-5.4		-1.9		0.453	0.478
Teacher's house	-0.5073	-0.6498	-0.2474	-0.4449	0.1678	0.1195
	-7.9	-11.0	-2.9	-5.6	0.374	0.324
OME			-0.2745	-0.2328	n.a.	0.4233
			-2.2	-1.8		0.210
State						
Piaui	0.1269	-0.0022	0.5494	0.6142	0.2938	0.351
	1.1	0.0	2.9	3.2	0.456	0.477
Ceara	-0.4816	-0.4351	-0.6570	-0.5403	0.2776	0.3352
	-4.9	-4.5	-3.8	-3.2	0.448	0.472
School Control						
State	-0.0865	-0.0543	0.0093	-0.0355	0.1172	0.1305
	-1.2	-0.8	0.1	-0.4	0.322	0.337
Federal	3.4163	3.4770	1.2382	1.4135	0.0043	0.0026
	0.4	0.4	0.1	0.1	0.066	0.050
Private	0.0679	-0.0317	-0.8603	-1.0040	0.0322	0.0102
	0.6	-0.3	-3.8	-4.7	0.176	0.101
Program states						
EDURURAL: Pernambuco	0.0991	0.0993	0.0353	0.1498	0.2558	0.1917
	1.6	1.6	0.4	1.5	0.436	0.394
EDURURAL: Piaui	-0.1963	-0.1412	-0.5154	-0.5276	0.2109	0.260
	-2.2	-1.6	-3.8	-3.9	0.408	0.439
EDURURAL: Ceara	-0.6663	-0.6841	-0.7754	-0.8456	0.1749	0.209
	-8.3	-8.6	-6.5	-7.2	0.380	0.407
Constant	0.3692	0.3721	1.0775	1.2508	1.00	1.00
	3.4	3.5	5.9	7.2		
Sample size	4,632	4,632	3,917	3,917		
Mean probability	0.591	0.591	0.697	0.697		
Log likelihood	-2645.3	-2666.6	-1645.0	-1665.0		

(a) Standard deviations are shown under the means.

Table C4-2: Probit Models of School Promotion, 1981, and 1983
(t-statistics underneath)

Variable	1981 (1)	1981 (2)	1983 (3)	1983 (4)	1981 Mean (a)	1983 Mean (a)
Personal characteristics						
Sex	0.2357	0.2393	0.1949	0.1968	0.587	0.6015
	3.0	3.1	2.8	2.8	0.493	0.490
Age	-0.0497	-0.0496	-0.0920	-0.0946	12.15	12.069
	-3.1	-3.0	-6.3	-6.4	2.41	2.55
Portuguese test	0.0104	0.0105	0.0138	0.0136	45.70	56.83
	5.6	5.6	7.2	7.0	27.61	23.86
Mathematics test	0.002	0.0023	0.0048	0.0051	42.94	48.47
	1.1	1.2	2.9	3.0	26.29	24.41
Family characteristics						
Mother's education	0.0271	0.0283	0.0376	0.0393	1.98	2.05
	1.7	1.7	2.7	2.8	2.11	2.30
Years in county	0.0068	0.0065	0.0078	0.0078	27.01	25.82
	3.0	2.9	3.8	3.7	15.89	15.51
School characteristics						
Number of students	-0.0014	-0.0014	-0.0042	-0.0042	89.76	91.69
	-2.5	-2.3	-6.5	-6.2	63.88	66.93
State						
Piaui	0.5538	0.6949	0.1683	0.3348	0.3398	0.442
	6.6	4.7	2.2	2.6	0.474	0.497
Ceara	0.2379	0.4132	-0.0112	0.0222	0.1578	0.1905
	2.7	2.9	-0.1	0.2	0.365	0.393
School control						
State		-0.0289		-0.0238	0.126	0.8279
		-0.3		-0.1	0.332	0.378
Federal		-0.1787		-0.0908	0.0073	0.161
		-0.5		-0.2	0.085	0.368
Private		0.2980		0.231	0.0267	0.0037
		1.3		0.3	0.161	0.060
Program status						
EDURURAL	-0.1473		-0.0503		0.605	0.6205
	-2.0		-0.1		0.489	0.485
EDURURAL: Pernambuco		-0.031		0.0518	0.2996	0.2187
		-0.3		0.5	0.458	0.413
EDURURAL: Piaui		-0.2181		-0.1684	0.234	0.3187
		-1.3		-1.6	0.423	0.466
EDURURAL: Ceara		-0.2828		-0.0146	0.0712	0.0831
		-1.7		-0.1	0.251	0.276
Constant	-1.8187	-1.9209	-1.1958	-1.211	1.00	1.00
	-7.7	-7.8	-5.5	-2.7		
Sample size	2737	2737	2730	2730		
Mean Promotion Probability	0.091	0.091	0.139	0.139		
Log Likelihood	-757.9	-755.8	-975.6	-974.1		

(a) Standard deviations are shown under the means.

Table C4-3: Probit Models of On-time Promotion, Migration, and Dropout Behavior, 1985-87
(t statistics underneath)

Variable	On-time Promotion (1)	On-time Promotion (2)	Migration (1)	Migration (2)	Dropout Behavior (1)	Dropout Behavior (2)
Sex	0.0209	0.0102	0.1644		-0.0715	-0.0761
	0.24	0.12	1.41		-0.50	-0.53
Age	-0.1087	-0.1145	0.0616		0.1786	0.1737
	-5.63	-5.76	2.62		5.49	5.38
Portuguese test	0.0124	0.0120	0.0072	0.0070	-0.0055	-0.0054
	4.08	3.89	1.95	1.96	-1.33	-1.31
Mathematics test	0.0037	0.0027	0.0033	0.0021	-0.0033	-0.0035
	1.56	1.14	1.04	0.72	-0.83	-0.91
Mother's education	0.0624	0.0584	0.0216		-0.0779	-0.0067
	3.27	3.03	0.85		-2.25	-1.93
Years in county	0.0072	0.0071	-0.0051	-0.0059	-0.0080	
	2.42	2.35	-1.31	-1.51	-1.59	
Number of students	0.0031	0.0037	-0.0005		-0.0002	
	5.71	6.27	-0.58		-0.16	
EDURURAL	-0.5247	-0.4957	0.0707		0.0411	
	-6.17	-4.65	0.62		0.29	
Family size		0.0090		-0.0491		
		0.59		-2.44		
Agricultural productivity		-0.1046		-1.639		
		-0.27		-3.60		
SES county		-1.422		-0.6118		
		-3.75		-0.56		
Not farmer		0.1824				-0.7427
		1.46				-2.51
Constant	-1.023	-0.7386	-2.229	-0.3226	-2.22	-2.289
	3.32	-1.84	-5.69	-0.91	-4.55	-4.86
Sample size	1,506	1,506	706	706	535	535
Mean probability	0.168	0.168	0.235	0.235	0.193	0.193
Log likelihood	-591.2	-580.6	-371.2	-366.5	-234.8	-232.3

Table C4-4: Ordered Probit Estimates of Promotion
Promotion to Grade Three or Grade Four, 1985-87
(t statistics underneath)

Variable	1985-87
Sex	-0.0374
	-0.26
Age	-0.1133
	-3.20
Portuguese test	0.0255
	5.93
Mathematics test	-0.0013
	-0.35
Mother's education	0.0686
	2.07
Years in county	0.0029
	0.54
Number of students	0.0010
	0.97
MU	1.371
	12.40
Constant	1.228
	2.39
Sample size	404
Mean promotion probability - Grade 3	0.322
Mean promotion probability - Grade 4	0.592
Log likelihood	-308.2

Table C5-1: Comparison of Alternative Estimation Strategies, Fourth Grade
Portuguese, 1981-83

	Level Form		Value-added Form		
Variable Description	OLS (1)	SELECT (2)	OLS (3)	SELECT (4)	IV-SELECT (5)
State					
Ceara	22.717	19.624	16.759	19.223	22.261
	4.44	1.36	3.59	3.46	3.56
Piaui	10.634	-0.675	10.324	11.977	14.092
	2.06	-0.05	2.20	1.90	2.07
OME	-9.091	-9.132	-7.191	-6.397	-10.600
	-1.41	-1.37	-1.23	-1.16	-1.84
Program states					
EDURURAL: Pernambuco	1.161	2.584	-0.320	-1.125	1.398
	0.26	0.24	-0.08	-0.25	0.27
EDURURAL: Ceara	-1.890	2.998	-6.454	-4.297	-6.768
	-0.33	0.24	-1.25	-0.70	-1.04
EDURURAL: Piaui	1.365	3.461	-0.541	-0.563	0.438
	0.33	0.41	-0.14	-0.14	0.10
Personal characteristics					
Female student	4.795	-0.287	7.385	7.889	5.740
	0.59	-0.02	1.00	1.05	0.74
Age	0.008	0.844	-0.081	-0.404	-0.470
	0.01	0.45	-0.16	-0.55	-0.56
Pupil works	-12.003	-11.648	-12.773	-12.712	-12.897
	-2.70	-2.61	-3.19	-3.37	-3.20
Joint characteristics: pupil and school					
Portuguese test score, 1981			0.237	0.285	0.303
			4.03	2.37	2.24
Mathematics test score, 1981			0.142	0.142	0.132
			2.64	2.07	1.71
Homework	6.900	6.185	4.760	4.524	4.425
	2.64	2.30	2.01	2.02	1.96
Male teacher/male student	-5.234	0.862	0.323	1.030	0.009
	-0.92	0.16	0.06	0.21	0.00
Female teacher/female student	-3.405	-3.993	-4.835	-5.430	-4.731
	-0.67	-0.76	-1.05	-1.25	-1.08
Peer influences					
Percent families not farming	14.502	16.225	13.948	13.970	14.468
	2.44	2.85	2.60	2.77	2.73
Relatively large landholders	10.339	7.689	7.500	7.368	8.262
	2.11	1.44	1.69	1.76	1.94

	Level Form		Value-added Form		
Variable Description	OLS (1)	SELECT (2)	OLS (3)	SELECT (4)	IV-SELECT (5)
Percent female classmates	5.901	7.420	9.996	8.453	8.019
	0.57	0.68	1.07	0.96	0.88
Female classmates when female student	1.638	0.840	-0.972	0.275	1.165
	0.14	0.07	-0.09	0.03	0.11
School characteristics					
Graded class	0.428	-1.334	-0.601	-1.680	-2.330
	0.14	-0.42	-0.22	-0.63	-0.83
Pupil-teacher ratio	0.141	0.160	0.116	0.123	0.132
	1.55	1.61	1.41	1.58	1.63
School hardware index	13.674	15.352	13.798	11.728	12.632
	2.44	2.50	2.72	2.36	2.51
School software index	0.481	0.460	-3.202	-3.020	-2.302
	0.08	0.07	-0.58	-0.57	-0.43
Teacher characteristics					
Years teacher's education	0.195	-0.453	-0.239	-0.334	-0.328
	0.41	-0.97	-0.55	-0.80	-0.75
Years teacher's experience	0.255	0.217	0.212	0.198	0.237
	1.69	1.45	1.56	1.54	1.74
Logos II teacher training	0.386	0.246	1.558	2.000	2.636
	0.12	0.07	0.53	0.71	0.92
Qualificacao teacher training	-1.150	0.586	0.871	1.022	0.246
	-0.33	0.17	0.28	0.35	0.08
Promotion selection		-24.970		5.537	6.797
		-1.34		0.52	0.58
School survival selection		-15.333		-6.075	-4.806
		-0.85		-0.87	-0.63
Constant	27.210	78.719	15.910	12.252	8.693
	2.34	1.83	1.50	0.49	0.32
Adjusted R squared	0.190	0.295	0.347	0.346	0.356
Number of cases	227	227	227	227	212
Mean of dependent variable	51.172	51.172	51.172	51.172	

Table C5-2: Comparison of Alternative Estimation Strategies, Fourth Grade
Mathematics, 1981-83

	Level Form		Value-added Form		
Variable Description	OLS (1)	SELECT (2)	OLS (3)	SELECT (4)	IV-SELECT (5)
State					
Ceara	14.889	12.627	9.597	11.224	13.731
	2.35	1.20	1.61	0.83	0.81
Piaui	7.456	0.568	9.855	18.384	20.938
	1.17	0.06	1.65	1.32	1.25
OME	-10.157	-10.288	-6.275	-5.118	-6.624
	-1.27	-1.32	-0.84	-0.69	-0.83
Program states					
EDURURAL: Pernambuco	8.020	8.924	7.673	4.987	8.932
	1.44	1.09	1.49	0.47	0.68
EDURURAL: Ceara	8.433	10.894	5.331	1.629	-2.615
	1.19	1.10	0.81	0.13	-0.18
EDURURAL: Piaui	5.558	6.769	2.622	0.558	1.937
	1.08	1.00	0.55	0.07	0.20
Personal characteristics					
Female student	-1.035	-4.057	3.192	7.922	5.834
	-0.10	-0.36	0.34	0.62	0.41
Age	-0.653	-0.120	-0.797	-1.704	-2.193
	-0.91	-0.09	-1.19	-0.91	-0.93
Pupil works	-6.964	-6.790	-6.826	-7.579	-7.583
	-1.27	-1.28	-1.34	-1.53	-1.44
Joint characteristics: pupil and school					
Portuguese test score, 1981			0.041	0.241	0.298
			0.55	0.76	0.75
Mathematics test score, 1981			0.319	0.340	0.373
			4.63	1.74	1.56
Homework	8.336	7.913	6.353	5.616	4.870
	2.57	2.53	2.10	1.93	1.68
Male teacher/male student	-0.956	2.615	3.696	2.913	3.704
	-0.14	0.38	0.56	0.45	0.56
Female teacher/female student	-3.519	-3.790	-5.924	-6.494	-6.835
	-0.56	-0.62	-1.01	-1.10	-1.14
Peer influences					
Percent families not farming	18.559	19.575	16.518	15.471	16.474
	2.52	2.80	2.41	2.38	2.46
Relatively large landholders	20.084	18.523	16.027	16.736	16.587
	3.31	3.10	2.83	2.92	2.90

Table C5-2 Cont'd

Variable Description	Level Form		Value-added Form		
	OLS (1)	SELECT (2)	OLS (3)	SELECT (4)	IV-SELECT (5)
Percent female classmates	26.626	27.852	26.805	27.089	28.214
	2.08	2.21	2.25	2.26	2.35
Female classmates when female student	-17.850	-18.571	-17.808	-17.893	-16.048
	-1.21	-1.31	-1.30	-1.33	-1.18
School characteristics					
Graded class	6.117	5.221	5.099	4.811	6.059
	1.63	1.39	1.47	1.33	1.56
Pupil-teacher ratio	0.278	0.289	0.206	0.200	0.199
	2.48	2.61	1.96	1.88	1.85
School hardware index	13.173	14.481	10.776	8.321	7.885
	1.90	2.06	1.66	1.30	1.24
School software index	0.614	0.534	-4.446	-5.580	-4.477
	0.08	0.07	-0.63	-0.79	-0.61
Teacher characteristics					
Years teacher's education	0.567	0.192	0.351	0.456	0.353
	0.97	0.33	0.64	0.84	0.63
Years teacher's experience	0.300	0.279	0.225	0.226	0.327
	1.61	1.56	1.30	1.31	1.79
Logos II teacher training	-0.783	-0.895	-0.556	0.720	1.573
	-0.19	-0.23	-0.15	0.19	0.41
Qualificacao teacher training	0.775	1.797	3.196	2.962	1.854
	0.18	0.43	0.80	0.74	0.47
Promotion selection		-15.380		22.396	27.589
		-1.23		0.85	0.85
School survival selection		-8.115		4.713	6.263
		-0.62		0.28	0.32
Constant	14.910	45.311	7.230	-37.530	-47.776
	1.03	1.47	0.53	-0.60	-0.64
Adjusted R squared	0.183	0.202	0.299	0.305	0.357
Number of cases	227	227	227	227	212
Mean of dependent variable	45.648	45.648	45.648	45.648	

259

Table C5-3: Comparison of Alternative Estimation Strategies, Fourth Grade
Portuguese, 1983-85

| | Level Form | | Value-added Form | | |
Variable Description	OLS (1)	SELECT (2)	OLS (3)	SELECT (4)	IV-SELECT (5)
State					
Ceara	23.124	21.794	19.212	18.674	18.650
	5.28	2.47	5.16	5.10	5.07
Piaui	15.233	14.025	15.718	16.583	16.530
	3.57	1.66	4.29	4.45	4.42
OME	3.398	7.813	8.131	8.040	7.894
	0.79	1.76	2.23	2.28	2.23
Program states					
EDURURAL: Pernambuco	6.923	13.742	11.978	11.884	11.816
	1.74	1.75	3.54	3.57	3.54
EDURURAL: Ceara	-4.587	0.503	-5.336	-6.694	-6.329
	-1.18	0.05	-1.64	-1.79	-1.66
EDURURAL: Piaui	-3.180	-0.966	-3.450	-4.289	-4.228
	-1.04	-0.13	-1.33	-1.54	-1.52
Personal characteristics					
Female student	6.346	2.814	4.762	4.702	4.946
	1.06	0.32	0.95	0.97	1.02
Age	-1.282	0.166	-1.346	-1.371	-1.394
	-2.81	0.14	-3.50	-3.08	-3.12
Pupil works	-5.182	-5.458	-5.671	-5.721	-5.643
	-1.02	-1.18	-1.33	-1.40	-1.37
Joint characteristics: pupil and school					
Portuguese test score, 1983			0.430	0.434	0.431
			8.39	6.59	6.51
Mathematics test score, 1983			0.129	0.132	0.131
			3.23	3.28	3.26
Homework	1.780	2.189	2.028	1.926	1.924
	0.88	1.14	1.20	1.18	1.17
Male teacher/male student	7.161	9.743	8.816	8.907	8.968
	1.39	2.15	2.04	2.14	2.15
Female teacher/female student	-0.421	-0.499	-0.811	-0.854	-0.862
	-0.10	-0.13	-0.24	-0.26	-0.27
Peer influences					
Percent families not farming	13.913	11.059	9.831	10.123	9.956
	2.49	2.02	2.08	2.23	2.18
Relatively large landholders	4.446	0.183	0.775	0.191	-0.009
	1.19	0.04	0.25	0.06	0.00

Table C5-3 Cont'd

Variable Description	Level Form		Value-added Form		
	OLS (1)	SELECT (2)	OLS (3)	SELECT (4)	IV-SELECT (5)
Percent female classmates	4.192	-0.193	-0.219	-0.483	-0.660
	0.69	-0.03	-0.04	-0.10	-0.13
Female classmates when female student	-2.490	-0.447	2.293	2.596	2.280
	-0.32	-0.06	0.35	0.41	0.36
School characteristics					
Graded class	-2.933	-2.128	-4.108	-3.873	-3.948
	-1.21	-0.69	-2.02	-1.95	-1.97
Pupil-teacher ratio	0.014	-0.068	-0.107	-0.107	-0.109
	0.20	-0.86	-1.80	-1.88	-1.89
School hardware index	3.401	10.003	7.813	8.778	8.690
	0.75	2.14	2.04	2.21	2.18
School software index	4.042	4.808	6.427	6.689	6.834
	0.92	1.09	1.73	1.87	1.91
Teacher characteristics					
Years teacher's education	-0.311	-0.128	-0.132	-0.134	-0.132
	-0.89	-0.39	-0.45	-0.48	-0.47
Years teacher's experience	0.076	0.058	0.052	0.063	0.066
	0.58	0.47	0.47	0.59	0.61
Logos II teacher training	-1.111	-0.719	-0.139	-0.224	-0.279
	-0.53	-0.37	-0.08	-0.13	-0.16
Qualificacao teacher training	-6.759	-3.172	-2.158	-2.211	-2.337
	-2.77	-1.17	-1.03	-1.10	-1.15
Teacher's Portuguese test score	0.226	0.223	0.172	0.172	0.174
	2.65	2.76	2.37	2.49	2.50
Teacher's mathematics test score	0.283	0.287	0.192	0.185	0.170
	2.49	2.34	2.01	2.00	1.80
Promotion selection		-24.214		0.309	0.084
		-2.19		0.08	0.02
School survival selection		-5.865		3.413	3.248
		-0.46		0.72	0.68
Constant	3.540	18.443	-22.357	-24.008	-21.812
	0.25	0.77	-1.84	-1.86	-1.66
Adjusted R squared	0.195	0.333	0.432	0.430	0.427
Number of cases	349	349	349	349	346
Mean of dependent variable	47.218	47.218	47.218	47.218	

Table C5-4: Comparison of Alternative Estimation Strategies,
Fourth Grade Mathematics, 1983-85

	Level Form		Value-added Form		
	OLS	SELECT	OLS	SELECT	IV-SELECT
Variable Description	(1)	(2)	(3)	(4)	(5)
State					
Ceara	22.832	23.560	21.911	23.775	23.645
	3.86	1.91	4.56	4.54	4.53
Piaui	5.756	0.174	12.703	9.779	9.800
	1.00	0.02	2.69	1.83	1.84
OME	-1.294	5.222	6.821	7.436	7.570
	-0.22	0.80	1.45	1.57	1.59
Program states					
EDURURAL: Pernambuco	-0.593	9.107	7.900	8.970	9.042
	-0.11	0.83	1.81	1.89	1.91
EDURURAL: Ceara	-6.629	6.505	-9.267	-3.997	-3.737
	-1.27	0.48	-2.20	-0.75	-0.70
EDURURAL: Piaui	4.619	11.480	1.288	4.325	4.284
	1.12	1.09	0.38	1.06	1.05
Personal characteristics					
Female student	-14.919	-19.268	-13.257	-13.582	-13.844
	-1.85	-1.58	-2.04	-2.08	-2.12
Age	-1.414	0.596	-1.806	-1.431	-1.432
	-2.30	0.36	-3.64	-2.26	-2.28
Pupil works	-6.092	-6.242	-7.030	-6.874	-6.934
	-0.89	-1.01	-1.27	-1.31	-1.31
Joint characteristics: pupil and school					
Portuguese test score, 1983			0.262	0.199	0.206
			3.96	1.85	1.94
Mathematics test score, 1983			0.486	0.464	0.465
			9.44	7.21	7.39
Homework	3.661	4.690	3.383	3.747	3.786
	1.35	1.83	1.55	1.79	1.80
Male teacher/male student	8.415	11.436	9.878	9.920	9.772
	1.21	1.78	1.77	1.83	1.79
Female teacher/female student	4.549	4.667	5.669	5.838	5.824
	0.84	0.89	1.30	1.39	1.38
Peer influences					
Percent families not farming	9.757	4.466	7.715	6.744	6.807
	1.29	0.59	1.27	1.14	1.15
Relatively large landholders	1.355	-1.585	-1.779	-0.405	-0.207
	0.27	-0.26	-0.44	-0.10	-0.05

Table C5-4 Cont'd

Variable Description	Level Form		Value-added Form		
	OLS (1)	SELECT (2)	OLS (3)	SELECT (4)	IV-SELECT (5)
Percent female classmates	-1.196	-5.870	-5.119	-4.662	-4.667
	-0.15	-0.71	-0.77	-0.72	-0.72
Female classmates when female student	5.131	6.542	8.504	7.407	7.692
	0.49	0.58	1.00	0.90	0.93
School characteristics					
Graded class	-3.986	-4.126	-5.767	-6.186	-6.322
	-1.22	-0.97	-2.20	-2.36	-2.39
Pupil-teacher ratio	0.110	-0.003	-0.061	-0.063	-0.060
	1.17	-0.03	-0.80	-0.85	-0.80
School hardware index	10.596	14.814	14.559	12.404	12.498
	1.73	2.24	2.94	2.38	2.39
School software index	10.379	10.220	11.964	11.028	10.895
	1.75	1.68	2.50	2.37	2.33
Teacher characteristics					
Years teacher's education	-0.341	-0.082	-0.102	-0.080	-0.079
	-0.73	-0.18	-0.27	-0.22	-0.22
Years teacher's experience	0.368	0.289	0.299	0.263	0.262
	2.07	1.66	2.09	1.89	1.87
Logos II teacher training	-0.668	0.305	0.430	0.655	0.691
	-0.24	0.11	0.19	0.30	0.31
Qualificacao teacher training	-14.094	-8.856	-6.282	-5.936	-5.850
	-4.28	-2.42	-2.32	-2.29	-2.24
Teacher's Portuguese test score	-0.067	-0.079	-0.186	-0.183	-0.187
	-0.58	-0.73	-2.00	-2.05	-2.09
Teacher's mathematics test score	0.595	0.630	0.485	0.518	0.531
	3.89	3.76	3.93	4.31	4.33
Promotion selection		-33.264		-5.838	-5.421
		-2.19		-0.90	-0.85
School survival selection		-24.101		-11.640	-11.779
		-1.31		-1.63	-1.66
Constant	7.241	33.512	-21.385	-10.208	-12.136
	0.38	1.01	-1.37	-0.54	-0.64
Adjusted R squared	0.206	0.357	0.488	0.491	0.489
Number of cases	349	349	349	349	346
Mean of dependent variable	48.209	48.209	48.209	48.209	

Table C5-5: Alternative Specifications of Value-Added Fourth-Grade Models,
Portuguese, 1981-83

Variable Description	(1)	(2)	(3)	(4)
State				
Ceara	19.223	19.180	20.449	19.028
	3.46	3.44	3.37	3.38
Piaui	11.977	11.845	12.652	10.689
	1.90	1.73	1.89	1.57
OME	-6.397	-6.415	-5.927	-6.241
	-1.16	-1.16	-1.07	-1.11
Program states				
EDURURAL: Pernambuco	-1.125	-1.133	-1.098	-1.761
	-0.25	-0.22	-0.23	-0.34
EDURURAL: Ceara	-4.297	-4.321	-4.119	-4.858
	-0.70	-0.63	-0.63	-0.72
EDURURAL: Piaui	-0.563	-0.538	-0.867	-0.917
	-0.14	-0.13	-0.21	-0.24
Personal characteristics				
Female student	7.889	7.887	8.237	6.349
	1.05	1.05	1.08	0.86
Age	-0.404	-0.399	-0.472	-0.400
	-0.55	-0.55	-0.59	-0.57
Pupil works	-12.712	-12.668	-12.330	-13.163
	-3.37	-3.33	-3.27	-3.47
Joint characteristics: pupil and school				
Portuguese test score, 1981	0.285	0.283	0.296	0.276
	2.37	2.36	2.23	2.38
Mathematics test score, 1981	0.142	0.142	0.135	0.144
	2.07	2.10	1.76	2.25
Homework	4.524	4.540	4.520	4.533
	2.02	2.03	2.03	2.04
Male teacher/male student	1.030	0.996	1.886	1.506
	0.21	0.20	0.38	0.31
Female teacher/female student	-5.430	-5.416	-5.632	-5.947
	-1.25	-1.23	-1.29	-1.36
Peer influences				
Percent families not farming	13.970	13.999	15.690	14.533
	2.77	2.77	2.99	2.88
Relatively large landholders	7.368	7.441	7.741	6.642
	1.76	1.75	1.84	1.56
Percent female classmates	8.453	8.489	7.935	7.179
	0.96	0.96	0.90	0.82

Table C5-5 Cont'd

Variable Description	(1)	(2)	(3)	(4)
Female classmates when female student	0.275	0.219	0.904	2.908
	0.03	0.02	0.09	0.29
School characteristics				
Graded class	-1.680	-1.673	-1.350	-1.596
	-0.63	-0.62	-0.50	-0.59
Pupil-teacher ratio	0.123	0.123	0.100	0.147
	1.58	1.57	1.25	1.84
School hardware index	11.728	11.847	11.744	
	2.36	2.33	2.37	
School furniture				-1.057
				-0.21
School facilities				8.550
				1.66
Water				4.712
				1.88
Electricity				0.350
				0.14
School software index	-3.020		-2.538	
	-0.57		-0.48	
Writing materials index		-1.428		-1.536
		-0.25		-0.26
Textbook used some days		-1.085		-1.087
		-0.33		-0.33
Textbook used every day		-1.663		-1.709
		-0.52		-0.54
Teacher characteristics				
Years teacher's education	-0.334	-0.333	-0.344	-0.402
	-0.80	-0.80	-0.82	-0.91
Years teacher's experience	0.198	0.195	0.171	0.200
	1.54	1.49	1.30	1.47
Logos II teacher training	2.000	2.003	2.264	1.847
	0.71	0.71	0.80	0.62
Qualificacao teacher training	1.022	1.043	0.844	0.400
	0.35	0.35	0.29	0.14
Teacher activity index			8.198	
			1.38	

Table C5-5 Cont'd

Variable Description	(1)	(2)	(3)	(4)
Teacher materials index			-3.074	
			-0.62	
Promotion selection	5.537	5.362	6.960	4.562
	0.52	0.51	0.60	0.44
School survival selection	-6.075	-6.000	-6.289	-6.934
	-0.87	-0.85	-0.82	-0.96
Constant	12.252	12.641	6.780	17.257
	0.49	0.50	0.24	0.68
Adjusted R squared	0.346	0.340	0.345	0.342
Number of cases	227	227	227	227
Mean of dependent variable	51.172	51.172	51.172	51.172

Table C5-6: Alternative Specifications of Value-Added Fourth-Grade Models
Mathematics, 1981-83

Variable Description	(1)	(2)	(3)	(4)
State				
Ceara	11.224	9.129	9.433	13.006
	0.83	0.76	0.71	0.99
Piaui	18.384	11.725	17.682	12.979
	1.32	0.92	1.30	0.94
OME	-5.118	-5.509	-6.239	-4.551
	-0.69	-0.76	-0.85	-0.63
Program states				
EDURURAL: Pernambuco	4.987	0.981	5.017	1.875
	0.47	0.10	0.48	0.18
EDURURAL: Ceara	1.629	-3.438	-0.166	-2.692
	0.13	-0.29	-0.01	-0.22
EDURURAL: Piaui	0.558	0.797	0.607	0.545
	0.07	0.11	0.08	0.07
Personal characteristics				
Female student	7.922	8.763	7.846	6.963
	0.62	0.74	0.62	0.57
Age	-1.704	-1.586	-1.595	-1.712
	-0.91	-0.98	-0.88	-0.98
Pupil works	-7.579	-6.979	-7.960	-7.654
	-1.53	-1.43	-1.62	-1.57
Joint characteristics: pupil and school				
Portuguese test score, 1981	0.241	0.211	0.239	0.237
	0.76	0.76	0.77	0.78
Mathematics test score, 1981	0.340	0.344	0.351	0.337
	1.74	2.03	1.84	1.82
Homework	5.616	6.008	5.722	6.400
	1.93	2.10	1.97	2.26
Male teacher/male student	2.913	2.657	2.311	2.082
	0.45	0.42	0.35	0.33
Female teacher/female student	-6.494	-6.893	-6.258	-7.256
	-1.10	-1.19	-1.07	-1.27
Peer influences				
Percent families not farming	15.471	16.602	12.726	16.550
	2.38	2.59	1.89	2.61
Relatively large landholders	16.736	18.409	16.576	18.166
	2.92	3.26	2.89	3.20

Table C5-6 Cont'd

Variable Description	(1)	(2)	(3)	(4)
Percent female classmates	27.089	27.571	27.872	26.065
	2.26	2.37	2.35	2.26
Female classmates when female student	-17.893	-19.427	-18.709	-16.064
	-1.33	-1.48	-1.40	-1.23
School characteristics				
Graded class	4.811	5.413	5.132	5.420
	1.33	1.53	1.42	1.55
Pupil-teacher ratio	0.200	0.183	0.211	0.192
	1.88	1.76	1.93	1.76
School hardware index	8.321	10.854	7.906	
	1.30	1.68	1.24	
School furniture				2.387
				0.37
School facilities				3.888
				0.56
Water				7.798
				2.25
Electricity				-4.802
				-1.36
School software index	-5.580		-5.959	
	-0.79		-0.85	
Writing materials index		6.385		2.808
		0.86		0.38
Textbook used some days		-9.587		-8.854
		-2.24		-2.08
Textbook used every day		-7.994		-7.782
		-1.92		-1.89
Teacher characteristics				
Years teacher's education	0.456	0.491	0.464	0.721
	0.84	0.92	0.86	1.28
Years teacher's experience	0.226	0.156	0.220	0.074
	1.31	0.91	1.24	0.40
Logos II teacher training	0.720	0.564	0.167	2.335
	0.19	0.15	0.04	0.59
Qualificacao teacher training	2.962	3.420	2.846	2.281
	0.74	0.88	0.72	0.59

Table C5-6 Cont'd

Variable Description	(1)	(2)	(3)	(4)
Teacher activity index			-8.121	
			-1.02	
Teacher materials index			9.072	
			1.40	
Promotion selection	22.396	19.044	21.738	21.011
	0.85	0.82	0.84	0.83
School survival selection	4.713	7.854	7.255	2.761
	0.28	0.53	0.45	0.18
Constant	-37.530	-31.672	-37.819	-31.677
	-0.60	-0.58	-0.62	-0.53
Adjusted R squared	0.305	0.314	0.304	0.332
Number of cases	227	227	227	227
Mean of dependent variable	45.648	45.648	45.648	45.648

Table C5-7: Alternative Specifications of Value-Added Fourth-Grade Models,
Portuguese, 1983-85

Variable Description	(1)	(2)	(3)	(4)
State				
Ceara	18.674	16.802	19.927	17.766
	5.10	4.26	5.42	4.43
Piaui	16.583	15.692	17.525	16.606
	4.45	4.13	4.67	4.30
OME	8.040	7.054	6.818	6.718
	2.28	1.95	1.94	1.83
Program states				
EDURURAL: Pernambuco	11.884	9.347	11.208	9.396
	3.57	2.41	3.37	2.43
EDURURAL: Ceara	-6.694	-7.932	-6.629	-8.855
	-1.79	-2.06	-1.78	-2.29
EDURURAL: Piaui	-4.289	-6.215	-3.801	-6.392
	-1.54	-1.96	-1.35	-2.01
Personal characteristics				
Female student	4.702	5.289	5.640	5.803
	0.97	1.09	1.17	1.18
Age	-1.371	-1.428	-1.435	-1.420
	-3.08	-3.20	-3.23	-3.12
Pupil works	-5.721	-5.573	-6.108	-5.349
	-1.40	-1.36	-1.51	-1.31
Joint characteristics: pupil and school				
Portuguese test score, 1983	0.434	0.432	0.445	0.430
	6.59	6.58	6.65	6.56
Mathematics test score, 1983	0.132	0.134	0.121	0.137
	3.28	3.34	2.95	3.39
Homework	1.926	1.882	2.267	2.180
	1.18	1.16	1.41	1.33
Male teacher/male student	8.907	8.871	7.715	8.980
	2.14	2.12	1.87	2.13
Female teacher/female student	-0.854	-1.506	-0.532	-1.903
	-0.26	-0.46	-0.17	-0.56
Peer influences				
Percent families not farming	10.123	9.981	9.523	10.525
	2.23	2.19	2.11	2.31
Relatively large landholders	0.191	0.547	-0.401	0.899
	0.06	0.17	-0.13	0.29

Table C5-7 Cont'd

Variable Description	(1)	(2)	(3)	(4)
Percent female classmates	-0.483	-0.784	1.488	-0.429
	-0.10	-0.16	0.30	-0.09
Female classmates when female student	2.596	2.907	0.012	2.734
	0.41	0.46	0.00	0.43
School characteristics				
Graded class	-3.873	-3.783	-3.753	-4.724
	-1.95	-1.90	-1.90	-2.31
Pupil-teacher ratio	-0.107	-0.111	-0.106	-0.104
	-1.88	-1.95	-1.87	-1.76
School hardware index	8.778	9.472	7.314	
	2.21	2.36	1.84	
School furniture				5.832
				1.64
School facilities				0.941
				0.25
Water				0.088
				0.05
Electricity				4.392
				2.29
School software index	6.689		6.142	
	1.87		1.73	
Writing materials index		7.821		8.266
		1.98		2.09
Textbook used in school only		0.999		0.716
		0.18		0.13
Textbook used school and home		2.150		1.892
		1.06		0.94
Teacher characteristics				
Years teacher's education	-0.134	-0.142	-0.216	-0.169
	-0.48	-0.51	-0.77	-0.59
Years teacher's experience	0.063	0.080	-0.035	0.068
	0.59	0.74	-0.32	0.63
Logos II teacher training	-0.224	-0.236	-0.831	-0.064
	-0.13	-0.14	-0.49	-0.04
Qualificacao teacher training	-2.211	-2.117	-2.902	-1.925
	-1.10	-1.05	-1.45	-0.95

Table C5-7 Cont'd

Variable Description	(1)	(2)	(3)	(4)
Teacher's Portuguese test score	0.172	0.162	0.159	0.141
	2.49	2.32	2.31	1.99
Teacher's mathematics test score	0.185	0.183	0.195	0.204
	2.00	1.98	2.11	2.18
Teacher activity index			9.118	
			2.02	
Teacher materials index			2.609	
			0.71	
Promotion selection	0.309	0.239	1.425	0.217
	0.08	0.06	0.35	0.05
School survival selection	3.413	3.779	4.044	4.143
	0.72	0.80	0.85	0.84
Constant	-24.008	-22.832	-28.873	-25.537
	-1.86	-1.77	-2.18	-1.97
Adjusted R squared	0.430	0.429	0.442	0.429
Number of cases	349	349	349	349
Mean of dependent variable	47.218	47.218	47.218	47.218

Table C5-8: Alternative Specifications of Value-Added Fourth-Grade Models, Mathematics, 1983-85

Variable Description	(1)	(2)	(3)	(4)
State				
Ceara	23.775	20.876	23.511	21.840
	4.54	3.73	4.43	3.83
Piaui	9.779	8.217	9.535	8.797
	1.83	1.52	1.76	1.59
OME	7.436	5.991	7.721	6.456
	1.57	1.24	1.61	1.31
Program states				
EDURURAL: Pernambuco	8.970	4.727	9.141	4.670
	1.89	0.87	1.91	0.86
EDURURAL: Ceara	-3.997	-5.984	-4.024	-6.348
	-0.75	-1.10	-0.75	-1.16
EDURURAL: Piaui	4.325	1.464	4.258	1.411
	1.06	0.32	1.02	0.31
Personal characteristics				
Female student	-13.582	-12.895	-13.765	-13.239
	-2.08	-1.97	-2.09	-1.99
Age	-1.431	-1.505	-1.419	-1.572
	-2.26	-2.37	-2.23	-2.44
Pupil works	-6.874	-6.575	-6.806	-6.251
	-1.31	-1.26	-1.29	-1.19
Joint characteristics: pupil and school				
Portuguese test score, 1983	0.199	0.197	0.197	0.197
	1.85	1.82	1.79	1.83
Mathematics test score, 1983	0.464	0.469	0.466	0.472
	7.21	7.27	7.10	7.32
Homework	3.747	3.774	3.682	3.695
	1.79	1.81	1.75	1.74
Male teacher/male student	9.920	9.450	10.183	8.951
	1.83	1.74	1.87	1.62
Female teacher/female student	5.838	4.895	5.779	5.422
	1.39	1.16	1.38	1.24
Peer influences				
Percent families not farming	6.744	6.839	6.828	7.417
	1.14	1.16	1.15	1.25
Relatively large landholders	-0.405	0.266	-0.300	0.374
	-0.10	0.07	-0.07	0.09

Table C5-8 Cont'd

Variable Description	(1)	(2)	(3)	(4)
Percent female classmates	-4.662	-5.269	-5.079	-4.441
	-0.72	-0.82	-0.78	-0.68
Female classmates when female student	7.407	7.904	7.925	7.420
	0.90	0.96	0.95	0.90
School characteristics				
Graded class	-6.186	-6.064	-6.235	-6.545
	-2.36	-2.32	-2.36	-2.43
Pupil-teacher ratio	-0.063	-0.071	-0.063	-0.079
	-0.85	-0.96	-0.85	-1.02
School hardware index	12.404	13.210	12.776	
	2.38	2.53	2.42	
School furniture				7.061
				1.53
School facilities				0.673
				0.13
Water				2.845
				1.28
Electricity				3.404
				1.36
School software index	11.028		11.114	
	2.37		2.37	
Writing materials index		12.651		12.716
		2.43		2.44
Textbook used in school only		-3.639		-3.585
		-0.52		-0.50
Textbook used school and home		3.487		3.470
		1.33		1.32
Teacher characteristics				
Years teacher's education	-0.080	-0.085	-0.067	-0.070
	-0.22	-0.24	-0.18	-0.19
Years teacher's experience	0.263	0.293	0.285	0.276
	1.89	2.09	1.96	1.95
Logos II teacher training	0.655	0.982	0.803	1.287
	0.30	0.44	0.36	0.56
Qualificacao teacher training	-5.936	-5.800	-5.782	-5.874
	-2.29	-2.24	-2.21	-2.26

Table C5-8 Cont'd

Variable Description	(1)	(2)	(3)	(4)
Teacher's Portuguese test score	-0.183	-0.205	-0.181	-0.220
	-2.05	-2.28	-2.01	-2.42
Teacher's mathematics test score	0.518	0.511	0.514	0.528
	4.31	4.27	4.22	4.34
Teacher activity index			-2.338	
			-0.39	
Teacher materials index			-0.209	
			-0.04	
Promotion selection	-5.838	-5.947	-6.084	-5.848
	-0.90	-0.92	-0.93	-0.91
School survival selection	-11.640	-11.319	-11.775	-11.804
	-1.63	-1.59	-1.64	-1.61
Constant	-10.208	-7.604	-8.874	-9.226
	-0.54	-0.40	-0.46	-0.49
Adjusted R squared	0.491	0.492	0.488	0.488
Number of cases	349	349	349	349
Mean of dependent variable	48.209	48.209	48.209	48.209

Table C5-9: Teacher Salary and Achievement - Value-added
Specifications for Fourth Grade, 1983

Variable Description	Portuguese		Mathematics	
	(1)	(2)	(3)	(4)
State				
Ceara	21.490	25.553	12.735	7.364
	4.18	3.60	0.99	0.52
Piaui	13.280	19.367	17.400	15.401
	2.24	2.54	1.30	1.07
OME	-5.060	-5.654	-2.959	-2.920
	-0.95	-1.06	-0.42	-0.41
Program states				
EDURURAL: Pernambuco	0.069	2.025	5.047	4.094
	0.02	0.42	0.49	0.38
EDURURAL: Ceara	-4.785	-4.912	1.441	2.458
	-0.81	-0.80	0.12	0.21
EDURURAL: Piaui	-1.126	-0.823	0.601	0.286
	-0.30	-0.21	0.08	0.04
Personal characteristics				
Female student	8.085	9.835	7.890	7.976
	1.09	1.29	0.63	0.63
Age	-0.331	-0.423	-1.602	-1.567
	-0.49	-0.59	-0.92	-0.90
Pupil works	-12.747	-12.712	-8.302	-8.393
	-3.41	-3.40	-1.69	-1.71
Joint characteristics: pupil and school				
Portuguese test score, 1981	0.248	0.260	0.229	0.230
	2.29	2.24	0.77	0.76
Mathematics test score, 1981	0.147	0.155	0.331	0.331
	2.38	2.31	1.80	1.79
Homework	4.291	4.570	5.598	5.814
	1.90	2.01	1.91	1.96
Male teacher/male student	-0.159	0.716	1.457	0.963
	-0.03	0.14	0.22	0.14
Female teacher/female student	-5.636	-6.665	-7.175	-6.899
	-1.31	-1.52	-1.24	-1.18
Peer influences				
Percent families not farming	13.517	13.868	16.502	15.873
	2.75	2.81	2.59	2.48
Relatively large landholders	6.873	7.009	17.350	17.431
	1.65	1.68	3.04	3.05

Table C5-9 Cont'd

Variable Description	Portuguese		Mathematics	
	(1)	(2)	(3)	(4)
Percent female classmates	8.384	9.352	25.729	25.817
	0.95	1.06	2.17	2.16
Female classmates when female student	-0.231	-1.167	-17.681	-18.305
	-0.02	-0.12	-1.33	-1.36
School characteristics				
Graded class	-2.826	-3.156	3.517	3.103
	-1.08	-1.18	1.02	0.88
Pupil-teacher ratio	0.078	0.046	0.185	0.192
	1.00	0.56	1.78	1.79
School hardware index	11.407	11.773	10.128	9.825
	2.40	2.48	1.65	1.60
School software index	-2.709	-3.961	-5.228	-4.952
	-0.52	-0.75	-0.76	-0.71
Teacher characteristics				
Teacher salary	0.023		0.023	
	1.23		0.82	
Teacher salary: Pernambuco		0.075		-0.001
		1.73		-0.02
Teacher salary: Ceara		0.044		0.156
		0.35		0.96
Teacher salary: Piaui		0.012		0.025
		0.60		0.84
Promotion selection	4.089	5.176	20.876	21.034
	0.42	0.50	0.83	0.83
School survival selection	-4.214	-3.707	3.755	3.998
	-0.66	-0.55	0.24	0.25
Constant	13.035	7.192	-29.619	-28.646
	0.57	0.29	-0.51	-0.49
Adjusted R squared	0.346	0.345	0.307	0.303
Number of cases	227	227	227	227
Mean of dependent variable	51.172	51.172	45.648	45.648

Table C5-10: Teacher Salary and Achievement - Value-added
Specifications for Fourth Grade, 1985

Variable Description	Portuguese		Mathematics	
	(1)	(2)	(3)	(4)
State				
Ceara	18.133	16.814	22.002	18.420
	4.71	3.75	4.02	3.00
Piaui	15.451	16.442	5.421	1.092
	3.98	3.59	0.97	0.17
OME	9.153	8.780	12.032	13.016
	2.57	2.43	2.49	2.69
Program states				
EDURURAL: Pernambuco	10.135	9.929	5.786	5.544
	3.05	2.97	1.21	1.18
EDURURAL: Ceara	-7.010	-7.563	-3.230	-3.797
	-1.82	-1.94	-0.59	-0.70
EDURURAL: Piaui	-5.571	-5.964	4.582	4.360
	-1.88	-1.99	1.06	1.02
Personal characteristics				
Female student	5.892	6.782	-12.123	-12.262
	1.18	1.35	-1.80	-1.82
Age	-1.591	-1.593	-1.114	-1.078
	-3.55	-3.54	-1.77	-1.73
Pupil works	-5.388	-5.622	-7.448	-6.602
	-1.29	-1.34	-1.37	-1.21
Joint characteristics: pupil and school				
Portuguese test score, 1983	0.466	0.466	0.224	0.232
	6.57	6.48	2.03	2.13
Mathematics test score, 1983	0.157	0.159	0.477	0.468
	3.65	3.65	7.24	7.18
Homework	2.109	2.197	3.707	4.079
	1.27	1.32	1.72	1.88
Male teacher/male student	10.061	11.133	11.108	10.264
	2.31	2.51	1.93	1.76
Female teacher/female student	-0.961	-1.037	3.465	3.361
	-0.29	-0.32	0.81	0.79
Peer influences				
Percent families not farming	7.898	7.726	3.125	3.098
	1.71	1.68	0.52	0.51
Relatively large landholders	0.706	0.926	0.629	-0.720
	0.22	0.28	0.15	-0.17

Table C5-10 Cont'd

Variable Description	Portuguese		Mathematics	
	(1)	(2)	(3)	(4)
Percent female classmates	-1.251	-0.047	-5.385	-5.778
	-0.25	-0.01	-0.81	-0.86
Female classmates when female student	2.278	1.195	8.708	8.634
	0.35	0.18	1.02	1.01
School characteristics				
Graded class	-4.579	-4.157	-8.814	-9.282
	-2.18	-1.95	-3.19	-3.31
Pupil-teacher ratio	-0.102	-0.093	-0.141	-0.133
	-1.87	-1.70	-1.98	-1.84
School hardware index	11.895	11.476	19.034	19.294
	3.08	2.96	3.71	3.78
School software index	5.183	5.203	6.434	6.916
	1.42	1.42	1.34	1.44
Teacher characteristics				
Teacher's salary	0.013		0.042	
	0.95		2.26	
Teacher's salary: Pernambuco		0.012		-0.013
		0.34		-0.29
Teacher's salary: Ceara		0.050		0.046
		1.62		1.17
Teacher's salary: Piaui		0.002		0.056
		0.12		2.38
Promotion selection	2.140	2.400	-6.003	-5.807
	0.49	0.55	-0.91	-0.89
School survival selection	4.141	4.690	-13.019	-11.678
	0.84	0.93	-1.76	-1.59
Constant	0.726	-0.411	18.267	19.114
	0.06	-0.04	1.05	1.12
Adjusted R squared	0.411	0.410	0.463	0.462
Number of cases	349	349	349	349
Mean of dependent variable	47.218	47.218	48.209	48.209

Table C5-11: Alternative Specifications of Cross-Section Second-Grade Models
for Portuguese and Mathematics, 1981
(t statistics underneath)

Variable Description	Portuguese				Mathematics			
	(1)	(2)	(3)	(4)	(1)	(2)	(3)	(4)
State								
Ceara	18.6692	17.6756	18.5009	18.4167	8.8213	4.7781	8.9588	14.2774
	10.849	8.226	10.868	15.584	5.372	2.338	5.524	12.729
Piaui	3.4240	-3.5222	4.1587	-0.9831	-5.2520	-14.8269	-4.4254	-6.8455
	1.893	-1.600	2.136	-0.795	-3.043	-7.078	-2.385	-5.832
School control								
State operated	-1.0004	-5.3697	0.9072	0.3112	-8.8370	-14.2771	-6.9460	-6.6474
	-0.644	-3.147	0.611	0.206	-5.962	-8.796	-4.907	-4.642
Federally operated	4.3664	3.4526	4.3138	3.6907	-0.4069	-1.2950	3.4750	1.2060
	0.732	0.581	0.714	0.606	-0.071	-0.229	0.604	0.209
Privately operated	0.0500	-0.5704	1.5633	0.5605	0.0056	-0.9694	0.9937	-1.3916
	0.022	-0.256	0.694	0.243	0.003	-0.458	0.463	-0.637
Program states								
EDURURAL: Pernambuco	6.2340	5.2342	6.3518		2.4408	0.8794	2.4911	
	4.748	3.942	4.826		1.948	0.696	1.987	
EDURURAL: Ceara	7.6786	7.1439	7.4693		10.6011	10.4959	11.2868	
	4.852	4.474	4.598		7.020	6.910	7.293	
EDURURAL: Piaui	-0.9512	-1.7708	-1.1744		1.4561	0.4189	0.7852	
	-0.565	-1.053	-0.672		0.906	0.262	0.471	
Personal characteristics								
Female student	-5.2806	-6.0929	-5.1130	-5.2216	-10.7798	-11.9827	-11.6216	-10.1573
	-1.639	-1.896	-1.584	-1.607	-3.506	-3.920	-3.780	-3.293
Age	0.7564	0.7173	0.7668	0.8448	1.1672	1.1205	1.1946	1.2728
	4.427	4.212	4.448	4.907	7.158	6.917	7.273	7.790
Pupil works	-0.5880	-0.5048	-0.6027	-1.1520	-2.1212	-2.1140	-2.2398	-2.8978
	-0.434	-0.374	-0.443	-0.848	-1.642	-1.647	-1.730	-2.248
Family characteristics								
Mother's education	0.4085	0.4048	0.3437	0.3397	0.4328	0.4307	0.3329	0.3162
	1.930	1.921	1.596	1.570	2.143	2.148	1.623	1.540
Father's education	0.7548	0.6959	0.7779	0.7514	0.7420	0.6673	0.7805	0.7674
	3.055	2.826	3.123	3.009	3.148	2.849	3.289	3.238
Family size	-0.3273	-0.3449	-0.3445	-0.3445	0.1578	0.1434	0.0979	0.1142
	-2.173	-2.298	-2.259	-2.252	1.098	1.004	0.674	0.786
Joint characteristics: pupil and school								
Days absent last two months	-0.3800	-0.3540	-0.3902	-0.3657	-0.3244	-0.2873	-0.3298	-0.3432
	-5.003	-4.670	-5.032	-4.701	-4.476	-3.985	-4.464	-4.648
School lunch some days	-0.0981	0.2716	0.2944	-1.0659	-1.7885	-1.3729	-1.8612	-2.2165
	-0.095	0.263	0.280	-1.014	-1.814	-1.400	-1.856	-2.221

Table C5-11 Cont'd

Variable Description	Portuguese				Mathematics			
	(1)	(2)	(3)	(4)	(1)	(2)	(3)	(4)
School lunch every day	-0.2721	-0.0520	0.1153	-0.7171	-0.6704	-0.5348	-0.8352	-0.4243
	-0.238	-0.045	0.099	-0.599	-0.614	-0.492	-0.752	-0.373
Male teacher/male student	-3.5916	-4.3858	-3.7880	-3.9464	-3.8954	-5.0266	-5.1495	-4.7162
	-1.515	-1.854	-1.600	-1.673	-1.722	-2.233	-2.283	-2.106
Female teacher/female student	6.2055	6.9516	4.9252	4.9868	4.8336	5.8341	4.5495	3.8088
	2.665	2.993	2.127	2.150	2.175	2.640	2.062	1.730
Peer influences								
Percent families not farming	-3.5836	-4.5401	-3.1967	-4.7044	-6.3485	-7.2498	-6.6398	-4.7354
	-1.231	-1.562	-1.083	-1.598	-2.285	-2.622	-2.361	-1.695
Relatively large landholders	11.5460	11.6320	12.0750	11.3900	11.4530	11.5000	11.9180	12.2510
	5.702	5.768	5.874	5.552	5.927	5.994	6.085	6.292
Percent female classmates	-5.9298	-6.9086	-7.2706	-7.6339	2.0918	0.6270	0.7122	1.9970
	-1.830	-2.136	-2.225	-2.328	0.676	0.204	0.229	0.642
Female classmates when female student	8.8255	8.9481	10.7906	10.9428	-0.6145	-0.2448	1.2866	-0.0159
	2.083	2.120	2.524	2.550	-0.152	-0.061	0.316	-0.004
School characteristics								
Graded class	-1.2224	-0.3495	-1.1538	-2.1961	0.0041	0.6534	-0.0712	-0.4422
	-1.218	-0.341	-1.136	-2.074	0.004	0.670	-0.074	-0.440
Pupil-teacher ratio	0.0458	0.0472	0.0664	0.0525	0.0003	-0.0002	0.0273	0.0331
	1.652	1.710	2.396	1.892	0.010	-0.007	1.035	1.258
School hardware index	8.1479	8.1768	8.9063		10.4786	10.4539	11.9641	
	4.011	4.042	4.318		5.406	5.432	6.088	
School furniture				-0.7815				0.1329
				-0.555				0.099
School facilities				7.0799				8.6306
				3.487				4.478
Water				1.4434				6.1276
				1.540				6.889
Electricity				2.7108				-1.3170
				2.534				-1.297
School software index	5.9688	4.9445	5.8963		5.8411	4.7165	4.8247	
	3.431	2.839	3.322		3.518	2.847	2.854	
Writing materials for some				-1.6473				-2.3943
				-1.772				-2.714

Table C5-11 Cont'd

Variable Description	Portuguese				Mathematics			
	(1)	(2)	(3)	(4)	(1)	(2)	(3)	(4)
Writing materials for all				0.7541 0.592				-2.0739 -1.715
Textbooks used in classroom				5.5163 4.369				5.6400 4.706
Teacher characteristics								
Teacher's salary	0.0292 2.870				0.0325 3.341			
Teacher's salary: Pernambuco		-0.0092 -0.704				-0.0251 -2.028		
Teacher's salary: Ceara		-0.0642 -1.606				-0.0008 -0.022		
Teacher's salary: Piaui		0.1114 6.537				0.1369 8.445		
Years teacher's education			0.5629 3.556	0.3541 2.254			0.5862 3.886	0.5167 3.465
Years teacher's experience			0.0184 0.297	-0.0123 -0.196			0.1936 3.277	0.1630 2.740
Logos teacher training			-0.8813 -0.675	-0.5536 -0.421			0.2596 0.209	0.5040 0.404
Teacher activity index			3.9291 1.538	3.1846 1.253			10.1539 4.171	7.2910 3.022
Teacher materials index			-8.0136 -3.668	-7.1845 -3.257			-9.1848 -4.412	-8.9764 -4.287
Constant	21.8148 5.898	26.4420 6.945	19.5418 4.943	26.8008 7.105	21.1470 5.991	28.0136 7.735	15.7545 4.183	16.3313 4.562
Adjusted R squared	0.1450	0.1520	0.1440	0.1395	0.1571	0.1692	0.1589	0.1609
Number of cases	4320	4320	4257	4257	4320	4320	4257	4257
Mean of dependent variable	48.860	48.860	48.568	48.568	45.878	45.878	45.624	45.624

Table C5-12: Alternative Specifications of Cross-Section Second-Grade Models for
Portuguese and Mathematics, 1983
(t statistics underneath)

Variable Description	Portuguese				Mathematics			
	(1)	(2)	(3)	(4)	(1)	(2)	(3)	(4)
State								
Ceara	14.1421	12.7396	14.4336	18.7064	5.7931	2.9090	7.4474	13.1583
	9.161	5.903	9.277	18.269	3.494	1.255	4.466	12.041
Piaui	11.2297	8.9135	11.7658	7.2205	-4.7660	-7.5830	-3.3911	0.1627
	6.289	3.849	6.447	6.316	-2.485	-3.049	-1.734	0.133
School control								
State operated	-0.8795	-1.6532	2.6035	2.6667	-1.4466	-2.1070	2.0210	0.4755
	-0.607	-1.084	2.057	2.056	-0.930	-1.287	1.490	0.344
Federally operated	1.1450	0.1422	3.7246	5.8481	-4.0246	-4.7705	-2.2677	-3.6132
	0.160	0.020	0.521	0.820	-0.524	-0.619	-0.296	-0.475
Privately operated	9.6805	9.5115	8.2688	7.6464	5.0740	4.9125	5.6548	3.8355
	2.717	2.668	2.304	2.127	1.326	1.283	1.470	1.000
OME	-2.3636	-2.2124	-1.6823	-5.1816	-7.2822	-7.0702	-6.7848	-8.1838
	-1.246	-1.165	-0.889	-2.920	-3.575	-3.466	-3.345	-4.321
Program states								
EDURURAL: Pernambuco	1.9320	1.4005	2.4010		-1.5911	-2.3618	-0.7228	
	1.357	0.950	1.684		-1.041	-1.492	-0.473	
EDURURAL: Ceara	10.0703	10.0159	11.1514		10.3953	10.7080	11.3762	
	7.134	6.937	7.900		6.857	6.907	7.518	
EDURURAL: Piaui	-1.6825	-1.7506	-1.7627		5.0836	5.0023	5.3810	
	-1.161	-1.208	-1.215		3.267	3.214	3.461	
Personal characteristics								
Female student	-2.0038	-2.3264	0.7869	0.6793	-11.5876	-11.9436	-8.9112	-9.0254
	-0.719	-0.833	0.285	0.245	-3.871	-3.981	-3.013	-3.051
Age	0.4147	0.4100	0.4257	0.6291	0.8924	0.8932	0.9283	1.1085
	2.735	2.703	2.814	4.201	5.481	5.484	5.725	6.936
Pupil works	-0.6918	-0.8427	-0.8958	-1.2285	0.8957	0.7194	0.5817	0.0948
	-0.624	-0.757	-0.809	-1.109	0.752	0.602	0.490	0.080
Family characteristics								
Mother's education	0.6099	0.6029	0.6236	0.5639	0.5514	0.5531	0.5605	0.5048
	3.436	3.393	3.515	3.179	2.893	2.899	2.947	2.667
Father's education	0.6920	0.6873	0.6842	0.6497	0.9337	0.9293	0.9065	0.9527
	3.232	3.210	3.201	3.040	4.061	4.042	3.956	4.176
Family size	-0.3259	-0.3232	-0.2871	-0.3021	0.0096	0.0163	0.0166	0.0498
	-2.496	-2.475	-2.214	-2.330	0.069	0.116	0.119	0.360

Table C5-12 Cont'd

	Portuguese				Mathematics			
Variable Description	(1)	(2)	(3)	(4)	(1)	(2)	(3)	(4)

Joint characteristics:
pupil and school

Homework	3.5006	3.5514	3.5280	4.2577	2.6681	2.7202	2.7201	3.5477
	4.973	5.041	5.034	6.041	3.530	3.596	3.621	4.717
School lunch some days	-3.4455	-3.4094	-5.2203	-6.1417	-3.2698	-3.2292	-5.1966	-5.5112
	-2.316	-2.292	-3.530	-4.156	-2.047	-2.022	-3.278	-3.494
School lunch every day	-4.2079	-4.3420	-5.7016	-5.9156	-4.6581	-4.7856	-6.5675	-5.8716
	-2.614	-2.694	-3.536	-3.642	-2.694	-2.765	-3.800	-3.387
Male teacher/male student	-1.2529	-1.5538	0.6358	0.5015	0.1212	-0.1990	2.0888	1.8858
	-0.633	-0.782	0.327	0.257	0.057	-0.093	1.002	0.907
Female teacher/female student	3.4961	3.6765	1.4176	0.8113	2.4257	2.6084	1.0477	0.2023
	1.975	2.074	0.804	0.458	1.276	1.370	0.554	0.107

Peer influences

Percent families not farming	4.2161	4.2936	3.7418	3.2103	-0.0025	-0.3783	-0.8027	-0.7532
	1.898	1.906	1.685	1.438	-0.001	-0.156	-0.337	-0.316
Relatively large landholders	5.7660	5.6450	6.3520	7.6740	4.0570	3.8290	4.5190	5.7160
	3.113	3.042	3.402	4.093	2.040	1.922	2.258	2.857
Percent female classmates	-3.4215	-3.4614	-3.3811	-4.8848	-0.0685	-0.2390	0.0219	-1.7832
	-1.136	-1.149	-1.125	-1.615	-0.021	-0.074	0.007	-0.553
Female classmates when female student	5.5610	5.7613	4.1175	5.4594	2.0751	2.3310	-0.3182	1.2907
	1.450	1.501	1.077	1.425	0.504	0.566	-0.078	0.316

School characteristics

Graded class	-4.2223	-4.0515	-3.9373	-3.9322	-2.4656	-2.3663	-1.9752	-0.5873
	-4.934	-4.690	-4.507	-4.275	-2.683	-2.551	-2.109	-0.598
Pupil-teacher ratio	-0.0789	-0.0754	-0.0726	-0.0684	-0.0531	-0.0481	-0.0406	-0.0292
	-2.713	-2.584	-2.521	-2.381	-1.699	-1.534	-1.315	-0.952
School hardware index	9.2711	9.2889	8.9685		6.9964	6.7838	6.3065	
	5.598	5.572	5.379		3.934	3.790	3.529	
School furniture				-5.6504				-11.2137
				-3.571				-6.641
School facilities				7.2277				1.8290
				4.317				1.024
Water				3.5126				6.6125
				4.449				7.847

Table C5-12 Cont'd

Variable Description	Portuguese				Mathematics			
	(1)	(2)	(3)	(4)	(1)	(2)	(3)	(4)
Electricity				1.2745				1.4130
				1.406				1.461
School software index	6.0302	5.9827	4.8637		3.9672	3.8568	2.5381	
	3.387	3.359	2.732		2.075	2.016	1.330	
Writing materials index				4.7026				3.2721
				3.483				2.271
Textbook used some days				7.6190				5.2955
				6.395				4.165
Textbook used every day				6.4029				4.2263
				5.704				3.528
Teacher characteristics								
Teacher's salary	0.0547				0.0642			
	5.715				6.245			
Teacher's salary: Pernambuco		0.0330				0.0350		
		1.880				1.856		
Teacher's salary: Ceara		0.0411				0.0858		
		1.309				2.542		
Teacher's salary: Piaui		0.0655				0.0736		
		5.633				5.894		
Years teacher's education			0.7943	0.8092			1.2223	1.2882
			5.613	5.758			8.058	8.589
Years teacher's experience			0.0003	0.0000			0.0973	0.0743
			0.005	0.000			1.567	1.194
Logos II teacher training			3.5942	3.5302			2.6200	2.8133
			3.345	3.281			2.275	2.450
Qualificacao teacher training			-0.1596	0.1065			-3.6203	-2.9333
			-0.154	0.103			-3.262	-2.656
Teacher activity index			5.9854	2.7093			4.9143	1.7678
			3.034	1.378			2.324	0.843
Teacher materials index			1.6012	2.4874			2.3701	4.1882
			0.935	1.449			1.292	2.287
Constant	32.3124	33.9760	26.0850	25.9224	32.4307	34.8301	23.3923	22.9925
	8.501	8.530	6.630	6.545	7.945	8.144	5.546	5.440
Adjusted R squared	0.1399	0.1400	0.1466	0.1442	0.1115	0.1118	0.1285	0.1337
Number of cases	3856	3856	3847	3847	3856	3856	3847	3847
Mean of dependent variable	58.66	58.66	58.78	58.78	51.15	51.15	51.24	51.24

Table C5-13: Alternative Specifications of Cross-Section Second-Grade Models for Portuguese and Mathematics, 1985
(t statistics underneath)

Variable Description	Portuguese						Mathematics					
	(1)	(2)	(3)	(3t)	(4)	(4t)	(1)	(2)	(3)	(3t)	(4)	(4t)
State												
Ceara	15.7660	20.9884	13.7798	14.1301	18.0368	17.4389	6.4259	7.2480	6.0837	6.1928	11.9537	11.7260
	8.946	9.568	7.590	7.681	14.897	14.046	3.629	3.289	3.339	3.353	9.759	9.334
Piaui	-0.9188	0.7559	-1.1175	-0.1160	4.0215	3.9845	-14.0855	-17.0901	-12.6998	-12.5898	2.0795	1.9768
	-0.456	0.327	-0.533	-0.054	3.418	3.260	-6.956	-7.364	-6.039	-5.890	1.747	1.598
School control												
State operated	-1.6318	-1.9761	-0.7371	-0.5046	-1.3510	-0.9944	-2.7187	-3.8683	-2.1343	-2.0697	-3.7071	-3.4714
	-1.189	-1.417	-0.530	-0.359	-0.983	-0.716	-1.972	-2.761	-1.528	-1.466	-2.666	-2.471
Federally operated	9.4174	8.7825	14.6749	13.5969	15.4351	14.2965	-5.3448	-8.4455	-2.1815	-3.4294	0.7383	-0.6218
	1.744	1.615	2.740	2.549	2.887	2.688	-0.985	-1.546	-0.406	-0.640	0.137	-0.116
Privately operated	3.7984	5.2313	4.9285	4.3300	4.4524	3.8181	3.6578	5.9113	3.7477	3.0037	2.6660	1.7917
	0.829	1.138	1.073	0.947	0.970	0.836	0.795	1.280	0.813	0.654	0.574	0.388
OME	-3.3321	-3.5883	-2.6817	-2.0433	-0.2391	0.3162	-9.3666	-8.1978	-8.9990	-8.9986	-3.1142	-3.5774
	-1.694	-1.799	-1.347	-0.998	-0.128	0.163	-4.740	-4.090	-4.504	-4.380	-1.644	-1.819
Program states												
EDURURAL: Pernambuco	-4.1163	-3.4474	-5.4435	-4.0701			-8.6353	-9.1291	-9.3091	-9.1284		
	-2.478	-2.050	-3.216	-2.336			-5.174	-5.405	-5.480	-5.218		
EDURURAL: Ceara	0.9820	-0.7156	-0.2890	0.0225			0.0088	-1.2901	-0.7451	-0.8207		
	0.744	-0.521	-0.215	0.017			0.007	-0.935	-0.552	-0.607		
EDURURAL: Piaui	2.3946	2.5437	0.9415	0.8411			12.9107	12.6829	11.2043	11.0897		
	1.522	1.617	0.581	0.514			8.165	8.026	6.887	6.748		

Table C5-13 Cont'd

Variable Description	Portuguese						Mathematics					
	(1)	(2)	(3)	(3t)	(4)	(4t)	(1)	(2)	(3)	(3t)	(4)	(4t)
Personal characteristics												
Female student	5.0076	5.0554	9.4476	7.1690	9.5921	7.1717	-5.7570	-6.2425	-3.2739	-5.5779	-2.5473	-4.9994
	1.661	1.679	3.072	2.301	3.122	2.305	-1.901	-2.064	-1.061	-1.783	-0.819	-1.588
Age	0.7686	0.7445	0.7632	0.7265	0.7483	0.7070	1.1723	1.1292	1.1951	1.2042	1.0854	1.0781
	4.833	4.684	4.752	4.463	4.700	4.389	7.336	7.070	7.414	7.369	6.740	6.614
Pupil works	-0.1609	-0.1052	-1.4218	-0.5028	-1.3526	-0.4169	2.0940	2.1369	1.2653	2.0791	2.0824	3.0225
	-0.101	-0.066	-0.887	-0.303	-0.845	-0.252	1.309	1.339	0.786	1.249	1.286	1.806
Family characteristics												
Mother's education	0.7337	0.7317	0.7852	0.6822	0.7781	0.6803	0.6118	0.6059	0.6368	0.5579	0.6276	0.5476
	3.872	3.870	4.103	3.495	4.067	3.490	3.213	3.190	3.315	2.848	3.243	2.776
Father's education	0.2835	0.3149	0.2584	0.2227	0.2797	0.2342	0.6350	0.6726	0.5973	0.5982	0.5996	0.5828
	1.314	1.462	1.178	0.998	1.274	1.049	2.930	3.108	2.713	2.669	2.701	2.580
Family size	-0.4711	-0.4940	-0.4553	-0.3803	-0.4529	-0.3777	-0.2105	-0.2234	-0.2037	-0.0981	-0.2063	-0.0853
	-3.551	-3.730	-3.402	-2.781	-3.387	-2.767	-1.580	-1.679	-1.516	-0.714	-1.525	-0.617
Joint characteristics: pupil and school												
Homework	3.3258	3.3774	3.3494	3.5554	3.1606	3.4029	1.7996	1.9115	1.8590	2.2056	1.7552	2.0917
	4.689	4.769	4.690	4.895	4.416	4.682	2.525	2.686	2.593	3.025	2.424	2.844
School lunch some days	-9.7692	-10.0061	-10.0675	-11.3237	-9.8454	-10.8755	-8.6490	-9.0467	-8.8732	-10.0701	-7.8039	-8.9821
	-2.864	-2.940	-2.934	-3.090	-2.869	-2.966	-2.524	-2.645	-2.577	-2.737	-2.248	-2.421
School lunch every day	-6.6934	-7.0722	-6.6774	-7.8543	-6.1718	-7.2249	-4.7125	-5.0339	-4.5133	-5.4768	-2.5737	-3.7216
	-1.942	-2.056	-1.928	-2.123	-1.780	-1.950	-1.361	-1.456	-1.298	-1.474	-0.734	-0.993

Table C5-13 Cont'd

Variable Description	Portuguese						Mathematics					
	(1)	(2)	(3)	(3t)	(4)	(4t)	(1)	(2)	(3)	(3t)	(4)	(4t)
Male teacher/male student	5.0814	5.0975	8.5917	7.9860	8.4533	7.8122	4.1646	3.3112	7.1320	5.2821	6.4790	4.5231
	2.257	2.257	3.619	3.315	3.564	3.249	1.841	1.459	2.993	2.184	2.700	1.859
Female teacher/female student	-0.5547	-0.5209	-3.9140	-3.2237	-3.8633	-3.1536	0.0289	0.6248	-1.9853	-0.7819	-1.9588	-0.6940
	-0.282	-0.265	-1.964	-1.601	-1.941	-1.570	0.015	0.316	-0.992	-0.387	-0.973	-0.341
Peer influences												
Percent families not farming	12.2612	12.3517	10.3978	10.5905	11.4930	11.1314	6.1678	5.9578	2.3787	1.8430	6.6749	6.0020
	4.929	4.974	4.082	4.069	4.589	4.353	2.468	2.388	0.930	0.705	2.635	2.320
Relatively large landholders	6.8270	7.2630	6.7560	6.5460	7.6970	7.4280	10.1600	10.7740	10.5150	10.2570	13.8260	13.6820
	3.411	3.629	3.285	3.113	3.789	3.575	5.053	5.358	5.094	4.858	6.727	6.508
Percent female classmates	3.9045	4.1525	4.1787	2.9197	5.1613	3.7960	4.8626	4.9181	4.2561	2.8012	6.1446	4.4412
	1.269	1.352	1.325	0.909	1.642	1.187	1.572	1.594	1.344	0.869	1.933	1.372
Female classmates when female student	2.3686	2.2051	0.7238	3.6187	0.3044	3.4003	1.5401	1.2683	0.8328	2.5187	-0.5540	1.2815
	0.591	0.551	0.177	0.872	0.075	0.822	0.383	0.316	0.203	0.605	-0.134	0.306
Percent seek 9 or more years school	7.6763	7.6812	7.9760	8.2109	8.9779	8.9413	6.3789	6.0376	7.1259	8.0919	8.9410	9.5407
	5.181	5.186	5.287	5.267	6.056	5.804	4.285	4.057	4.706	5.171	5.962	6.121
School characteristics												
Graded class	0.2617	0.4312	0.5017	0.5490	0.5181	0.6443	-1.7852	-1.8287	-1.0990	-0.9363	-0.6028	-0.4448
	0.324	0.533	0.607	0.652	0.611	0.746	-2.197	-2.251	-1.325	-1.107	-0.703	-0.509
Pupil-teacher ratio	0.0374	0.0203	0.0772	0.0766	0.0747	0.0693	-0.0276	-0.0218	-0.0090	0.0046	0.0102	0.0217
	1.134	0.608	2.330	2.201	2.255	1.997	-0.832	-0.650	-0.269	0.130	0.304	0.618

288

Table C5-13 Cont'd

Variable Description	Portuguese						Mathematics					
	(1)	(2)	(3)	(3t)	(4)	(4t)	(1)	(2)	(3)	(3t)	(4)	(4t)
School hardware index	-2.7271	-2.1388	-2.3766	-2.3197			0.5220	1.0028	0.4617	0.3725		
	-1.605	-1.258	-1.354	-1.274			0.306	0.587	0.262	0.204		
School furniture					0.7849	1.2029					1.0827	1.7312
					0.459	0.682					0.626	0.971
School facilities					-5.9780	-7.0957					-5.4583	-6.1190
					-3.401	-3.917					-3.070	-3.338
Water					-0.2832	-0.0379					2.4851	2.4496
					-0.355	-0.047					3.082	2.988
Electricity					0.5937	0.7387					-0.2448	-0.1609
					0.669	0.811					-0.273	-0.175
School software index	9.2199	9.1566	10.9996	10.9698			7.3734	7.9372	7.6978	7.2186		
	4.583	4.547	5.366	5.282			3.648	3.923	3.741	3.462		
Writing materials index					2.1835	3.5870					4.7500	6.1339
					1.384	2.132					2.975	3.602
Textbook used in school only					6.7156	7.0632					-3.2748	-4.1030
					2.934	3.054					-1.414	-1.753
Textbook used school and home					6.5417	6.2620					2.4995	1.8806
					5.500	5.212					2.077	1.547

Table C5-13 Cont'd

Variable Description	Portuguese						Mathematics					
	(1)	(2)	(3)	(3t)	(4)	(4t)	(1)	(2)	(3)	(3t)	(4)	(4t)
Teacher characteristics												
Teacher's salary	0.0460						0.0397					
	5.588						4.805					
Teacher's salary: Pernambuco		0.0739						0.0093				
		4.539						0.569				
Teacher's salary: Ceara		-0.0771						-0.0658				
		-2.577						-2.189				
Teacher's salary: Piaui		0.0492						0.0614				
		5.017						6.232				
Years teacher's education			0.1809	0.0089	0.2552	0.0775			0.5912	0.5372	0.7730	0.6840
			1.296	0.061	1.836	0.531			4.219	3.660	5.499	4.629
Years teacher's experience			0.0058	-0.0073	0.0023	-0.0131			0.0438	0.0517	0.0403	0.0504
			0.101	-0.125	0.041	-0.225			0.762	0.887	0.694	0.856
Logos teacher training			1.4555	1.8555	1.1421	1.5662			1.2735	1.7968	0.2302	0.6610
			1.480	1.844	1.165	1.563			1.290	1.778	0.232	0.652
Qualificacao teacher training			0.6777	0.5964	0.9940	0.9128			1.3798	1.4285	2.1805	2.0397
			0.679	0.594	1.004	0.915			1.378	1.416	2.177	2.021
Teacher activity index			-4.7327	-5.0161	-4.2871	-4.7494			0.7373	0.1886	0.9846	0.6213
			-2.235	-2.325	-2.040	-2.226			0.347	0.087	0.463	0.288

Table C5-13 Cont'd

Variable Description	Portuguese						Mathematics					
	(1)	(2)	(3)	(3t)	(4)	(4t)	(1)	(2)	(3)	(3t)	(4)	(4t)
Teacher materials index			2.3352	1.4703	2.0099	1.2675			1.1544	0.3119	0.4001	-0.3614
			1.387	0.856	1.202	0.744			0.683	0.181	0.237	-0.210
Teacher's Portuguese test score				-0.0823		-0.0803				-0.1555		-0.1592
				-2.718		-2.650				-5.116		-5.190
Teacher's mathematics test score				0.1347		0.1319				0.1243		0.1265
				5.752		5.649				5.285		5.352
Constant	31.7038	30.2676	32.9880	29.7434	29.7787	27.1316	30.9572	32.3916	26.5748	28.8133	15.7568	17.9037
	6.185	5.864	6.188	5.229	5.732	4.896	6.011	6.247	4.966	5.045	2.998	3.193
Adjusted R squared	0.1685	0.1722	0.1658	0.1760	0.1669	0.1784	0.1435	0.1474	0.1448	0.1571	0.1324	0.1463
Number of cases	4095	4095	4014	3828	4014	3828	4095	4095	4014	3828	4014	3828
Mean of dependent variable	59.33	59.33	59.34	59.54	59.34	59.54	48.94	48.94	48.78	49.00	48.78	49.00

Table C5-14: Effect of Health Status on Achievement in Ceara, 1987
(t statistics underneath)

Variable	Portuguese			Mathematics		
	Value-added Full sample	Value-added Bottom 40%	Cross-section Bottom 40%	Value-added Full sample	Value-added Bottom 40%	Cross-section Bottom 40%
Portuguese test, 1985	0.296	0.287	n.a.	n.a.	n.a.	n.a.
	8.40	3.34	n.a.	n.a.	n.a.	n.a.
Mathematics test, 1985	n.a.	n.a.	n.a.	0.257	0.281	n.a.
	n.a.	n.a.	n.a.	6.33	2.21	n.a.
Second grade in 1987	4.745	13.909	9.292	11.412	16.980	17.268
	1.42	2.28	1.51	2.50	2.26	2.26
Third grade in 1987	6.679	17.458	16.260	8.931	14.472	14.942
	2.41	3.18	3.86	2.33	2.07	2.11
Fourth grade in 1987	10.176	17.468	19.118	15.671	21.539	22.618
	3.70	3.13	3.31	4.14	3.03	3.14
Age	-1.263	-1.998	-1.781	-1.740	-2.376	-2.183
	-3.77	-2.87	-2.48	-3.76	-3.09	-2.81
Sex	0.264	-1.562	-1.581	-4.990	-3.805	-3.125
	0.19	-0.55	-0.54	-2.57	-1.03	-0.84
EDURURAL	4.110	8.424	9.336	12.587	14.610	14.803
	3.00	2.99	3.21	6.65	4.34	4.34
Skinfold-for-age: 50%-60% of normal	-3.224	-8.199	-6.964	-6.316	-7.344	-6.902
	-1.76	-2.14	-1.76	-2.48	-1.71	-1.58
Skinfold-for-age: below 50% of normal	-3.640	-15.099	-11.578	-6.064	-14.884	-14.741
	-1.76	-3.22	-2.44	-2.13	-2.89	-2.83
Height-for-age	-0.316	-0.772	-0.448	0.149	0.206	0.258
	-1.99	-2.25	-1.44	0.68	0.53	0.65
Visual: 60% of normal	-0.857	0.767	1.882	-3.942	-9.046	-11.406
	-0.37	0.18	0.42	-1.22	-1.65	-2.09
Weight-for-age: 80% of normal	-0.807	-6.510	-5.158	1.961	3.372	4.900
	-0.39	-1.56	-1.20	0.68	0.64	0.92
Weight-for-height: below 75% of normal	0.902	0.192	-0.882	-0.471	1.796	0.550
	0.37	0.04	-0.18	-0.14	0.33	0.10
Constant	102.560	148.509	133.025	53.707	49.879	50.489
	5.930	4.089	3.558	2.247	1.158	1.156
Adjusted R squared	0.271	0.252	0.194	0.277	0.282	0.261
Number of cases	377	143	143	377	148	148

Table C5-15: Effect of Nutritional Status on Portuguese Achievement
in Ceara, 1987
(t statistics underneath)

	Model 1 (a)		Model 2 (b)		Model 3 (c)	
	Full sample	Bottom 40%	Full sample	Bottom 40%	Full sample	Bottom 40%
Portuguese test, 1985	0.28	0.19	0.28	0.23	0.37	0.33
	8.02	2.23	8.13	2.73	9.14	3.42
Mathematics test, 1985	n.a.	n.a.	n.a.	n.a.	n.a.	n.a.
	n.a.	n.a.	n.a.	n.a.	n.a.	n.a.
Second grade in 1987	4.58	11.88	4.66	12.55	0.91	8.26
	1.37	1.91	1.40	2.05	0.25	1.20
Third grade in 1987	7.00	16.29	6.97	16.67	7.22	17.66
	2.53	2.93	2.53	3.04	2.54	2.74
Fourth grade in 1987	11.03	19.93	10.70	17.66	9.40	18.60
	4.07	3.58	3.94	3.18	3.35	2.78
Age	-1.03	-1.71	-1.05	-1.59	-0.62	-2.16
	-3.27	-2.50	-3.32	-2.38	-1.79	-2.69
Sex	-0.53	-3.72	-0.21	-2.70	-1.02	-4.87
	-0.39	-1.35	-0.15	-1.00	-0.74	-1.81
EDURURAL	3.97	7.49	4.09	8.23	7.39	24.89
	2.93	2.64	3.02	2.97	2.04	3.38
Skinfold-for-age: 50% to 60% of normal	n.a.	n.a.	-2.57	-6.58	-1.01	-0.13
	n.a.	n.a.	-1.42	-1.75	-0.54	-0.03
Skinfold-for-age: below 50% of normal	n.a.	n.a.	-2.65	-12.63	-1.01	-7.95
	n.a.	n.a.	-1.34	-2.81	-0.48	-1.43
School dummies	No	No	No	No	Yes	Yes
Constant	69.69	74.57	70.27	73.13	57.89	67.54
	11.94	5.94	11.97	5.87	8.57	4.56
Adjusted R squared	0.27	0.19	0.27	0.23	0.41	0.45
Number of cases	377	142	377	143	377	143

(a) Nutrition status variables were not used.
(b) Nutrition status variables were used.
(c) Both nutrition status variables and school dummies were used.

Table C5-16: Effect of Nutritional Status on Mathematics Achievement
in Ceara, 1987
(t statistics underneath)

	Model 1 (a)		Model 2 (b)		Model 3 (c)	
	Full sample	Bottom 40%	Full sample	Bottom 40%	Full sample	Bottom 40%
Portuguese test, 1985	n.a.	n.a.	n.a.	n.a.	n.a.	n.a.
	n.a.	n.a.	n.a.	n.a.	n.a.	n.a.
Mathematics test, 1985	0.25	0.33	0.26	0.33	0.41	0.43
	6.23	2.65	6.52	2.73	7.47	3.01
Second grade in 1987	11.80	15.34	11.87	15.84	5.80	9.16
	2.57	2.01	2.62	2.14	1.26	1.17
Third grade in 1987	9.31	14.15	9.22	14.25	2.39	2.99
	2.42	2.00	2.42	2.07	0.65	0.40
Fourth grade in 1987	16.92	22.39	16.13	20.77	11.24	14.93
	4.50	3.13	4.25	2.96	3.09	2.06
Age	-1.81	-2.87	-1.86	-2.56	-1.23	-1.46
	-4.12	-3.87	-4.25	-3.50	-2.71	-1.89
Sex	-5.81	-5.99	-4.89	-4.09	-5.67	-6.92
	-3.11	-1.90	-2.61	-1.17	-3.19	-2.17
EDURURAL	12.41	14.70	12.70	15.64	17.58	35.85
	6.59	4.40	6.82	4.78	3.76	3.47
Skinfold-for-age: 50% to 60% of normal	n.a.	n.a.	-6.40	-6.84	-3.92	-3.43
	n.a.	n.a.	-2.57	-1.62	-1.62	-0.83
Skinfold-for-age: below 50% of normal	n.a.	n.a.	-6.40	-14.75	-3.98	-6.64
	n.a.	n.a.	-2.36	-2.94	-1.45	-1.28
School dummies	No	No	No	No	Yes	Yes
Constant	66.98	72.87	68.60	69.97	49.53	42.99
	8.43	4.95	8.68	4.84	5.61	2.78
Adjusted R squared	0.26	0.25	0.28	0.29	0.49	0.57
Number of cases	377	147	377	148	377	148

(a) Nutrition status variables were not used.
(b) Nutrition status variables were used.
(c) Both nutrition status variables and school dummies were used.

Table C6-1: Cost-effectiveness of Inputs for Portuguese Achievement, 1981, 1983 and 1985

Grade level/input	Cost (US$)	Achievement change in Portuguese associated with input presence (a)			Achievement gain per U.S. dollar spent		
		1981	1983	1985	1981	1983	1985
Second grade (b)							
Infrastructure inputs							
Water	1.81	(1.433)	3.513	(-0.283)	(0.79)	1.94	?
School furniture	5.45	(-0.782)	-5.650	(0.785)	?	?	(0.14)
School facilities	8.80	7.080	7.228	-5.978	0.80	0.82	?
Hardware	16.06	8.906	8.969	(-2.377)	0.55	0.56	?
Material inputs							
Textbook usage	1.65	5.516	6.403	6.542	3.34	3.88	3.96
Writing material	1.76	(-0.893)	4.703	(2.184)	?	2.67	(1.24)
Software	3.41	5.896	4.864	11.000	1.73	1.43	3.23
Teacher salary (c)	0.39	0.029	0.055	0.046	0.07	0.14	0.12
Alternative teacher education strategies							
Curso de Qualificacao	2.50	n.a.	(-0.160)	(0.678)	n.a.	?	(0.27)
Logos II	1.84	(-0.881)	3.594	(1.456)	?	1.95	(0.79)
4 years primary school	2.21	2.252	3.177	(0.724)	1.02	1.44	(0.33)
3 years secondary school	5.55	1.689	2.383	(0.543)	0.30	0.43	(0.10)
Fourth grade (d)							
Infrastructure inputs							
Water	1.81		(4.712)	(0.088)		(2.60)	(0.05)
School furniture	5.45		(-1.057)	(5.832)		?	(1.07)
School facilities	8.80		(8.550)	(0.941)		(0.97)	(0.11)
Hardware	16.06		11.728	8.778		0.73	0.55
Material inputs							
Textbook usage	1.65		(-1.709)	(1.892)		?	(1.15)
Writing material	1.76		(-1.536)	8.266		?	4.70
Software	3.41		(-3.020)	(6.689)		?	(1.96)
Teacher salary (c)	0.39		(0.023)	(0.013)		(0.06)	(0.03)
Alternative teacher education strategies							
Curso de Qualificacao	2.50		(1.022)	(-2.211)		(0.41)	?
Logos II	1.84		(2.000)	(-0.224)		(1.09)	?
4 years primary school	2.21		(-1.336)	(-0.536)		?	?
3 years secondary school	5.55		(-1.002)	(-0.402)		?	?

Ratios in parentheses reflect statistically insignificant coefficients in the underlying
regression models; question marks reflect negative coefficients.
(a) Source as indicated in notes b and d.
(b) Based on the cross-section (level) models shown in full in appendix tables C5-11 to
C5-13 columns 3 and 4 (except column 1 for salary).
(c) A one percent increase in teacher salary expressed as a percentage of the minimum wage
prevailing in October, 1983 (30,600 cruzeiros).
(d) Based on the value-added (longitudinal) models shown in full in appendix tables
C5-5 and C5-7 (columns 1 and 4), and C5-9 and C5-10 (column 1).

Table C6-2: Cost-effectiveness of Inputs for Mathematics Achievement

Grade level/input	Cost (US$)	Achievement change in Mathematics associated with input presence (a)			Achivement gain per U.S. dollar spent		
		1981	1983	1985	1981	1983	1985
Second grade (b)							
Infrastructure inputs							
Water	1.81	6.128	6.613	2.485	3.39	3.65	1.37
School furniture	5.45	(0.133)	-11.214	(1.083)	(0.02)	?	(0.20)
School facilities	8.80	8.631	(1.829)	-5.458	0.98	(0.21)	?
Hardware	16.06	11.964	6.307	(0.462)	0.74	0.39	(0.03)
Material inputs							
Textbook usage	1.65	5.640	4.226	2.500	3.42	2.56	1.52
Writing material	1.76	(-4.468)	3.272	4.750	?	1.86	2.70
Software	3.41	4.825	(2.538)	7.698	1.41	(0.74)	2.26
Teacher salary (c)	0.39	0.033	0.064	0.040	0.08	0.16	0.10
Alternative teacher education strategies							
Curso de Qualificacao	2.50	NA	-3.620	(1.380)	NA	?	(0.55)
Logos II	1.84	(0.260)	2.620	(1.274)	(0.14)	1.42	(0.69)
4 years primary school	2.21	2.345	4.889	2.365	1.06	2.21	1.07
3 years secondary school	5.55	1.759	3.667	1.774	0.32	0.66	0.32
Fourth grade (d)							
Infrastructure inputs							
School furniture	1.81		7.798	(2.845)		4.31	(1.57)
School facilities	5.45		(2.387)	(7.061)		(0.44)	(1.30)
Hardware	8.80		(3.888)	(0.673)		(0.44)	(0.08)
	16.06		(8.321)	12.404		(0.52)	0.77
Material inputs							
Textbook usage	1.65		(-7.782)	(-3.470)		?	?
Writing material	1.76		(2.808)	12.716		(1.60)	7.23
Software	3.41		(-5.580)	11.028		?	3.23
Teacher salary (c)	0.39		(0.023)	0.042		(0.06)	0.11
Alternative teacher education strategies							
Curso de Qualificacao	2.50		(2.962)	-5.936		(1.81)	?
Logos II	1.84		(0.720)	(0.655)		(0.39)	(0.36)
4 years primary school	2.21		(1.824)	(-0.321)		(0.83)	?
3 years secondary school	5.55		(1.368)	(-0.241)		(025)	?

Ratios in parentheses reflect statistically insignificant coefficients in the underlying regression models; question marks reflect negative coefficients.

(a) Source as indicated in notes b and d.

(b) Based on the cross-section (level) models shown in full in appendix tables C5.11 to C5-13, columns 3 and 4, (except column 1 for salary).

(c) A one percent increase in teacher salary expressed as a percentage of the minimum wage prevailing in October, 1983 (30,600 cruzeiros).

(d) Based on the value-added (longitudinal) models shown in full in appendix tables C5-6 and C5-8 (columns 1 and 4), and C5-9 and C5-10 (columns 3).

Table C6-3: The Determinants of Teacher Salary: Raw Form Regressions
for 1981, 1983, 1985 and Pooled Years
(t statistics underneath)

	1981	1983	1985	1985 w.TT	Pooled	Pooled w.TT
Teacher sex	-7.918	-16.653	-12.373	-12.890	-12.836	-12.921
	-1.63	-3.20	-2.15	-2.22	-4.18	-4.20
Teacher experience	0.730	0.539	0.913	0.887	0.766	0.758
	3.67	2.60	4.08	3.96	6.27	6.20
Teacher education	4.468	4.204	3.751	3.511	4.242	4.153
	9.81	8.21	7.09	6.50	14.73	14.33
Logos II	3.277	9.259	2.517	1.912	4.522	4.268
	0.85	2.29	0.66	0.50	2.02	1.90
Qualificacao		-6.491	-3.088	-2.615	-3.590	-3.150
		-1.74	-0.84	-0.71	-1.51	-1.32
Benefits		-2.860	13.318	12.156	4.638	3.729
		-0.44	2.09	1.90	1.09	0.88
Portuguese test score				0.225		0.229
				1.85		2.06
Mathematics test score				0.037		0.046
				0.33		0.46
Contract status	18.324	16.977	22.263	22.074	19.323	19.300
	5.26	3.85	4.86	4.83	8.08	8.08
Regular status	8.390	6.451	14.381	14.040	8.354	8.271
	1.84	1.25	2.56	2.51	2.85	2.82
Fourth grade teacher	3.994	5.129	7.028	5.617	5.054	4.535
	1.55	1.75	2.32	1.80	3.05	2.71
Graded classroom	4.059	8.180	11.377	10.487	7.426	7.121
	1.37	2.60	3.60	3.30	4.16	3.99
Pupil-teacher ratio	0.089	0.592	0.137	0.139	0.140	0.140
	2.03	5.65	1.51	1.52	3.61	3.62
Federal school	30.814	67.650	131.824	130.680	138.483	136.691
	1.88	2.65	6.65	6.60	7.64	7.55
State school	50.432	63.874	45.929	45.540	53.513	53.374
	11.73	12.89	8.10	8.05	18.53	18.50
Private school	-5.145	-0.127	43.619	43.100	5.591	5.321
	-0.74	-0.01	2.72	2.69	0.91	0.86

Table C6-3 Cont'd

	1981	1983	1985	1985 w.TT	Pooled	Pooled w.TT
SES of Municipio	37.495	28.469	15.104	15.751	28.091	28.350
	6.33	4.02	1.95	2.03	7.00	7.07
EDURURAL	-3.442	-4.774	-5.411	-4.893	-4.295	-4.144
	-1.32	-1.65	-1.76	-1.58	-2.58	-2.49
Piaui	2.645	8.979	19.492	19.234	10.815	10.792
	0.67	2.02	4.43	4.38	4.42	4.42
Ceara	-28.762	-27.497	-29.212	-30.446	-29.002	-29.474
	-8.98	-7.17	-7.15	-7.40	-13.61	-13.79
Federal school, 1981					-113.424	-111.549
					-4.45	-4.38
Federal school, 1983					-77.123	-75.098
					-2.47	-2.41
Constant	0.306	2.413	-9.545	-24.994	-2.323	-21.668
	0.04	0.28	-0.98	-2.03	-0.43	-2.33
Year 1981					4.102	24.610
					1.297	2.87
Year 1983					6.151	27.165
					3.166	3.23
Adjusted R squared	0.56	0.59	0.50	0.50	0.54	0.54
Number of observations	726.00	726.00	764.00	764.00	2216.00	2216.00

Note:
Dependent variable is teacher salary expressed as a percentage of
regional minimum wage.

Table C6-4: The Determinants of Teacher Salary: Log Form Regressions
for 1981, 1983, 1985 and Pooled Years
(t statistics underneath)

	1981	1983	1985	1985 w. TT	Pooled	Pooled w. TT
Teacher sex	-0.105	-0.203	-0.219	-0.220	-0.166	-0.164
	-1.09	-2.16	-2.26	-2.28	-2.99	-2.95
Teacher experience	0.166	0.083	0.167	0.162	0.147	0.146
	2.00	2.41	4.48	4.34	7.14	7.07
Teacher education	0.492	0.512	0.512	0.476	0.521	0.509
	2.00	8.12	8.24	7.55	14.69	14.29
Logos II	0.058	0.146	0.099	0.089	0.099	0.094
	0.75	1.98	1.51	1.35	2.42	2.33
Qualificacao		-0.061	-0.054	-0.045	-0.065	-0.057
		-0.90	-0.87	-0.74	-1.50	-1.32
Benefits		-0.014	0.147	0.134	0.040	0.031
		-0.29	2.99	2.73	1.20	0.94
Portuguese test score				0.238		0.228
				1.80		1.77
Mathematics test score				0.119		0.139
				0.12		1.45
Contract status	0.312	0.281	0.279	0.276	0.280	0.279
	4.41	3.49	3.52	3.49	6.35	6.35
Regular status	0.251	0.162	0.195	0.192	0.179	0.179
	2.70	1.73	2.03	2.01	3.33	3.34
Fourth grade teacher	0.084	0.200	0.155	0.124	0.135	0.123
	1.62	3.79	3.03	2.38	4.49	4.08
Graded classroom	0.129	0.298	0.270	0.255	0.232	0.227
	2.16	5.26	5.08	4.77	7.18	7.01
Pupil-teacher ratio	0.184	0.173	0.097	0.100	0.143	0.144
	4.58	3.71	2.09	2.16	5.64	5.68
Federal school	0.835	0.569	1.182	1.152	1.214	1.176
	2.53	1.24	3.53	3.46	3.70	3.59
State school	0.829	0.818	0.501	0.492	0.726	0.723
	9.64	9.12	5.22	5.14	13.88	13.84
Private school	-0.132	0.141	0.855	0.840	0.091	0.085
	-0.95	0.57	3.16	3.12	0.81	0.76

Table C6-4 Cont'd

	1981	1983	1985	1985 w. TT	Pooled	Pooled w. TT
SES of Municipio	0.159	0.137	0.012	0.016	0.099	0.101
	5.70	4.86	0.44	0.58	6.11	6.22
EDURURAL	-0.275	-0.249	-0.280	-0.266	-0.269	-0.265
	-5.28	-4.78	-5.36	-5.10	-8.90	-8.78
Piaui	0.022	0.080	0.094	0.091	0.071	0.071
	0.28	0.98	1.23	1.19	1.57	1.58
Ceara	-0.917	-1.162	-1.104	-1.129	-1.061	-1.071
	-14.00	-17.22	-15.95	-16.24	-27.49	-27.71
Federal school, 1981					-0.597	-0.560
					-1.29	-1.21
Federal school, 1983					-0.614	-0.572
					-1.09	-1.01
Constant	2.150	2.339	2.247	0.804	2.193	0.630
	9.35	9.62	8.88	1.41	15.15	1.20
Year 1981					0.029	1.624
					0.63	3.12
Year 1983					0.074	1.664
					2.1	3.21
Adjusted R squared	0.62	0.67	0.61	0.61	0.62	0.62
Number of observations	726.00	726.00	764.00	764.00	2216.00	2216.00

Note:
Dependent variable is log of teacher salary expressed as a percentage of
regional minimum wage.

sas\data\sep90tab\an6-4

Table C6-5: Flow Improvements: Alternative Estimates of Years Saved Per Dollar Invested,
1981-83, 1983-85, and 1985-87
(best estimates)

	Software	Hardware	Teacher Salary	Logos	4 Years of Primary Education	3 Years of Secondary Education
Rural Northeast						
81-83 promotion probabilities						
81 2nd grade achievement coefficients	0.1312	0.0472	0.0062	0.0000	0.0817	0.0246
83 2nd grade achievement coefficients	0.0929	0.0424	0.0117	0.1462	0.1238	0.0378
85 2nd grade achievement coefficients	0.2349	0.0000	0.0093	0.0521	0.0371	0.0111
83 4th grade achievement coefficients	0.0000	0.0553	0.0048	0.0766	0.0120	0.0036
85 4th grade achievement coefficients	0.1707	0.0471	0.0038	0.0052	0.0000	0.0000
83-85 promotion probabilities						
81 2nd grade achievement coefficients	0.1860	0.0707	0.0091	0.0000	0.1189	0.0360
83 2nd grade achievement coefficients	0.1197	0.0599	0.0173	0.2053	0.1868	0.0575
85 2nd grade achievement coefficients	0.3265	0.0000	0.0134	0.0673	0.0620	0.0186
83 4th grade achievement coefficients	0.0000	0.0781	0.0070	0.1037	0.0265	0.0079
85 4th grade achievement coefficients	0.2578	0.0709	0.0064	0.0114	0.0000	0.0000
85-87 promotion probabilities						
81 2nd grade achievement coefficients	0.1499	0.0542	0.0071	0.0000	0.0937	0.0283
83 2nd grade achievement coefficients	0.1059	0.0486	0.0134	0.1670	0.1419	0.0434
85 2nd grade achievement coefficients	0.2675	0.0000	0.0107	0.0594	0.0428	0.0128
83 4th grade achievement coefficients	0.0000	0.0633	0.0055	0.0875	0.0141	0.0042
85 4th grade achievement coefficients	0.1954	0.0540	0.0044	0.0061	0.0000	0.0000
Low-income Rural Northeast						
81-83 promotion probabilities						
81 2nd grade achievement coefficients	0.1696	0.0612	0.0080	0.0000	0.1058	0.0319
83 2nd grade achievement coefficients	0.1203	0.0549	0.0151	0.1890	0.1601	0.0490
85 2nd grade achievement coefficients	0.3031	0.0000	0.0120	0.0675	0.0481	0.0144
83 4th grade achievement coefficients	0.0000	0.0716	0.0062	0.0991	0.0155	0.0046
85 4th grade achievement coefficients	0.2205	0.0610	0.0050	0.0067	0.0000	0.0000
83-85 promotion probabilities						
81 2nd grade achievement coefficients	0.2403	0.0916	0.0118	0.0000	0.1538	0.0467
83 2nd grade achievement coefficients	0.1548	0.0776	0.0224	0.2651	0.2412	0.0745
85 2nd grade achievement coefficients	0.4206	0.0000	0.0173	0.0871	0.0803	0.0241
83 4th grade achievement coefficients	0.0000	0.1011	0.0090	0.1342	0.0343	0.0103
85 4th grade achievement coefficients	0.3325	0.0918	0.0083	0.0148	0.0000	0.0000
85-87 promotion probabilities						
81 2nd grade achievement coefficients	0.1938	0.0702	0.0092	0.0000	0.1212	0.0366
83 2nd grade achievement coefficients	0.1370	0.0629	0.0174	0.2158	0.1834	0.0563
85 2nd grade achievement coefficients	0.3450	0.0000	0.0138	0.0770	0.0555	0.0166
83 4th grade achievement coefficients	0.0000	0.0820	0.0071	0.1132	0.0182	0.0054
85 4th grade achievement coefficients	0.2523	0.0700	0.0058	0.0079	0.0000	0.0000

Table C6-6: Partial Benefit-Cost Ratios: Alternative Estimates of Dollars Saved
Saved Per Dollar Invested, 1981-83, 1983-85, and 1985-87 (best estimates)

	Software	Hardware	Teacher Salary	Logos	4 Years of Primary Education	3 Years of Secondary Education
Rural Northeast						
81-83 promotion probabilities						
81 2nd grade achievement coefficients	3.935	1.417	0.185	0.000	2.452	0.739
83 2nd grade achievement coefficients	2.788	1.272	0.350	4.387	3.714	1.134
85 2nd grade achievement coefficients	7.048	0.000	0.279	1.563	1.113	0.333
83 4th grade achievement coefficients	0.000	1.660	0.144	2.297	0.359	0.107
85 4th grade achievement coefficients	5.120	1.412	0.115	0.155	0.000	0.000
83-85 promotion probabilities						
81 2nd grade achievement coefficients	5.581	2.122	0.273	0.000	3.568	1.081
83 2nd grade achievement coefficients	3.591	1.797	0.519	6.160	5.604	1.726
85 2nd grade achievement coefficients	9.796	0.000	0.401	2.018	1.861	0.559
83 4th grade achievement coefficients	0.000	2.344	0.209	3.111	0.795	0.238
85 4th grade achievement coefficients	7.733	2.126	0.193	0.343	0.000	0.000
85-87 promotion probabilities						
81 2nd grade achievement coefficients	4.497	1.627	0.213	0.000	2.810	0.848
83 2nd grade achievement coefficients	3.178	1.457	0.402	5.010	4.257	1.303
85 2nd grade achievement coefficients	8.026	0.000	0.320	1.783	1.285	0.385
83 4th grade achievement coefficients	0.000	1.900	0.165	2.624	0.422	0.126
85 4th grade achievement coefficients	5.862	1.621	0.133	0.182	0.000	0.000
Low-income Rural Northeast						
81-83 promotion probabilities						
81 2nd grade achievement coefficients	5.088	1.836	0.240	0.000	3.174	0.958
83 2nd grade achievement coefficients	3.608	1.647	0.454	5.671	4.803	1.469
85 2nd grade achievement coefficients	9.094	0.000	0.361	2.024	1.442	0.432
83 4th grade achievement coefficients	0.000	2.149	0.186	2.973	0.466	0.139
85 4th grade achievement coefficients	6.615	1.829	0.150	0.201	0.000	0.000
83-85 promotion probabilities						
81 2nd grade achievement coefficients	7.208	2.747	0.354	0.000	4.615	1.401
83 2nd grade achievement coefficients	4.644	2.327	0.673	7.953	7.237	2.235
85 2nd grade achievement coefficients	12.617	0.000	0.520	2.612	2.409	0.724
83 4th grade achievement coefficients	0.000	3.034	0.271	4.025	1.030	0.308
85 4th grade achievement coefficients	9.974	2.753	0.250	0.445	0.000	0.000
85-87 promotion probabilities						
81 2nd grade achievement coefficients	5.813	2.107	0.276	0.000	3.636	1.099
83 2nd grade achievement coefficients	4.111	1.887	0.521	6.474	5.503	1.688
85 2nd grade achievement coefficients	10.349	0.000	0.414	2.309	1.664	0.499
83 4th grade achievement coefficients	0.000	2.461	0.214	3.396	0.547	0.163
85 4th grade achievement coefficients	7.569	2.100	0.173	0.236	0.000	0.000

Table C6-7: Lower Bound Estimates of Years Saved Per Dollar Invested,
1981-83, 1983-85, and 1985-87

	Software	Hardware	Teacher Salary	Logos	4 Years of Primary Education	3 Years of Secondary Education
Rural Northeast						
81-83 promotion probabilities						
81 2nd grade achievement coefficients	0.0796	0.0259	0.0035	0.0000	0.0474	0.0142
83 2nd grade achievement coefficients	0.0661	0.0261	0.0066	0.0903	0.0661	0.0201
85 2nd grade achievement coefficients	0.1467	0.0000	0.0055	0.0000	0.0000	0.0000
83 4th grade achievement coefficients	0.0000	0.0340	0.0000	0.0000	0.0000	0.0000
85 4th grade achievement coefficients	0.0000	0.0255	0.0000	0.0000	0.0000	0.0000
83-85 promotion probabilities						
81 2nd grade achievement coefficients	0.1304	0.0470	0.0061	0.0000	0.0813	0.0245
83 2nd grade achievement coefficients	0.0922	0.0421	0.0116	0.1453	0.1232	0.0376
85 2nd grade achievement coefficients	0.2335	0.0000	0.0092	0.0000	0.0157	0.0047
83 4th grade achievement coefficients	0.0000	0.0476	0.0000	0.0000	0.0000	0.0000
85 4th grade achievement coefficients	0.0467	0.0468	0.0016	0.0000	0.0000	0.0000
85-87 promotion probabilities						
81 2nd grade achievement coefficients	0.0744	0.0242	0.0033	0.0000	0.0443	0.0133
83 2nd grade achievement coefficients	0.0619	0.0244	0.0061	0.0845	0.0619	0.0188
85 2nd grade achievement coefficients	0.1374	0.0000	0.0052	0.0000	0.0000	0.0000
83 4th grade achievement coefficients	0.0000	0.0318	0.0000	0.0000	0.0000	0.0000
85 4th grade achievement coefficients	0.0000	0.0239	0.0000	0.0000	0.0000	0.0000
Low-income Rural Northeast						
81-83 promotion probabilities						
81 2nd grade achievement coefficients	0.1030	0.0336	0.0046	0.0000	0.0614	0.0184
83 2nd grade achievement coefficients	0.0856	0.0338	0.0085	0.1168	0.0856	0.0260
85 2nd grade achievement coefficients	0.1896	0.0000	0.0072	0.0000	0.0000	0.0000
83 4th grade achievement coefficients	0.0000	0.0441	0.0000	0.0000	0.0000	0.0000
85 4th grade achievement coefficients	0.0000	0.0330	0.0000	0.0000	0.0000	0.0000
83-85 promotion probabilities						
81 2nd grade achievement coefficients	0.1686	0.0609	0.0080	0.0000	0.1052	0.0317
83 2nd grade achievement coefficients	0.1193	0.0546	0.0150	0.1879	0.1593	0.0487
85 2nd grade achievement coefficients	0.3013	0.0000	0.0120	0.0000	0.0203	0.0060
83 4th grade achievement coefficients	0.0000	0.0616	0.0000	0.0000	0.0000	0.0000
85 4th grade achievement coefficients	0.0605	0.0606	0.0021	0.0000	0.0000	0.0000
85-87 promotion probabilities						
81 2nd grade achievement coefficients	0.0964	0.0314	0.0043	0.0000	0.0574	0.0172
83 2nd grade achievement coefficients	0.0801	0.0316	0.0080	0.1093	0.0801	0.0243
85 2nd grade achievement coefficients	0.1777	0.0000	0.0067	0.0000	0.0000	0.0000
83 4th grade achievement coefficients	0.0000	0.0412	0.0000	0.0000	0.0000	0.0000
85 4th grade achievement coefficients	0.0000	0.0309	0.0000	0.0000	0.0000	0.0000

Table C6-8: Lower Bound Estimates of Dollars Saved Per Dollar Invested, 1981-83, 1983-85, and 1985-87
(at US$30 per student year saved)

	Software	Hardware	Teacher Salary	Logos	4 Years of Primary Education	3 Years of Primary Education
Rural Northeast						
81-83 promotion probabilities						
81 2nd grade achievement coefficients	2.387	0.778	0.105	0.000	1.422	0.427
83 2nd grade achievement coefficients	1.983	0.782	0.197	2.708	1.983	0.602
85 2nd grade achievement coefficients	4.401	0.000	0.166	0.000	0.000	0.000
83 4th grade achievement coefficients	0.000	1.020	0.000	0.000	0.000	0.000
85 4th grade achievement coefficients	0.000	0.765	0.000	0.000	0.000	0.000
83-85 promotion probabilities						
81 2nd grade achievement coefficients	3.911	1.410	0.184	0.000	2.439	0.735
83 2nd grade achievement coefficients	2.766	1.264	0.348	4.360	3.696	1.129
85 2nd grade achievement coefficients	7.005	0.000	0.277	0.000	0.470	0.140
83 4th grade achievement coefficients	0.000	1.427	0.000	0.000	0.000	0.000
85 4th grade achievement coefficients	1.400	1.405	0.048	0.000	0.000	0.000
85-87 promotion probabilities						
81 2nd grade achievement coefficients	2.233	0.727	0.098	0.000	1.330	0.399
83 2nd grade achievement coefficients	1.856	0.731	0.184	2.534	1.856	0.563
85 2nd grade achievement coefficients	4.123	0.000	0.155	0.000	0.000	0.000
83 4th grade achievement coefficients	0.000	0.954	0.000	0.000	0.000	0.000
85 4th grade achievement coefficients	0.000	0.716	0.000	0.000	0.000	0.000
Low-income Rural Northeast						
81-83 promotion probabilities						
81 2nd grade achievement coefficients	3.089	1.008	0.137	0.000	1.842	0.553
83 2nd grade achievement coefficients	2.568	1.014	0.256	3.504	2.568	0.780
85 2nd grade achievement coefficients	5.689	0.000	0.215	0.000	0.000	0.000
83 4th grade achievement coefficients	0.000	1.322	0.000	0.000	0.000	0.000
85 4th grade achievement coefficients	0.000	0.991	0.000	0.000	0.000	0.000
83-85 promotion probabilities						
81 2nd grade achievement coefficients	5.058	1.826	0.239	0.000	3.156	0.952
83 2nd grade achievement coefficients	3.579	1.637	0.451	5.636	4.780	1.462
85 2nd grade achievement coefficients	9.038	0.000	0.359	0.000	0.609	0.181
83 4th grade achievement coefficients	0.000	1.848	0.000	0.000	0.000	0.000
85 4th grade achievement coefficients	1.814	1.819	0.062	0.000	0.000	0.000
85-87 promotion probabilities						
81 2nd grade achievement coefficients	2.891	0.943	0.128	0.000	1.723	0.517
83 2nd grade achievement coefficients	2.403	0.948	0.239	3.280	2.403	0.729
85 2nd grade achievement coefficients	5.330	0.000	0.201	0.000	0.000	0.000
83 4th grade achievement coefficients	0.000	1.236	0.000	0.000	0.000	0.000
85 4th grade achievement coefficients	0.000	0.927	0.000	0.000	0.000	0.000

Table C6-9: Partial Benefit-Cost Ratios by Region of Brazil
(Dollars saved per dollar invested at US$30 per student year saved)

	Software	Hardware	Teacher Salary	Logos	Teacher Training Strategies	
					4 Years More Primary School	3 Years Secondary Education
Fourth grade mean results						
Brazil	0.81	0.47	0.04	0.37	0.07	0.02
Rural Brazil	1.56	0.92	0.08	0.72	0.13	0.04
Low-income rural Brazil	2.86	1.67	0.15	1.33	0.24	0.07
Rural northeast	3.12	1.84	0.16	1.45	0.26	0.08
Low-income rural northeast	4.02	2.39	0.21	1.88	0.34	0.10
Rural center-west	1.30	0.76	0.07	0.60	0.11	0.03
Low-income rural center-west	1.72	1.01	0.09	0.79	0.14	0.04
Rural southeast	1.24	0.72	0.06	0.57	0.10	0.03
Low-income rural southeast	2.02	1.19	0.10	0.94	0.17	0.05
Rural south	0.80	0.46	0.04	0.37	0.07	0.02
Low-income rural south	1.75	1.03	0.09	0.81	0.15	0.04
Urban southeast	0.60	0.35	0.03	0.28	0.05	0.01
High-income urban southeast	0.52	0.30	0.03	0.24	0.04	0.01
Second grade mean results						
Brazil	1.40	0.28	0.08	0.60	0.76	0.23
Rural Brazil	2.70	0.54	0.16	1.16	1.48	0.45
Low-income rural Brazil	4.93	0.99	0.30	2.13	2.71	0.82
Rural northeast	5.38	1.08	0.33	2.32	2.96	0.90
Low-income rural northeast	6.96	1.39	0.42	3.00	3.83	1.17
Rural center-west	2.24	0.44	0.13	0.96	1.23	0.37
Low-income rural center-west	2.97	0.59	0.18	1.28	1.62	0.49
Rural southeast	2.13	0.42	0.13	0.92	1.17	0.35
Low-income rural southeast	3.49	0.69	0.21	1.50	1.92	0.58
Rural south	1.37	0.27	0.08	0.59	0.75	0.22
Low-income rural south	3.03	0.60	0.18	1.30	1.66	0.50
Urban southeast	1.03	0.20	0.06	0.44	0.56	0.17
High-income urban southeast	0.90	0.18	0.05	0.38	0.49	0.15

Table C7-1: EDURURAL's Effect in Piaui, 1981, 1983, and 1985

	1981	1983	1985
Second grade Portuguese			
Hardware			
Estimated effect (coefficient)	8.906	8.969	-2.377
Mean Difference (EDURURAL - OTHER)	0.125	0.051	0.059
EDURURAL Effect	1.113	0.457	-0.140
Software			
Estimated effect (coefficient)	5.896	4.864	11.000
Mean Difference (EDURURAL - OTHER)	-0.033	0.002	0.249
EDURURAL Effect	-0.195	0.010	2.739
Effect of unmeasured EDURURAL Variables	-1.174	-1.763	0.942
Total effect of EDURURAL Program	-0.3	-1.3	3.5
Fourth grade Portuguese			
Hardware			
Estimated effect (coefficient)		11.728	8.778
Mean Difference (EDURURAL - OTHER)		0.078	0.068
EDURURAL Effect		0.915	0.597
Software			
Estimated effect (coefficient)		-3.020	6.689
Mean Difference (EDURURAL - OTHER)		0.004	0.254
EDURURAL Effect		-0.012	1.699
Effect of unmeasured EDURURAL Variables		-0.538	-6.215
Total effect of EDURURAL Program		0.4	-3.9

Table C7-1 Cont'd

	1981	1983	1985
Second grade Mathematics			
Hardware			
Estimated effect (coefficient)	11.964	6.307	0.462
Mean Difference (EDURURAL - OTHER)	0.125	0.051	0.059
EDURURAL Effect	1.496	0.322	0.027
Software			
Estimated effect (coefficient)	4.825	2.538	7.698
Mean Difference (EDURURAL - OTHER)	-0.033	0.002	0.249
EDURURAL Effect	-0.159	0.005	1.917
Effect of unmeasured EDURURAL Variables	0.785	5.381	11.204
Total effect of EDURURAL Program	2.1	5.7	13.1
Fourth grade Mathematics			
Hardware			
Estimated effect (coefficient)		8.321	12.404
Mean Difference (EDURURAL - OTHER)		0.078	0.068
EDURURAL Effect		0.649	0.843
Software			
Estimated effect (coefficient)		-5.580	11.028
Mean Difference (EDURURAL - OTHER)		0.004	0.254
EDURURAL Effect		-0.022	2.801
Effect of unmeasured EDURURAL Variables		0.797	1.464
Total effect of EDURURAL Program		1.4	5.1

SOURCE: Estimated effect (coefficient) from appendix tables C5-11 to C5-13 (columns 3) for second grade and appendix tables C5-5 to C5-8 (column 1) for fourth grade. Mean differences (EDURURAL - OTHER) from supplementary tables available from the authors.

Table C7-2: EDURURAL's Effect in Ceara, 1981, 1983, and 1985

	1981	1983	1985
Second grade Portuguese			
Hardware			
Estimated effect (coefficient)	8.906	8.969	-2.377
Mean Difference (EDURURAL - OTHER)	-0.050	-0.048	0.010
EDURURAL Effect	-0.445	-0.430	-0.024
Software			
Estimated effect (coefficient)	5.896	4.864	11.000
Mean Difference (EDURURAL - OTHER)	-0.105	0.196	0.027
EDURURAL Effect	-0.619	0.953	0.297
Effect of unmeasured EDURURAL Variables	7.469	11.151	-0.289
Total effect of EDURURAL Program	6.4	11.7	-0.0
Fourth grade Portuguese			
Hardware			
Estimated effect (coefficient)		11.728	8.778
Mean Difference (EDURURAL - OTHER)		0.023	-0.076
EDURURAL Effect		0.270	-0.667
Software			
Estimated effect (coefficient)		-3.020	6.689
Mean Difference (EDURURAL - OTHER)		0.190	0.032
EDURURAL Effect		-0.574	0.214
Effect of unmeasured EDURURAL Variables		-4.321	-7.932
Total effect of EDURURAL Program		-4.6	-8.4

Table C7-2 Cont'd

	1981	1983	1985
Second grade Mathematics			
Hardware			
Estimated effect (coefficient)	11.964	6.307	0.462
Mean Difference (EDURURAL - OTHER)	-0.050	0.048	0.010
EDURURAL Effect	-0.598	0.303	0.005
Software			
Estimated effect (coefficient)	4.825	2.538	7.698
Mean Difference (EDURURAL - OTHER)	-0.050	0.196	0.027
EDURURAL Effect	-0.241	0.497	0.208
Effect of unmeasured EDURURAL Variables	11.287	11.376	-0.745
Total effect of EDURURAL Program	10.4	12.2	-0.5
Fourth grade Mathematics			
Hardware			
Estimated effect (coefficient)		8.321	12.404
Mean Difference (EDURURAL - OTHER)		0.023	-0.076
EDURURAL Effect		0.191	-0.943
Software			
Estimated effect (coefficient)		-5.580	11.028
Mean Difference (EDURURAL - OTHER)		0.190	0.032
EDURURAL Effect		-1.060	0.353
Effect of unmeasured EDURURAL Variables		-3.438	-5.984
Total effect of EDURURAL Program		-4.3	-6.6

SOURCE: Estimated effect (coefficient) from appendix tables C5-11 to C5-13 (columns 3) for second grade and appendix tables C5-5 to C5-8 (column 1) for fourth grade. Mean differences (EDURURAL - OTHER) from supplementary tables available from the authors.

Table C7-3: EDURURAL's Effect in Pernambuco, 1981, 1983, and 1985

	1981	1983	1985
Second grade Portuguese			
Hardware			
Estimated effect (coefficient)	8.906	8.969	-2.377
Mean Difference (EDURURAL - OTHER)	-0.073	-0.157	-0.074
EDURURAL Effect	-0.650	-1.408	0.176
Software			
Estimated effect (coefficient)	5.896	4.864	11.000
Mean Difference (EDURURAL - OTHER)	0.006	0.274	0.269
EDURURAL Effect	0.035	1.333	2.959
Effect of unmeasured EDURURAL Variables	6.352	2.401	-5.444
Total effect of EDURURAL Program	5.7	2.3	-2.3
Fourth grade Portuguese			
Hardware			
Estimated effect (coefficient)		11.728	8.778
Mean Difference (EDURURAL - OTHER)		-0.166	-0.071
EDURURAL Effect		-1.947	-0.623
Software			
Estimated effect (coefficient)		-3.020	6.689
Mean Difference (EDURURAL - OTHER)		0.263	0.246
EDURURAL Effect		-0.794	1.645
Effect of unmeasured EDURURAL Variables		-1.133	9.347
Total effect of EDURURAL Program		-3.9	10.4

Table C7-3 Cont'd

	1981	1983	1985
Second grade Mathematics			
Hardware			
Estimated effect (coefficient)	11.964	6.307	0.462
Mean Difference (EDURURAL - OTHER)	-0.073	-0.157	-0.074
EDURURAL Effect	-0.873	-0.990	-0.034
Software			
Estimated effect (coefficient)	4.825	2.538	7.698
Mean Difference (EDURURAL - OTHER)	0.006	0.274	0.269
EDURURAL Effect	0.029	0.695	2.071
Effect of unmeasured EDURURAL Variables	2.491	-0.723	-9.309
Total effect of EDURURAL Program	1.6	-1.0	-7.3
Fourth grade Mathematics			
Hardware			
Estimated effect (coefficient)		8.321	12.404
Mean Difference (EDURURAL - OTHER)		-0.166	-0.071
EDURURAL Effect		-1.381	-0.881
Software			
Estimated effect (coefficient)		-5.580	11.028
Mean Difference (EDURURAL - OTHER)		0.263	0.246
EDURURAL Effect		-1.468	2.713
Effect of unmeasured EDURURAL Variables		0.981	4.727
Total effect of EDURURAL Program		-1.9	6.6

SOURCE: Estimated Impact (coefficient) from appendix tables C5-11 to
C5-13 (columns 3) for second grade and appendix tables C5-5 to C5-8
(column 1) for fourth grade. Mean differences (EDURURAL - OTHER) from
supplementary tables available from the authors.

Table C7-4: Years-Behind-Grade by Year, Grade, and Program Status,
1981, 1983, and 1985

	1981		1983		1985	
	EDURURAL	OTHER	EDURURAL	OTHER	EDURURAL	OTHER
Full Cross-section samples						
All states						
Second Grade	2.22	1.99	2.63	2.15	2.47	2.41
Fourth Grade	2.38	2.31	2.71	2.48	2.70	2.51
Piaui						
Second Grade	2.23	2.40	2.41	2.44	2.26	2.76
Fourth Grade	2.20	2.71	2.66	2.27	2.62	2.68
Ceara						
Second Grade	2.88	2.10	3.38	2.26	3.42	2.65
Fourth Grade	3.02	2.32	3.44	2.91	3.15	2.53
Pernambuco						
Second Grade	1.75	1.73	2.10	1.81	1.58	1.90
Fourth Grade	2.28	2.13	2.38	2.36	2.36	2.35

	1981-83		1983-85		1985-87(Ceara)	
	EDURURAL	OTHER	EDURURAL	OTHER	EDURURAL	OTHER
Matched longitudinal samples						
(Fourth grade only)						
All States	2.47	1.92	2.80	2.44		
Piaui	2.81	1.69	2.79	2.58		
Ceara	2.40	2.15	3.61	2.29	3.87	2.77
Pernambuco	2.02	2.00	2.33	2.43		

Notes

Chapter 1

1. Education decisions are clearly made within the context of much other expenditure, and deciding on the appropriate level is very difficult. Even though we find the overall level of spending in rural northeast Brazil to be appallingly low, we do not directly address that issue.

The distribution of educational services and outcomes similarly is extremely important for policy decisions. While our study has direct bearing on the issue (especially through the analysis in chapter 6), the analytical methods employed here cannot substitute for informed political decisionmaking. Our starting point remains, however, that, regardless of the distributional goals, more is always preferred to less, a view emphasizing the need for efficient allocation of resources.

2. This analysis is not the traditional analysis of quantity that focuses on years of school completed. Instead, we consider the probabilities of continuing at any point in time.

Chapter 2

3. Alternative theories are built on ideas of screening (for example, Berg 1970, Spence 1973, or Riley 1979), of luck (for example, Jencks and others 1972), or of the influences of social structure (for example, Bowles and Gintis 1976). None of these alternatives, however, offers any guidance on evaluating the performance of schools.

4. The typical analysis estimates the independent effect of test score differences on earnings after accounting for differences in years of schooling and other factors. Most of this evidence is developed for small and nonrandom samples of workers, making generalizations somewhat difficult. In these analyses, the direct effect of test scores generally tends to be rather small. There is, however, a larger indirect effect through the impact of achievement differences on continuation in schooling. See the review in Hanushek (1986).

5. The evidence on direct returns to achievement differences in developing

countries tends to be considerably stronger than for developed countries. The larger relative earnings implications of test differences could simply reflect short-ages in minimal skills in developing countries. See, for example, Behrman and Birdsall (1983), Jamison and Moock (1984), Boissiere, Knight, and Sabot (1985), and Knight and Sabot (1987).

6. In developed countries, the original work on agricultural productivity was done by Welch (1970). This has been followed up in developing countries by Lockheed, Jamison, and Lau (1980) and Jamison and Lau (1982). Direct links with total, nonagricultural productivity changes and economic growth are more difficult to document, but commonly hypothesized; see, for example, Denison (1974). Solmon (1985), while concentrating on expenditure differences, reviews various aspects of the linkage of schooling and growth. One suggestive quanti-tative analysis linking productivity growth to test performance over time for the United States is Bishop (1989). A very different approach for developing coun-tries similarly attributes large differences in productivity to school quality mea-sured by test scores. See Knight and Sabot (1987).

7. This discussion relies heavily on the extensive review of U.S. studies found in Hanushek (1986, 1989). Other reviews and perspectives on this body of work can be found in Bridge, Judd, and Moock (1979); Glasman and Biniaminov (1981); and Murnane (1981b).

8. In addition, differences in educational financing and in the opportunity costs of decisions to leave school make it difficult to extrapolate the behavioral responses observed in United States secondary schools to the situation of primary schools in developing countries.

9. This is contrasted to a more common approach in educational research of *process-outcome* studies, in which attention rests on the organization of the curriculum, the methods of presenting materials, the interactions of students, teachers, and administrators, and the like. An entirely different approach—true experimentation—has been much less frequently applied, particularly when in-vestigating the effects of expenditure differences.

10. There were also extensive analyses of the report's methodology and of the validity of its inferences. See, for example, Bowles and Levin (1968), Cain and Watts (1970), and Hanushek and Kain (1972).

11. Recently, a specialized form of statistical modeling has been employed to treat explicitly the normal clustering of sampled students in specific classrooms and schools. These models, labeled variously multilevel linear models, hier-archical linear models, or random coefficient models, have incorporated spe-cialized functional forms for different relationships and have focused consider-able attention on the correct estimation of components of variance in student performance. They have not, however, yielded results on the effects of specific school inputs, thus limiting their usefulness in policy debates. For a general dis-cussion of these alternative approaches, see Raudenbush (1988).

12. As discussed at length elsewhere (Hanushek 1979, 1986), a variety of empirical problems enter into the estimation and the subsequent interpretation of results. The most significant general problems are the lack of measurement of innate abilities of individuals and the imprecise measurement of the history of educational inputs. Both the quality of the data and the estimation techniques

are very important in interpreting any specific findings, but these problems have less effect on the aggregate findings illuminated here. We return to these issues in chapter 5 when we discuss our empirical specifications.

13. A qualified study was defined as a production function estimate that (1) is published in a book or refereed journal; (2) relates some objective measure of student output to characteristics of the family and the schools attended; and (3) provides information about the statistical significance of estimated relationships. Note that a given publication can contain more than one estimated production function by considering different measures of output, different grade levels, or different samples of students. Different specifications of the same basic sample and outcome measure, however, count as only one study. This is an expanded version of tabulations in Hanushek (1981, 1986) and covers studies published through late 1988.

14. The tabulations, when stratified by grade level, by whether individual or aggregate data were used, by output measure, and by value-added or level form of estimation, yield the same qualitative conclusions.

15. In any statistical analysis, which necessarily relies on a sample of all possible students and classroom environments, an estimated relationship may not be real but only perceived to be so because of the specific sample. Standard regression techniques provide ways of estimating the likelihood of being fooled by sampling into thinking there is a relationship when in fact there is not. The shorthand term "statistical significance" implies that less than 5 percent of the time, when there is really no relationship, would we get an estimate as large as the one obtained. In other words, when the estimate is statistically significant, we are quite confident that some relationship does indeed exist.

In all cases, however, the estimates of statistical significance assume that the correct relationship is being estimated; that is, that the model of achievement is properly specified to include the relevant factors determining performance. This is obviously a strong assumption.

16. Recent critiques of standard regression approaches to analyzing educational achievement have concentrated on the fact that sampled students are clustered in classrooms and schools. This clustering implies that conventional methods of analyzing statistical significance may be biased. Unfortunately, the magnitude and even the direction of bias in the estimated variance of the coefficients are unknown. A variety of techniques for estimating such models (often called hierarchial or multilevel models) have been proposed, but the actual applications have provided little direct information about either the effects of individual resources or the reliability of estimated relationships. For a general discussion of the modeling approach, see Raudenbush (1988).

17. Tabulated results are adjusted for variables being measured in the opposite direction; for example, the sign for estimated relationships including student-teacher ratios is reversed.

18. It would be extremely difficult to provide information on quantitative differences in the coefficients because the units of measure of both inputs and outputs differ radically from one study to another. One attempt to provide quantitative estimates of varying class sizes is Glass and Smith (1979). This work,

however, has been subjected to considerable criticism, largely because of the ultimate difficulties in doing such analyses.

19. Teacher-pupil ratios are treated here as being synonymous with class sizes. This is not strictly the case and, in fact, could be misleading in current studies. Several changes in schools, most notably deriving from the introduction of extensive requirements for dealing with handicapped children in the mid-1970s, have brought in new instructional personnel without large changes in typical classes. Since much of the evidence here refers to the situation before such legislation and restrictions, it is reasonable to interpret the evidence as relating to class sizes.

20. Not all studies report the sign of insignificant coefficients. For example, forty-five studies report insignificant estimated coefficients for teacher-student ratios but do not report any further information.

21. Note that only 113 studies report evidence about teacher education. Since data on teacher education are so readily available, it seems likely that a number of additional studies investigated teacher education effects but discarded the results without reporting them after finding negative or insignificant effects.

22. There are two reasons for possible biases in the opposite direction. First, the effect of experience may be nonlinear (for example, the first year or two of experience may be much more important than any subsequent years of experience); this implies that linear models might misestimate the true importance of some experience. In these tabulations, however, any underlying study investigating such possibilities and finding any range of positive (significant) experience effects was recorded as a positive (significant) result. Second, and more important, experience measures may confuse the differences in performance accruing to experience for any individual teacher with differences in performance across groups of teachers. For example, if the best teachers all leave teaching within the first five years, any teacher with more experience will simply be a remaining (poorer) teacher. Both factors are subsequently considered in our own empirical work.

23. Information on each of these is less frequently available. This is partially explained by common reliance on administrative records, which do not record them (except perhaps teacher salaries). The level of the analysis and sampling frame for some studies offer another explanation; for example, since expenditure per student is generally measured for districts, the analyses that rely on data for a single district would find no variation in this input and thus could not include it.

24. The interpretation of expenditure and salary estimates is sometimes clouded by including them in addition to teacher experience, education, and class size. Also, because prices can vary across the samples in the separate studies, it is more difficult to interpret the dollar measures than the real input measures. Finally, eight of the thirteen significant positive expenditure results in table 2-1 come from the different estimates of Sebold and Dato (1981). In this analysis, imprecise measurement of family inputs suggests that school expenditure may be mainly a proxy for family background.

25. When estimated salary effects are translated into policy conclusions, special care is required. Most of the salary results refer to what happens when in-

dividuals move to different levels of a given salary schedule. They do not indicate what would happen if the entire schedule was shifted out, raising the salary of individuals at all different levels.

26. These studies are analyses of covariance or the equivalent, which use individual teacher (or school) dummy variables in addition to measures of prior student achievement, family background factors, and other explicitly identified inputs in a regression format. See Hanushek (1971, 1992); Murnane (1975); Armor and others (1976); and Murnane and Phillips (1981).

27. Hanushek (1992) provides a direct analysis of the stability of teacher effects over time and the possibility of interactions between classroom composition and teacher skill. The evidence there, although limited, suggests that classroom differences result chiefly from differences in teacher skill.

28. An important sidelight of the production function investigations is that decisionmakers might be able to identify with fair accuracy underlying differences in skills among teachers. Murnane (1975) and Armor and others (1976) find that principals' evaluations of teachers were highly correlated with estimates of total effectiveness (that is, adjusted mean gains in achievement by the students of each teacher). This is exactly what is needed to implement a merit pay scheme.

29. One interesting subset of these analyses, however, involves investigating more detailed aspects of family structure and size. The large changes in birth rates and divorce rates of the past two decades have created a concern about their potential effects on learning and achievement. General discussions and reviews of the issues can be found in Easterlin (1978) and Preston (1984). For the most part, these ignore influences of schools on achievement, although it may not be too problematical in a time series context. A preliminary investigation of family factors based upon simple time allocation models can be found in Hanushek (1992).

30. Since the publication of the Coleman Report, there has been a fascination with the question of whether families, peers, or schools are most important in determining the performance of students. However, such questions simply cannot be answered very easily within the production function framework. The primary information provided by knowledge of the production function is how much student performance will change when given inputs are varied; or what will be the marginal effect on achievement from changing the level of a particular input. On the other hand, questions of the relative importance of, say, the inputs of families to education versus the inputs of schools commonly refer to decompositions of the variation in student achievement. These decompositions, while bearing some relationship to the marginal effect of each variable, also involve the sample variations of the observed inputs and make it impossible to evaluate specific policies. Moreover, from a policy perspective, most attention is concentrated on inputs that are malleable through policy explicit decisions.

31. See, for example, Hanushek (1972), Winkler (1975), Henderson, Mieszkowski, and Sauvageau (1976), and Summers and Wolfe (1977).

32. Assessing the importance of desegregated schooling has been especially difficult because such studies demand historical information on the course of desegregation—data that are seldom available—along with the other information needed for production function studies.

33. The discussion of the analysis of private schools in Coleman, Hoffer, and Kilgore (1982) highlights these issues. See, for example, Murnane (1983) or the compendium of analyses in *Sociology of Education* 55 (April/July 1982).

34. Tabulations similar to those in table 2-1 indicate thirty-one studies that have analyzed teacher verbal scores. Of these, eight find positive and significant relationships and another ten find positive but insignificant relationships.

35. The idea of skill differences among teachers is not the only possible interpretation of the data. Differences in achievement across classrooms could reflect differences in teachers, in other classroom-specific factors, or in a combination of both. The teacher skill interpretation is suggested by the fact that principals' ratings of teachers are correlated with the covariance estimates of classroom differences; see note 28. Direct evidence of the stability of teacher effects is found in Hanushek (1992). Further discussion of skill differences in the production function context can be found in Hanushek (1986).

36. One way of framing this issue has been to contrast the relative importance of family and school inputs—a line of inquiry stimulated by the Coleman Report in the United States, which emphasized the overwhelming importance of families in the achievement process. The hypothesis of large effects of school resources in developing countries, developed over some time by Stephen Heyneman of the World Bank and some of his associates, has an empirical basis in international comparisons of educational achievement.(See Heyneman and Loxley [1983] and the bibliographical references in that paper.) A weak form of this hypothesis is that variations in family background are noticeably less important in determining the performance of children in poor countries. A strong form is that variations in school resources have a more powerful effect on student performance in developing countries than in developed countries. This line of inquiry has generated considerable controversy; see, for example, Riddell (1989), who questions the general conclusions based on a multilevel analysis of achievement. Because the analytical focus of this entire line of inquiry differs noticeably from that in our study, however, we provide only tangential evidence about the hypothesis.

37. In regression analysis, the precision with which any relationship can be estimated is directly related to the variation of the variable in the sample. The reason for this is intuitively clear: if a factor takes on widely different values, its effect on the dependent variable will be large, or at least larger than if little variation in the factor is observed.

38. Avalos and Haddad (1979), Fuller (1985), Lockheed and Hanushek (1988), Lockheed and Verspoor (1991).

39. While U.S. teacher salaries are determined chiefly by experience and education levels of teachers, salaries in some of these countries may be determined by a variety of other characteristics. Therefore, the linkage of the first three characteristics in the table and expenditures may be less strong.

40. The specific concern is that the reported results for developing countries are biased in one way or another toward the presentation of statistically significant results. Many of the underlying studies, done in the field as governmental reports, are primitive by usual quality standards.

41. Again, because the tabulation relies on other reviews, it is impossible to divide the insignificant results according to sign.

42. In general, we are most confident in interpreting the results from regression analyses when we restrict ourselves to the range of observations presented in the data. Extrapolations of results to other circumstances introduces added uncertainty. The U.S. results on class sizes pertain roughly to a range between fifteen and forty students, while the developing country results cover a much broader range.

43. See Jamison, Searle, Galda, and Heyneman (1981); Heyneman, Jamison, and Montenegro (1984); and Lockheed, Vail, and Fuller (1987). Discussions of textbooks have frequently considered costs, a test to which few of the other potential policies have been submitted on any rigorous basis. In policy terms, past research suggests that providing textbooks also appears to be very cost-effective. See the reviews and discussion in Lockheed and Hanushek (1988) and Lockheed and Verspoor (1991).

44. See Friend, Searle, and Suppes (1980); Oxford and others (1986); and Friend, Galda, and Searle (1986). Cost estimates are compared with the effectiveness estimates in Lockheed and Hanushek (1988).

45. What we call flow efficiency is sometimes called internal efficiency, but we reserve that latter term for situations where quality of performance and costs are both considered.

46. A much shorter review of available evidence is found in Jamison (1978). That review contrasts the available analysis on promotion and dropout behavior. The materials on dropout behavior, while more extensive, tend also to leave out consideration of students' scholastic performance. There is, however, more evidence on the relationship between years of schooling attained and achievement: see, for example, Cochrane and Jamison (1982) and Jamison and Lockheed (1987).

47. The interpretation requires a little care. These inputs may be just as important in developed countries. In developed countries, however, the variation in these inputs across schools is less, and resources are supplied at a very different level (presumably much above any minimally adequate level). Both factors make identification of the separate effects of these factors very difficult.

Chapter 3

48. Brazil's northeast region, as officially designated by the IBGE (Instituto Brasileiro de Geografia e Estatística, the national statistical office) comprises nine states and the Federal Territory of Fernando de Naronha. The nine states, in alphabetical order, are: Alagoas, Bahia, Ceará, Maranhão, Paraíba, Pernambuco, Piaui, Rio Grande do Norte, and Sergipe. The combined land area is some 1.5 million square kilometers, roughly 18 percent of Brazil's total land mass. All nine states were included in the EDURURAL project, although, as described below, only three were included in the research and evaluation effort.

49. These, of course, were not the first efforts to address the relative deprivation of the northeast or to improve education there and in other poor areas. The efforts of the 1980s were, however, more extensive than any previous efforts, especially in the extent to which the federal government was directly involved in a domain normally reserved for state and local action.

50. For an interesting account of these trends, see Merrick and Graham (1979).

51. Statistical information in this section is drawn variously from (a) the 1979 and 1982 household surveys—Pesquisas Nacional por Amostrade Domicílios (PNAD)—and the 1980 census, both produced by IBGE, and (b) "Brazil: Economic Survey Report: Northeast Region: Development Issues and Prospects," World Bank data.

52. This is the approximate equivalent in U.S. dollars of twice the officially designated regional minimum wage. In Brazil one regional minimum wage per adult in a household is often used as a proxy for the poverty line.

53. The ano de alfabetização usually extends for at least a year, frequently with intermittent attendance. In light of different recordkeeping practices among states (exacerbated by varying compliance at the school level with whatever rules the states establish), there is no reliable way to discriminate consistently between youngsters being prepared for first grade and those already in first grade. In our data they are simply included within the first grade numbers. As mentioned below, this anomaly in the formal grade structure in the rural northeast precluded sampling from first grades, despite the obvious desirability of doing so for methodological reasons.

54. The enrollment rates in table 3-2 are calculated on a gross basis—that is, the numerators include all students enrolled irrespective of age—while the denominator refers exclusively to the primary school age group of seven to fourteen years. The large differences, especially for the rural northeast, in attendance information between table 3-2 and table 3-3 and 3-4 are attributable to sharply different regional patterns of under-and over-age children in school.

55. These findings are all drawn from the innovative work by Philip R. Fletcher and Sergio Costa Ribeiro (1989) on the 1982 Brazilian household sample survey (IBGE various years). For more extensive data on progression see appendix tables C3-3 and C3-4.

56. Access to education would also be provided directly, through the construction of new schools for unserved populations.

57. Roughly analogous to an education department of local government elsewhere, an OME comprises an appointed manager and technical staff, all employed full time, with a mandate to provide pedagogical assistance and supervision as well as administrative inspection. Prior to the advent of the OME, schools in the typical rural county of northeast Brazil enjoyed only such administrative support as the county executive (prefeito) himself chose to offer, and no pedagogical assistance whatsoever.

58. In fact, toward the end of the originally planned implementation period, it became clear that exchange rate and other changes in economic circumstances would result in an unused balance in the loan account. The EDURURAL project was then extended to 152 additional counties, bringing the overall total to 370. Because these counties were added very late, they were never eligible for inclusion in the evaluation research component of EDURURAL, and are thus not mentioned further here.

59. The federal Ministry of Education and Culture selected a group of researchers from two departments—Education, and Statistics and Applied Math-

ematics—of the Federal University of Ceará to undertake the fieldwork, in close association with the secretariats of education in the involved states. The ministry of education provided financing, in part with proceeds from the World Bank loan in support of EDURURAL. Technical collaboration in the design and conduct of the work was obtained from the Carlos Chagas Foundation in São Paulo (also financed by the ministry of education, in part with World Bank loan funds) and from World Bank staff and consultants (financed from the World Bank's administrative budget by its Research Committee). A grand total from all sources of approximately US$1.4 million, equivalent to about 1.5 percent of the total costs of the EDURURAL project, was spent on the evaluation research program in the period 1980–89.

60. Again, the desirability of collecting information from all grades in all schools on each of the four occasions was recognized, but financial and logistical constraints required sampling schools and grades. Because of the difficulty in distinguishing first grade from ano de alfabetização, data collection was begun at the second grade.

61. At the same time, it was recognized from the outset that this design was not pure in the sense that the selection of counties into the EDURURAL and OTHER groups was not intended to be random. While the poorest and educationally the most deserving counties were supposedly included in EDURURAL, counties were selected for the project in 1979 and 1980 on the basis of the very limited information then available. These factors are considered in the evaluation work in chapter 7.

62. More detailed data are provided in the appendixes. See tables C3-1 and C3-2.

63. For many years before 1983, county executives had been appointed by the state governors, themselves appointed by the federal government. Because of the election in 1983, all county executives changed at the same time and patronage-related shifts in teachers were almost certainly greater than in a non-election year.

64. Note that having a fourth grade was a prerequisite for inclusion in the original 1981 sample.

65. As discussed later, the 1987 survey attempted to trace a selected sample of 1985 second graders to their precise grade. The percentage of students in surviving schools and still in the second grade two years later is 4.5 percent for 1983–85 and 5.0 percent for 1985–87.

66. A more satisfactory attempt was made for the reduced sample in Ceará in 1987. But, contrary to our expectations, the analytical findings on this variable were not robust, possibly because of the smaller sample sizes in 1987 and the continuing imprecision of measurement.

67. The use of this information to relate costs of inputs to their effectiveness in producing desired results is discussed in chapter 6.

68. The agricultural productivity variable is constructed from information on the cruzeiro value of production per hectare. The socioeconomic status indicator is a complex variable incorporating information on the value of output per worker, the proportion of the labor force outside agriculture, the proportion of

the population receiving income above the poverty line, the proportion literate, and the prevalence of houses with electricity and of medical doctors. See appendix B for a complete description of data construction.

Chapter 4

69. The actual outcome depends upon a number of factors whose importance is uncertain. Who decides on promotion? Do existing promotion patterns reliably reflect performance differences among students? Are there other causes and effects of retention beyond achievement? The general topic of wastage, the combination of dropouts and grade repetitions, has been the focus of extensive policy discussions in developing countries. A review of the evidence on the various important relationships is found in Haddad (1979). One part of those discussions has been whether mandatory promotion policies should be followed, but the existing evidence is ambiguous.

70. A significant, if not fully satisfying, exception to this rule is the work by Jere Behrman and Nancy Birdsall (1983) with data drawn from the 1970 Brazilian census. Their work, however, explores the relationship between quantity and quality of schooling in the context of earnings functions and derivative rates of return and not with respect to actual education production.

71. It is of course not surprising that these tradeoffs have received so little attention. Data on students' performance and promotion patterns have been virtually nonexistent (see Haddad 1979). The exception is found in the analyses of Jamison (1978, 1980).

72. As explained in chapter 3, the sampling in 1987 differed significantly from that in prior years. It can be described more as a student-based sample design in which the primary factor driving the data collection was finding students who had been sampled in 1985. In this section, both the samples and the analytical models pertain directly to the 1981, 1983, and 1985 data. The final sections of this chapter turn to the unique aspects of the 1987 data.

73. Additionally, there were two groups of students stuck in their initial grades. They were second graders who had not been promoted and fourth graders who had not been promoted in the two-year period between data collections.

74. This figure ignores dropout with subsequent reentry paths. While these might be relevant, they cannot be observed in our data, which capture on-time promotions.

75. The most serious effect of this measurement error probably occurs in the analysis of achievement in the next chapter, when corrections are undertaken for biases possibly introduced by sample selectivity.

76. Probit models can be thought of as similar to standard regression techniques except that they recognize the special dichotomous nature of the dependent variable, in this case school survival. Schools in a sample are observed either to exist or not in the follow-up period. These observations are assumed to be the result of an underlying probability process that follows a normal distribution. The parameters relating the exogenous factors to the probabilities of survival are estimated by maximum likelihood techniques. See, for example, Hanushek and Jackson (1977).

77. The probit estimates provide a nonlinear relationship between the various explanatory factors and the probability of survival. Because of this, the estimation of probability effects of changing any given variable depends upon where the function is evaluated. Throughout this chapter, probability evaluations are done at the mean values for each of the variables. Each of the separate estimated coefficients is interpreted as the independent effect of the variable, holding constant the other variables in the estimated equation. See Hanushek and Jackson (1977).

78. The complete estimates of the basic results of the probit models for school survival, along with variable means and standard deviations are presented in appendix table C4-1.

79. Certainly the true relative agricultural productivity of the counties in 1983–85 cannot be captured very well by a variable constructed from data relating to 1979/80, which consequently cannot reflect the inevitably significant changes experienced in the intervening drought years. Further, it seems plausible that the old adage "the higher they climb the farther they fall" could apply to agricultural product. Specifically the drought may very well have substantially reduced the variance in agricultural productivity: the high-productivity areas were probably hurt relatively more than those areas of always low productivity. The negative and significant coefficient may possibly be reflecting the effect on school survival of rapid decreases in productivity, due to the drought, in the areas most well-to-do in 1979/80.

80. As noted in chapter 3 (see table 3-12) and appendix B, this overall SES index is a complex variable constructed from data from around 1980 on six separate partial indicators of socioeconomic status.

81. We suspect the interaction of the drought and local politics is indirectly responsible for this bogus effect. The proportion of schools with drinking water on the premises declined from 72 percent in 1981 to 39 percent in 1983 (and recovered only slightly to 46 percent in 1985; see note 186). Schools that survive without water are likely to be particularly robust in other ways. By contrast, one important reason for closing a school surely is the disappearance of its source of water. Suppose that the ways in which the "always dry schools" are peculiarly robust are not fully captured in the other variables in the model and that the "newly dry schools" are not special in these same unmeasured ways. In this situation, the water variable would proxy relatively unstable or fragile schools— that is, those with the highest propensity to close when adversity strikes. Among the many unmeasured ways in which the "always dry schools" could differ from others and the "newly dry schools" need not differ systematically is in greater protection against the whim of local politicians. A teacher might have personal connections to the local power structure; or a school could be more visible, for example, by location on or near a rural road of greater proximity to the county seat. This explanation for an unexpected result may seem tortured, but it is plausible in the context of rural northeast Brazil.

82. OMES became reasonably prevalent only after 1982. Only the 1983 and 1985 surveys collected data on the OMES. Thus this factor enters only the 1983– 85 models.

83. These probabilities are additive such that in 1983–85 a Ceará program

324Notes

school would be 46.2 percent (-0.202 plus -0.260) less likely to survive than a
similar school in the OTHER portion of Pernambuco.

84. Estimates of bivariate probit models that allow for correlations of the errors in the school survival and promotion equations were also done, but the
correlation of errors was never over 0.001. Therefore, the results reported here
are based on simple probit estimates for each equation.

85. The complete probit models of promotion are displayed in appendix table
C4-3, along with means and standard deviations of the variables.

86. If school size has an independent effect on promotion possibilities, this
is mixed with the sampling effects. There is no clear reason, however, why size
per se would affect promotion. The separate estimates found in appendix table
C4-2 are not shown in the summary tables.

87. Unlike the situation in the school survival models, the separately estimated
within-state effects of schools being located in EDURURAL counties are all statistically insignificant. Conditional probabilities for a global EDURURAL effect are thus
reported here. The separately estimated coefficients are, however, shown in appendix table C4-2. As the models there show, differences in the control of schools
(state, federal, or private as opposed to county) have no effect on student promotions.

88. As shown in the figure, an attempt was also made to trace the schooling
status of migrants. Such information, however, was available for fewer than half
of the migrants, suggesting that any analysis of this group would be unreliable.

89. The promotion models consider three possible grades and are estimated
by ordered probit. This technique presumes that the same basic factors that
determine promotion from second to third also determine promotion from third
to fourth. By combining the two separate promotions and using the fact that
there is a natural ordering to the outcomes, more efficient estimates are obtained
than would be if the promotions were analyzed separately. See Hanushek and
Jackson (1977).

Chapter 5

90. Chapter 4 provides evidence that promotion is related to achievement on
the tests of curricular objectives.

91. Administration of trial tests originally developed for students in the second
and fourth grade in the south indicated that they would not provide reliable
discrimination among the students of the northeast.

92. In 1987 the special samples of Ceará students were given the 1985 second-
grade tests. Information on performance and reliability of these is found later in
this chapter.

93. Appendix A presents the distribution of questions and test points across
different conceptual objectives. It also provides a detailed analysis of test reliability.

94. The raw test item response data needed for constructing the reliability
estimates were unavailable for the 1981 tests. They were inadvertently discarded
before any reliability analysis had been conducted.

95. Since the EDURURAL counties differ somewhat from the OTHER counties in the northeast, it would be necessary to use an analysis of covariance design that accounts for the nonrandom assignment of schools to treatment and control groups. See the discussion in chapter 7.

96. As discussed shortly, it is often better to include A_t. as one of the explanatory variables instead of simply looking at the difference. The principle is, however, the same.

97. If two measures of prior achievement are available, it is possible to incorporate both "level" and "growth" effects directly. Boardman and Murnane (1979) develop this for the case where achievement is measured at three distinct points in time, but multiple measurements of prior achievement at a single point in time will generally suffice.

98. Specifically, in order to obtain unbiased estimates of the effects of the measured inputs, the expected value of each error term, conditional upon exogenous variables, must be zero for each student. When there are important unmeasured factors, as discussed above, this requirement will generally not hold.

99. The selection bias problems arise because of unmeasured achievement factors that are related to sample selection.

100. Note that similar measurement errors in final achievement, A_{it}, do not cause the same problems. The error term in the equation, ϵ_t, can accommodate measurement errors as long as they are not systematically related to the explanatory factors.

101. If there is an independent estimate of the error variance, an alternative technique is available. The classical correction procedures (Maddala 1977) essentially use the estimated error variance to adjust the observed variance in prior achievement before the regression analysis is performed. With test scores, it is possible to use estimates of test reliability to estimate the error variance. An example of this approach in the value added achievement context is found in Hanushek (1992).

102. Consistent with the discussion in chapter 4, the term school survival throughout, implies that the second grade student attends a school that still exists and that has a fourth grade. This is consistent with the analysis in chapter 4.

103. The procedures are described in Heckman (1979) and Maddala (1983). As described in the previous chapter, these two selection factors appear independent of each other. Therefore, the model estimation simply enters the two separate inverse Mills ratios without considering any selection correlations. If they were not independent, the second-stage estimation of the achievement models would have to take the interrelationships into account. This procedure does rely heavily on the assumption that the probit errors are normally distributed.

104. Factors that affect the level of performance (for example, second-grade scores) but not the growth in achievement can arise from two different relationships: (1) the factor has an effect only early in life or schooling; or (2) the factor has an effect at all ages but the differences over short periods of time are too small to detect within our samples. In most situations, the latter explanation is the more plausible one.

105. These calculations reflect the fact that the sum of the entering achievement scores in the value-added models is close to 0.6 across years and tests except for 1981–83 Portuguese, where it is closer to 0.4. Since both second-grade tests enter each of the value-added models, the rough range of fourth-grade output effects from a 3 to 6 percentage point increase in second-grade scores is 1.8 to 3.6 percentage points.

The small cumulative effects identified here imply very tiny differences in growth each year, making the value-added finding of no parental effects quite understandable.

106. The specific measures of family economic status investigated included whether the family worked in farming, owned land, owned livestock, sold part of its crop or livestock, or had family members earning income on second jobs.

107. In all fourth-grade models, both earlier mathematics and earlier Portuguese achievement are included. This circumvents the problems of disentangling past inputs and ability variations discussed by Boardman and Murnane (1979).

108. The 1981 survey included a measure of student absences, but it was deemed too unreliable to be included in subsequent surveys. The 1981 cross-sectional analysis of second-grade performance (appendix table C5-11) does, however, indicate that even this imprecise measure provides information about student learning of the kind expected: the higher the reported days a student was absent, the lower the recorded academic achievement.

109. All fourth graders had to have been promoted on time between second and fourth grades to be included in our value-added models.

110. Work behavior of students is quite crudely measured, employing a dummy variable reflecting employment status. This measure does not indicate the wide variations in time commitments, in strenuousness of the activity, or in effects on attendance or homework. Therefore, some imprecision in the estimates would be expected.

111. These farms are large only in a relative sense. Farms are measured against an estimate of how large a farm must be in each county to support fully a family. "Large" here is defined as being 35 percent of this minimal size.

112. The specific measures included in the table are the proportion female and the proportion female times the dummy variable for females. This form allows the effect of sex composition to differ between boys and girls.

113. Our data contain a number of classrooms in which all sampled students are female. These may not, however, be true single-sex classrooms because the sampling of students within schools may select only the females from a mixed gender classroom.

114. Because it is possible to measure the achievement composition of classes on the basis of prior test scores, direct investigations of the importance of peer academic achievement can be conducted. If only a cross-section is observed, the average achievement of the other members of the class will include the effects of school and teacher quality. Thus, they would distort the entire analysis, making it difficult to distinguish between true achievement composition effects and other inputs to education. This specific analysis therefore is only conducted for the fourth-grade value-added models.

115. Previous investigations of such issues in developed countries include Hanushek (1972), Henderson, Mieszkowski, and Sauvageau (1976), and Summers and Wolfe (1977).

116. In all cases, these were calculated for all students in the second grade in the initial year, not just for those who appear in the matched longitudinal samples.

117. The components of the hardware index include the availability of specific kinds of physical plant: more than one classroom, kitchen, sanitary facilities, storage space, offices; of specific items of furniture: desks and chairs for pupils, table for teacher, bookcases; of water; and of electricity.

118. The writing materials variable, as used, is an index capturing the availability of specific items supplied by the EDURURAL program (such as chalk, notebooks, pencils, erasers, and crayons). The actual components of the index differ slightly from one year to the next, as does the precise wording of the questions on the survey instruments. In all years, the value of the index ranges from 0 to 1; in 1983 and 1985 these values represent, respectively, students having access to none of the index components and students having access to all of them. In 1981, however, the writing materials coefficient in table 5-11 represents adequate materials for all students compared to none, while the full results in appendix table C5-11 also include a measure of writing materials for only some students compared with none (which has a significant negative relationship with both Portuguese and mathematics performance).

119. The actual measures of textbook use also vary from year to year. In 1981, the textbook measure indicates whether or not the teacher reports textbooks are used in class. In 1983, the textbook measure in table 5-11 indicates texts are used every day; the full estimates (appendix tables C5-5, C5-6, and C5-12) also include positive and significant effects of textbooks being used only some days. Finally, in 1985, textbooks in table 5-11 refer to having them available in school and at home; appendix tables C5-8, C5-9, and C5-13 show that having texts at school only was also positive and significantly related to Portuguese, but was insignificantly negatively related to mathematics performance.

120. The specific measure of homework used here is given a value of 1 if the student reports always doing homework, and 0 otherwise—that is, if the student reports never or only irregularly doing homework; this information from the pupils is available only for 1983 and 1985. All three surveys also sought information from the teacher concerning the frequency of assigning homework. In the earliest modeling trials, however, this was never a significant determinant of achievement, possibly because the hypothesized effect comes not so much from the teacher assigning homework as from the student actually doing it. Therefore we did not further consider the teacher-derived homework variable.

121. Consideration of homework policies has been popular in part because assigning more homework appears to entail no incremental costs. This assumes that there is no interaction between assigning (and correcting) homework and teacher salaries. It also assumes that the time students spend doing homework has no significant opportunity cost. If either of these assumptions fail, the cost-effectiveness presumption might change.

122. The coefficient for Portuguese performance at fourth grade in 1985, while

marked insignificant in the table, is statistically significant at the 10 percent level.

123. At times there are several graded classes that simultaneously share a single teacher.

124. Both the negative 1985 Portuguese coefficient and the positive 1983 math coefficient are significant at the 90 percent level.

125. The mean teacher salary for the reduced sample in the longitudinal value-added models is between two-thirds and three-fourths of a minimum wage, somewhat higher than the average for all teachers in our sample. This slight difference is attributable to weighting of the teachers in the analytical samples by the numbers of students they have, and to a tendency for longer established—and thus marginally higher paid—teachers to be associated with schools and students that survive over each two-year period. None of this should obscure the main point: teachers are abysmally paid in rural northeast Brazil, receiving only a fraction of the minimum wage, which itself is equivalent to only about half the Brazilian poverty line for a family with two adults.

126. Note that in this section only, different estimated models are employed. Each of the other identified effects simply extracts coefficients from a common model. But here, since we replace specific measures of teacher characteristics with salary terms, separate estimates of the entire model are employed. See appendix tables C5-9 to C5-13.

127. The essential question is whether we are observing different teachers arrayed along a single salary schedule or observing differences across a variety of salary schedules. The results are undoubtedly a combination of both.

128. These factors command attention for three reasons. First, if shown to be important for student achievement, they are convenient policy instruments because they can be readily manipulated. Second, they have been the subject of frequent past policy, even in the absence of information about their importance. Third, as shown in chapter 6, they are frequently related closely to salary differences.

129. Studies of education in developed countries, as summarized in chapter 2, have reached similar conclusions about the unimportance of quantitative differences in teacher education. But the level and range of teacher education is very different in those situations. Virtually all teachers in those studies are college graduates, and the variations pertain only to the amount of graduate work by teachers. For developing countries, past studies have shown variations in teacher's education to be more consistently related to students' performance.

130. Very few teachers had actually completed either program at the time of the surveys. Any who had were included with those receiving training.

131. Both indexes were constructed from questionnaire items about whether or not the teacher used a set of materials (for example, magazines and newspapers or books other than the text) or engaged in specific activities (for example, storytelling or drama). The results from this estimation are included in appendix tables C5-5 to C5-8 and C5-11 to C5-13 but are not reported in the text.

132. Unfortunately, administration of the achievement tests to the teachers was feasible only in 1985, so that the consistency of findings across years cannot be checked.

133. As described earlier in this chapter and in appendix A, tests were criterion-referenced to concepts and objectives actually revealed in the official texts and supporting materials. They were deemed by local teachers and administrators to constitute a minimally acceptable standard of performance. The teachers completed the tests at the same time their students were doing so under the direction of the field interviewers.

134. For a more complete discussion of the ideas of skill differences and of their implications for interpreting these models as production functions in the economists' sense, see Hanushek (1986).

135. These differ substantially from the means and standard deviations on second-grade tests administered to second graders in 1981, 1983, and 1985. Even though the 1987 scores refer to a second-grade-level test, most of the sample by 1987 had progressed to the third or fourth grade.

136. Grade level in 1987 is included as a series of dummy variables comparing grade-specific achievement to that of the twenty-four students who had dropped out by 1987 but were nevertheless located by the survey team and tested.

137. This formulation is frequently referred to as a covariance specification, since it analyzes variations in mean differences after allowing for other measurable differences among the sampled students. The analysis relies on the fact that the 1987 survey collected data on concentrations of students from specific schools. In theory, of course, similar analyses could have been conducted using the value-added models for fourth-grade achievement in 1983 and 1985. In practice, however, for those years, the number of cases is too small, and the dispersion of children among schools and classrooms is too great, for this to be feasible. Too few degrees of freedom would be left in the statistical models.

138. If we knew the specific factors that were important and how they interacted with each other in the educational process, we would prefer the explicit modeling of the achievement. This would provide direct estimates of individual factors that might be modified through policy decisions. However, given our lack of exhaustive knowledge of specific input factors, the covariance approach is superior.

139. This analysis is appropriate as long as there are not wide variations of inputs within schools or classrooms. If resources vary within the schools, the correct analysis would identify the relevant groupings of students receiving the same inputs.

140. The calculations rely on the full sample regression results reported in appendix tables C5-15 and C5-16 and involve comparing the residual variance when school dummies are included (model 3, full sample) with the case when they not included (model 2, full sample). Except for the inclusion of two additional anthropometric variables (treated in the following section), the analytical model is exactly that outlined above.

141. More precisely, the reference group for comparisons comprises students attending the twenty-one schools from which in 1987 three or fewer pupils were tested.

142. By selecting schools on the basis of the estimated school quality parameters, which contain some sampling errors, we will tend to overstate the differ-

ences in performance. Even allowing for this, however, the remaining differences are huge.

143. The previously estimated regression coefficients for hardware provide achievement weights for the mean differences in hardware. The uncertainty of data measurement implies, however, that exact estimation of the achievement effects would potentially give a false impression of the evidence.

144. Developed countries also often provide food to schoolchildren at public expense, but typically the targeting is on the individual child, not the whole school. Even the wealthiest school districts in the United States operate such programs. For example, Montgomery County in Maryland offers free breakfasts to students from poor (often immigrant or racial minority) families as well as subsidized lunches to a larger slice of the student population.

145. In some areas, the school feeding program does not operate in the months immediately following the harvest, when food supplies are relatively plentiful.

146. For reviews of evidence on the relation between malnutrition and the various facets of education, see Leslie and Jamison (1990). The policy implications for educational planning is found in Jamison and Leslie (1990). Work on malnutrition and school performance can be found in Jamison (1986) and Moock and Leslie (1986)

147. Because this information is available only for 1987, it could not be used in the general models of chapter 4 to test for the possible effect of health and nutritional status on pupil flows: promotion and dropout. Further, direct tests of the availability of school lunches in the 1983 and 1985 achievement models do not show different effects. This could, however, simply reflect the limited variability of our crude measures of availability.

148. Special measuring devices for height, weight, and skinfold thickness were supplied to the teams of interviewers, who were trained specifically in their use. The norms are the median values for a large population of U.S. children surveyed for the purposes of developing standards by the U.S. National Center for Health Statistics (NCHS). Separate norms are used for males and females.

149. Following the work of E. Sounis (*Manual de Higiene e Medicina do Trabalho*, no date), information required to compute his index of vital capacity was also obtained. The formula is height in centimeters less the sum of weight in kilograms plus thorax perimeter in centimeters. Sounis defines seven levels of vital capacity on this basis. While this variable demonstrated substantial variation in the data, it was never significant in our trial regressions and does not figure in the results reported here.

150. Several alternative specifications of each of these indicators of nutritional and health status were tried, beginning in all cases with a simple continuous form of the variable. In the subsequent statistical analyses, specification as dummy variables capturing the most extreme states generally gave the most interesting results.

151. Put differently, once the variation of achievement attributable to these control variables is accounted for in the estimated regression equations, we have set a quite stringent test of the independent effect of health and nutritional variables.

152. For full results from these several specifications of this regression model see appendix table C5-14.

153. One significant difference in model specification is the inclusion of students in different grades—something that could not be done in the earlier survey years. By comparison to the dropouts, achievement generally increases with grade level; the occasional discontinuities in the progression are likely due to the varying times at which the dropouts occurred.

154. When attempting an overall assessment of the effect of the EDURURAL program in chapter 7, we note but do not make much of this anomalous though intriguing result. We speculate that the nonrandom sampling of schools in 1987 is at the heart of the matter.

155. In the cross-section models reported in appendix table C5-14, however, visual acuity is significant and in the expected direction for mathematics: visual capacity of 60 percent or less of normal incurs an achievement penalty of about 12 percentage points.

156. The proportion of variance explained increases dramatically in both samples and academic subjects; the change is greater for the children with the most to learn (the bottom 40 percent of the achievement distribution in 1985) and for mathematics. As we saw earlier, the school in which a student is enrolled is an enormously important predictor of achievement gains.

157. They do, however, uniformly retain the correct sign and generally maintain about the same relative sizes across the two samples and subjects and indicators of nutritional status.

Chapter 6

158. The numbers would change a little, but not the overall conclusions, if four years, not three, were deemed the standard time to reach fourth grade. This would make nominal provision (as Brazilian law does not) for the de facto kindergarten, represented by primary enrollees in the ano de alfabetização. Full data on progression in schools is available in appendix tables C3-3 and C3-4, from which table 3-5 is extracted.

159. We use the term "graduate" loosely here to denote a student who arrives in fourth grade. The true flow efficiency of the system for each student who completes fourth grade is even less than indicated, because both repetition and dropout occur during the fourth-grade year as well as earlier in the primary cycle.

160. Jane Armitage was initially responsible for our explorations into cost-effectiveness. She developed the unit cost information and first calculated cost-effectiveness ratios. Her preliminary results have here been updated by basing them on the more elaborate underlying analytical models of achievement determination.

161. Full detail of the calculations are available from "Annex 5: Estimates of Costs of Educational Inputs in Ceará State," in Jane Armitage and others (1986)

162. Ten percent, for example, is the discount rate used in U.S. government analyses of capital expenditures; see also Levin (1983). Others (for example, Gramlich 1981) have argued for use of lower discount rates—say, 3–4 percent—

in the United States; these same arguments would, however, lead to higher discount rates for use in developing countries.

163. The chief reason that average and marginal costs differ is the existence of excess capacity. For any given school or policy, excess capacity could imply that the added costs from an expansion were low, but such situations would not be expected to exist over long periods of time.

164. In those cases where the estimated impact of the input on achievement is negative, the cost-effectiveness ratio is not calculated and a question mark is entered in table 6-2. Where the estimated effect is positive but statistically insignificant, the cost-effectiveness ratio is enclosed in parentheses.

165. Appendix tables C6-3 and C6-4 contain the full specifications. This analysis was conducted using our teacher file—that is, the information collected from each teacher during the surveys. While the definitions of the variables are identical to those used in analyses dealing with students, the means of the teacher variables are of course different from those reported elsewhere, since at the student level the teacher variables are weighted by the number of students associated with each teacher.

166. A rigorous test of the equality of coefficients between the separate year and pooled year estimates in appendix tables C6-3 and C6-4 reveals that the estimates are statistically different. For practical purposes, however, the evident differences are typically small, and reliance on the pooled data does not materially change the conclusions. For that reason, only the pooled results are recapitulated in table 6-3.

167. João Batista Gomes-Neto, our statistical consultant and data base manager throughout the study, derived the underlying mathematical relationship and constructed the complicated spreadsheet programs used in this section to implement empirically the concept of a partial benefit-cost ratio.

168. In project evaluation, it is frequently necessary to resort to cost-effectiveness analysis because benefits (in this case achievement gains) cannot be easily valued in dollar terms. Cost-effectiveness ratios will provide guidance about which potential projects or inputs yield the largest gains in output, but other information is needed before it can be decided whether any project should be pursued. Benefit-cost analysis, on the other hand, is used when benefits can be valued in dollar terms. Such analysis provides direct information not only on which of several options are best but also on whether options should be undertaken. See Lockheed and Hanushek (1988, 1991) for a discussion of efficiency concepts.

169. Note that a given investment in an input typically has a simultaneous effect on both Portuguese and mathematics achievement. Therefore, the calculation of promotion probabilities will be the sum of the effects of improved Portuguese performance and of improved mathematics performance.

170. The estimated marginal probability associated with any input investment will vary, depending on where the probit models are evaluated. As described in chapter 4, the marginal probability associated with a change in a given input is the probit coefficient times the ordinate of the normal distribution evaluated at

the initial probability. For these calculations, we evaluate the probit models at the initial probabilities used in the fourth step above.

171. The correspondence between promotion or dropout probabilities and years expended on schooling can be calculated by following a cohort through school until everybody either has been promoted or has dropped out. This can be derived mathematically, and the formula is used throughout these calculations.

The promotion and dropout probabilities used for different regions come directly from the Profluxo model of P. Fletcher and S. Costa Ribeiro (1989), which employs data from the 1982 Brazilian household survey (IBGE various years). The basic transition probabilities (and the subsequent calculation of student flows) are based on individual grades. Our probit models, however, indicate on-time promotion between second and fourth grade. To apply these probit estimates, we assume: (a) that any change in promotion probability is evenly distributed between the second and the third grades; and (b) that changes in the total promotion probability are proportional to the estimated change in the on-time promotion probability.

172. This figure combines the mean teacher salary from our sample data with the complete hardware and software packages (identified in appendix B) costed out at the values in table 6-1.

173. See Xavier and Marques (1984). Their equivalent work on schools in the center-west states is reported in World Bank (1986), 29, table 10.

174. These cost calculations assume that marginal costs—the incremental dollar savings that would result from one fewer student-year—are the same as average costs.

175. Using data from the 1982 household sample survey (IBGE various years), P. Fletcher and S. Costa Ribeiro, in elaborating their Profluxo model, further subdivide the normal geographical classification of IBGE into income groups, defined consistently across all Brazilian households included in the 1982 survey on the basis of regionally determined minimum wages and selected socioeconomic characteristics of the family.

176. As discussed, a variety of teacher factors are not included here. For example, the teacher's command of the subject matter, revealed in our earlier analyses to be among the most important determinants of the learning achievement of children, is not among the inputs to schooling selected for partial benefit-cost analysis. In the absence of a fully specified supply function for teachers, it is not feasible to calculate the cost of providing teachers with some incremental amount of subject matter knowledge.

177. The partial benefit-cost ratios are all directly proportional to this figure; the figures in table 6-4 for years saved per dollar invested are all multiplied by US$30 to arrive at dollars saved per dollars invested. In fact, any change in the cost per student-year will alter all the partial benefit-cost ratios in exact proportion but leave their relative magnitudes unchanged. While the precise numbers would be different, the overall conclusions would not be materially different unless the cost parameter were changed radically.

178. We do not report results of recalculating the benefit-cost ratios at the upper bound of the 90 percent confidence interval on the Portuguese and math-

ematics achievement coefficients, since our concern is with the possibility of spuriously overstating what already appears to be an extraordinary payoff to certain kinds of investments in school quality. Further, note that evaluating the benefit-cost ratios with both these coefficients set at their 90 percent lower bound is a very stringent test. However, there is no more reason for presuming that our probit coefficient estimates could be biased systematically upward than that they could be biased downward. Basing conclusions on the lower-bound results rather than on the best estimates themselves introduces as much risk of vastly understating the payoffs to investments.

179. We return to a discussion of teacher salary later. The results here indicate, however, that simply increasing the pay of teachers (within the current structure of salaries) continues to be, in relative terms, the most unattractive investment strategy. This is followed by giving teachers complete secondary schooling. Indeed, given other available alternatives, these are low-priority avenues and will not be further explored in the context of partial benefit-cost ratios.

180. These examples are provided to illustrate the point about needed knowledge of teacher supply and are not to be taken as policy proposals at this point. More will be said on alternatives later.

181. There is one general caveat to this. It is not possible to lower the total career salary that potential teachers face without affecting the supply of teachers. For example, it is not feasible to dictate that all teachers, regardless of experience or qualifications, will henceforth receive the pay of an entry teacher without affecting the supply of teachers. Prospective teachers would in such a case see that their lifetime earnings in teaching would be lower, and thus they would be more likely to go into other professions.

182. Requiring teachers to pass examinations based on the material that the students are supposed to learn does not seem to be an outrageous policy. Indeed, many school systems around the world require teachers to pass examinations. Manski (1987) argues that more general testing of teachers in the United States may also be an appealing policy. The important thing here is that we show directly the strength of teacher knowledge on the learning of students.

183. Again, the evidence available here relates to the existing salary structure, and not to what might be observed if there were significant changes either in the incentives for teachers or in the available pool of teachers.

184. The interpretation of the experience results is subject to alternative interpretations because of entry and exit of teachers from teaching. If, for example, the best teachers tend to leave teaching for other occupations, measured experience could be unrelated to student performance even though teachers get better at their job over time. In this case, experience would be at least partly reflecting who stayed in teaching.

Chapter 7

185. In a strict sense, of course, expanded access would occur only if promotion rates increased more rapidly than dropout rates declined. Put differently, constant (or declining) promotion rates combined with an increase in retention

(reduction in dropouts) would simply further clog up the schools, thereby reducing rather than increasing access, if no other changes were made.

186. The actual data from which the conclusions on resources are drawn are available from the authors on request. These data are of two kinds. The first set (five tables) summarizes the availability of learning resources to children in the full sample of schools in which data were collected in the three major survey years. But the sample of schools changes somewhat in each of the three survey years. So the second set (again five tables) summarizes the availability of learning resources in 1981 and 1983 to children in those schools that existed in both those years, and in 1983 and 1985 to children in the schools that existed in both those years.

Because some of the data are gathered at the school or teacher level, while learning resource availability is a concept most appropriately related to individual children, the calculated means in all these tables are weighted by the number of sampled students in each school.

Further, the first table in each set presents, for these full and matched samples respectively, the mean values for these school quality variables for data pooled for all three states for 1981, 1983, and 1985. The same information is disaggregated by state in the second table in each set. Finally, the remaining three tables in each set contain, again for the full and matched samples respectively, a breakdown of the values of the school quality variables for each state for each of the three observation years by project status (EDURURAL and OTHER).

187. The children who appear in the 1985–87 matched sample may well be a rather special subset of all children who were to benefit from the program, since no attempt was made in the 1987 reduced Ceará survey to sample schools randomly.

188. These mean differences are derived from the absolute levels that appear in the ten learning resource tables available from the authors. See note 186.

189. The coefficients are consistent estimators of population parameters irrespective of their statistical significance, which is a measure of the stability or reliability of the coefficients if repeated samples were to be drawn from the same population. For purposes of evaluation, we ignore statistical significance.

190. Reference must be made to the full results displayed in appendix tables C7-1 to C7-3 in order to see the separate influence of measured and unmeasured factors. In addition to skepticism regarding the educational improvement strategy embodied in the EDURURAL project, the evaluation results also imply skepticism concerning sample surveys as reliable sources of information on the availability of learning resources and on learning achievement. Despite an immense effort, probably unprecedented in environments such as northeast Brazil, a lot that is evidently important did not get measured, or was poorly measured.

191. In practice, no school is flow-perfect—that is, the distribution of enrollments over grades is never absolutely even. Repetition may be reduced but not often entirely eliminated, unless there is a policy of automatic promotion. Dropouts typically increase with age and grade, as opportunity costs of school attendance increase; this is clearly important in northeast Brazil. And growing numbers of school-age children may increase the numbers who enter the system each year. For these reasons, first-grade enrollments will likely be somewhat

greater than those in subsequent years. The proportion in first grade in our data, however, clearly far exceeds this putative "frictional" amount.

192. In this study, we define years-behind-grade as age less age-at-entry-to-school less grade.

193. More detailed breakdowns are available from the authors. Although not shown in table 7-12, it is useful to note that, for all years and samples, more than one-fifth of the students are four years or more behind grade, a figure that uniformly exceeds the proportion who are precisely on time—that is, those with zero years-behind-grade.

194. Care is needed in examining table 7-12 to make the correct comparisons: between the 1983 (1985) fourth-grade figure and those for 1981–83 (1983–85).

195. See the first two tables mentioned in the sets of data referred to by the authors in note 186. The mean differences for hardware (and other) inputs shown there are themselves derived, for second and fourth grade respectively, from the last three tables in each set.

196. The appropriate measures vary across grades because of differences in the underlying regression models. For the second-grade cross-section models, it is appropriate to use the information on availability of learning resources for the full sample of schools. For the fourth-grade value-added models, where the sample is limited to children who appear in two successive surveys, the learning resource information must be taken from the much smaller matched samples.

Chapter 8

197. None of this discussion delves into the politics of governmental decisions or into the overall level of support for schools. Such considerations do offer a cautionary note. When efficiency improvements release funds from schools, the released funds may not be plowed back into the educational sector but might, instead, go into other areas. If this happens systematically, school officials may have little incentive to pursue efficiency improvements. Indeed, they may actually have disincentives to do so.

198. For technical reasons related to the method of constructing our samples of schools, the loss rate of schools between 1983 and 1985 underestimates the expected losses for the entire region (p. 62).

199. There is some uncertainty about the exact interpretation of this finding. The drought led to considerable relocation of families, so that closing schools could simply reflect a lack of sufficient numbers of local students remaining in the area.

200. The calculation incorporates the average number of student-years resulting from repetition of the first grade plus time spent by students who never enter the second grade. These calculations do not distinguish between any kindergarten or alfabetização training and true first graders. The standard cumulative period to reach the second grade (with perfect promotion rates and no dropouts) would be one year, not 4.5 years.

201. Students in the primary schools can be quite old and thus capable of

productive employment. The average second grader in our complete sample is some twelve years old, and 10 percent are fifteen or older.

202. Migration does not necessarily imply that a student will drop out of school. In areas where there is such a tenuous attachment to schooling, however, disruptions in progress will frequently operate to stall or end schooling careers.

203. The most important feature is the use of value-added models, that is, models that examine what causes different rates of growth in achievement over time. Additionally, however, the school survival models and promotion models can be used to correct for nonrandom sampling (p. 84).

204. The results pertaining to behavioral models of school survival, student promotion, and student achievement are all derived from multivariate statistical analyses. In each instance, findings are presented on the marginal effect of a factor, holding the effects of other systematic influences constant.

205. In our samples, the proportion of students attending school in teachers' houses declined between 1981 and 1985. This decline, however, reflects in part the way that new schools were added to the data base over time and therefore does not indicate what is happening to this kind of schooling.

206. The quality of the support staffs of the OMES is measured by both the numbers of staff members and their qualifications.

207. The estimation method does combine the effects of both teachers and other school-specific factors such as quality of facilities. Therefore, the total differences among schools could overstate the influences of just the teachers. A separate analysis, employing the results of estimated achievement models for 1983 and 1985, indicates, however, that measured differences in school facilities and materials are a relatively minor part of these aggregate differences. In other words, while the evidence is indirect, the major differences in classroom performance appear to result from differences in overall skill of teachers.

208. A different strand of argument has advanced a somewhat similar position for developing countries. On the conceptual side, it has noted that the level of resources available to developing country schools is so far removed from that in developed countries that variations in resource availability would likely be much more important in developing countries than in developed countries. The empirical implementation has considered the relative explanatory power of family background and school resource measures in models of student achievement; see Heyneman and Loxley (1983).

The analysis presented here is quite different because it focuses on the absolute amount of leverage of teachers in affecting student achievement and does not rely on explicit measures of school and teacher resources.

209. As noted in chapter 2, beginning on page 22, one of the strongest relative findings in past work on schooling in developing countries is that variation in teacher education is important, although the evidence that exists is not persuasive on its own.

210. The tests are criterion-referenced tests designed to capture knowledge students are expected to master in the fourth grade. A priori, one might expect all teachers to achieve at this level, yet the average teacher score on the fourth-

grade Portuguese test was less than 80 percent. This is another statement of the poor overall quality of schools in this region.

211. This analysis relied on survey data from individual teachers and did not include any direct observations of teacher behavior.

212. The source of these differences is unclear. The special analyses of patterns through schools in the 1985–87 sample of selected Ceará schools suggest that a large part of this might be reduced dropout probabilities. This in turn seems to reflect higher opportunity costs of boys on the farms. This evidence is somewhat weak, however, and we do not want to overemphasize it.

213. Because students included in the sample are a subset of those present in the classroom, almost 20 percent of the sampled students have only female classmates within that sample, although they are not necessarily in single-sex classrooms.

214. Rural settings do present constraints. There may simply not be enough students to achieve an efficient scale.

215. A notable exception, with important lessons for many countries, is Colombia, where primary schooling in rural areas is increasingly provided through the *Escuela Nueva*, a program involving specially developed curricula and multigrade teaching methods and supportive instructional materials and teacher training. Schools in the Escuela Nueva program have produced academic performance superior to that of schools operating in the traditional graded classroom mode.

216. A separate analysis also used teacher salary as a summary measure of teacher attributes in the estimation of achievement models (p. 106). While salaries were positively related to student performance, the magnitude of the estimated effects was minute, suggesting again that salaries are very imperfect measures of differences in teacher abilities.

217. Again, we concentrate solely on efficiency issues and leave aside the very important political questions about where monies from efficiency gains would be directed. Of course, decisions on the use of funds so generated will typically imply a set of incentives for school administrators and teachers. In some cases, these incentives could completely eliminate any desire on the part of school officials to seek efficiency gains. Therefore, the way funds are used is not entirely independent of the ultimate efficiency of the system.

218. The range of estimates comes from the average coefficients in cross-sectional models of second-grade performance in 1981, 1983, and 1985 and the average coefficients in the value-added models of fourth grade performance in 1983 and 1985. The calculations are described in chapter 6, beginning on page 145, and a discussion of the alternative estimation approaches is found in chapter 5, beginning on page 84.

219. Estimates of lower bounds were made that incorporate very conservative allowances for the uncertainty in the estimation of the promotion effects of achievement differences. The lower-bound estimates suggest the possibility that such investments would not completely pay for themselves. For hardware, the range would be US$0.82–US$1.36; for software, it would be US$0.30–US$4.40. Even if the lower bounds were to hold, however, there would be increased

achievement by the students and there would be additional cost savings (in the fourth grade and later) that do not appear in these calculations.

220. This is strictly true only over a significant period of time, during which the cost-saving efficiency gains are generated. The annual budget requirements early in the period needed to prime the investment savings are, of course, significant. Assuring their provision is an obvious role for external development assistance.

221. In most situations, the use of test score results for hiring, promotion, and other management purposes—whether scores by teachers or by their students—faces serious implementation problems. One must be certain of the content of the exams, that is, whether or not they properly reflect desired skills. But, more important, one must be concerned about the incentives generated by the tests. Whenever tests are used administratively, scores will be expected to improve, but this improvement of scores may simply reflect learning the specific tests and not more fundamental factors that are desired.

222. In fact, just the opposite: there are many examples, at least in the United States, of merit pay systems that were either ineffective or discarded over time; see Murnane and Cohen (1986).

223. This offers some support to the Heyneman hypothesis that schools are relatively more important in low-income countries where there is less educational support in the home—see chapter 2 and Heyneman and Loxley (1983). There are, however, other interpretations including both measurement problems and the indirect leverage of parents on students through continuation rates in school.

224. A variety of different approaches can be pursued to elevate attention to school performance. These go far beyond merit pay proposals and include ways to involve parents and students in the decision process. For a discussion in the United States context, see Chubb and Hanushek (1990).

225. The EDURURAL design, which sampled second and fourth graders in waves separated by two years, was restricted to analysis of just those promoted on time. The special Ceará sample of 1987 is an exception because it changed to a student-based sampling design that relied on following a subset of the second graders sampled in 1985.

226. The special 1987 Ceará sample also followed students who had dropped out. However, because of the nature of the survey, the additional modeling suggested here could be done only in a crude way.

227. The general covariance analysis provides estimates of the mean gain in student performance in each classroom after allowing for the prior achievement of students and family inputs into education. Thus it provides direct estimates of the total effect of teachers without relying upon specific measurements of the characteristics or behaviors that go into good teaching.

Bibliography

Armitage, Jane, João B. F. Gomes-Neto, Ralph W. Harbison, Donald B. Holsinger and Raimundo H. Leite. 1986. "School Quality and Achievement in Rural Brazil." Education and Training Department Discussion Paper EDT25. Population and Human Resources Department, World Bank, Washington, D.C.

Armor, David, Patricia Conry-Oseguera, Millicent Cox, Niceima King, Lorraine McDonnell, Anthony Pascal, Edward Pauly, and Gail Zellman. 1976. *Analysis of the School Preferred Reading Program in Selected Los Angeles Minority Schools*. R-2007-LAUSD. Santa Monica, Calif.: Rand Corporation.

Avalos, B., and Wadi D. Haddad. 1979. "A Review of Teacher Effectiveness Research in Africa, India, Latin America, Middle East, Malaysia, Philippines, and Thailand: Synthesis of Results." IDRC Manuscript Reports IDRC-MR10.

Behrendt, Amy, Jeffrey A. Eisenach, and William R. Johnson. 1986. "Selectivity Bias and the Determinants of SAT Scores." *Economics of Education Review* 5(4):363–71.

Behrman, Jere R., and Nancy Birdsall. 1983. "The Quality of Schooling: Quantity Alone is Misleading." *American Economic Review* 73(5):928–46.

———. 1987. "Comment on Returns to Education: A Further International Update." *Journal of Human Resources* 22(4):603–05.

Behrman, Jere R., and Barbara L. Wolfe. 1984. "The Socioeconomic Impact of Schooling in a Developing Country." *Review of Economics and Statistics* 66(2):296–303.

Beiker, Richard F., and Kurt R. Anschel. 1973. "Estimating Educational Production Functions for Rural High Schools: Some Findings." *American Journal of Agricultural Economics* 55(August):515–19.

Berg, Alan. 1981. *Malnourished People: A Policy Review*. World Bank Poverty and Basic Needs Series. Washington, D.C.

Berg, Ivar. 1970. *Education and Jobs: The Great Training Robbery*. New York: Praeger.

Birdsall, N. 1985. "Public Inputs and Child Schooling in Brazil." *Journal of Development Economics* 18(1):67–86.

Bishop, John. 1989. "Is the Test Score Decline Responsible for the Productivity Growth Decline?" *American Economic Review* 79(1):178–97.

Boardman, Anthony E., Otto A. Davis, and Peggy R. Sanday. 1977. "A Simultaneous
Equations Model of the Educational Process." *Journal of Public Economics*
7(1):23–49.

Boardman, Anthony E., and Richard J. Murnane. 1979. "Using Panel Data to Improve Estimates of the Determinants of Educational Achievement." *Sociology
of Education* 52(April):113–21.

Boissiere, Maurice X., John B. Knight, and Richard H. Sabot. 1985. "Earnings,
Schooling, Ability, and Cognitive Skills." *American Economic Review* 75(5):
1016–30.

Bowles, Samuel. 1970. "Toward an Educational Production Function." In W. Lee
Hansen, ed., *Education, Income and Human Capital*. New York: National
Bureau of Economic Research.

Bowles, Samuel, and Herbert Gintis. 1976. *Schooling in Capitalist America*. New
York: Basic Books.

Bowles, Samuel, and Henry M. Levin. 1968. "The Determinants of Scholastic
Achievement—An Appraisal of Some Recent Evidence." *Journal of Human
Resources* 3(1):3–24.

Bridge, R. Gary, Charles M. Judd, and Peter R. Moock. 1979. *The Determinants
of Educational Outcomes: The Impact of Families, Peers, Teachers, and
Schools*. Cambridge, Mass.: Ballinger.

Brown, Byron W., and Daniel H. Saks. 1975. "The Production and Distribution
of Cognitive Skills Within Schools." *Journal of Political Economy* 83(3):
571–93.

Burkhead, Jesse V. 1967. *Input-Output in Large City High Schools*. Syracuse,
N.Y.: Syracuse University Press.

Cain, Glen G., and Harold W. Watts. 1970. "Problems in Making Policy Inferences
from the Coleman Report," *American Sociological Review* 35(2):328–52.

Carnoy, M. 1971. "Un enfoque de sistemas para evaluar la educacion, ilustrado
con datos de Puerto Rico." *Revista del Centro de Estudios Educativos* 1(3):
9–46.

Chubb, John E., and Eric A. Hanushek. 1990. "Reforming Educational Reform."
In Henry J. Aaron, ed., *Setting National Priorities: Policy for the Nineties*.
Washington, D.C.: The Brookings Institution.

Cochrane, Susan H., and Dean T. Jamison. 1982. "Educational Attainment and
Achievement in Rural Thailand." *New Directions for Testing and Measurement: Productivity Assessment in Education* 15(September):43–59.

Cohn, Elchanan. 1968. "Economies of Scale in Iowa High School Operations."
Journal of Human Resources 3(4):422–34.

Cohn, Elchanan, with Stephen D. Millman. 1975. *Input-Output Analysis in Public
Education*. Cambridge, Mass: Ballinger.

Coleman, James S., Ernest Q. Campbell, Carol J. Hobson, James McPartland, Alex-
ander M. Mood, Frederic D. Weinfield, and Robert L. York. 1966. *Equality of*

Educational Opportunity (Coleman Report). Washington, D.C.: U.S. Government Printing Office.

Coleman, James S., Thomas Hoffer, and Sally Kilgore. 1982. *High School Achievement: Public, Catholic, and Private Schools Compared.* New York: Basic Books.

Denison, Edward F. 1974. *Accounting for United States Economic Growth, 1929–1969.* Washington, D.C.: The Brookings Institution.

Dolan, Robert C., and Robert M. Schmidt. 1987. "Assessing the Impact of Expenditure on Achievement: Some Methodological and Policy Considerations." *Economics of Education Review* 6(3):285–99.

Dynarski, Mark. 1987. "The Scholastic Aptitude Test: Participation and Performance." *Economics of Education Review* 6(3):263–73.

Easterlin, Richard A. 1978. "What will 1984 Be Like? Socioeconomic Implications of Recent Twists in Age Structure." *Demography* 15(4):397–421.

Eberts, Randall W., and Joe A. Stone. 1984. *Unions and Public Schools: The Effect of Collective Bargaining on American Education.* Lexington, Mass.: Lexington Books.

Fletcher, Philip R., and Sérgio Costa Ribeiro. 1989. "Modelling Education System Performance with Demographic Data: An Introduction to the Profluxo Model." Brasília, March 8.

Friend, Jamesine, Klaus Galda, and Barbara Searle. 1986. "From Nicaragua to Thailand: Adapting Interactive Radio Instruction." *Development Communication Report* 52(winter).

Friend, Jamesine, Barbara Searle, and Patrick Suppes, eds. 1980. *Radio Mathematics in Nicaragua.* Stanford, Calif.: Institute for Mathematical Studies in the Social Sciences, Stanford University.

Fuller, Bruce. 1985. "Raising School Quality in Developing Countries: What Investments Boost Learning?" Education and Training Department Discussion Paper EDT7. Population and Human Resources Department, World Bank, Washington, D.C.

Fundação Cearense de Pesquisas e Cultura. Various years. "Relação de Tabelas Referentes a Ficha de SEEC/MEC." (Data elaborated by the EDURURAL research team at Federal University of Ceará, Fortaleza, from the yearly educational statistics collection of the state education secretariats.) Fortaleza.

Glasman, Naftaly S., and Israel Biniaminov. 1981. "Input-Output Analyses in Schools." *Review of Educational Research* 51(4):509–39.

Glass, Gene V., and Mary Lee Smith. 1979. "Meta-Analysis of Research on Class Size and Achievement." *Education Evaluation and Policy Analysis* 1(1): 2–16.

Gramlich, Edward M. 1981. *Benefit-Cost Analysis of Government Programs.* Englewood Cliffs, N.J.: Prentice-Hall.

Greenberg, David H., and John McCall. 1974. "Teacher Mobility and Allocation." *Journal of Human Resources* 9(4):480–502

Haddad, Wadi D. 1979. *Educational and Economic Effects of Promotion and Repetition Practices.* World Bank Staff Working Paper 319. Washington, D.C.

344   Bibliography

Hanushek, Eric A. 1971. "Teacher Characteristics and Gains in Student Achievement: Estimation Using Micro-Data." *American Economic Review* 61(2): 280–88.

———. 1972. *Education and Race: An Analysis of the Educational Production Process.* Cambridge, Mass.: Heath-Lexington.

———. 1979. "Conceptual and Empirical Issues in the Estimation of Educational Production Functions." *Journal of Human Resources* 14(3): 351–88.

———. 1981. "Throwing Money at Schools." *Journal of Policy Analysis and Management* 1(1):19–41.

———. 1986. "The Economics of Schooling: Production and Efficiency in Public Schools." *Journal of Economic Literature* 24(September):1141–77.

———. 1989. "The Impact of Differential Expenditures on School Performance." *Educational Researcher* 18(4):45–51.

———. 1992. "The Trade-off Between Child Quantity and Quality." *Journal of Political Economy* 100(February):84–117.

Hanushek, Eric A., and John E. Jackson. 1977. *Statistical Methods for Social Scientists.* New York: Academic Press.

Hanushek, Eric A., and John F. Kain. 1972. "On the Value of 'Equality of Educational Opportunity' as a Guide to Public Policy." In Frederick Mosteller and Daniel P. Moynihan, eds., *On Equality of Educational Opportunity.* New York: Random House.

Heckman, James S. 1979. "Sample Selection Bias as a Specification Error." *Econometrica* 47:153–61.

Heim, John, and Lewis Perl. 1974. *The Educational Production Function: Implications for Educational Manpower Policy.* Institute of Public Employment Monograph 4. Ithaca, N.Y.: Cornell University.

Henderson, Vernon, Peter Mieszkowski, and Yvon Sauvageau. 1976. *Peer Group Effects and Educational Production Functions.* Ottawa, Economic Council of Canada.

Heyneman, Stephen P., and Daphne Siev White. 1986. *The Quality of Education and Economic Development.* Washington, D.C.: The World Bank.

Heyneman, Stephen P., and William A. Loxley. 1983. "The Effect of Primary School Quality on Academic Achievement across Twenty-nine High- and Low-Income Countries." *The American Journal of Sociology* 88(6):1162–94.

Heyneman, Stephen P., Dean T. Jamison, and Xenia Montenegro. 1984. "Textbooks in the Philippines: Evaluation of the Pedagogical Impact of a Nationwide Investment." *Educational Evaluation and Policy Analysis* 6(summer): 139–50.

Hough, J. R. 1991. "Input-Output Analysis in Education in the U.K.—Review Essay." *Economics of Education Review* 10(1):73–81.

IBGE (Instituto Brasileiro de Geographia e Estadística). Various years. *Pesquisa Nacional ao Domicilio* (PNAD). Rio de Janeiro.

Jamison, Dean T. 1978. "Radio Education and Student Repetition in Nicaragua." In Patrick Suppes, Barbara Searle, and Jamesine Friend, eds., *The Radio Math-*

ematics Project: Nicaragua, 1976–1977. Stanford, Calif.: Institute for Mathematical Studies in the Social Sciences, Stanford University.

———. 1980. "Radio Education and Student Failure in Nicaragua: A Further Note." In Jamesine Friend, Barbara Searle, and Patrick C. Suppes, eds., *Radio Mathematics in Nicaragua.* Stanford, Calif.: Institute for Mathematical Studies in the Social Sciences, Stanford University.

———. 1986. "Child Malnutrition and School Performance in China." *Journal of Development Economics* 20:299–309.

Jamison, Dean T., and Lawrence J. Lau. 1982. *Farmer Education and Farm Efficiency.* Baltimore, Md.: Johns Hopkins University Press.

Jamison, Dean T., and Joanne Leslie. 1990. "Health and Nutrition Considerations in Education Planning: 2. The Cost and Effectiveness of School-Based Interventions." *Food and Nutrition Bulletin* 12(September):204–14.

Jamison, Dean T., and Marlaine E. Lockheed. 1987. "Participation in Schooling: Determinants and Learning Outcomes in Nepal." *Economic Development and Cultural Change* 35(2):279–306.

Jamison, Dean T., and Peter R. Moock. 1984. "Farm Education and Farm Efficiency in Nepal: The Role of Schooling, Extension Services and Cognitive Skills." *World Development* 12:67–86.

Jamison, Dean T., Barbara Searle, Klaus Galda, and Stephen Heyneman. 1981. "Improving Elementary Mathematics Education in Nicaragua: An Experimental Study of the Impact of Textbooks and Radio on Achievement." *Journal of Educational Psychology* 73(4):556–67.

Jencks, Christopher S., and Marsha Brown. 1975. "Effects of High Schools on their Students." *Harvard Education Review* 45(August):273–324.

Jencks, Christopher S., Marshall Smith, Henry Acland, Mary Jo Bane, David Cohen, Herbert Gintis, Barbara Heyns, and Stephen Michelson. 1972. *Inequality: A Reassessment of the Effects of Family and Schooling in America.* New York: Basic Books.

Jimenez, Emmanual, and Marlaine E. Lockheed. 1989. "Enhancing Girls' Learning Through Single-Sex Education: Evidence and a Policy Conundrum." *Educational Evaluation and Policy Analysis* 11(summer):117–42.

Jimenez, Emmanuel, Marlaine E. Lockheed, and Nongnuch Wattanawaha. 1987. "The Relative Efficiency of Private and Public Schools in Enhancing Achievement: The Case of Thailand." *World Bank Economic Review* 2(2):139–64.

Katzman, Martin T. 1971. *Political Economy of Urban Schools.* Cambridge, Mass.: Harvard University Press.

Keisling, Herbert. 1965. "Measuring a Local Government Service: A Study of Efficiency of School Districts in New York State." Unpublished Ph.D. thesis, Harvard University, Cambridge, Mass.

———. 1967. "Measuring a Local Government Service: A Study of School Districts in New York State." *Review of Economics and Statistics* 49(August):356–67.

Kenny, Lawrence W. 1982. "Economies of Scale in Schooling." *Economics of Education Review* 2(1):1–24.

King, Elizabeth N., and Lee A. Lillard. 1983. "Determinants of Schooling Attainment and Enrollment Rates in the Philippines." N-1962-AID. Santa Monica, Calif.: The Rand Corporation.

Knight, John B., and Richard H. Sabot. 1987. "Educational Policy and Labour Productivity: An Output Accounting Exercise." *The Economic Journal* 97(March):199–214.

————. 1990. *Education, Productivity, and Inequality: The East African Natural Experiment.* New York: Oxford University Press.

Lee, Valerie E., and Marlaine E. Lockheed. 1990. "The Effects of Single-Sex Schooling on Student Achievement and Attitudes in Nigeria." *Comparative Education Review* 34(2):209–32.

Leslie, Joanne, and Dean T. Jamison. 1990. "Health and Nutrition Considerations in Education Planning: 1. Educational Consequences of Health Problems among School-Age Children." *Food and Nutrition Bulletin* 12(September):191–204.

Levin, Henry M. 1970. "A New Model of School Effectiveness." In U.S. Office of Education, *Do Teachers Make a Difference?* Washington, D.C.: U.S. Government Printing Office.

————. 1975. *Cost Effectiveness.* Beverly Hills, Calif.: Sage.

————. 1976. "Concepts of Economic Efficiency and Educational Production." In Joseph T. Froomkin, Dean T. Jamison, and Roy Radner, eds., *Education as an Industry.* Cambridge, Mass.: National Bureau of Economic Research.

————. 1983. "Cost Effectiveness in Evaluation Research." In Marcia Guttentag and Elmer Struening, eds., *Handbook of Evaluation Research*, vol. 2. Beverly Hills, Calif.: Sage.

Link, Charles R., and James G. Mulligan. 1986. "The Merits of a Longer School Day." *Economics of Education Review* 5(4):373–81.

Link, Charles R., and Edward C. Ratledge. 1979. "Student Perceptions, IQ, and Achievement." *Journal of Human Resources* 14(winter):98–111.

Lockheed, Marlaine E. 1987. "School and Classroom Effects on Student Learning Gain: The Case of Thailand." Education and Training Department Discussion Paper EDT98. World Bank, Population and Human Resources Department, Washington, D.C.

Lockheed, Marlaine E., Josefina Fonacier, and Leonard J. Bianchi. 1989. "Effective Primary Level Science Teaching in the Philippines: Achievement Effects of Group Work, Testing, and Laboratories." Policy, Planning and Research Working Paper 208. World Bank, Population and Human Resources Department, Washington, D.C.

Lockheed, Marlaine E., and Eric A. Hanushek. 1988. "Improving Educational Efficiency in Developing Countries: What Do We Know?" *Compare* 18 (1): 21–38.

————. 1991. "Concepts of Educational Efficiency and Effectiveness." In Torsten Husén and T. Neville Postlethwaite, eds., *International Encyclopedia of Education.* Supplementary vol. 2. Oxford: Pergamon.

Lockheed, Marlaine E., and André Komenan. 1987. "Teaching Quality and School Effects on Student Achievement in Africa: The Case of Nigeria and Swaziland." *Teaching and Teacher Education* 5(2):93–113.

Lockheed, Marlaine E., Dean T. Jamison, and Lawrence J. Lau. 1980. "Farmer Education and Farm Efficiency: A Survey." *Economic Development and Cultural Change* 29(1):37–76.

Lockheed, Marlaine E., and Alastair G. Rodd. 1990. "World Bank Lending for Education Research, 1982–89." Policy, Research, and External Affairs Working Paper 583. World Bank, Population and Human Resources Department, Washington, D.C.

Lockheed, Marlaine E., Stephen C. Vail, and Bruce Fuller. 1987. "How Textbooks Affect Achievement in Developing Countries: Evidence from Thailand." *Educational Evaluation and Policy Analysis* 8(4):379–92.

Lockheed, Marlaine E., and Adriaan Verspoor. 1991. *Improving Primary Education in Developing Countries.* New York: Oxford University Press.

Maddala, G. S. 1977. *Econometrics.* New York: McGraw-Hill.

———. 1983. *Limited-Dependent and Qualitative Variables in Econometrics.* New York: Cambridge University Press.

Manski, Charles F. 1987. "Academic Ability, Earnings, and the Decision to Become a Teacher: Evidence from the National Longitudinal Study of the High School Class of 1972." In David A. Wise, ed., *Public Sector Payrolls.* Chicago: University of Chicago Press.

Maynard, Rebecca A., and David Crawford. 1976. "School Performance." In *Rural Income Maintenance Experiment Final Report.* Madison, Wisc.: University of Wisconsin Institute for Research on Poverty.

Merrick, Thomas W., and Douglas H. Graham. 1979. *Population and Economic Development in Brazil: 1800 to the Present.* Baltimore, Md.: Johns Hopkins University Press.

Michelson, Stephen. 1970. "The Association of Teacher Resources with Children's Characteristics." In U.S. Office of Education, *Do Teachers Make a Difference?* Washington, D.C.: U.S. Government Printing Office.

———. 1972. "For the Plaintiffs—Equal School Resource Allocation." *Journal of Human Resources* 7(summer):283–306.

Moock, Peter R., and Joanne Leslie. 1986. "Childhood Malnutrition and Schooling in the Terai Region of Nepal." *Journal of Development Economics* 20(1): 33–52.

Murnane, Richard J. 1975. *Impact of School Resources on the Learning of Inner City Children.* Cambridge, Mass.: Ballinger.

———. 1981a. "Teacher Mobility Revisited." *Journal of Human Resources* 16(winter):3–19.

———. 1981b. "Interpreting the Evidence on School Effectiveness." *Teachers College Record* 83(fall):19–35.

———. 1983. "How Clients' Characteristics Affect Organization Performance: Lessons from Education." *Journal of Policy Analysis and Management* 2(spring):403–17.

Murnane, Richard J., and David K. Cohen. 1986. "Merit Pay and the Evaluation Problem: Understanding Why Most Merit Pay Plans Fail and a Few Survive." *Harvard Education Review* 56(February):1–17.

Murnane, Richard J., Rebecca A. Maynard, and James C. Ohls. 1981. "Home Resources and Children's Achievement." *Review of Economics and Statistics*
63(3):369–77.

Murnane, Richard J., and R. J. Olsen. 1988. "Will There Be Enough Teachers?"
Paper presented at American Economic Association meetings, New York, N.Y.

Murnane, Richard J., and Barbara F. Phillips. 1981. "What Do Effective Teachers
of Inner-City Children Have in Common?" *Social Science Research*
10(March):83–100.

National Research Council. 1987. *Toward Understanding Teacher Supply and
Demand: Priorities for Search and Development, Interim Report.* Washington,
D.C.: National Academy Press.

Nelson, Richard R., and Edmund S. Phelps. 1966. "Investment in Humans, Technology, Diffusion, and Economic Growth." *American Economic Review*
56(May):69–75.

Ngay, Aben. 1984. "An Assessment of Educational Inequality in the Ivorian Primary Schools." Ph.D. diss., Stanford University, Stanford, Calif.

Oxford, R., J. Clark, J. Hermansen, P. Christensen, and M. Imhoff. 1986. *Final
Report: Evaluation of the Kenya Radio Language Arts Project.* Washington,
D.C.: Academy for Educational Development and Center for Applied Linguis-
tics.

Perl, Lewis J. 1973. "Family Background, Secondary School Expenditure, and
Student Ability." *Journal of Human Resources* 8(spring):156–80.

Preston, Samuel H. 1984. "Children and the Elderly: Divergent Paths for America's
Dependents." *Demography* 21(November):435–57.

Psacharopoulos, George. 1981. "Returns to Education: An Updated International
Comparison." *Comparative Education* 17(3):321–41.

———. 1985. "Returns to Education: A Further International Update and Implications." *Journal of Human Resources* 20(4):583–604.

———. 1989. "Time Trends of the Returns to Education: Cross-National Evidence." *Economics of Education Review* 8(3):225–31.

Psacharopoulos, George, and Ana Maria Arriagada. 1989. "The Determinants of
Early Age Human Capital Formation: Evidence from Brazil." *Economic Development and Cultural Change* 34(4):682–708.

Raudenbush, Stephen W. 1988. "Educational Applications of Hierarchical Linear
Models: A Review." *Journal of Educational Statistics* 13(2):85–116.

Raymond, Richard. 1968. "Determinants of the Quality of Primary and Secondary
Public Education in West Virginia." *Journal of Human Resources* 3(fall):
450–70.

Ribich, Thomas I., and James L. Murphy. 1975. "The Economic Returns to
Increased Educational Spending." *Journal of Human Resources* 10(winter):
56–77.

Riddell, Abby Rubin. 1989. "An Alternative Approach to the Study of School
Effectiveness in Third World Countries." *Comparative Education Review*
33(4):481–97.

Riley, John G. 1979. "Informational Equilibrium." *Econometrica* 47(March):
331–59.

Schiefelbein, E. J., and J. Farrell. 1982. *Eight Years of Their Lives: Through Schooling to the Labor Market in Chile*. Ottowa: IDRC.

Sebold, Frederick D., and William Dato. 1981. "School Funding and Student Achievement: An Empirical Analysis." *Public Finance Quarterly* 9(1):91–105.

Smith, Marshall. 1972. "Equality of Educational Opportunity: The Basic Findings Reconsidered." In Frederick Mosteller and Daniel P. Moynihan, eds., *On Equality of Educational Opportunity*. New York: Random House.

Sociology of Education. 1982. Symposium on "High School and Beyond" study. Volume 55(April/July).

Solmon, Lewis C. 1985. "Quality of Education and Economic Growth." *Economics of Education Review* 4(4):273–90.

———. 1986. "The Quality of Education and Economics Growth: A Review of the Literature." In Stephen P. Heyneman and Daphne Siev White, eds., *The Quality of Education and Economic Development*. Washington, D.C.: The World Bank.

Sounis, E. No date. Manual de Higiene e Medicina do Trabalho.

Spence, A. Michael. 1973. "Job Market Signaling." *Quarterly Journal of Economics* 87(August):355–74.

Strauss, Robert P., and Elizabeth A. Sawyer. 1986. "Some New Evidence on Teacher and Student Competencies." *Economics of Education Review* 5(1):41–48.

Summers, Anita A., and Barbara L. Wolfe. 1977. "Do Schools Make a Difference?" *American Economic Review* 67(September):639–52.

Tan, J. P. 1982. "Research Components in World Bank Education Projects." Education Department, World Bank, Washington, D.C.

Tuckman, Howard P. 1971. "High School Inputs and Their Contributions to School Performance." *Journal of Human Resources* 6(fall):490–509.

Welch, Finis 1970. "Education in Production." *Journal of Political Economy* 78(January-February):35–59.

Winkler, Donald K. 1972. "Production of Human Capital: A Study of Minority Achievement." Ph.D. diss. University of California, Berkeley, Calif.

———. 1975. "Educational Achievement and School Peer Group Composition." *Journal of Human Resources* 10(spring):189–204.

World Bank. 1986. *Brazil: Finance of Primary Education*. Washington, D.C.

Xavier, Antônio Carlos da R., and Antônio Emílio Semdim Marques. 1984. "Custo Direto de Funçãionamento das Escolas Públicas de Primer Grau na Regio Nordeste." Brasília: CHRH/IPES, July 1984 (under terms of MEC/SEPS/SEAC V Acordo MED/BIRD).

Works by EDURURAL Evaluation Research Team Members

Conty, R. 1987. "Um Levantamento das Condições de Funcionamento e Estrutura dos Órgãos Municipais de Educação no Program EDURURAL: Os Casos de Assaré e Canindé." Comunicação no VII Encontro de Pesquisa de Educação no Nordeste, Aracaju. e na 40a. Reunio da SBPC, São Paulo, 1988.

Dallago, Maria Lúcia Lopes. 1985. "Exploração das Condições dos Alunos com Maior Defasagem Entre a Idade Cronológica e a Série em Escolas Rurais do Nordeste."

Ferreira, Helena Maria de Sousa, and Silene Barrocas Tavares. 1985. "A Escola na Casa da Professora: as Caraterísticas e o Impacto Sobre o Aluno."

Fundação Carlos Chagas. 1987. "Relatório Técnico do Estudo do Rendimento Escolar dos Alunos," 1983 x 1981.

Gomes-Neto, João Batista F., Ralph W. Harbison, Eric A. Hanushek, e Raimondo Hélio Leite. 1991. *Educação Rural: Liçóes EDURURAL.*

Gomes-Pereira, Antônio, and João Batista Ferreira Gomes-Neto. 1987. "Academic Performance and Family Variables in Rural Areas of Northeast Brazil." Paper presented at the 31st annual meeting of the Comparative and International Education Society, Washington, D.C.

Leite, Raimundo Hélio. 1985. "A Eficiência na Escola Rural de Primeiro Grau do Nordeste Brasileiro."

———. 1988. *Educação—Temas para Refletir* (Colab. Mesquita, V.). Fortaleza, Edições UFC.

Lian Sousa, Sandra Maria Zakia. 1987. "O Processo de Avaliação das Açoes de Capacitação de Recursos Humanos do Programa EDURURAL/NE: Origem e Perspectiva Atual." *Capacitação de Profissionais da Educação: Perspectivas para Avaliação*. Ministério da Educação, Fundação de Assistência ao Estudante, Instituto de Recursos Humanos João Pinheiro, Projeto Capacitação de Recursos Humanos/EDURURAL/NE. Belo Horizonte, Brazil.

Lisa Sousa, Sandra Maria Zakia, e Dyla Tavares de Sá Brito. 1987. "Subsídios para avaliacão do Projeto Capacitação de Recursos Humanos/Programa EDURURAL/NE," *Capacitação de Profissionais da Educação: Perspectivas para Avalíação*. Ministério da Educação, Fundação de Assistência ao Estudante, Instituto de Recursos Humanos João Pinheiro, Projeto Capacitação de Recursos Humanos/EDURURAL/NE. Belo Horizonte, Brazil.

Lins de Matos, Consuelo. 1985. "Os Papéis Femininos na Educação Rural do Nordeste Brazileiro."

Tavares, Silene Barrocas. 1986. "A Casa da Professora Enquanto Instituição Escolár do Nordeste Brasileiro." Comunicação na 4ª, Conferência Brasileira de Educação. Goiânia, Brazil.

Therrien, Ângela. 1985. "The Impact of Family Background on Achievement."

Therrien, Jacques. 1985. "The Impact of School Quality on Enrollments."

———. 1987a. "Algumas Lições da Avaliação do Programa EDURURAL/NE." *Capacitação de Profissionais da Educação: Perspectivas para Avaliação*. Ministério da Educação, Fundação de Assistencia ao Estudante, Instituto de Recursos Humanos João Pinheiro, Projeto Capacitação de Recursos Humanos/EDURURAL/NE. Belo Horizonte, Brazil.

—. 1987b. "As Lições do EDURURAL/NE e a Problemática da Educação Básica no Meio Rurál." Conferência apresentada no Seminário sobre a Problemática da Educação Básica. Secretaria de Educação do Ceará. Fortaleza, Brazil.

—. 1987c. "As Práticas Pedagógicas nos Movimentos Sociais e a Compreensão da Escola Rural." Apresentado da Mesa Redonda sobre Educação e Movimentos Sociais no VII Encontro de Pesquisa em Educação do Nordeste. Aracaju, Brazil.

—. 1987d. "Formulação de Políticas e Programas Educacionais para o Meio Rural e a Experiência do EDURURAL/NE. Conferência no Encontro de Secretários Estaduais de Educação do Nordeste, SUDENE. Recife, Brazil.

—. 1987e. "Os Movimentos Sociais e a Compreensão da Escola no Meio Rural: Um Eixo de Análise." *Revista Educação em Debate* 10(4). Fortaleza, Brazil: EUFC.

—. 1988a. "Políticas de Educação para o Meio Rural: O Papel do Estado e a Produção do Saber." *Anais da IV* CBE: Educação e Constituinte, Cortez Edit. São Paulo, Brazil.

—. 1988b. "Trabalho, Saber e Educação na Fala dos Camponeses," Apresentado em Painel na V Conferência Brasileira de Educação. Brasília, Brazil.

—. 1988c. "Educação Basica no Meio Rural," Apresentado no VIII Encontro de Pesquisa de Educação do Nordeste. Maceió, Brazil.

Universidade Federal do Ceará. 1982a. "Descrição do Trabalho de Campo," Relatório Técnico No. 1.

—. 1982b. "Acesso e Eficiência na Escola Rural," Relatório Técnico No. 2.

—. 1982c. "Descrição da Amostra," Relatório Técnico No. 3.

—. 1982d. "Comparações Básicas," Relatório Técnico No. 4.

—. 1982e. "Estudo do Rendimento Escolar,"Relatório Técnico No. 5.

—. 1984. "(1) "Introdução," (2) "Avaliação Programas de Educação Rural Básica," (3) O Acesso à Escola de lo Grau na Zona Rural", (4) "A Administração e a Organização do Ensino Rural," (5) "As Condicoes de Vida dos Alunos," (6) "Eficiência," "Anexos," Relatório Técnico No. 7.

Index

Academic achievement. *See* Student performance

Access to schooling: determinants of, 9, 78; EDURURAL and, 34, 36, 53, 183–85; quantity of schooling and, 57; school survival and, 184, 192–93

Achievement differentials, 170–77

Achievement models, 90, 93, 120–22, 141, 331 n153; EDURURAL, 84–88; partial benefit-cost ratios and, 150–51

Achievement tests. *See* Mathematics test results; Portuguese test results

Administrative records, 16, 316 n23

Age: dropout behavior and, 76, 335 n191; grade level and, 48, 51, 53; promotion and, 77; student performance and, 97–98

Agricultural productivity: measurement of, 321 n68, 323 n79; promotion and, 74–75; schooling and, 14, 82, 314 n6; school survival and, 63–64

Ano de alfabetização ("year of literacy training"), 31, 320 n53

Armitage, Jane, 240, 331 n160, 331 n161

Armor, David, 317 n26, 317 n28

Arriagada, Ana Maria, 33

Attendance, school: compulsory, 27, 57–58; in EDURURAL schools, 45; employment and, 195; feeding programs and, 124; measurement of, 42–43; in northeast Brazil, 32–33; patterns of, 190, 213; quality of learning and, 57–58; student performance and, 97, 326 n108; in United States, 14–15

Avalos, B., 318 n38

Behrman, Jere R., 191, 313 n5, 322 n70

Benefit-cost considerations, summarized, 156–57

Berg, Ivar, 313 n3

Biniaminov, Israel, 314 n7

Birdsall, Nancy, 191, 313 n5, 322 n70

Birth rates, 317 n29

Bishop, John, 314 n6

Boardman, Anthony, 325 n97, 326 n107

Boissiere, Maurice X., 191, 313 n5

Bowles, Samuel, 313 n3, 314 n10

Brazil: compulsory schooling in, 31, 57; educational policy in, 4, 29, 53, 319 n49; living standards in, 30; public works programs in, 64; redemocratization in, 39; school feeding programs and, 124–25; socioeconomic conditions in, 29–34

Brazil, northeast: description of, 319 n48; earnings in, 30; education in, 4, 31–34, 45, 47, 190–92; educational policy for, 53; literacy in, 31–32; poverty of, 53, 58; pupil-teacher ratios in, 107–08; school enrollment rates in, 32–33; school survival in, 39–41, 78–79, 193–94; socioeconomic conditions in, 29–34, 47; student performance in, 115–16; teacher salaries in, 142. *See also* Ceará, Pernambuco, Piaui

Brazilian Institute for Geography and Statistics (IBGE), 43, 319 n48

Bridge, R. Gary, 314 n7

Cain, Glen, 314 n10

Capital costs, 136